THE BRIGHT TWENTIES

The author, aged 29.
From a painting by Denholm Davis in the Council Room, Nottingham University.

THE BRIGHT TWENTIES

Being the third book of an Autobiography

1920–1929

by

CECIL ROBERTS

"Gladly as I would undertake immortal works and show posterity that I have lived, I am obliged to earn my living."—Leonardo da Vinci to the Duke of Milan

HODDER AND STOUGHTON

Copyright © 1970 by Cecil Roberts
First printed in 1970

ISBN 0 340 10635 2

13503
920

Printed in Great Britain for Hodder and Stoughton Limited,
St. Paul's House, Warwick Lane, London, E.C.4,
by The Camelot Press Ltd., London and Southampton

To
William C. Ballance

CONTENTS

7

ILLUSTRATIONS

9

KEY TO ACKNOWLEDGEMENTS

[1] Frick Museum Library, New York

[2] *Chicago Tribune*   [4] Popperfoto Library

[3] Baron de Meyer   [5] National Gallery, Warsaw

PREFACE

THE first volume of this autobiography, *The Growing Boy*, covered the years 1892–1908; the second volume, *The Years of Promise*, the years 1908–1919, my youth. Now in this volume I cover the decade 1920–1929, bright and hopeful after the shadow of war, and a time of my early manhood. The curtain rises on a varied scene where every prospect pleased and man, after the holocaust of 1914–1918, was now less vile, we hoped. I was twenty-seven when the decade opened, youthful, tireless, egotistically ambitious. With Wordsworth I could exclaim—

> *Bliss was it in that dawn to be alive,*
> *But to be young was very heaven.*

Half a century has not dimmed that early zest. I have attempted to convey something of it despite great difficulties. My diaries of those heady years were lost in the bombing of London and I fear there will be errors, for which I seek forgiveness and correction.

As in the preceding volumes of this autobiography I have given details of my earnings. I hope I shall not be accused of being mercenary; if I were I should not have chosen a notoriously ill-rewarded profession, eighty per cent of whose members have to exist on the income of a village grocer. In my case the battle for independence was reinforced by grim memories that inculcated thrift and the determination to be at no man's behest.

The picture is changed today. The rake's progress of vote-catching Governments has made nonsense of thrift. The young do not save. They spend their money before it is further devalued. The

11

sums I earned during the Twenties must be multiplied five or six times to represent their equivalent value today. Crushing income-tax, punitive estate duties and recurrent devaluations of the currency have made a football of thrift. After fifty years of careful living a man discovers that his life-savings have shrunk to a fifth of their value. During life, and at death, he is plundered to finance a Chancellor of the Exchequer's desperate Budget. Modern youth knows that life begins today and not tomorrow, which will always be more expensive. My figures point a cautionary tale.

Lastly, an expression of thanks to many who have helped me. My story could not have been told except for the help of those, some hundreds, from whom I have sought corroboration and information. My friends credit me with a phenomenal memory but often the things we are most sure of prove fallacious. The response to my enquiries has been generous. Alas, down the long corridor of half a century many doors have closed for ever and there can be no answer.

Among those who have readily responded to my opportuning I would like to mention, particularly, the late Lady (Norman) Birkett, Lord Drogheda, Mr. Robert Lutyens, Mr. George Maddocks, the Prince of Pless, Mr. Reginald Pound, Mr. Graham Greene, my cousin Mr. Walter Roberts, Mr Trevor Allen, and Mr. Douglas Woodruff, C.B.E. Without the assistance of Countess Isa Potocka and Prince Alphonse Clary the Polish chapters could not have been written; they have helped me to decipher the heroic Polish palimpsest that records a vanished world.

C. R.

CHAPTER ONE

The New World

I

ON THE VERGE of Christmas, 1919, aged twenty-seven, I set forth on a new adventure, a lecture tour across the United States in the role of a poet and ex-war correspondent. I sailed to New York from Liverpool. There was something singular in the fact that I was setting forth from the very city to which I had come, only four years earlier, to my first post in journalism, on the staff of the *Liverpool Post*. Here I had got my foot on the first rung of the ladder to fame and fortune, as I regarded it hopefully. Within the last five years I had been an editorial assistant, a schoolmaster, a literary editor and dramatic critic, a civil servant, a London journalist and a special correspondent with the Royal Navy, the Air Force and the Army. I had marched with our victorious troops into Germany, visited Denmark on the eve of the Schleswig-Holstein plebiscite, and had been an Examiner to the Civil Liabilities Commission, charged with the rehabilitation, in their professions and businesses, of returned soldiers who, during service, had seen their livelihood disappear. In this period I had made something of a reputation as a public speaker and had published five books of verse and a fledgling novel. On the more personal side I had made some rewarding contacts, with Winston Churchill, John Masefield, Joseph Conrad, Arnold Bennett, Laura Knight, Leonide Massine, Grant Richards and Holbrook Jackson. It had been an exciting journey, Liverpool to Liverpool, in the space of four years. I was now a little more assured, and a little better off. I was beginning to conquer the obsessive fears of my hard-driven adolescence.

In this last month I had completed another cycle in my career.

Five years earlier, in desperation, I had burned my boats, escaping from a municipal office stool, and had forced myself into the editorial office of the *Nottingham Journal* as an unpaid pupil, with nothing to sustain that role except ambition and audacity. And now, by a quirk of fate, I would be returning presently to that same newspaper as its editor. I would be the youngest editor of one of the oldest newspapers in the country, founded in 1710, at about the same age as J. M. Barrie, who, coming down from Edinburgh University, had begun his ascent to fame on this newspaper at a salary of three guineas a week. My salary, some forty years later, was to be fourteen pounds. *Da capo*—back to the beginning, but what a different beginning now!

As I stood, on a chill December afternoon, at the taffrail of the Cunard liner, watching Liverpool glide from view as we made for the open sea beyond the Mersey bar, I counted other assets in my brief span of life. Somehow I had saved my first thousand pounds. The penury of my early years, when my father's tragic death had left me stranded, compelling me and my mother to exist on less than one pound a week, had gone, a nightmare that had not left me unscarred. It was in no vainglorious spirit that I made a review of the events of the past five years. I had sufficient experience of life to know that without some luck all effort can be vain. Standing at the taffrail on this darkening afternoon, I reviewed my achievement. Ambitious and young, I was not blind to *hubris*; some apprehension accompanied me into the future. I was destined never to be quite free of it.

Even so, it was a miracle to be young and alive in a world that had just made a hecatomb of its youth. Fate or luck had placed me in the centre of great events. I was no longer a penniless boy heady with dreams in the back street of a provincial town. I had lived in London and felt the pulse of a great city, I had been an eye-witness of a titanic struggle at sea, on land and in the air. Thus early I was rich in experience.

Our liner sailed majestically seawards. The Egremont Promenade, along which I had walked to my office from my lonely lodgings at Seacombe only three years ago, glided by. Now came the twinkling evening lights of New Brighton. It was my last view of land. England faded in grey mist. The ship's engines were audible as we crossed the

THE NEW WORLD

bar. Here was a new experience. The only deck of a great ship I had known had been that of a battleship with its menacing guns. This was my first liner, safely transporting its passengers in comfort across the Atlantic, lately submarine-infested and a graveyard for many.

Thinking of the new continent to which I was sailing, I tried to analyse my apprehension. It did not arise from fear of the public platform, to which I was now accustomed. It came, rather, from the vastness of the scene into which I was about to step. There would not be one familiar face amid those millions in that new world. I should find myself in many strange cities and all I had to offer was an ability to tell my story and tell it so that it would hold an audience for two hours. It would not be an easy task. The actor has the assistance of a play's structure, of words he has learned by heart, of scenery, of a supporting cast, of restful intervals between the acts. Mine was a solitary, unbroken, impromptu performance. Hostility might be encountered. The opening lecture in New York of my colleague Philip Gibbs had provoked a riot. The unforgiving Irish, nursing grievances imbibed with their mothers' milk, were there in force. Gibbs was a former war correspondent with a large public but he was British and, therefore, not to be listened to while Ireland lacked Home Rule. He told me that he had only just begun his first lecture when a man in a front stall shouted something offensive. Thereupon a woman sitting behind gave him a whack on the head with a folded newspaper. This was a signal for general uproar and free fights between the pro-Irish and the pro-British factions until the police moved in and restored order. In Chicago it had been worse. He had been howled down. Certainly, I was going to encounter some unusual audiences. I could not foresee that I was destined to return to the United States many times in the next forty years, to face hundreds of audiences in most of the States of the Union, and to remain as astonished by the American character at the end of those years as at the beginning.

I was making my first tour at a singular time. I left an England exhausted by a great war but hopefully expecting years of rewarding peace after four of bloodshed. The titanic effort to preserve our liberty had left us financially impoverished and drained of our

15

youth. It was not so with the United States. The war had brought America great wealth, great invigoration and, though she knew it not, the dominant role among the nations of the world. Enormous man-power, enormous energy and illimitable resources were at her command. Her navy was now near parity with ours. The liabilities that would load her inheritance of leadership were as yet unfelt. All Europe was in her debt. She had still to reap the abuse that greets the lender who asks to be repaid. We had not yet soured her with repudiation of debts, called her "Uncle Shylock" instead of "Uncle Sam", and reminded her of a profitable tardiness in entering the war. My embarkation was made while there was hope for unity between the Allies. The embryo League of Nations had not yet been repudiated. The great President who had conceived it was not yet a vilified paralytic.

The last light had gone from the sky, the ship's engines throbbed, we were gaining the open sea. I went below to unpack. I shared a cabin with a New Zealander who, after an adventurous life in the Solomon Islands, where he was a District Officer, was sailing to America to seek his fortune. Hector Macquarrie was young, intelligent and agreeable. On going to the dining-room to find my table the head steward, consulting his list, informed me that I was at the Captain's table. I did not then know that this was supposed to be a mark of distinction conferred on the eminent and socially elect, or that failure to make this grade often caused much resentment among those who were sure they were somebodies. I asked to be seated with my cabin companion and found myself at a table of eight. It proved a rewarding choice. The Captain's table, with a dotty peer, a breasty, doll-faced film actress, two jowly American business men with flashy wives, a diplomat, a faded Honourable with her companion; seemed very dull. No laughter came from their table. On the contrary ours was noisy with mirth. We had drawn an American widow and a paunchy president of a Chicago company that made ladies' panties, of which he recurrently brought models for exhibition. The company's trade mark was 'Venus'. "But I'll bet she never wore any," he observed. He sat surrounded by bottles. Prohibition was being enforced soon after our landing and he was "taking in" all he could against that dire day. Though he ate little and drank copiously he was never drunk. Vulgar, loud-mouthed, he exuded benevolence and took us all by storm. He insisted on calling our sallow-faced Cockney steward "Jumbo". We had a knight's widow at our table. He always addressed her as "Ladyship", and she thought him delightful. "You come and visit us. My Maggie'll eat you up. She's a culture-bug, Women's Club lectures, and a good dresser." We felt sorry for the élite at the Captain's table. We wondered what would have been the effect on them of the 'Venus' panties president. I believe he would have conquered them.

The second night out I was missing from the table, the world's worst sailor. For me this Atlantic crossing meant my body wrapped up in a rug on a deck chair, a cold nose and hands, chicken broth at eleven, and a dread of going below when darkness fell. Since that initial trip I have made a score of Atlantic crossings, all purgatorial. The aeroplane has been my salvation. But a ship provides the proper initiation to the United States. The water-entry of New York is stupendous. The entry by air, as everywhere, is a skyey commonplace.

My advent in the New World was not unprepared. A volume of *Poems*, with a preface by John Masefield, would appear on my arrival. I could not have had a better introducer. Masefield was famous, personally known and much loved.* I knew something about his early years in America. After leaving the cadet training ship *Conway*, an "old ironside" moored in the Mersey, he made only one voyage on a sailing ship and never served before the mast. He had a brief experience as an officer on an Atlantic liner. This gave him all the sea-sense he displayed in *Salt Water Ballads*, *Mainsail Haul* and *The Dauber*. Quitting the sea, he went ashore in New York, and gravitated to Greenwich Village's "Bohemia". He was twenty-eight, a penniless wanderer. One of the jobs he found was working in a bar for ten dollars a month, including board and lodging.

While Masefield talked to me one spring day about his American experiences he looked out of a window into his Oxfordshire garden.

---

* John Masefield (1878–1967). Poet Laureate, 1930. Order of Merit, 1935. Author of *The Everlasting Mercy*, *The Widow in the Bye Street*, *The Dauber*, *Tragedy of Nan*, *Sard Harker*, etc.

There was a wistfulness in his voice as he talked. This son of a Ledbury solicitor, born in one of the loveliest small towns of England, had now reached the middle years. He was famous, his position assured and he found pleasure in these recollections of his adventurous youth. "America is a good place and a great adventure for a young man. You will enjoy it," he said.

He had provided me with the best letter of introduction any Englishman could have had. Two of his greatest admirers were Florence and Thomas Lamont. The latter was president of the great financial house of J. Pierpont Morgan and thereby at the fulcrum of power. Quiet, smooth-mannered, Lamont had a soft-voiced, smiling wife. They were ardent Anglophiles, stalwarts of the English-Speaking Union and the new League of Nations Association. The best way for anyone to enter the United States was through the portal of their New York mansion. They enjoyed a prestige greater than that of Mrs. Vanderbilt, leader of the Four Hundred, for they were more than social, they were rich without ostentation, they cultivated persons renowned in the arts, of which they were generous patrons. When a British ambassador visited New York from Washington for some public occasion he invariably stayed with them. Their guest-list was a Who's Who of Europe and America. Warm-hearted, they established a personal relationship with their guests. John Masefield was an old friend. In the grounds of his home at Boar's Hill they had built for him a little theatre in which to produce his plays. His letter of introduction established a firm friendship for me that lasted until their deaths nearly forty years later.

I carried other letters of introduction. Philip Gibbs had two brothers living in America, one Major Arthur Hamilton Gibbs, M.C., the other, Cosmo Hamilton. They were both authors. The latter was one of the most successful dramatists of the day. I also had a note from Ivor Novello to his mother, Madam Clara Novello Davies, who was living in New York, teaching voice production. Thus armed, I entered on the conquest of this new continent in the dual roles of poet and ex-war correspondent. I noticed on the brochure sent out by my lecture agent, written with embarrassing exaggeration, that I would lecture on "The March to the Rhine", and give readings of my poems. Twelve lectures and six readings had been booked. I would have preferred it the other way round, for I had finished with "Our Special Correspondent". Moreover it was easier to read poetry than to speak extemporaneously, as was my habit, entailing nervous exhaustion.

The outlook as I drew near my destination was not encouraging. My agent, Lee Keedick, warned me that the bookings to-date would not cover expenses. I was not going to find any gold mine. He hoped I would pick up some more engagements when I arrived. I refused to be dismayed or to accept his hint that I might wish to cancel the tour. I believed in my star and would accept any risk. Even if at the end of the tour I could only say, "I came, I saw, but did not conquer," it would have been worth it. I have always been avid of adventure.

The days on board ship passed pleasantly. I read, I dozed, bundled up in rugs on my deck-chair, I gossiped. Next to me there sat an agreeable Englishman of about thirty-five, married, with two small children, a daughter Elizabeth, aged five, and a son, Colin, about four. My deck-chair companion was named Hugh Lofting, a civil engineer by profession. Born in Maidenhead, he was half-Irish and had been educated at a Jesuit boarding school in Derbyshire. At the age of eighteen he had gone to America to attend the famous Massachusetts Institute of Technology. After nearly two years there he returned to England for a course at the London Polytechnic. He subsequently worked in Canada, West Africa and Cuba. He later settled in U.S.A., being then twenty-six. There he met his first wife, an American, the mother of his two children. The World War breaking out, and America entering it in 1917, he joined the British Army and served with the Irish Guards in Flanders. He was seriously wounded and invalided out in 1918. His wife having died, leaving his two children motherless, he had married again in 1918. But fate was not kind to him for she died within ten years. I learned these details later, as also that, fifteen years after I had met him, he married a third time. By this wife he had a son, Christopher.

While he was fighting in France Lofting wrote letters to his infant children, Elizabeth and Colin. They were very simple letters and as they were too young to read he illustrated them with his own drawings.

It being wartime the censorship restricted his subjects, so he wrote letters about animals of which he and his children were fond.

I enjoyed talking to Hugh Lofting. Every evening about six he got up from his steamer chair. "I have to go. My kids expect me to tell them a bedtime story," he said. "What sort of stories do you tell them?" I asked. "Oh, I've invented a character called Dr. Dolittle —it's a nickname I've given to my little boy—who has set himself up as a doctor for sick animals and has all sorts of adventures with them."

One day, curious, I asked, "Do you write out your stories?" "I do now but at first they were just letters," he answered. "Would you let me see some of them? I'm interested. I'm an author, making my first lecture tour in America." Responding to my request, he brought me a sheaf of manuscript. I read through it, engrossed, and was charmed by his illustrations. I noticed that he had taken Dr. Dolittle's snub nose from his own little boy. "You should have these stories published," I said. He looked surprised. "Do you think they're good enough?" he asked. "Indeed I do. Look, let me give you a letter to my New York publishers, Frederick Stokes and Co," I said. I gave him the letter. Within twelve months I received an inscribed copy of *The Story of Dr. Dolittle*. Lofting was on the road to fame and fortune, writing subsequently *The Voyages of Dr. Dolittle, Dr. Dolittle's Circus, Dr. Dolittle's Post Office*, and other books in this popular series.

When Lofting died in 1947, he left his copyrights to his third surviving wife. She died and these passed to their son, Christopher, with no rights in them for his half-brother, the original Dr. Dolittle, and his half-sister. Lofting never foresaw that on a far distant day his Dr. Dolittle books would attract a film company and thereby a fortune. In January, 1968, walking by the Baths of Diocletian in Rome, I was startled to read on great placards *È'in Arrivo! Il Favoloso Doctor Dolittle* (Coming! *The Fabulous Dr. Dolittle*). The film had been made by the 20th Century-Fox Company, with Rex Harrison playing Dr. Dolittle. A few yards further on I came to a store. The whole window was occupied with a double-headed white llama, a feature of Dr. Dolittle's Circus. At its foot was a thousand-page book, the Italian collected edition of the Dolittle works. I could not help reflecting on the vagaries of fate, that I should be walking past the flamboyant notices of Dr. Dolittle's gigantic success in the film world, with the author, my agreeable companion in the deck chair, long dead, his fame having gone round the globe. And in this evocation of his memory there was a note of irony too. The original Dr. Dolittle, now fifty-two, commenting on the prospect that his half-brother, Christopher, owner of the Dolittle copyrights, might become a millionaire, said, when interviewed in New York by a correspondent of the London *Daily Express*, "As we say over here, Chris picked up all the marbles and has been handling everything. But I have absolutely no ill feelings."

II

One evening, going up on deck, I was surprised by the intense coldness of the air, it stung one. We seemed to have entered an Arctic zone, having left the Gulf Stream. It was thought we should dock about ten o'clock the next morning. I could not sleep that last night on board for excitement. I was up and about on deck at seven o'clock. It was a crystal-clear morning with a cloudless sky of steel. The intense cold made me glad of my fur coat, the coat with the astrakhan collar, that had invoked the derision of my brother because of its Diaghilevian note of the impresario. There was land on the horizon, the flat coastline of Long Island. Near me stood an English girl whom I had come to know, a vivacious, delicate brunette from Manchester. She was going out to marry an American boy whom she had met when he was a soldier in England. I saw tears running down her face as she stood by me at the taffrail. Was it from the cold or from her emotion? She turned and forcedly smiled at me. "It's silly—I'm happy really!" she said, wiping her eyes. I asked if anyone was coming to meet her. "Oh, yes. My fiancé's coming to collect me," she answered. Collect! The word chilled me. Poor girl, she seemed so very much alone. I asked her where she would be living. In Minneapolis, Minnesota. It sounded terribly far away and emphasised her loneliness.

After breakfast we were in the Narrows, and then, of all things, the Statue of Liberty, dark, towering, came into view. It looked unreal while familiar, as if it were a picture postcard in a forgotten collection. We slowly passed it. The grey serrated skyline was New York, but before anything was clearly visible the ship stopped. The Health and Immigration officers were boarding us. With them came the Press. A group of young men, reporters and photographers, bore down on me in the lounge. They seemed to know all about me except that they would address me as "Sir Roberts". How long was I staying? I had been in the march to the Rhine—had I seen the Kaiser? "No, he left before I arrived in Spa but I saw the bed he slept in."

"Before his abdication?"

"The Kaiser never really abdicated, he was pushed out. While he was dithering over the terms a telephone message from Berlin informed him that the Chancellor had announced to the Press his abdication. That was two days before the Armistice. He held a Council at the Hotel Britannique and protested vigorously against the Chancellor's high-handed act. But it was all over. He signed a statement putting on record that he abdicated from the Imperial throne but not from the throne of Prussia. Then he slipped over the Dutch frontier. This limited abdication was not accepted by the new German Reich. On November 28th, at Amerongen in Holland, the Kaiser was compelled to sign a statement that he abdicated from both the Imperial and Prussian thrones."

The pencils were busy. "Were you there?" asked a reporter.

"No, but I was in the Hotel Britannique, which had been Hindenburg's headquarters, a week later, and got the story from a German colonel who was at the last Council."

"Say, that's some history!" exclaimed a cigar-chewer.

"It's a foretaste of my lecture, but I'm reading my poems also," I added, feeling I was getting a little off track.

"Do you make money out of poetry?"

"Well, perhaps a little more than did Shelley or poor Keats," I replied.

A sharp-eyed youth looked me over. "Who's your tailor, Sir Roberts—the Prince of Wales's?"

"That's a good guess," I replied. The pencils were busy again. Was I married? "No." Was I looking for a wife in America? "I won't put any geographical limit on that," I answered. Later that reply produced a startling newspaper headline—"Trigger-quick British poet won't limit heiress hunt". But it was preferable to "Royal-tailored bard wows the Press". I was soon to learn what not to say. They wanted me on deck for a photograph. When I got there I found I had some competition. The cameras were busy on the film star and the dotty peer. The latter was having a field-day. He had been a constant entertainment on board with his clothes. He had an immense wardrobe and kept his valet busy. We had come to like him. He was as friendly and amiable as a spaniel. He now produced a masterpiece. He wore a light grey cloth deer-stalker's hat and a tweed overcoat with cape. He looked like Sherlock Holmes. One reporter was quick to see it. "The Hound of the Baskervilles Arrives," ran the caption over his photograph.

"What do you think of New York?" asked a reporter.

"I haven't seen it yet," I replied evasively.

"Waal, it's there over your shoulder," he said, jerking his head.

I turned. The ship was sailing past Battery Park. A gigantic skyline had towered up.

A photographer eyed my fur coat. "Is that British?" he asked.

"No, Russian," I replied. I was about to say it had belonged to a dead Russian prince, penniless, who had shot himself in the Pera Palace Hotel in Constantinople, but I was getting wiser and kept my mouth closed.

"Mighty fine!" he commented, chewing. "Will you raise your hat saluting America."

He stood back. I raised my hat. The cameras clicked.

"Glad to see ya!" said a little fat reporter, on leaving.

I was now alone and able to look at New York steadily coming into view. There are no adjectives to describe the experience. It was like landing on a new planet, terrifying in its immeasurable majesty. This was not a city, it seemed like a sun-glazed dinosaur that might become aggressive. Then it changed shape and I saw steel canyons, shuttered with light and shadow, and cascades of windows, diamond bright. As our ship nosed into its berth, vista followed vista; fluted pinnacles, dove-grey pyramids, stone mausoleums and steam-plumed obelisks shining beneath the snowy grandeur of sun-lit cumuli. I felt then, as I was to feel through the next forty years, that I was seeing one of the great cities of the earth, and

23

one of the most beautiful if one confined the choice to cities that owe little to their location and everything to man. What great good fortune it was for me to see it from a ship gliding up the River Hudson, an eye-level view no air approach can provide! The Cave of Aladdin could not have matched this vision of shining marvels.

So much majesty and then, in the landing formula, so much crudity. We docked by a large open Customs shed. We were told to proceed to a letter under which our baggage was placed, and there to await the Customs officer. The shed was half open. It was twenty degrees below freezing, the place was an ice-box. These were the days of ponderous iron-bound wardrobe trunks. They opened vertically revealing coat hangers and drawers. They belonged to an era of numerous porters. Air passage had not yet established the twenty kilogram limit and the feather-weight portmanteau. I found my trunk, but in the scramble no Customs officer came. Under 'R' I was far down in the alphabet. I might be an icicle before the officer reached me. I looked for the dotty peer in his deer-stalker hat and cape. He was an R. He must have had half-a-dozen trunks. There was no sign of him. Later I learned that even in the democratic United States the aristocracy had privileges. A peer was a member of the House of Lords and thereby was entitled to diplomatic immunity as a member of the Government. The privilege he could not exercise in his native land served him abroad.

At last I received some attention. A grim, tough official, pulling my Customs Declaration out of a sheaf, fastened his eyes on my fur coat. Where had I bought it, how long had I had it, how many dollars had I paid for it? Satisfied by my reply he turned to my wardrobe trunk and portmanteau which I had unlocked. I believe he was about to ask me, half-frozen, to open them when a smiling man appeared. "I'm Glass of the Keedick Lecture Bureau," he exclaimed, holding out his hand. In the next ten weeks I came to know this extraordinary man very well. My life was at his disposal. He nodded to the Customs officer. "One of your lions, eh?" said the latter. Without further ado, he stuck labels on my belongings and went off to his next victim. Glass, a huge man with a humorous, rugged face, took charge of me. He asked if I had had a pleasant crossing and gave me an envelope. "Here's fifty dollars in case you've

no cash," he said. "There's a friend waiting for you at the barrier."
"A friend?" I repeated, surprised. The awful loneliness I felt had
vanished in the presence of my agent; and now there was a friend to
meet me! But who? As I went towards the barrier holding back a
crowd awaiting the passengers, I caught a glimpse of the girl who
had been in tears that morning. There was a tall, bronzed lad standing with her. Seeing me, she waved her hand and gave me a radiant
smile. So all was well, her fiancé had "collected" her. In after years
I never heard the name Minneapolis without wondering what was
her fate.

Over the barrier someone waved a hat and called my name. At
once I knew who the friend was. It was a former colleague of the war
years at the Ministry of Munitions, de Burgh Whyte, who had
arranged accommodation for me at the Columbia University Club.
English, he had been educated at Columbia and had married an
American girl. He had given his services to the Ministry, being a
man of means. I had thought he was still in London but he had
returned a few months earlier and was living in New York. His
automobile, with a Negro chauffeur, awaited us. Bidding Glass
goodbye I was soon speeding through the traffic-thronged chasms of
New York. Whyte settled me in at the club and said he would call
for me at seven o'clock. He had arranged a small dinner party for me.
It was New Year's Day.

My room, high up, was over-heated. All the time I was in America
I seemed to go from an iceberg into an oven. Was that why so many
American women had frizzled white hair? After unpacking I turned
to a pile of letters. There was a large number of invitations from
societies and persons I had never heard of, guest-cards for clubs,
greetings from publishers with books, and, most surprising of all, a
card attached to a great bouquet of flowers from the Lamonts.
Masefield must have written to them. One book parcel gave me a
thrill. It contained a dozen copies of my *Poems*, bound in green cloth.
This was the first sight of my book. A letter enclosed had a list of
bookshops at which it had been arranged for me to autograph it.

There was a tap on the door. A genial man introduced himself,
clearly pronouncing his name, following the excellent habit of
Americans as opposed to our nonchalant mumbling. He was the

25

club's secretary. They were delighted to have me with them. They would take care of anything I required. Did I play squash? There were courts on the roof. He would be glad to fix me up with racquet and togs and to introduce me to players. I thanked him. When he left I sat in a chair, looked at the cards, letters, books and flowers, a little overwhelmed. It was cheering to feel wanted. Two hours ago I had feared I was going to find myself in depressing loneliness, and here I was, in a flood of friendliness.

One letter was from my lecture agent. The Bureau was closed as it was New Year's Day. They would be glad to see me tomorrow morning. So Glass had broken his holiday to greet me. There was a list enclosed of my lecture bookings. I opened at the Brooklyn Institute. Three lectures were in New York, the others in Newark (N.J.), Bedford (Mass.), Philadelphia, Boston, Grand Rapids, Lansing (Michigan), Chicago, Pittsburgh, Kalamazoo (where on earth was that?), Baltimore, Buffalo, Washington, Richmond (Virginia), St. Louis (Missouri), etc. I looked at a map. The distances were tremendous. It seemed to me that all my fees would be swallowed up in travelling expenses. There were two singular things about this list. Sometimes the lecture fee sank to $80, sometimes, but not often, it soared to $300. And the bookings were not in geographical sequence. If I was to be in Baltimore on the 18th why was I shot over to Boston on the 20th, then south again to Richmond, back to Washington, and West again to St. Louis? Happily I was unaware that I was to be a shuttle, spending my nights in trains. "We shall try to fill in, picking up where we can," explained Glass when I queried the bookings.

After lunch I went out on to Fifth Avenue. I learned something surprising. It was five miles long! The lower end, at Washington Square, ran into Bohemia, a maze of little streets, bars, studios, and brownstone houses. The upper end ran alongside snow-covered Central Park and the sprawling Metropolitan Museum. From 45th Street up, on the left side, was Millionaires Row, a line of pseudo-French châteaux housing the industrial tycoons and wizards of high finance. In these palaces also lived the élite, the arbiters of elegance, the leaders of the exclusive Four Hundred whose daughters were raffled off to the impoverished princes, dukes, earls, counts and barons of the Old World, sometimes with safeguards, sometimes

26

without—as in the case of gay Count Boni de Castellane, who ran through the twelve-million-dollar *dot* of his wife Anna Gould.* Frightened American fathers-in-law took precautions. When an excited youth of the French nobility triumphantly announced that he was going to marry one of the great heiresses of America, Count Boni asked—"Can she say the Lord's Prayer?" The astonished youth asked why that was necessary. "Because if she can't say 'Our Father which art in Heaven' you won't see a dollar," replied the denuded and divorced spendthrift.

Along the row of these Fifth Avenue mansions spread the Vander-bilt clan. I was fated some twenty-five years later to be a witness in the library, at the request of the widow of Cornelius Vanderbilt, to the deed of sale of the last of these mansions, marked for demolition under the pressure of building development. Shops and towering offices now occupy the site of the mansion whose owner had once called, in his yacht, on a Czar, an Emperor and a King. In turn he had entertained the most illustrious and famous figures in Europe. In 1944 I attended a farewell ball in this house now trapped in by skyscrapers like a mouse in a tallboy.

Twenty-two years were to pass before I became the guest of Mrs. Cornelius Vanderbilt, or "Grace" as she was called among her friends. She was a fair little woman, famous for the bandeau she always wore. She was extremely hospitable, and gave lunch and dinner parties for twenty or thirty guests. All this was in the future. I gazed now in wonder at the façades, railings and portes-cochères of these million-aires' mansions. Some of them were copies of French châteaux, Italian palaces or Tudor baronial mansions.

* He built, at a cost of eight million dollars, a house, 'The Palais Rose' near the Bois de Boulogne. One day he returned to find it locked up. His wife and children had departed. He was divorced. Except for one occupant, during the Second World War, the German Governor of Paris, General von Stülpnagel, it remained shut up until sold for its original cost, in 1969, the house pulled down for an apartment site. Anna Gould after the divorce became the Duchess de Talleyrand. Though unlucky in her first marriage, this daughter of an unscrupulous railrood tycoon was favoured by fate. One day about to drive to a charity bazaar and ball called 'Old Paris', she was delayed chatting with the Duke de Luynes. She arrived late, to find the hall burned down in a fire in which over a hundred members of the élite of Paris perished.

Such was this world of 1920, all unaware of its doom, for the great wealth amassed from the First World War was to prove a cataclysmic cause of the terrible Wall Street crash nine years later. Within twenty years these private mansions on Fifth Avenue would have vanished, their sites occupied by immense office blocks and shops backed by the gigantic architectural concept of Rockefeller Center rising behind a Plaza with fountain and skating rink.

As promised, de Burgh Whyte called for me at seven o'clock. A few minutes later I was shot up in the elevator of a Park Avenue apartment house to the twelfth floor. I found myself in a large bright drawing-room. There were a dozen dinner guests. What I recall most clearly was the advent of a little daughter dressed in a long white nightgown, fairy-like, who came in to kiss parents and guests good-night, her blue eyes smiling under a halo of fair hair.

I returned to Park Avenue the next night, this time as the guest of Cosmo Hamilton, my old colleague Sir Philip Gibbs's brother. He had dropped the name Gibbs. What surprised me in these great apartment houses was that when you had ascended them you stepped straight out of the elevator into a private vestibule. Cosmo Hamilton, then in the heyday of his success as a dramatist, lived in considerable luxury in a duplex apartment. Down the years he occupied many splendid houses, including the 'Duke of York's' lobby flat in Albany, Piccadilly. He was destined to end in a tiny Surrey cottage, penniless, alone, forgotten. He showed a serene face to ill-fortune and never complained. It had always been his ambition to be taken for a Guards officer. Tall, erect, handsome, well-groomed, this was not difficult. When he lavishly entertained me he had two plays running on Broadway and commanded £500 a time for his short stories in the leading American magazines. He was prolific in output and wrote a beautiful clean script that almost rivalled that of another calligraphic artist, Arnold Bennett. His kindness to me was over-whelming. Aware of my apprehension, he and his wife accompanied me to my opening lecture at the Brooklyn Institute. He put his secretary at my disposal to deal with correspondence, and gave me valuable advice. Thus early, I was being made aware of the great American tradition of hospitality.

CHAPTER TWO

The Lecture Tour

I

THE MORNING AFTER my arrival the telephone rang incessantly. Had I seen the newspapers, asked my agent. I had not. He wished me to call at once. "You are speaking at the annual banquet of the Book and Play Club in the ballroom of the Biltmore Hotel tonight, at eight o'clock, full dress. Important. I'll explain when you come round," he said. I went to his office off Fifth Avenue. The walls were covered with posters of the celebrities the bureau handled. Glass introduced me to Lee Keedick with whom I had a short chat and then took me into his inner office and showed me the press interviews, with photographs, on board ship. The write-ups staggered me. Everything seemed a little off-truth and blown up. I had a "clipped speech"—I discovered later that this was a fixed obsession concerning the English—I was obviously "an aristocrat", "aloof and alert". "A bright bachelor but not wife hunting." "Nice fellow to talk to if you can understand that Oxford accent." "Gets his highlife clothes made by the Prince of Wales's tailor of whom he is an intimate friend." (Did this mean I was the friend of the Prince or of the tailor?) "Published his first book of poems at fifteen" (I was eighteen), "Filled London's largest hall when twenty." This was taken erroneously from the lecture brochure—"He took the Bechstein Hall at twenty-one to give a recital of his poems."

Glass smiled at me. "Pretty good, eh?" he asked. I felt like a plucked fowl. "We've had a lot of calls about you—*The Times* account is good—dignified. Now, here's something important. Miss Emma Mills has called. She runs the Book and Play Club. She wants to know if you are related to Lord Cecil Roberts. I said—"

29

"Does she mean Lord Robert Cecil? I'm not related at all!" I protested. "Did you tell her that?"

"I said I didn't know—don't bother about that!"

In the next few weeks I bothered a lot, Lord Cecil Roberts, Lord Robert Cecil, it was a bogy that kept popping up. As a variant I became "Sir Roberts".

"Now, Emma Mills wants you at her dinner tonight—it's the annual banquet of her club at the Biltmore," said Glass. "Quite a big affair, three or four hundred. There's a long speakers' list, including a Russian Grand Duke, but she'll put you in at the end. She'll give you five minutes. It's a full dress show. She doesn't pay but it is good publicity. You'll take it?"

I agreed to take it. What should I speak about, I asked. Glass grinned. "Oh, that doesn't matter. She'll give you a build-up. They just want to look at you, a new face."

The more I saw of Glass, the driving spirit of that bureau, the more I marvelled and came to like him. He had an avuncular manner. Nothing perturbed him. He was a prodigious worker. I often wondered when he went to bed. He was often in his little cluttered room at midnight. He never made errors with dates, trains, hotel bookings. He knew by heart the connections on the remotest railway lines, and the buses, if buses were necessary. What a book he could have written on the inside stories of the celebrities he had handled! He had been an assistant to John Cowper Powys's manager when that amazing author astonished America. "Don't open your tour like he did," warned Glass, reminiscing. "He went to Rochester and said to the Women's Club, 'Ladies, we all like to have our sexual life go on pleasantly.' No, I don't advise you to start like that tonight. And if you get any hot fans pursuing you, don't date 'em. Tell 'em to call you up. It's easier to say 'No' on the phone. Amundsen said he felt safer at the South Pole than at some places on tour. Well, good luck. Emma's a celebrity-eater, tough or tender."

I came to know Emma Mills very well in the next thirty years. I complained that she often put me last on her list of speakers. "Yes, dear Cecil. You're a corpse-reviver. When the other speakers have left my audience dead you bring it back to life," she asserted. I tolerated this treatment because I admired her. She managed a

THE LECTURE TOUR

large collection of women, sensible or silly, and thereby supported herself and an invalid brother. She could be as hard as a walnut but the kernel was soft if you reached it. She died in harness, turned seventy.

When I arrived at the Biltmore Hotel I found a mob of men and women entering the great ballroom. There appeared to be acres of tables under brilliant chandeliers. The noise was terrific, four hundred American-throat-power. Someone seized me, threaded me through the tables and took me to Miss Mills. "How nice of you to come. I'll call on you to speak. Five minutes," she said, firmly. Did she think I would take fifty, unpaid at that? She introduced me to a group around her. One was a very tall, handsome man, with trim beard. She presented me as "Sir Cecil Roberts", so I was knighted again. I was given no opportunity to correct her; at least I wasn't Lord Cecil. An assistant gave me a programme-menu and a numbered ticket. Presently a gong sounded, the crowd sought their seats. "Wait for the procession," said a man near me, his name clearly labelled on the lapel of his coat. He looked at my card. "You're at the end," he said.

Our procession moved to the Speakers' Table down one side of the glittering ballroom. My place was No. 22. I was at the very end of the table. We all sat down. The handsome giant was seated on Emma Mills's right. She was the chairman with gavel and board. Unlike in England there was no red-faced ex-guardsman, in a brass-buttoned crimson tail coat, standing behind the chair to bellow "My Lords, Ladies and Gentlemen, Pray silence for the Chairman, the Right Honourable the Viscount . . . etc." I reflected that my last chairman, in far-away London, had been my friend Sir Burton Chadwick, at the complimentary dinner given for me at the Holborn Restaurant before I sailed for the United States. Sir Philip Gibbs had proposed and youthful Alec Waugh had responded to the toast, "The Younger Generation". It had been all very cosy, with some fifty friends gathered for my send-off. And here I was, utterly alone and unknown in this great mob of Americans.

I looked at the programme. There were nine speakers! I was not on the list, probably too late for the printers. At the head of the list there was the Russian Grand Duke. On the table, at my left, I noticed a place card—"Princess Something-ski". Addressing her in French, to break the ice, I asked her if the gentleman on Miss Mills's right was the Grand Duke. "You don't have to speak French, I'm an American, married to a Pole," she said. "Yes, that's the Grand Duke. Isn't he a lovely man! I heard him last Wednesday." I enquired what was his subject. "The Religion of Love. Very interlecktewaal and too deep for me!" she said laughing. I liked the little woman. She gave me her life story. She was born in Omaha and had married a Polish prince she had met in Paris a year after her first husband died. "You're English? I know that by your lovely voice." "Thank you," I said, "And my clipped speech?" "Sure!" she replied.

The dinner went on. Towards the end someone sang. Then a Negro stood up in the orchestra and played a trombone solo. No one stopped talking. Now and then the cameras flashed. When coffee came, the Chairman hammered for silence. She introduced, name by name, "Our very distinguished guests." Following the Grand Duke, we all got up in turn and bowed. Then after coffee was finished the Chairman introduced the Grand Duke, glowingly. The handsome giant rose and spoke. I wondered how he had survived the Russian Revolution, whether he was destitute, what adventures he had experienced in that terrific maelstrom from which Lenin and Trotsky had now emerged, all Russia in the grip of the Bolsheviks. I looked at the Grand Duke, a vehicle of tremendous history. We should now have a personal description of the great drama. Alas, there was not a word of all this. Calmly, in quite good English, he spoke. His delivery was fair but I found his subject matter banal and incomprehensible. He kept repeating "But divine love is . . ." The audience in the great ballroom was politely silent. When he sat down there was a great burst of applause. "What a lovely man," said the Princess, "so cultured!" It was half-past eleven when I, the tenth and last speaker, was called upon. The audience was now moribund.

The next morning Glass telephoned me. "I've had Emma on the phone. You must have done a great job last night, she's quite excited. She loves you. Let's hope it does something for us." It did. In the next four days we had three more local bookings. And when the lively Princess tried to date me, I did not resist despite Glass's advice.

II

I was not the only visiting lecturer on the scene. There seemed to have been a boat load of us. I went to call on John Drinkwater who was staying at the Algonquin Hotel, the favourite haunt of the literary and theatrical worlds. He was there with his wife, at the very peak of success. His play *Abraham Lincoln*, which had run in London for a year, was now a hit on Broadway. Inspired by Lord Charnwood's *Lincoln*, it had caught the tide of the Anglo-American *entente* born of the united war effort. I found Drinkwater as calm and pompous as ever, with his trained voice, and monocle on a cord. We had both, aged fifteen, been office boys in Nottingham. He greeted me cordially and gave me an autographed copy of his poems, just published in America. I went to a reading he gave at a theatre matinée under distinguished auspices. He read well and was mobbed afterwards by feminine lion-hunters. He told me he was booked up for lectures at $600 a time.

At twenty-four Drinkwater had married Kathleen Walpole, an actress whom he had met when at the Birmingham Repertory Theatre. She was a charming woman, now very much in the shadow of her famous husband. The wives of all famous men hold an unenviable position. "It isn't me, it's Philip they want to see," said Lady Gibbs, with patient resignation. Alas, fame destroyed Drinkwater. From this peak-year Fate took him downhill. He separated from his wife four years later to marry Daisy Kennedy, the violinist ex-wife of Benno Moiseiwitsch, the pianist. Touched by *folie de grandeur*, living on too large a scale, he saw his vogue vanish. He ended his life, poor fellow, nigh bankrupt, at the age of fifty-five. Happily all this was unforeseen in those bright days of acclaim in America.

Other visiting lecturers were enjoying their celebrity, some of them very remuneratively. Among them were Sir Oliver Lodge, Sir Arthur Conan Doyle, Maurice Maeterlinck, W. B. Yeats, Alfred Noyes, Robert Nichols, and Siegfried Sassoon. Jessica Rittenhouse, of the Poetry Society of America, to whose annual dinner I was invited, recorded our presence in her autobiography *My House of Life*.

"It was our constant pleasure to entertain poets from other

countries, especially England and Ireland, and our annual dinners were nearly always distinguished by such visitors. The dinner of 1920 may be cited as the extreme instance of an assembling of a group of foreign poets and we had as guests of honour William Butler Yeats, Siegfried Sassoon, Laurence Housman, Cecil Roberts and Yone Neguchi, all of whom spoke. Cecil Roberts declared that it had come to a point where, if one wished to see one's writing friends, one must come to New York."

I was astonished to find how readily Americans went to hear poets read their verses. In England not a score of persons would tolerate such a thing. I had indeed established something of a record, long before the Sitwells' enterprise with *Façade*, by taking in 1914, at the age of twenty-one, the Bechstein Hall in London (later the Wigmore Hall), and inducing some three hundred persons to buy tickets to hear me read my poems. I was regarded generally as a curiosity who had pulled off an audacious fluke. Only the Poetry Bookshop, with much publicity and no "overheads", had been able to make the experiment. In America the scene was quite different. Here we were, Yeats, Noyes, Drinkwater, Sassoon, drawing enthusiastic audiences. It was a phenomenon noticed by Rebecca West: "When I first went to America in 1923 I was struck by the way that Americans listened to poetry being read aloud, often by its authors, in the same way that the Germans and Austrians and the French did, but not the English."

One evening at a dinner party I met W. B. Yeats. He was a legendary figure to me. He had a tall, grave, handsome presence, his brow draped in long black hair. He had recently married. Some years ago he had acquired a gaunt half-ruin, a Norman tower on the bank of the Ballylee in Ireland. He was now in the process of doing it up for a home, having given up his bachelor quarters off Woburn Place, London, where he had lived for twenty-five years. Repairing and furnishing Thoor Ballylee, as it was called, with winding stairs, venetian windows and great stone fireplace, was proving costly. He was therefore making an extended lecture tour to raise funds. He was at the height of his fame, and there was no difficulty in booking him for large fees. "Just to look at him is worth the money!" said an Irish lady.

"In spite of all expenses and the high rate of living," wrote Yeats to Lady Gregory, "I hope to bring home more money than ever before. My agent Pond is sending at once £100 for the roof." Yeats was commanding a fee of $1,000 a reading, as compared with Noyes' and Drinkwater's $600. There were a few who complained of his manner of reading, and his choice of poems. He would not read any "personal" poems. "My private emotional life is my own," he told Pond, when the point was raised. As for his reading, it was inanimate and to one person who complained he retorted, "I read my poetry as all the great poets from Homer down read their poetry." As no one living could say they had heard Homer that reply stopped any argument.

I admired Yeats as an artist but I found some of his conversation incomprehensible. He was "spooky", as was then the post-war fashion, with Sir Oliver Lodge's amazing stories of the psychic world. After dinner, the conversation turned to this subject and Yeats began to wave a necromancer's wand over us. Was it possible that he believed the stories he told, or did he hypnotise himself with his wordy incantation? We accepted the flights of fancy, too polite to contest his statements or interrupt the imaginative journey on which he embarked, intoning like some priest in a temple at Karnak. Masefield, who visited him in his Woburn Place lodging, told me it was a magician's cave. Yeats described to him an experience he had had which made him believe in the occult. While he lay awake one night a coat-hanger came out of his wardrobe, travelled across the end of his bed and went back again. It emerged the next night, this time carrying one of his jackets. On the third night it came out of the wardrobe and disappeared, after a circuitous journey, into the wall. The effect of these manifestations did not disturb Yeats's nervous system. On the contrary he found that he had recovered his lost potency.

At our dinner party there was no coat-hanger story but he told us that he had seen succubi* around his bed. They exuded a green light and faded away when he pronounced a Gaelic incantation over them. One of the company was inspired to ask if he would read some of his poems and produced a book of them. He sat silent for some minutes

* *Succubi*, demons who have sexual intercourse with sleeping men.

and then, without opening the book, began to declaim his verses. He put an enchanter's spell upon us. It was difficult to believe later that we drove home in a taxi through New York. We had been on "The Lake Isle of Innisfree", and "in a bee-loud glade".

Two days later Yeats stepped into the lift at the Algonquin Hotel as I was going up to the Drinkwaters' room. I greeted him. He peered at me, raven-like. "I know you? I know you?" he asked. I mentioned where we had met. He looked at me a little dazed, then shook his noble head. "I am sorry," he murmured. The lift arrived at his floor and a determined lady accompanying him glared at me as she pushed him out. I was infringing proprietorial rights, and perhaps she suspected I was heavy-footed.

> But I, being poor, have only my dreams;
> I have spread my dreams under your feet;
> Tread softly, because you tread on my dreams.

It was here in New York that I met another poet whose name and work were familiar to me, Alfred Noyes. Still young, highly popular and famous, he was a splendid reader of his verses. Endowed with dramatic power, he was able to give every delicate shade to them. I was delighted, therefore, one day, lunching at the Harvard Club, when a powerfully-built man came over to my table and introduced himself. "I'm Alfred Noyes. I want to thank you for some splendid reviews of my books," he said. From that meeting our friendship flowered.

III

I saw and heard quite a number of my fellow lecturers. The chasm of the war years bridged, they came over to the United States, unscarred by the war and bursting with gold. Most of the visiting lecturers profited from this prosperity and the American passion for seeing and hearing famous European figures whose visits the four years of the war had prevented. One of them above all others made a triumphant entry into the New World. This was Maurice Maeterlinck, but what began as a triumph ended in tragedy.

One morning as I was about to leave my lecture bureau Glass picked up a ticket. "Would you like to hear Maeterlinck? He's just arrived and is giving his opening lecture this afternoon at Carnegie Hall." I thanked him and took the ticket. I had heard about Maeterlinck's sensational arrival on Christmas Eve on his first visit to America. His advent seemed to have convulsed New York. It was in the throes of a *Blue Bird* mania. As soon as the liner *Paris* came past the Statue of Liberty, entering New York, a dozen aeroplanes of the wartime Lafayette Squadron flew over the vessel, their wings painted blue. The quayside was hung with banners proclaiming "Welcome to Maeterlinck!" The streets put out French and Belgian flags, the public never being quite sure whether the Nobel Prize winner was French or Belgian. Shops had special *Blue Bird* window displays. These had surprised me as I walked down Fifth Avenue. For the next two weeks hostesses fought for the famous author. He had agreed on behalf of a Belgian charity to autograph his books, but when he saw the crowd waiting in line he was so appalled that he refused to sign a single copy. It was given out that he was suffering from neuritis in his right hand.

Every ticket was sold for the *Blue Bird* Ball, devoted to charities for French and Belgian war orphans, organised by a committee presided over by Mrs. Cornelius Vanderbilt. There was not a seat obtainable when the opera *L'Oiseau Bleu* was performed at the Metropolitan Opera House on December 27th, 1919. The music was by Albert Wolff the Met's French conductor. The bewildered blue-eyed Belgian sat in the box of honour with the Belgian Ambassador and his wife. He hated music, was tone-deaf, and had hitherto refused to hear opera, including that of his *Pelléas and Mélisande*, set to music by Debussy, but the pressure of fame was too great, and a month after the *L'Oiseau Bleu* production he attended a performance of *Pelléas and Mélisande*, with Mary Garden leading the cast. *Noblesse oblige.* The next day he wrote to her a graceful tribute: "Yesterday I violated my vow and I am a happy man. For the first time I have entirely understood my own play, and because of you!" The shade of Debussy was at last avenged. Some thirty-five years later when Mary Garden was in retirement, old and poor, in Scotland, she raised £600 with that letter.*

* *Maurice Maeterlinck* by W. D. Hulls (The Clarendon Press).

37

When I arrived at Carnegie Hall to hear Maeterlinck lecture on "Immortality" (Life-after-Death was then all the fashion, Conan Doyle and Oliver Lodge assisting) the hall was sold out. Ambassadors, millionaires with a sprinkling of divines sat on the platform. Alas, the lecture was a débâcle. The young son of an American impresario, Maeterlinck's neighbour at his Riviera villa above Monte Carlo, had tried to teach Maeterlinck a phonetic English. The poet had been very reluctantly co-operative. Like a parrot he learned the English, not understanding a word of it. He had only been lecturing a few minutes when the audience became restive, for his language was neither English nor French but a sheer gibberish. There were cries of "Louder! Louder". Maeterlinck raised his voice and the gibberish became worse. "Talk French!" shouted members of the audience. "No, talk English!" shouted others. A riot broke out at the back of the hall. "Imbécile!" screamed a disappointed ticketholder. The chairman intervened. It was decided that Maeterlinck should deliver his lecture in French, with intervening translation into English. But the text was at the poet's hotel. The audience, now rampageous, had to await its arrival. Many had left the hall, demanding their money back at the box office. When the Press reports appeared the next day there were cancellations of bookings across the United States. A quarrel broke out with Major Pond, the lecture agent. Maeterlinck changed to another agent. Pond issued an injunction. Fortunately for the poet the lawyers found a flaw in the contract. Pond, whom young Winston Churchill, lecturing under his promotion twenty years earlier and disappointed in the receipts, called "a dreadful hooligan", went bankrupt. His agency had been the foremost in the country and had handled world celebrities with much success. Luck did not altogether desert Pond. One day at a friend's house he heard a young woman giving some character sketches of her own devising. He was impressed and suggested she should give them in public. He booked her and had such great success that it put his agency back in business. Her name was Ruth Draper. It was fortunate that at the time of this Maeterlinck débâcle I was with another agency.

I was lecturing in Chicago in February and there I had my last glimpse of Maeterlinck. I was taken by my hostess, Mrs. Rockefeller McCormick, to a reception given for him by the Arts League, that had its rooms on Michigan Avenue. I was surprised to learn from my hostess that some ladies had refused to attend the reception. A scandal was pursuing Maeterlinck. It was said that, having discarded one mistress, Mlle Georgette Leblanc, the actress, after living with her for twenty-three years, he was now travelling with another, a very young French girl whom he was said to be trying to pass off as Madame Maeterlinck. She was at the reception, a very pretty blonde young woman, with dark eyes and a brilliant complexion. Like all the wives of famous men no one wanted to bother with her, and she kept in the background. There was no truth in the charge that she was Maeterlinck's mistress, which a great disparity in their ages seemed to support, for he was a white-haired man of fifty-eight and Renée Dahon was twenty-six, younger even in appearance. "Barbe-bleu, no Oiseau-bleu" gibed a New York journalist. They had been married a year when they arrived in America. It proved to be a completely happy marriage, and when Maeterlinck lay dying at eighty-seven his last words to her were: "It's all over with me. I have only one regret—that's leaving you."

Maeterlinck made an almost regal journey across the United States. Sam Goldwyn enticed him to Hollywood. He sent his special railway coach for him, once used by President Wilson. A strange cavalcade set off from New York. It consisted of Goldwyn's representative, M. and Mme Maeterlinck, two friends, a typist-secretary, a Japanese butler, a Chinese chef, a quadroon chamber-maid and a Negro page boy. Goldwyn hoped that Maeterlinck would make the films more "intellectual". He was reported to have told someone who said that there were too many old clichés in a scenario, "Then get some new clichés". To this Goldwyniana could be added his retort, when one of his scriptwriters complained that there were too many lesbians in the story they had bought—"Good Lord! We've plenty of Czechs, Arabs, Poles, Germans and Italians on the set, why not Lesbians?" In this new milieu Maeterlinck was lost. He wrote three scenarios that were never produced though he was handsomely paid for them. As Goldwyn remarked to me twenty years later, giving his latest scriptwriter lunch: "I've had 'em all, and most of 'em were dumb!"

In May, 1920, Maeterlinck was back in France, vowing he would never visit America again. But Fate willed otherwise. In 1940 he returned, a refugee from the Nazi storm. The author of *The Burgomaster of Stilemonde* and other anti-German works felt Europe was not safe. For seven years America provided him with a comfortable refuge.

Two other lecturers dealing in "the other world" met with much success. I did not hear Sir Arthur Conan Doyle. He lectured on spiritualism, then a growing vogue following the abnormal deaths of millions of young men on the battlefields, leaving behind a multitude of bereft parents and friends. "You'd have thought he would have chosen Sherlock Holmes, but the spook-business is in fashion just now," said Glass. "Maeterlinck says there are no dead, and Sir Oliver goes one better, he's talking with them. Well, Sir Arthur's seen fairies painting the colours on flowers—and he's photographed them! Well, well. The hall's sold out every time."

The catch of the season was Sir Oliver Lodge. He had created a sensation with his book *Raymond, or Life and Death*. Sir Oliver was an imposing figure. Six-feet three-inches in height, he weighed 200 lb. Walter Tittle, the portrait painter, called him "a great oak-tree of a man with a head like the dome of St. Paul's". One of the foremost physicists of the world, the father of six sons and six daughters, he lived to be eighty-nine, mentally vigorous to the end and in no way perturbed by the derision with which his belief in psychic phenomena was received.

Now sixty-nine, he had just retired from being the Principal of Birmingham University. He was a past President of the British Association, a Faraday Medallist, and a pioneer in wireless telegraphy. Loaded with honours, he was a highly respected, eminent man of science, of unimpeachable integrity. During the First World War he had published *Raymond*, parts of which seemed incredible and at times absurd. He had avowed his belief in spiritualism, announcing that he had held conversations, via a medium, with his son Raymond who had been killed in the war. Thousands of bereaved parents clutched at this revelation of life after death.

The examples he gave of communications with his son stretched credulity to breaking point. A table, tilted via a medium, spelt out astonishing messages. "Father, tell Mother she will have her son with her on Christmas Day. There will be thousands and thousands of us back in our homes that day," said the "passed-over" Raymond. He was reported as saying still more foolish things. "A chap came over the other day who asked for a cigar—it was produced. There are laboratories over here and they manufacture all sorts of things in them. Not like you do, out of solid matter but out of essences and ethers and gases. They were able to manufacture what looked like a cigar. The chap jumped at it. Some want meat and strong drink, they call for whiskies and sodas. Don't think I am stretching it when I tell you that they can manufacture even that . . . The heavenly mansions are made of bricks and when I touch them they feel like bricks."*

After Sir Oliver's return from America Alfred Noyes went to stay with him. He told Noyes that when he and his wife were alone queer things began to happen. The furniture started moving about. "The sofa behaved very affectionately towards Lady Lodge—some of its advances were grotesque," said Sir Oliver. He did not find this at all unusual. "If you were a shipwrecked sailor on a raft you might try to attract attention by waving your shirt in any way you could," he explained. Noyes was glad when the visit was over. "The place was spooky—I felt I was in a mental home," he said.

I went to Sir Oliver's opening lecture in New York. Carnegie Hall was crammed. He was an impressive figure on the platform, calm and positive, but there was little of note in his subject matter. He disappointed the audience by excluding any sensationalism although he stuck by the statements in his book. "I have not the slightest doubt that I have talked to my son Raymond. There are no dead." Perhaps, unknowingly, he echoed the words of a character in *The Blue Bird*, written by the dramatist who had come to disaster on the same platform.

Sir Oliver refused to be cornered or rocked by the Press. Only once during the lecture did he appear ruffled. Two women in the front stalls sat knitting. He stooped and addressed them severely. "If you ladies must knit, please do it elsewhere. It is not courteous to me or my subject." Rebuked, they stopped knitting. The audience, disappointed and bored after a time, behaved well but the applause at the end was coolly polite. Glass reported an incident in the artistes'

* *Raymond, or Life and Death*, by Sir Oliver Lodge (Methuen).

41

room, filled with autograph and celebrity hunters. "Oliver, put your name in my book, I'm Laura!" said an elderly woman, thrusting it forward. Sir Oliver took her book, pen in hand. "Laura what?" he asked. "Surely you know me!" exclaimed Laura. "I was your wife in our last reincarnation." Sir Oliver signed without a word. "Oh boy!" said Glass, raising his hands.

On my tours there was one name that always came up—John Cowper Powys. He seemed to have left a ripple in every town from the Atlantic to the Pacific Coast. We had the same agent, and one day when he came into the bureau Glass introduced me. He was an impressive and extraordinary figure. "Hard-fleshed, keen-boned, lean-bellied, not beautiful with his loose coherent mouth, simian forehead villainously low, beaked nose, high-toned Red Indian cheeks—a beauty of transfiguring power for those who saw and heard him." Thus wrote a lifelong friend, Louis Wilkinson. It described him as I saw him, aged about fifty. I was to see him only once again, in 1924, although he lived long enough for me to send him a congratulatory telegram on his ninetieth birthday. He sent me through his friend Frederick Davies, a book of his, inscribed "John Cowper Powys, who recollects in his ninetieth year the Nineteen-Twenties when he and Cecil Roberts lectured across the United States".

As we greeted one another in Glass's office, he a platform veteran, I a novice, he said, booming—"So you are the fellow who's trying to snatch my mantle!"

He had no rival on the platform. The legend of him pervaded everywhere. I felt the reverberation of his presence in the houses I stayed in, where he had preceded me. He magnetised his audiences by sheer intellectual force. Exuberant egotism, and necessity, drove him on like a tornado. He loved and hated the United States in which he was a travelling circus for over twenty years. When he first set foot in Theodore Roosevelt's America in 1907, "I howled and whimpered and chanted and burbled like a Dervish", he recorded. He had not then made his mark as a novelist. He was the eldest of a prolific novel-writing trio of brothers bred in a vicarage. Powys made £1,000 a year lecturing each winter and spent his summers with his family in England. Tortured by gastric ulcers, he lived in the utmost discomfort in cheap hotel bedrooms in order to transmit money home to his family. Maurice Browne, the theatrical producer who saw much of him in America, gives us a vivid sketch of the magician.*

He was incomparably the finest public speaker I have heard, not excepting John Burns at the turn of the century or Winston Churchill. He was like a trumpet calling to battle. When he lectured on Huysmans at Lincoln Center, a social settlement on Chicago South Side, sparks seemed to fly from his fingers, which were handling, like an obscene object, a Bible lying on the lectern before him, and the audience hated his guts, as he intended. Once I heard him talk on Thomas Hardy for over two hours to an audience of more than two thousand in a large auditorium in the heart of the Chicago slums. Throughout there was no sound from his listeners save an occasional roar of applause or laughter, and when he had finished speaking we rose like one person on our feet, demanding more. The man was a great actor.

When Powys lectured he wore a voluminous black gown. "He looks like a necromancer and you wonder what he's going to conjure up, what voodoo he has up his wide sleeve. I've never met such a flood of intellect," said Glass. Somehow, during the years when he flew like Mercury through the American scene, he wrote two gigantic novels, *Wolf Solent* and *A Glastonbury Romance*, and an autobiography. When I last met him in 1924 he had another forty-one years in front of him. Despite his playful admonishment I had no ambition to snatch his mantle. It would have been a thing quite beyond me. He was a meteor crossing my path. I blame myself, now, that in the following forty years I never made the effort to go and see him.

IV

When Prohibition came into force on January 16th, 1920, the club bar could sell only soft drinks. This Draconian law was fiercely opposed throughout the United States and had disastrous results. A vast illicit traffic grew up. The law came into contempt and the amount of secret drinking became prodigious. It promoted the cocktail habit. A network of bootleggers covered the United States and vast

* *Too Late to Lament*, by Maurice Browne (Gollancz).

43

fortunes were made from the peddling of liquor. Soon along the coast of Florida fleets of rum-runners just outside the three-mile limit successfully ran the gauntlet of Customs officers. I had not been five minutes in my hotel in Detroit when my telephone rang. An unknown voice greeted me. Did I require any whisky, gin, rum? The price was named. It could be delivered at my bedroom door within a few minutes. Obviously there was connivance with the reception desk which must have informed them of the new guest. In Chicago, "the wickedest city in the world", during Prohibition there were 703 gang murders arising directly from the drink traffic.

The revolt against Prohibition never died down; it grew, despite the fact that "The 18th Amendment" to the Constitution had been passed by an 80 per cent majority in the Senate and a 70 per cent majority in the Lower House. This Amendment caused more bitter controversy than any since the slavery issue of pre-Civil War days.

After a trial of fourteen years, Prohibition was scrapped. It proved unworkable, created widespread corruption and turned the country into a nation of alcoholics addicted to secret drinking. Its disastrous effects reached into subsequent history. When the Japanese swooped down on the American fleet in Pearl Harbor, Honolulu, at 7.55 a.m., on Sunday, December 7th, 1941, they knew that the crews were sleeping off the effects of their customary Saturday night "binge". A Japanese spy in Honolulu despatched a coded message informing Tokio what American naval ships were in harbour that Saturday. It was picked up by the U.S. Navy but not decoded, and put aside for later attention. The admiral of the Pacific Fleet was dismissed for negligence.

V

Before leaving New York I paid a call on Madam Clara Novello Davies. Once, years earlier, in the stalls at the St. James's Theatre I had seen Eddie Marsh with a young man of about my age. He was in uniform, black-haired, slim, somewhat Italianate in appearance. During the interval Marsh introduced his companion. He must have been one of the handsomest young men in England, Rupert Brooke having died during the war in a blaze of glory. His name was Ivor

Novello Davies. Despite appearance, he had no Italian blood. His mother had added Novello to her name in admiration of a famous singer. Her son had already won renown as the composer of a highly popular war song, "Keep the Home Fires Burning", which earned him £15,000, using the name Ivor Novello. When a boy he had been a chorister of Magdalen College, Oxford, and had published his first composition at fifteen. His mother was eminent in the musical world. Ivor was her only child.

When we met he had not yet gone on the stage. His good looks, flawless profile and dark luminous eyes were enhanced by a nature of much sweetness and generosity. He had before him a very great success as an actor-producer of his own musical plays, and until the day of his death, aged fifty-seven, he delighted large audiences, playing the lead in his own creations. His first film role was in a version of Robert Hichens' Sicilian novel *The Call of the Blood* which his Italianate face suited perfectly. Seven years after I first met him he began his career as author-actor-producer with *The Rat*, written in conjunction with Constance Collier. It made him famous. He had a spell in Hollywood, which did not suit his temperament, and then came back to the London stage for a long career of unbroken success. All this, which would have turned the soundest head, never affected his delightful character. An idol of the theatre, he never became vain or spoilt though he thoroughly enjoyed the adulation that enveloped him. In sheer kindness of heart he would cast old actors and actresses to give them employment. In all things, despite the artistic temperament, he was level-headed.

During the Second World War Ivor had a collision with the Government over petrol for his Rolls-Royce car. It was a stupid affair on both sides, with a vicious note on the part of the authorities, who sent him to prison following the British delight in vilifying "those bloody artistic blokes", a tradition running from Oscar Wilde to Noël Coward and Compton Mackenzie, all victims of British "justice". Although the audience gave Ivor a terrific welcome when he stepped from a prison cell on to the Drury Lane stage this official brutality shortened his life. He died very suddenly one night in his Adelphi flat just after returning from the theatre.

I had last seen him when, with Naomi Jacob and Mrs. Patrick

45

Campbell, we motored to lunch with him in Verona. The conjunction of Ivor and Mrs. Pat at the lunch table was epic. Ivor attracted the attention of all in the restaurant, being debonair, handsome and beautifully dressed in his easy bohemian style, but it was Mrs. Pat, matriarchal, deep-voiced, who commanded the scene. Old and broken, her financial position a nightmare, she was still a reigning queen and exacted the homage of all within her circle.

Ivor's mother, Madam Clara Novello Davies, on whom I called soon after arriving in New York, was now living there and teaching voice production. She was a woman of some fascination and presence. At that time I had no idea what a lifelong trial she was to Ivor. She was one of those women with no sense of money, whose plans always go awry, who eat cake when they should be content with bread and butter. She was, to use a horrid word, a leech on her generous, loving son. Deeper and deeper he plunged his hand into his pocket to rescue her from a new crisis. She was always his darling mother, impervious to repeated protests in which he mingled gentleness with despair. Happily she died before him. When I called on her she was full of plans to found a school of voice production, about which she was charmingly vague and optimistic.

VI

A fortnight after my arrival in New York, I left on my lecture tour, if that name could be applied to what was a shuttle-service in which I bobbed in and out of various cities and states following a crazy pattern of bookings. I now became acquainted with the American sleeping-car, or Pullman. No trains were visible in the New York Central Railroad Station, a building with the majesty of a cathedral. It had a vast nave, and above it rose a star-encrusted dome. In this great hall, which might have been borrowed from the Baths of Caracalla at Rome, on a shining marble floor, the diminutive booking offices looked like illuminated choir stalls from which rose a faint hymn to Mercury, the god of travel. Along one wall were a number of gateways, each portal having an illuminated number and route-indication scroll. You chose your number, went down a chute and found your train housed in a long metal shed. The cathedral

46

illusion was maintained by Negro porters wearing dark suits and red caps, who acted as vergers showing you to your "pew". The local trains had aisles, which you traversed in almost a religious silence. In a long-distance train you went "Pullman", seated in an individual divan chair on a swivel, the whole floor carpeted. Each car carried a Negro "verger", clad this time in a white jacket. These long-distance trains were enormous in length and so high up off the ground that at smaller stations you climbed up into them using a small footstool supplied by the car attendant.

The sleeping cars provided an adventure. They were ingenious contrivances, with wide seats that by night were converted into double-decker beds. They were like catacombs, so restricted that you could not sit upright in them. Undressing and dressing became an acrobatic feat behind drawn green curtains. To gain the upper berth the Negro attendant provided a ladder. You swivelled your legs into your catacomb, drew the curtains and away went the ladder, which you asked for in the morning when you wished to go to the washroom at the end of your car. Because of this climbing up and down my agent strove to get me a lower instead of an upper berth. The tycoons travelled in "drawing rooms", private sleeping apartments equipped with everything. Strange to relate, I came to like these sleeping berths. Once in them you had a private domain. The bed was very wide and soft. There was an overhead reading light. There was a window, with a drawn blind in the lower berth, which was almost hermetically sealed, for a good reason. If you contrived to open the window only an inch there was such an Arctic blast that you were in peril of being frozen. The upper berths had no ventilation. The heat of the car was controlled by the Negro attendant, and he, with reminiscences of his African home-land, kept it tropically high. I generally ended the night without a sheet over me, parched.

Such was the mode of travel in the nineteen-twenties. All night these green-curtained incubators roared across the vast snow-bound continent, over plains, ravines, deserts, rivers, and mountains. You could travel two thousand five hundred miles east–west, and one thousand five hundred miles north–south, still in the same country but with varying climates. On this continent of

47

mammoth railways there was one very singular fact. Owing to some financial or territorial battle between railway giants you could not travel from the east across to the west through Chicago without changing. The line was severed there. The company provided its passengers with a bus service joining the severed ends. It seemed to me an incredible inconvenience, in a country that prided itself on its mechanical efficiency, that the line at Chicago should be bisected like a chopped worm, entailing a tiresome and time-wasting connection via a bus service. "The railroad tycoons have got us tied up," said Glass when I commented on this. Twenty years later transcontinental air services abolished this absurdity. They have almost abolished the sleeping car since New York and Los Angeles are now only five hours and not four days and three nights apart. Only one hundred years earlier this transcontinental passage had entailed a three or four months' journey in an ox-wagon, braving floods, torrents, blizzards, prairies, deserts and the menace of hostile Indians, something like a Fenimore Cooper saga of peril and courage.

There was one great blessing derived from the trip by sleeping car. You were alone, you could not be invaded by telephone calls, reception committees, the Press, or merciless hostesses showing you off. It was romantic for me, a stranger, young and eager, to go roaring through the snowy landscape, to peep out on strange villages bathed in moonlight, and to hear the sad wail of the train whistle that evoked the ghosts of dead pioneers who had opened up this great continent. The only drawback was the car coupling connections, made with such violence that you seemed likely to have your neck dislocated.

VII

It was a great relief to find my audiences responsive and warmhearted. My impression from the opening Brooklyn lecture was confirmed. English audiences are politely reserved. Not until the end is one aware what impression one has made. American audiences are spontaneous in their reaction. You feel as if you had put your foot on the accelerator of a high-powered car. They imbibe lectures with gusto and are quick to express themselves, sometimes in surprising terms. "My, that English voice! I haven't understood what you said but it's how you say it!" cried a Texan, wringing my hand. I discovered certain obsessions. Almost every press report referred to my "clipped English speech". Also it is firmly embedded in the American mind that we are devoid of humour. "Despite the fact that he is English he has a vivid sense of humour . . ." they reported.

I was often embarrassed by an excess of enthusiasm. My Trenton chairman took me to the station. He was unusually silent until the train came in. Then he gripped my hand and said, "Sir, if I'd a gift of eloquence like yours I'd turn myself into a power station and light up New York!" Occasionally there was unrestrained comment. One newspaper, Hearst-owned and therefore anti-British, wrote—"He exuded hauteur and patronage like a Bourbon talking to hicks." This was balanced by a lady in Kalamazoo saying, as I came off the platform, "I think you're cute. I'd like to kiss you!" She did.

Some of the newspaper headings were startling. It seemed I had a sadistic passion for "flaying" my audiences. "Roberts flays us for not joining the League." "Roberts flays Prohibition." "Writer flays Clubwomen" (I had expressed surprise at how they found time to do so many things, this by way of compliment). "America called Naughty Nation." "Poet tells why we are cordially hated." "Scoffs at Democracy. Says we're mob-minded." "Despotic English-man damns ballot box." All this was rather shattering. I thought I had been very tactful, an unofficial ambassador of my country. But I was heartened by other headlines. "Noted Briton brilliantly addresses Seminary at Graduation." "American bathrooms lauded as temples." "Superlative charm, wit, eloquence." "Best-dressed, best-spoken of the British Invaders." This in Chicago, whose mayor had threatened to "bust King George on the snoot", was a real compliment.

Visiting Grand Rapids, I had a new experience. I slept in a wooden house, a luxurious steam-heated pseudo-Doric villa such as are common in New England. It was at Grand Rapids that I made an unusual headline. I had such a welcome from my hostess and friends, gathered to meet me after the lecture, that an excited wire-terrier dog nipped me in the calf, drawing blood. Everyone showed tremendous concern lest I should die of rabies. Hot water, iodine and bandages were brought. I refused to have a doctor called and maintained there was no cause for alarm. The next morning's local paper recorded the mishap. "Distinguished Guest Shows British Phlegm." Arising out of the incident I had a lesson on how careful one should be and how small the world is. I wrote some articles on my tour and one of them appeared some months later in *The Christian World*, to which English journal I was a regular contributor. Somehow a copy of the paper, containing my article describing the Grand Rapids incident, reached that town. It was reproduced in the local paper, of which a copy was sent to me. "Courteous Englishman Does Not Tell on His Host's Dog", ran the heading. I had omitted the mishap in my account.

VIII

In Montgomery, Alabama, I met in my hotel a Cornell graduate, a young giant of childlike ingenuousness, travelling about in search of experiences for a thesis he planned to write on social conditions in the southern states. He had been working in an Alabama lumber camp. "It's living with savages," he said. "They can't read, they can't write, they can only booze. One of 'em's gone blind on bootleg liquor. If any poor devil fails to hitch up a log on the moving chain, up comes the boss and gives him a nick with a razor. If he puts up a hand to defend himself, he shoots him in the arm."

"Do you mean to say he can treat Negroes in that fashion?" I asked.

"Negroes be damned—they're Poor Whites—not niggers!"

"But the law?"

He laughed and emptied his flask of bootlegger gin. "We've had two Sheriffs in nine months. They didn't shoot quick enough."

I told him I could not believe it. "Come back with me tomorrow," he said. "I've been here to see a doctor about a poisoned foot. I didn't believe it until I saw it."

Incredible—but I recalled something I had found in the New York Public Library. Perhaps things had not changed very much. One day, passing by the library, I went in. I was curious to learn whether it had yet heard of me, full of the young author's urge to be recognised. Would it have my *Poems*, just out? It had, but in consulting the index I was astonished by two things. There were also my four earlier books published in England. It had something else, an error surely, a book by me called *Adrift in America*. This title had a sinister note. I was not exactly adrift, and I had written no such book. Was there another Cecil Roberts who had had a difficult time here? I asked for the book. The title and the name were quite correct but my predecessor had been here in America long before me. The book had been published in London in 1891, the year before I was born. This other Cecil Roberts, born in 1860, died in 1894.

I read the book. What a story he had recorded of his adventures in the United States! He had gone to sea when about twenty-two in the *Soukir* (1,300 tons) of the Shaw Savill Line. After having rounded the Cape he became Second Mate of the *Babington*, of the same line. Finding a seaman's lot miserable and hard, he decided to go West and try his fortune in the United States. With little money, from New York he made his way to South Bend, Indiana, where he worked as a farm-hand for $15 a month. He found the people so terribly bigoted and sunk in religious mania that he left. They ostracised him as immoral for referring to "legs" instead of "limbs". He set out for Fargo, North Dakota, where he was told he might find work. He was in such poverty, being often without food, that he travelled by jumping freight trains. (One recalls that W. H. Davies, the "Tramp Poet", lost a leg in the U.S.A. in the same fashion.) After many wretched experiences entailing very hard labour he decided to go south, away from the extreme cold. He heard that his elder brother, Morley Roberts, who was to win fame later as a novelist, was also in America. Then about thirty, Morley Roberts had been a rancher in Australia and had sailed before the mast. Cecil found him in Colorado City. When he saw his brother he could hardly believe his eyes, he looked so disreputable and down and out. They found work as shepherds and cattle-minders forty miles south of Colorado City. The younger brother became so ill with dropsy that he was warned that he must get to a less inclement clime, with better food. Saying goodbye to his brother, whom he was destined not to see again until six years later in England, Cecil set out, tramping and freight-car jumping. He became very ill, and was so destitute that he was arrested for vagrancy. He was sentenced to ninety days' hard labour and sent to a chain gang. The labour consisted of street-sweeping

51

under a guard with a gun. He had an iron fetter on his right leg, attached to a bar of iron, part of a railway line, weighing 28 lb. He had to pick this up and carry it each time he moved. But a chance arose and he escaped, hiding the bar up his trouser leg. He came upon a sympathetic farmer who unfettered him and gave him work. In due course he worked his way to Kansas City, Minneapolis and St. Paul, then by canal boat through to Pittsburgh and finally reached New York. Here a man gave him a drink that was drugged. He was shanghaied on board a boat off the Bowery. Risking his life, he jumped overboard and swam to a Norwegian ship in the Hudson River, anchored there prior to its voyage to Glasgow, where he landed with thirty shillings in hand. He wrote his reminiscences, which probably his brother, now a rising novelist, got published for him. It is a plain narrative with some literary merit. His terrible experience seems to have undermined his health. He died three years later, aged thirty-four. Poor Cecil Roberts!

Having read *Adrift in America* I left the library. There were steps, guarded by stone lions, leading down to Fifth Avenue. I stood there in bright sunshine, looking at the concourse of traffic where 42nd Street intersected the Avenue. I thought how strange and terrible it would be if I were that other Cecil Roberts, thirty years ago, sick, lonely, impoverished, unwanted and unknown, doomed to die at thirty-four. Here I was, young, healthy, known and welcomed in the United States that had treated him so cruelly. Save for a trick of fate I might have been that Cecil into whom I now imaginatively projected myself. But I was not adrift in America, I was alive, happy and grateful to fortune which had so favoured me.

I thought of that poor lad, long dead, when the Cornell graduate told me about the Alabama lumber camp. It would seem things had not changed so greatly. But the other side of the picture could not be ignored. For thousands this was a land of hopes fulfilled, of prosperity and security.

IX

On, on I went, Philadelphia, Detroit, Niagara Falls, Baltimore, Richmond, St. Louis, Chicago, Lexington, Montgomery. On I went, with the most astonishing adventures. Masefield had given me a letter to friends in Philadelphia. My hostess there put me up in her father's duplex apartment in a modern skyscraper block. It might have been an historic mansion, from the illusion of space and decoration. After being "vetted" by a house detective, I ascended to the top floor and entered a marble hall with a pool of goldfish. Beyond rose a marble staircase. Then the lounge came into view, in the style of a baronial hall, with a carved Elizabethan fireplace, tapestries and pictures. I went from painting to painting in the drawing-room, dining-room and study. I began to believe that my host was a member of an art syndicate that imported masterpieces from Europe. There were works by Tintoretto, Titian, Guardi, Canaletto, Corot, Degas, Constable, Gainsborough, Raeburn, Hogarth, and Turner. I went up the staircase to the bedroom floor. In my own suite I found a bed that Shakespeare's patron, the Earl of Southampton, had slept in, with carved headpiece, footboard and canopy. I could not sleep for a time, feeling like little Tom Thumb in the Castle of the Giant. In the morning the butler, the only servant I saw, asked me if I would like to see the Italian roof garden. He opened a window. We stepped out. There was a large garden, high over the Square. It had a pergola, a *pozzo*, marble benches, and statues. Under a blue sky the illusion was complete save that the air was Arctic on this February day. It was as if a part of the Villa Medici had been transported to the roof of this Philadelphia apartment house.

I never saw the owner of this palace, he was away on business in Los Angeles. I wrote expressing my delight in his home and received a letter in which he apologised for his absence. I discovered something about him. He was a Scot by birth who had made a fortune in Philadelphia as a cotton broker. He had a passion for paintings. These, wisely bought, were worth several million dollars, and on his death, went to enrich various public galleries. The butler showed me a catalogue. It gave the source and prices paid for many of the masterpieces, together with press clippings recording the sensation created by his purchases.

To his married daughter I owed a rewarding friendship. One day she took me, learning of my interest in the piano, to visit a friend, a

53

professional concert pianist, Mrs. Ethel McKenzie. She was the wife of the celebrated Canadian sculptor, Tait McKenzie. When later I visited his studio I was captivated by his work. He had specialised in modelling athletes, and was the first occupant of the chair of Physical Education at the University of Pennsylvania. The university commissioned him to make studies of American athletes, for which purpose he visited universities, took measurements and made statues of youths of good physique.*

I felt he should have an exhibition of his art in London. On my return from World War I I had been commissioned by the Fine Art Society Galleries, New Bond Street, to write the notes for a de luxe edition of Raemaeker's famous war cartoons. Many had appeared originally in the *Amsterdam Telegraaf*. The cartoons got under the skins of the Germans, and the artist had felt it safer to live in England. I was delighted when the Fine Art Society held, early in 1920, an exhibition of Tait McKenzie's work. Sir Philip Gibbs wrote a preface to the catalogue. The exhibition was a great success and led to several commissions including the Cambridge War Memorial, with its noble figure of a typical East Anglian soldier. The memorial was unveiled by the Duke of York (later King George VI). McKenzie also made the splendid Scottish-American War Memorial in Princes Street Gardens, Edinburgh. Our warm friendship ended only on his death.

My experiences on tour were so varied that I was not surprised by anything. I was thumped on the back, called "Ceecil" after five minutes' acquaintanceship, a "good guy", and "a stiff-necked British snob", by a Hearst newspaper. I encountered the American aristocracy, the Daughters of the American Revolution. Wearing orchids in their corsages, they were freezingly solemn. I had a feeling we had not yet been forgiven for Lord North and George III. They were

---

* "The importance of Tait McKenzie's sculpture lies in its being the first considerable *œuvre* since the time of the Greeks to take as its subject and purpose the athletic ideal. The old sports of the chase have produced an illustrative, reminiscent art—hunting pictures for example—much valued by sportsmen. And countless artists have on occasion represented episodes of sport. But McKenzie is the first man of our civilisation to translate athletic actions into plastic beauty."—Christopher Hussey, *Tait McKenzie. A Sculptor of Youth.* (Country Life Ltd.)

admirable ladies, full of good works, with an old-world courtesy. It was odd to discover later that the Dames of the Colonial Wars thought themselves of better vintage, more exclusive. I regretted that I was not engaged to address "The Ancient Order of Nobles of the Mystic Shrine". I saw members of the Order assembling for a banquet in an Alabama hotel. They were dressed as if they had just left the Seraglio, without yashmaks but in voluminous trousers. They could not compete, however, with the Pittsburgh "Shriners", wearing crimson plush Turkish trousers and tasselled tarbooshes. A town in Indiana gave me a surprise. I had ordered a taxi. "Isn't he late?" I asked, afraid of losing my train. "Yes, but he's probably been delayed in Court." "In Court—is he in trouble?" "Oh no! He's conducting a case for a client." "But surely a man who's a lawyer doesn't drive a taxi?" "Let me explain, Mr. Roberts. You're in Hoosier-Land.* Here any man who's of good character can practise in the courts. It comes down from pioneer days when the accused could nominate a friend to take charge of his defence if he didn't feel capable himself."

Five minutes later my lawyer-taximan drove me past the High School. It had a swimming pool, gymnasium and an auditorium to hold eight hundred, with a stage for theatrical productions. All this in a town of ten thousand. "Is it paid for?" I asked. "No, we do it with Bonds. Our future prosperity will pay." It did, everywhere.

It would be wrong for me to leave an impression of eccentricity only. How admirable were those university faculty clubs, their members quiet, cultivated and delightful to talk with; and how efficient were those clubwomen, motoring their children to and from school, organising lectures, concerts and charity drives. How smoothly they ran their servantless houses! On a bedside table in my room stood two vacuum jugs. "Iced water" said a label on one.

* The State's inhabitants have been immortalised by the native poet, James Whitcomb Riley, in his poem *Little Orphant Annie*:

Little Orphant Annie's come to our house to stay,
To wash the cups an' saucers an' brush the crumbs away,
An' shoo the chickens off the porch, an' dust the hearth an' sweep,
An' make the fire, an' bake the bread, an' earn her board an' keep.

55

"Hot milk" said a label on the other. There was an adjustable lamp, an eye-shade, a pencil and a memo pad thoughtfully placed there by the professor's wife. I have long remembered the warm bedrooms (too warm at 88 degrees) with rocking-chair, books, chintz curtains, double-glazed windows dashed with crystallized snow, bright candle-wick counterpane, bath-gown, slippers, a bedside tin of biscuits, and a view, the blind raised, on moonlit fields and hills snow-covered, and the distant moan of a train as it crossed the valley, so many miles and miles and miles away from England.

X

Breakfasting one morning in a Chicago hotel with Witter Bynner, the American poet, I mentioned that I was leaving to lecture at Niagara Falls. "Then you must stay with some friends of mine," he said, and sent off a telegram at once. Thus it was that instead of going to an hotel I found myself in the home of Mrs. Franchot, a lady of French-Polish descent. Witter Bynner had told me that he had once gone there for two days and stayed six weeks. That was the sort of house it was. You were enfolded in kindness and luxury. I arrived there out of a February blizzard. There were children in the house, the more enchanting because they were invisible until you called for them; a baby, a boy aged ten, a girl aged twelve. Little Stanislas had romped with John Masefield who had stayed there. He was half-way through a recital in my honour of Masefield's "Beauty" when he disappeared on being told that his French mistress had arrived.

I stayed two nights, not six weeks, and was taken to see the Falls. They were not in full force being partly frozen, but an engineer of the hydro-electric station clad me in oilskins and high boots and took me along a perilous promenade to a white world of ice, thundering walls of water and spray. I was driven halfway across the great bridge to see Canada, which began on the other half. I was delighted and astonished when I learned that the American train in which I departed later for Detroit ran for a short distance over Canadian soil and stopped briefly in Windsor, Ontario, which was no greater distance from Detroit than is the Tower of London from Piccadilly.

I solemnly descended and remounted so that I could say that I had set foot in Canada.*

The Franchot brother and sister were matched later when I was taken to see another home in Baltimore. My hostess departed for a few moments leaving me in the drawing-room. A cosy log fire crackled in the open grate, the window panes were frosted in the setting of a wintry sun. Presently a very small boy appeared on an upper balcony and solemnly inspected me. Probably I was the first Englishman he had ever seen wearing spats and with a ribbon to his glasses. There was a stunned silence, then in a husky voice he addressed his sister somewhere behind. "Polly, come right here— there's an Englishman downstairs with ankle-mitts and danglums!" In that same drawing-room, following dinner, I read my poems to the assembled guests. There was a large green parrot in a cage behind me and I was apprehensive that it might screech and shatter some delicate passage I was reading but it behaved beautifully. Later, I expressed my gratification at the bird's model behaviour. My hostess laughed loudly. "It's a stuffed one! We put it there when the old parrot died!"

My nine-week tour came to an end. I had addressed forty audiences in thirty cities, towns and odd places. My last lecture, a survey of the economic future of Europe, a subject right outside my syllabus, was to a gathering of bankers in a private auditorium kept by a Wall Street financier, who invited speakers to address his selected audience. I had travelled incessantly, slept twenty nights on trains and been interviewed by dozens of newspapers. Radio and television were not yet added to this ordeal, nor air travel that robs the lecturer today of blessed periods of rest and seclusion. I had done my best to be a creditable ambassador of my country. I never showed boredom at interminable lunch and dinner parties. Americans are gluttons for speeches. They want them off the platform as well as on them. "You'll

* There is an amusing footnote to this. Fearing that my memory might have tricked me, I sent this description to the Town Clerk of Windsor, Ontario, asking "Will you kindly inform me if this is correct, or whether my memory across fifty years has betrayed me." Back came my own letter, stamped "Received, City Clerk, Windsor," with written in pencil at the foot— "Dear Cecil, your memory did not fail you." It was unsigned.

say a few words, won't you?" asked a hostess, and I pulled myself together to say a few words. Sometimes after a lecture I was whisked away to a gathering of the local American Legion, or to sign books, with much handshaking. I never omitted writing to thank a hostess. At twenty-seven one is wonderfully resilient; a night's sleep, even in a train, recharges the battery, but I found the social part much more exhausting than the platform. It would all have been easier if I had had a set piece, like an actor, but I was an extemporaneous performer and always had to start from scratch. After a time my conscience began to trouble me. In an atmosphere of exaggeration it is so easy to become a charlatan, to take seriously one's inflated reputation. When I arrived in Boston, the *Boston Evening Transcript* began a three-column review of my *Poems* with the statement: "During a season of invasion of foreign authors, the two most romantic personalities among them are the Spanish novelist Blasco Ibáñez and the English poet Cecil Roberts." Ibáñez was the world-famous author of *Blood and Sand* and *The Four Horsemen of the Apocalypse*. I had not "invaded" in any sense nor could I consider myself a "romantic personality". I possessed too much "British phlegm", as one newspaper had said.

XI

I had kept the last few days after my tour free of any engagements. In London during the war I had formed a friendship with a young American, a Carolinian; soft-voiced, employed in the American Consulate there. He had returned to America and was taking a law course at Harvard University. He insisted that I should visit him. So one dark evening in March a taxi deposited me at the gate of a large brick quadrangle, by name Smith Dormitory. I was boisterously welcomed and taken into a cheerful room with a log fire burning. It was a double suite, shared with a student who happened to be away, consisting of a large sitting-room, two bedrooms and a bathroom. Here I was installed. There followed five delightful days. We rough-housed, played poker, danced and sang absurd songs. One night, the atmosphere being frowsty, I suggested a run. We changed into shorts and vests and set off, towards midnight, in a hard frost, with snow on the ground, for a three-mile run along the bank of the River Charles, Longfellow's river, where he "stood on the bridge at midnight as the clocks were striking the hour". The previous day I had been taken to the poet's old home to have tea with white-haired Miss Longfellow. She was the "grave Alice" who, with her young sisters, "Laughing Allegra and Edith with golden hair", had rushed in on their father and made him a prisoner in his chair, as his poem related.

Over our room there dwelt a lad with a mop of black curly hair, who often burst in upon us full of laughter and then disappeared to practise on his violin. Of French descent, the son of an owner of orange groves in Florida, I called him Le Roi Philippe, metonymising his name, Phillips. There was also a footballer with a Praxitelean physique, bearing an aura of glory. He was naïve and puppyish. He told me his people in California could not read, so he telephoned them twice a week! A friend assured me he was not pulling my leg.

It was a delightful interlude, to be nobody, free of formality. We made waffles for breakfast, then unknown in England. We sat around in pyjamas. Le Roi Philippe sometimes joined us, clad in a yellow bathrobe, looking like a young Buddhist monk but breaking the illusion by a "shimmy" dance.

And then came the end. They all went into Boston to see me off and I climbed aboard a train that roared through the night to New York. My last task there was to write a long review in the *New York Times Book Review* of Philip Gibbs's *Now it Can Be Told*. Free of censorship, my colleague had told the grim story of the World War as he had seen it. It was a terrifying account written with a skill that has made it a classic.

The Lecture Bureau wanted me to return the next winter. "You've made quite a name. We could book you up at increased fees." I said I could not return so soon. I was going home to take over the editorship of a newspaper. Perhaps I would come back in three or four years. When our accounts were settled my American adventure turned out better than I had expected. I sailed with nearly £1,300 in hand. Twenty years earlier another Englishman, then almost of my age, had made his first lecture tour and netted only a little more. But he had advantages unknown to me, for his name was Winston Churchill and Mark Twain had taken the chair at his opening lecture in

New York.* I had also sold for £800 to *Colliers Weekly* six articles on my impressions of the United States. The happy prosperity of post-war America was marked by a surprising incident. Before sailing I had to obtain an income-tax clearance. The tax official calculated that, less liberal expenses, I owed $280. I got out my cheque book. "Aw, forget it, mister!" he said, signing a cancellation.

As my liner went down the Hudson River and the fantastic outline of New York, grey-towered, sun-smitten, faded behind me, I felt almost tearful, for much kindness received, many friendships made. Down in my cabin I found a great basket of fruit, with an enormous silk bow to which was pinned a card. It was from the imperturbable Mr. Glass. "Bon Voyage. Come again!" he had written on it.

During the Atlantic crossing I was alone at last. I breakfasted in bed. There were no telephone calls, no railway journeys, Press interviews, reception committees and audiences. The atmosphere of America had been electric in every sense. When I slipped out of my fur coat I produced sparks at my finger tips, my hand crackled on door knobs, the carbon paper from the sheets in my typewriter flew across the room and attached itself to the window pane. I now experienced a let down, mentally and physically. In the unnatural quiet and privacy of my cabin, I could possess my soul and meditate upon the life I had left behind and the life towards which I was going. The sense of adventure was still with me after five incredible, crowded years that had taken me from obscurity and penury into a life of increasing experience and rewards. I took stock of my position. I was returning to my home town to edit a newspaper at a comfortable salary. In May I should enter my twenty-eighth year. On my sixteenth birthday, living with my mother, indigently, I had made a

* "Even while he was still in South Africa Churchill had been attracted by offers to give lectures on the war and his experiences . . . I would not go to the United States unless guaranteed at least a thousand pounds a month for three months and I should expect a great deal more. Five thousand pounds is not too much for making oneself so cheap."—*Winston S. Churchill.* Randolph S. Churchill, Vol. I (Heinemann). In the event he went without any guarantee, had scenes with Pond, his lecture agent, and, for a seven weeks' tour, made £1,600.

vow, recording it in my diary, that I would have saved ten thousand pounds at thirty-five, life's halfway, and be at no man's command. I had seven years to go to reach that goal. I was on my way. The bogy of poverty that had haunted me since I was fifteen was dead. I should be able to keep my mother in some comfort after the privation she had so gallantly endured. My delightful scholarly father, dead at forty-nine, had never earned more than £80 a year. At little more than half his age I now had, with odd commissions added, over £1,000 a year and £3,000 in hand.* As I lay in my bunk, hearing the sea lapping the ship's side, I reviewed my journey so far. I had resisted temptation. In New York a banker had offered me £4,000 a year starting salary. I declined the offer, determined not to be deflected from my set course. A man is always poor doing what he does not wish to do.

The editorship I was now taking up had fallen into my lap through a chance encounter with the owner of the paper. It would not be the end of the story. It was only the beginning. It was my dream to be able, one day soon, to write at my own free will just what I wanted to write. It might seem conceited—and what man ever achieved his goal without belief in his ability?—but I regarded myself as a born writer, dedicated to my pen. I had no intention of being consumed by journalism, perpetually climbing its sandhills that collapsed under one's feet. I had neither the disposition nor the toughness. I had learned enough in Fleet Street, exhilarating as it was, to wish to escape its fetters. I wanted my own business under my own control, whatever the risks.

I had already made a start along the road I wished to travel. Four years earlier I had sketched out a novel, its material gathered from experience. The seed had been planted when I was a boy. I had visited the local art gallery and seen a bronze statue labelled "Narcissus". The original had been unearthed at Pompeii. It was the prototype of my *Scissors*. Some years later, in 1917, reviewing for a paper, I found a suggestion for the opening of my story in a book describing its author's journey across Asia Minor. The idea thus fertilised, I wrote the first few pages of my projected novel. Pressure

* £1 in 1920 equalled £7 or more in 1970. The *en pension* rate at Geneva's best hotel in 1920 was £1, in 1970 £14.

61

of journalistic work had caused postponement. Now, crossing the Atlantic, with leisure, I resumed the long delayed story, determined to carry it to completion. Such was my ambitious plan, but I must first address myself to a practical task, my editorship. Lying there in my bunk, I set my course.

Our liner's first call was Plymouth, where I landed. It was a soft spring evening of the first of April, with low-lying clouds over the Hoe. Never had I seen a land so lovely, back from exile however kind.

> Red of the Devon loam,
> Green of the hills,
> April, and I am home!
> God! my heart thrills.
> Far have I travelled
> And great beauty seen
> But, oh, out of England
> Is anywhere green?

CHAPTER THREE

The Editor

I

IN THE FIRST week of April, 1920, I walked into my editorial office and was introduced by the general manager to the staff of the *Nottingham Journal*. I was almost the youngest person on the newspaper. I had wondered, with some anxiety, how I should be received by veterans who could recall the youth of five years ago who, without a penny, had forced himself on the paper in the guise of an "unpaid pupil". Would they resent my presence and authority? My fears were groundless. Throughout my editorship I never had less than kindness and loyalty from my colleagues.

Newspapers, like ships, are complex things and can easily run into danger. One had to be lynx-eyed. In five years we were threatened with four libel actions. These actions are often begun by persons in search of publicity. Not one of the four threats took us into court or entailed dispensing any damages. One was the case of a baronet with shady financial transactions. He loudly briefed a famous council. We stood firm in face of his bluff and the case never went into court. Another libel threat was from a charlatan with a bogus American medical degree. I put the British Medical Association on his track and he vanished without paying the solicitor who wrote suggesting a "settlement".

Journalism is an unrivalled school of training in humanity. There is no other profession which has such a diversified experience of life. You see human beings in many unsavoury aspects, their meanness, treachery, vanity and gullibility. Dignitaries of the Church creep up your stairs to stiletto colleagues, politicians offer betrayal of their friends without asking for thirty pieces of silver, philanthropists making gifts ensure that adequate publicity will be given, the "broad-minded" person spits venom with every sentence he writes, the leader of society avows she hates publicity but hates you if you do not give it to her; the editor is familiar with all these, and with a few who redeem the race. The most tiresome of all are the religious cranks. The theological controversies that periodically break out in the Press, evoking an avalanche of letters, reveal a volcano that never ceases to erupt. One recalls the Prayer Book controversy of 1927 with its perfervid debates on the floor of the House of Commons. The road to salvation is full of potholes and crowded with disputatious travellers. People are generally ignorant of the fact that the size of newspapers is not controlled by the amount of news available but by the amount of advertisements. These must be laced by reading matter; a parliamentary recess affords a field day for events that would usually go unnoticed.

The chairman of my company, Sir Charles Starmer, who had engaged me after our contact at a public dinner on the eve of my departure for America, was the managing director of some forty provincial newspapers. A Darlington boy who had come up the hard way, he knew his business thoroughly. The strength of the provincial Press lies in two factors; it covers the home field more lengthily than its London rivals and it can go to press with later news. It also benefits from local advertisements. Even so, the dominance of the London Press is almost supreme. My own policy was to maintain as much independence as possible. I wrote my own leaders, two or three every night, and soon found a following. We went to press at midnight for district distribution and ran a final 2 a.m. local edition, thus beating the London Press with later news which it could not provide in its own early provincial editions.

I inherited an extraordinary chief sub-editor. Very able, he was a source of alarm. He had been trained in the blood-and-thunder school of journalism. He exulted in murders, suicides, rapes, burglaries and earthquakes. It was a poor night that did not supply some horror or calamity. The mildest of men, he had a lurid mind. "A good evening," he would say on appearing for our conference. "Two murders, one a horrible thing, man who cut the throat of his wife and of his two children and gassed himself. And a factory fire—

wall collapsed and killed two firemen. Churchill's thinking of retiring."

When I went upstairs to the "setting" room the murder had the headlines. I cut the story to a third of a column, transferred it, with the dead firemen, to an inner page, brought Churchill forward, and gave headline place to a speech on the League of Nations by Lord Robert Cecil. These nightly transpositions and my lack of a sense of "news value" troubled the poor fellow. I never dared to go home without seeing the display poster. One night, out speaking at a dinner, I missed seeing it. The next morning I jumped. "Drugged Girl Raped. Archbishop Protests." The archbishop's protest was not about the rape but about Sunday football matches.

I was fortunate in my very able editorial assistant, a young man with a long, pointed nose. He was a ferret for news. He burrowed in pubs and came back with astonishing information. There is a boy called Pinocchio in a very popular Italian fairy tale whose nose grows longer every time he tells a lie. My assistant's nose seemed to grow longer every time he ferreted out a new story.

The human relationship with my staff provided problems and pleasures. I had to allay friction, to maintain discipline. We had an excellent chief reporter, alert, hardworking but, alas, the bottle proved irresistible. It came to a point when after many years of good service dismissal had to be threatened. He had a wife and family. I talked to him like a father, though in years he could almost have been mine. One day on a fifth occasion for reprimand, at a stage where finality had been reached, I called him in after two weeks' suspension. "Look, you've brought me to the verge of despair," I said. "If I am compelled to dismiss you I shan't sleep for a month. The only alternative is for me to resign as I can't manage the situation properly."

"If you did that the boys would kill me, sir," he replied. "There's nothing we won't do for you."

"Thank you—but the bottle controls this situation. One more lapse and it drives either you or me out of this office. I am quite serious in this." There was no more trouble.

For the most part my staff was young. I gave them their heads as much as possible. There was a tall bright lad, sometimes a little too bright, and occasionally I jerked the leash. Thirty years later I felt rewarded when he wrote me a reminiscent letter of gratitude. He was now an editor himself. There was a Russian youth on the staff. One did not know from what stresses and strains he had emerged. He had the handicap then attached to anyone of foreign origin. I felt this worried him. He was astonished when I put him, at twenty-one, in charge of our sub-office in another town. The experiment was wholly successful. Later he became the diplomatic correspondent of a London paper.

All told, we had a happy office, humming with enterprise. I was fortunate, too, in the general manager, an extremely able young man, who had charge of the commercial side. His main task was to procure advertisements and control the finances. There is often friction between manager and editor. Our relations were harmonious, with give and take between us. In some newspaper offices, the manager, the bringer in of revenue, is often all-powerful. A weak editor allows his authority to be infringed. It was perhaps indicative of our mutual respect that we always tapped on each other's door before entering. I was particularly fortunate in one respect, our chairman, Sir Charles Starmer, in London, never interfered. I was given a free hand and a sympathetic hearing. Equally considerate was a fellow director, J. B. Morrell. Shrewd, gentle, twice Lord Mayor of York, for fifty years a power in that city, he had become a director at twenty-five of the famous Rowntree company.

II

The *Nottingham Journal*, founded in 1710, recorded many great events, such as the victory at Waterloo (see opposite).

It was not possible to sit in my editorial chair without thinking of former occupants. Foremost among these was Sir James Barrie. By this time, aged sixty-two, the dramatist was now a legendary figure. He dwelt, a little aloof, among the bright stars of the literary firmament: Kipling, Wells, Shaw, Bennett, Conrad, Chesterton, Galsworthy, they were an impressive group filling the Edwardian-Georgian scene, but something about Barrie, something unhappy and withdrawn, set him in lonely eminence. He had just been awarded

POSTSCRIPT.
Battles between the Duke of Wellington and Buonaparte.

OFFICIAL BULLETIN.

"DOWNING STREET, *June* 22, 1815.

" The Duke of Wellington's dispatch, dated Waterloo, the 19th of June, states, that on the preceding day Buonaparte attacked, with his whole force, the British line, supported by a corps of Prussians; which attack, after a long and sanguinary conflict, terminated in the complete Overthrow of the Enemy's Army, with the loss of ONE HUNDRED and FIFTY PIECES of CANNON and TWO EAGLES During the night, the Prussians under Marshal Blucher, who joined in the pursuit of the enemy, captured SIXTY GUNS, and a large part of Buonaparte's BAGGAGE. The Allied Armies continued to pursue the enemy. Two French Generals were taken."

the Order of Merit. He made few appearances. He was reputed to be rich, careful with the "bawbies", a shy baronet but still fecund, as recent plays *Mary Rose* and *Shall We Join the Ladies* proved. He had been kissed by fame and kicked by tragedy. Far distant now seemed those days when, an eager young man, he had come down from Edinburgh to take his first journalistic post, in February, 1883, as leader-writer and editor of the newspaper I now edited. Subsequently he had become England's leading playwright, author of the immortal *Peter Pan, What Every Woman Knows, Quality Street, Dear Brutus,* a procession of successes in the theatre. In the year 1897 his British and American royalties for *The Little Minister* had brought him in £80,000, a sum he repeated with five subsequent plays. Gone were those early days of struggle when, relinquishing his Nottingham post, he threw himself on London as a freelance. When the first cheques began to come in, the friend with whom he shared a twelve-shilling a week lodging noticed his habit of tucking them along the edge of the mantelpiece mirror. They grew and grew until the mirror became almost invisible. When his friend protested Barrie shyly confessed he feared to bank them. It might not be safe. The young man with whom he had shared his lodgings in Nottingham at eight shillings a week, a stockbroker's clerk, did not appear to have imparted his early know-how to Barrie. This room-mate became a leading Midlands stockbroker, was knighted, and died a millionaire.

At sixty-two Barrie could sit back, an "immortal", with as much success as is good for any man. Critically considered, he failed as a novelist. Today there is not one of his novels in print, or worth recalling, though they ran through many editions soon after they appeared. He was fortunate in his hour. He made a false start with *Better Dead*, published at his own expense, possibly it was too prophetically named. He was fortunate in being taken up by a fellow Scot, Sir William Robertson Nicoll, a nonconformist minister turned journalist, then a powerful critic editing the *British Weekly*, which serialised *When a Man's Single*, Barrie's "Nottingham novel". Hodder and Stoughton, who owned the paper, published his novels. Nicoll pulled the wires. Barrie was established and never looked back. He soon realised he was not a novelist but a dramatist. As Arnold Bennett discovered with *Milestones*, "the play's the thing" wherein to make the money.

The little Scot was shrewd, too. When years later he presented the Peter Pan statue to Kensington Gardens he thereby took a lease of them, and without asking permission. But fate tricked him. He married an actress, a publican's daughter. She went off with his handsome young secretary, Gilbert Cannan, who turned novelist and came to a sad end in an asylum. It was a shattering blow for Barrie. The divorce in 1909 was the talk of London. Bennett, returning from lunch with Mrs. Belloc Lowndes, recorded in his *Journal* —"Most of our talk about Wells's scandals and Barrie's scandals. Surprised to learn that the little Scotsman had given his wife Mary £3,000 a year for a dress allowance." The absconding wife was twenty years older than Cannan. To add to the injury she did Barrie, she went off with his sheep dog, "Nana". One weekend Barrie had stayed in a house where a huge dog acted as a Nannie to the children. Barrie came downstairs the next morning and said the dog had given him an idea for a play: it was called *Peter Pan*. So "Nana" was a very special animal and its abduction must have increased Barrie's distress. Horrified by the publicity, he retreated into his shell. Magnanimous, he made the Cannans an annual allowance. With a typical Barrie touch he presented it to them at a little dinner *à trois* given on the anniversary of his marriage to the erring lady.

It was fortunate that Barrie's wife did not go off with the original manuscript of *Peter Pan*. He presented it to the actress, Maude Adams, who had had such a resounding success in the title role. He inscribed it "To Maude Adams, the MS of *Peter Pan*, from her humble servant and affectionate friend, J. M. Barrie." The manuscript which carried no title page being simply headed "Anon", had only eighty-three pages, bearing the dates of its beginning and completion: Nov. 23, 1903—Mar. 1, 1904. In 1936 when Scribner's Sons, Barrie's American publishers, acquired the manuscript they informed him. Barrie, who had long wondered what had happened to it, immediately cabled "Greatly interested about discovery of long-lost manuscript. Thought I had given it to Maude Adams but uncertain. Want to buy it back from you. Kindly cable suggesting terms." Before the transaction could be completed Barrie died. Eventually it came into the possession of the Indiana University Library at Bloomington, U.S.A., where it now reposes.

When Barrie came to employ a new secretary he played for safety. He took Lady Cynthia Asquith, the brilliant daughter of an earl and daughter-in-law of ex-Prime Minister Asquith. From her he received devoted service. The scar of the Cannan affair remained with a traumatic effect. Lady Cynthia relates how one morning she found him pale, with a haunted look. She discovered that he had had a dream in which he struggled on his sofa with a body that tried to push him off it and yet was somehow his own. The dream-figure obsessed him. It recurs in his plays such as *Dear Brutus*. One wonders what Freud would have deduced from this obsession.

When we were bringing out a special edition of *The Nottingham Journal*, to which he had contributed when on its staff many articles under the name of "Hippomenes", I wrote asking whether he would send us a message on the fortieth anniversary of his joining the paper. He responded at once and invited me to call on him one day.

Soon after I had left the *Journal* and was living again in London
I suggested calling and he replied that he would be happy to see me
at 1.30 p.m. On the appointed day, encountering John Drinkwater,
I somewhat proudly informed him that I was on my way to lunch
with Barrie. "You're lunching with Barrie! What an ordeal! He
won't say a word to you the whole time," he said. Barrie lived at the
bottom of Robert Street, Adelphi, in an eyrie flat overlooking the
Thames. Arnold Bennett in his *Journal* recorded dining there in the
company of Thomas Hardy. "Dined at his flat in Robert Street.
Barrie has an ugly manservant and the finest view of London I ever
saw." He was quite correct. When the lift had taken me to the top
floor of the building, mostly offices, and I emerged, I was received in
a small hall by Barrie's bullet-headed, squat manservant. He took
my coat and hat and hung them in the hall that divided the flat.
The hour was precisely one-thirty. Barrie smiled a welcome as I
entered his large study. It was, possibly, a former studio with high
wide windows commanding the curving sweep of the river beyond the
Waterloo Bridge as far as St. Paul's and the Tower Bridge. It was a
stupendous view on this sharp March day of sunflecked steeples and
river, like a canvas by Canaletto.

I examined my host, curious to see what time had done to him
since he left Nottingham to win fame and fortune. He was tiny, with
a large head, sharp nose, thin mouth, greying hair and keen eyes. He
wore an old brown suit, unpressed, and stood with his back to a
large open fireplace. I knew something about him for he was a
public legend. A ship-wrecked marriage, no children, fame, wealth,
all these comprised a lonely little man. A recluse, every one of his
movements drew the limelight. He still wielded a magic pen. Only
recently he had made a Rectorial Address at St. Andrews University
entitled *Courage* which had enchanted everyone with its deep wisdom.
He had kept a kind heart, and having no children of his own it went
out to others. He was the fairy godfather of a children's hospital,
to which he ultimately left much of his fortune, and he had taken
under his wing two small boys who had lost their father in the war.
They had tragic ends. One was killed in the Second World War,
the other committed suicide.

Barrie looked at me keenly. There were wooden settles on either side of the fireplace. He pointed to one and sat down opposite me. In the shadow, diminutive, he looked like a dormouse. He folded his small hands over a tubby stomach. His little feet just seemed to reach the floor. After he had cross-questioned me a little I began to ask him about his life in Nottingham.

"Well, I was happy there, quite happy," he said, picking up a poker and stirring a log on the fire. "The owner never interfered with me. I wrote whatever I wished. One innovation of mine went unapplauded. You see how every newspaper at the beginning of the year now presents its readers with a survey of the events of the past twelve months—well, I was the first to do that. How I laboured at it! I wrote the whole thing. Did the world gasp? No! Not even the proprietor made any comment!"

"All for three pounds a week?" I asked.

"Three guineas," corrected Sir James.

Drinkwater's prophecy was quite wrong. Barrie talked easily. He was reminiscent and inquisitive. He kept poking the fire and talking. But I was getting hungry, indeed I was rumbling internally. It was now past two o'clock. At last, as I was describing a visit to Max Beerbohm at Rapallo, the little manservant came in and announced lunch. I stopped my narration.

"Do go on, finish your story," said Barrie, as I half rose.

Resuming my seat I finished my story. At last Barrie stood up and led the way to lunch. As we crossed the hall he picked up my coat, helped me into it and turned towards the lift which his manservant had summoned. He held out his hand. "Well, it's been a pleasure. I hope ye'll come again," he said. I entered the lift. He watched it descend. Down in the quiet dead-end street, I stood paralysed. Then my senses returned. "Lunch with Barrie! Lunch with Barrie!" I repeated. Holding on to a lamp-post I fell into uncontrollable laughter.

A little after this I saw Drinkwater and told him about my experience. "I thought you were a little optimistic when you told me Barrie was giving you lunch. One day I met him near the Savoy Hotel. We walked together to Robert Street. All the way he uttered hardly a word. When we got to Robert Street he stopped and took a bit of wet paper out of his mouth. It had a stamp on it. He carefully pulled off the stamp and put it in his wallet. 'It's been nice seeing ye,' he said, as we shook hands and parted."

III

The first problem that confronted me on returning to Nottingham was one of housing. The war had caused a great shortage and in 1920 houses were at a premium. My mother was quite happy in the little home she had made for herself after I had uprooted her from her former home in Grove Villas, taking her to Liverpool when I went there in 1916 to my first journalistic post. Her present abode, one of a row of two-storey houses with only a parlour, scullery and two bedrooms, was too small for us but she counselled me not to be rash and enter into heavy commitments. "Wait and see how you like your post," she said. The suggestion that my editorship might be only a transient thing rather startled me. When I protested she said quietly, "Nothing lasts. We're Time's playthings. I've learned that. I'm quite content here. Let's wait and see." So we remained in that little box in a dreary row of houses in a depressed district. There was something piquant in this defiance of the address snobs. I thought of the millionaire's apartment in Philadelphia in which I had recently stayed. Well, variety is the spice of life.

I was determined not to be buried in the provinces and lose my London connections. I therefore bought a season ticket for London and kept a pied-à-terre in South Kensington. London is always a good investment for an ambitious young man.

One morning, breakfasting there, I saw in my newspaper the advertisement of an auction to be held in a house near by. "Splendid Steinway Grand Piano", I read. It was the last "Private View" day. The auction was on the morrow. I had always coveted a Steinway grand piano. The advertisement proved irresistible. The fact that I had not owned a piano since my father's death and the loss of our home twelve years ago, had always been a grievance. I was getting out of practice.

I ate my breakfast, reading the advertisement over and over. What would the Steinway fetch? I was willing to give a hundred pounds for it. The sale seemed to be a small one. If no piano-hungry bidders were there I might get a bargain, but my naturally cautious spirit said: "Leave it alone. A Steinway in a terrace house with only a parlour whose door opens directly off the street—are you crazy?" The room would not hold both a Steinway and a dining-table, and Steinway grands did not go with an oven and hob-kitchen grate. Like the girl who buys herself a pair of expensive shoes and finds she must have a new costume, I should have to buy a house large enough for a grand piano.

I poured myself a second cup of tea, still debating. My room was about the size of our parlour. How long was a Steinway grand? I rang up the Steinway company, who gave me the measurements. I then walked from wall to wall. My guess was that there would be four feet to spare. Not exactly. Since the front door opened into the room there must be leeway. I calculated the door would just clear the piano stool.

Half an hour later I went to the house where the sale was to take place. The Steinway in the drawing-room had a padded satin cover. Furniture had been piled on top of it. I lifted the cover and raised the lid of the keyboard. The ivory keys were not discoloured. I cleared a space, sat down and ran my fingers from the bass to the treble and back. Then I tried the pedal action. It seemed perfect. I played a Chopin *Mazurka*. The tone was excellent. The piano gave no signs of being worn, though the floral satin cover was faded. As I played, an auctioneer's workman stood by in a white apron, smoking a cigarette. He had been stacking furniture to make room for the sale on the morrow. He listened. When I ceased playing he said, "Sounds orl right to me, guv'nor!" I agreed. I would have to take a chance as to how the lid looked and on the condition of the hammer-felts. Perhaps the piano would be uncovered at the sale. I left, picking up a catalogue. The sale began the next morning at ten o'clock. It looked as if Lot 78 would come up about noon.

On the way back to my room I thought the matter over. I would go to £100 for it. But for that sum I could buy a motor-car! Also the instrument would take up all the space in our small room. "You're crazy!" I said to myself. But I longed so much for a piano. We should not remain long in that tiny house. I had money in the bank. For once why should I not let myself go and have what I wanted?

73

Selfishly, not for one moment did I think of my poor mother wedged in with a grand piano.

I returned the next morning a little before eleven. I was in plenty of time. The drawing-room was packed with the curious crowd that haunts a saleroom. There were old dowagers and beady-eyed dealers and the lunatic fringe that puts up a fight over a mouldy article, with the heated winner paying a ridiculous price. About noon, the Steinway piano came up. It was not wheeled into view, or uncovered. "A magnificent instrument, in perfect condition, by Steinway, the finest make in the world—along the wall there, on the left," said the auctioneer. All heads turned round to look. I felt a resentment at such an undignified presentation of this Steinway grand piano, for it now had two chairs and a gilt overmantle on it. "Shall we say—fifty guineas?" asked the auctioneer. There was a heavy silence. "Fifty guineas!" he cried, nodding at someone. In a few minutes the price had risen to ninety guineas. I went in and got the piano for a hundred guineas.

I called up the Steinway company. Yes, they would arrange delivery to Nottingham. When the next day I arrived home and reported what I had bought my tranquil mother, accustomed to shocks throughout her life, showed not a tremor. "Are you sure it will get in?" she asked. "Just," I said, having measured the room. "And the dining-table?" "We shall have to let a flap down and fit it in the belly of the piano," I replied.

"Well, it's better than having a Great Dane," observed my mother. "Why a Great Dane?" I asked. "You once said you'd like a Great Dane," she answered.

A week later a pantechnicon drew up. From its cabin a small man and an enormous man came out. The latter had a paper in his hand. He seemed doubtful whether the address was correct. I assured him it was. Where did I want the piano taken? "Not anywhere—here!" I answered. "Here!" he exclaimed. I invited him in. He looked round and made no comment. Obviously he thought he had encountered a lunatic. "I've delivered pianos all over the kingdom, for all the great artists—" he began to tell me. "I'm not a great artist!" I said. "No, sir—very well, sir, now we'll see what we can do."

They got the piano out of the van down a slide. It seemed to fill the street, to have grown in size en route. I became fearful. People began to linger on the pavement. The neighbours came out. Never had there been such a sight. The piano went in through the door sideways. The fat man got trapped getting the instrument on its feet. It had just cleared the opening of the street door. When all the swathings had been removed I raised the great lid. It was a noble sight. I sat down and played. The tone was superb but I realised that, *fortissimo*, I should be heard to the end of the street. The van men listened. When I tipped the huge fellow on departing I said, "I suppose you've never delivered a Steinway to a place like this?" "Never, sir!" he replied, emphatically. "It's—it's a record. And I've been moving pianos for twenty years!"

A month later it chanced that Marion Keighley Snowden, of the musical family in Auriol Road, Kensington, which had been so hospitable to me in my first years in London, came to Nottingham to give a recital. I took her home. "But I never knew you could play!" she exclaimed, surveying the piano. "I kept it a dark secret, I didn't dare to play in your house," I replied, "I used to practise at Mrs. Val Prinsep's in Holland Park."

She sat down and played. When she had finished, I said, "Well?" "It's near perfect—what a bargain!" she replied, with a final *glissando*.

CHAPTER FOUR

Compton Mackenzie, Alfred Noyes, Evan Morgan

I

ONE OF THE pleasures of the return to my native city was that I could again see my old friends. First, there was dynamic old William Kiddier, with his mane of silver hair, his brilliant eyes and ever warm heart. In all the trying years of my youth when I had been like a young caged lion struggling for freedom he had never failed me. He still spent much of his time in the attic studio above his shop in the Market Place, where he painted his landscapes. But I found he was not as free as he had been before his son was killed in the war. He had now to give more time to his business. He solved this problem later by presenting it to the local Institute for the Blind. Although he was still full of spirit I saw that he had aged, but he was still sympathetic to those who took their problems to him, as I had done. I could not see him often as I had a newspaper on my hands. The fascination and the nightmare of journalism is that you may never relax. My paper had to renew itself every morning. The daily Press is a quicksand. Relax for one hour and it engulfs you.

I had four other close friends of my youth whom I now began to see again, Duncan Macpherson, John Grosvenor Laing, and two artists, Helen Stiebel and gentle Denholm Davis, both still hospitable in their skyey studios. I was again in and out of the Laing house, that museum piece of Victorianism, with its morning prayers and be-ribboned maidservants.*

* For those living in an era in which maidservants are no more it may be recorded that their morning uniform was a pink-striped print frock and blouse, and in the afternoon a black skirt and bodice, to which were added starched white cuffs and collar, and a white bow crowning the hair. They rose at 6.30, had one afternoon off and ten to fifteen shillings a week. To obtain a post a

76

I had to plan my day carefully. Leaving my editorial office, having seen the paper to press, I reached home about 2 a.m., but instead of going to bed I went to my desk and wrote for two hours. I had to earn my living at the *Journal* but I firmly resolved to keep something of myself apart. I already had in view my route of escape into personal freedom. I was determined not to be shackled for life to an editor's chair. While I was young and fresh I wanted to create my individual career, so each night on my return from the office I sat at my desk and wrote. I had begun in earnest the career of novelist; I was writing *Scissors*. Steadily the story progressed and, like most first novels, it was in part autobiographical. It was the story of a boy who lost his father young, who had faced necessity, escaped out of a hateful office, became in turn a journalist, a civil servant and a war correspondent. I had no lack of material.

I rose and breakfasted about eleven. Then I examined other newspapers to see if we had missed anything, marking our own copy. To provide myself with exercise I joined a rowing-club whose boat-house was pleasantly situated only fifteen minutes distant over Trent Bridge. I rowed a skiff up-stream a couple of miles most days. On Saturday afternoons I was one of a crew of six, with cox. We took our boat as far as the foot of Clifton Grove, the haunt of Kirke White, the young doomed poet. It was a sylvan setting used by D. H. Lawrence in *Sons and Lovers*. We climbed the steep wooded hillside to the ancestral domain of the Clifton-Bruce family, taking tea at one of the thatched cottages in a village as yet unravaged, with Hall, Rectory and a large Green with a Georgian brick dovecote. We rowed home, singing in the twilight. This was the river and scene of my early prize-poem, *The Trent*. Friendship, youth, health, and starry ambition; I fondly recall those years of a lost enchantment.

On normal days I was at my office by two o'clock, when I dealt with correspondence, discussed plans with my editorial assistant and chief reporter, and gave interviews to various callers. About four o'clock I took my rowing exercise. Sometimes I varied the

reference was necessary from a clergyman or former employer. There was no escape except by marriage. After thirty or forty years of service they might be remembered or forgotten in their deceased employer's will. They seemed quite content and happy. Well-trained, they made good wives and mothers.

programme and practised on my Steinway. I was memorising Schumann's *Carnaval*. At times my mother would peer out of the window and say: "Do you know you've got an audience?" One thing worried her. She thought I was not getting enough sleep. Sleep! It seemed a dreadful waste of time. There was so much I wanted to do.

From time to time I went to London. That summer the Russian Ballet returned and opened its season at Covent Garden. The Company had not greatly changed. It had come from Paris, having had much success with *Les Sylphides*, in which Karsavina now made a reappearance after a long absence and received an ovation. The male role was taken by Leonide Massine. He had long coveted the part, one of the last of Nijinsky's triumphs. Now Diaghilev let him essay it. He was equal to the opportunity being, as Grigoriev recorded, "handsome, elegant and poetic". At Covent Garden they produced three new ballets *The Nightingale*, *Pulcinella* and *The Artful Ladies*, all Massine productions. He seemed to go from triumph to triumph, dancing superbly, sure in command, and only just twenty-five. Owing to his heavy engagements and my own absences from London I did not see much of him that season but our friendship was as cordial as ever. The company was received with great fervour. Karsavina, Tchernicheva, Idzikowsky, Woidzikowsky, Sokolova, what a galaxy of talent, inspired and controlled by Diaghilev the despotic magician who appeared and disappeared, taciturn, and aloof.

My friend Zadia was as alluring and elusive as ever. Not since that night in 1918 when she had appeared at my lodging in Upper George Street, getting me out of bed after midnight because she had forgotten her key, had I ever been sure of my relationship with her. She could be infuriatingly evanescent, spasmodically possessive and devoted. She was not dancing this season, having torn a tendon.

One evening when I took her home after seeing the ballet she said, in the taxi, "I am leaving for Warsaw on Friday. I'm going to my aunt's. I must rest. Why don't you come to Warsaw?" She could not think why my newspaper should prevent my going to Warsaw. "My aunt would love you," she said. I told her that I was not at all interested in being loved by her aunt. My reply set her off in a peal of laughter. I did not believe she had any intention of going to Warsaw. She did not speak of it again.

I was astonished two weeks later to get a letter from Warsaw. So she really had gone. "I have shown your photograph to my aunt and she says you look a handsome, clever boy. She invites you to visit us. I am teaching her English so that she can talk to you," she wrote.

I answered that I could not come. I heard no more from Zadia again but from a friend of hers who returned with the Diaghilev Ballet the next year, I had news. I learned she was dancing with a Spanish company touring South America. I wrote. Silence. Twenty-four years later, leaving the Colony Restaurant in New York, someone called my name. I turned and saw a lady, accompanied by a gentleman, smile at me. "It is Cecil, surely?" she cried. Still I did not know who she was. She held out her hand. "I'm Zadia!" she exclaimed. And then I recognised her. She introduced me to her husband. Three nights later we dined together. She had given up dancing years ago and had married an Argentine banker. They had four children and were very happy, living in Buenos Aires. She was no longer the sylph in a tutu, she had thickened and a pirouette or an "elevation" would have been beyond her. But her eyes were as beautiful as ever. It was clear that she had an adoring husband.

The Diaghilev season had an unhappy finale. The Maestro was in a fractious mood that summer. I heard that in Rome he and Massine had disagreed over the treatment of a new ballet. This time Massine would not give way. A rift opened. Diaghilev had also had a quarrel with Picasso over *Pulcinella,* for which Stravinsky had done the music and Picasso the décor. And then in London, towards the close of the Covent Garden season, a dispute over money arose between Diaghilev and the management. Lawyers were brought in, without success. Suddenly in a rage Diaghilev cancelled at the eleventh hour the last performance which was to have been in the nature of a gala. Flowers had already arrived for the final curtain.

The company dispersed for the holidays. Diaghilev departed for his beloved Venice. He was very adversely criticised for his high-handed conduct. There had been a strained atmosphere throughout the season. I saw that Massine, as others, was tense. To add to this malaise a provincial tour of England arranged for the autumn was not a success. The next year when the Russian Ballet returned, Massine was not with it. He had been peremptorily dismissed. With him absent, and Zadia vanished, my chief contacts with the Diaghilev Ballet Company were lost.

II

Three months after the purchase of the Steinway piano I bought my first small car. One of my places of call was Thrumpton Hall, not far from Clifton Grove, situated on the banks of the River Trent. It was a brick mansion with an Italian loggia and a Grinling Gibbons staircase. Here quietly lived the Reverend Lord Byron and his wife. She was the daughter of the Reverend Lord Charles Fitzroy, so they were both "in the cloth" as it were. They were a gentle couple. Lord Byron was the local vicar. The church nestled among the trees beyond his garden. From the front terrace could be seen and heard the sparkle and roar of a weir. Lord Byron was the nephew of the ninth baron and younger son of the seventh, who was first cousin, two removes, of the poet. A distant descent, but not much more so than that of Lord Nelson from the first Lord Nelson, or the Duke of Marlborough from the first Duke. The Byron peerage dated from 1643, when Sir John Byron, descended from the Sir John who had fought at the battle of Bosworth Field in 1485, was Member of Parliament for Nottingham and a devoted officer of Charles the First.

At the time that I visited Lord Byron he was a scholarly, grey-haired man of sixty. They had no children but the title is still extant. One day I told him that I had seen the Regatta of Venice from the balcony of the Palazzo Mocenigo, where Byron had lived. He showed me a drawing of the palazzo which the poet had sent to a cousin. "I fear he led a very disreputable life there," said Lord Byron, sadly. He was the only man I ever knew who could approach a peacock, stroke its head and cause it to expand its gorgeous tail feathers.*

* Count Robilant, the present owner of the Palazzo Mocenigo, told me that sometimes, when he stands on the balcony, gondoliers, rowing tourists, point up and say "Beeron!" "The tourists gape and raise their cameras. I always bow," he said.

Nearly thirty years later I returned to the Hall to open a church garden fête. A young couple living there were striving to keep the place going by opening it to visitors. I seemed to feel the ghost of the gentle old vicar haunting the rose beds and stroking his peacocks. There were two notable events in the first year of my editorship. Sir Jesse Boot, later Lord Trent, wholly paralysed, and retired from the chairmanship of the great chain of chemists' shops he had founded, was given the Freedom of the City of which he had been such a benefactor. I watched Sir Jesse—wheeled in his chair into the Council Chamber in the old Exchange Hall. He sat there, white-haired, patriarchal, while the Mayor (the city had not yet got a Lord Mayor) called on the Town Clerk to read the illuminated scroll creating the new Freeman. How incredulous I should have been had someone told me that one day, in a neo-classic Council House that replaced the Regency Exchange, with a Lord Mayor presiding, I should listen to the Town Clerk reading the scroll that conferred the City's Freedom on me! Near the Mayor sat the Sheriff of Nottingham in his robes of office. Shades of Robin Hood, Friar Tuck and Maid Marion in Sherwood Forest, of which Noyes had sung in his poem of the name!

Friar Tuck and Little John are riding down together
With quarter-staff and drinking-can and grey goose feather.
The dead are coming back again, the years are rolled away
In Sherwood, in Sherwood, about the break of day.

There came to the city that year the foremost young novelist of the day, Compton Mackenzie, to rehearse a play of his at the Repertory Theatre. Compton Mackenzie's mother, the widow of Edward Compton whose touring Comedy Company had been for many years a school for young actors, had settled in Nottingham and launched a bold enterprise.* Entirely at her own expense she had

* "In December, 1888, Edward Compton, a young English actor who had his own troupe and had for ten years been touring the British Isles playing old comedies and costume pieces, wrote to Henry James. His wife, Virginia Bateman, an American actress, had read an article suggesting James's novel *The American* would make a play . . . This started James, having financially failed as a novelist, off as a dramatist." *Henry James: The Middle Years*, by Leon Edel (R. Hart-Davis).

bought and refitted a decayed theatre in a depressed suburb of the city, and founded there a repertory company. It was an act of courage for an elderly woman.

There was already a vivid local interest in the drama. Amateur theatricals were supported by a lively Playgoers Club. Mrs. Compton was an indomitable little woman, famous in her day when she had acted with her husband. All her children were distinguished. She had three daughters: Fay, one of the foremost actresses on the London stage, Viola and Ellen. I gave Mrs. Compton's enterprise the utmost support.

There was considerable excitement when we learned, in the autumn of 1920, that she was going to produce a first play by her son, Compton Mackenzie, called *Columbine*, a stage version of his novel *Carnival*. It was a good play, with lively dialogue. I attended the first night and wrote the critique. It was launched hopefully, but unhappily the London Press was hostile and it had a short run when it went to the West End. D. H. Lawrence wrote to Mackenzie from his Sicilian abode: "Heard from my sister who saw *Columbine* and liked it. Heard from my elder sister that Nottingham thought it a great success."

I did not meet the author of *Sinister Street*. I refrained in order to preserve my independence as a critic, and he observed the same convention. It was pleasant to learn, forty-six years later, when he came to write *Octave Five* of his autobiography, that my goodwill had not gone unnoticed.

My memory of directing the rehearsals of *Columbine* at Nottingham that autumn (1920) is cloudy. However, I do remember sharply an extremely sympathetic and extremely able young editor of *The Nottingham Journal* whose name was Cecil Roberts. He wrote a "Silhouette" of me in his paper from which I hope the Cecil Roberts of today will not mind my quoting a line or two—"I have reviewed all his novels with the exception of the first, for which task my youth alone incapacitated me, and I have yet to experience a better thrill of anticipation than that aroused by the publisher's advance copy."

Like Compton Mackenzie I was to experience a production at the same repertory theatre. The poetic drama *A Tale of Young Lovers*, which I had written to relieve my loneliness in my Liverpool lodgings in 1917, had been accepted by Sir George Alexander for presentation at St. James's Theatre. Its production was cancelled by his death.* Now Mrs. Compton said she would like to produce it. It was a costume drama set in Genoa in the sixteenth century. I accepted her offer.

The great handicap of the repertory theatre is that it has little time for production since it must provide a series of plays acted by the same company for practically the same audience. Time for rehearsal is necessarily short. My own play was put into rehearsal on Tuesday and produced the following Saturday! Any changes in the text were therefore impossible. I have always marvelled at the phenomenal memorisation which is involved, and the pace of production. In the case of my own play I was fortunate in having a clever young lead in Lester Matthews. He had an inborn sense for verse. He had also a good technique, a handsome presence and an excellent voice. When I was in Hollywood twenty years later I was surprised one day when he called at my hotel. He was now very successful in the films. "How I wish I had had the experience I have now, when I had that wonderful opportunity with your lines," he said, and reeled off the speech with which he had brought down the final curtain. "They think it's from one of the Elizabethan dramas—Shakespeare, Webster, Jonson!" "I fear it was an echo of them all!" I replied. Compton Mackenzie's two sisters, Ellen and Viola, were in the cast, and the producer was W. G. Fay, of Abbey Theatre fame, who had produced for Synge and Yeats.

The play ran ten days and then had to come off for the next production. There was no field for poetic drama, I believed, but I was wrong. The play never quite died. It was published by Heinemann and I had the pleasure of dedicating it to Joseph Conrad. "Let me at once congratulate you affectionately on the charm and skill and beauty in your work," he wrote. In subsequent years it was intermittently produced in England and America, but the net profit from it was £280! Another reason for banishing one's muse.

In a very different sense I rang up the curtain of the Nottingham Repertory Theatre. After the first enthusiasm created by Mrs.

* Vide *The Years of Promise*. Ch. 3. XII.

Compton's enterprise a severe struggle for survival ensued. Within two years she was in serious financial difficulty. She had sunk a large part of her personal fortune in the venture. Worry brought on a nervous breakdown and she had to retire from active management, leaving her two daughters in command.* They put up a gallant fight. A day came when all the money was gone. I was made aware of this late one night by the sudden appearance at my office of Viola Compton, accompanied by their manager, W. G. Fay. They explained their mission. Funds were required immediately if the theatre was to keep open. They had not enough to meet the wages of the cast at the end of the week. They had come to me in desperation. I asked them what was the minimum sum required. Two thousand pounds. I sat back in my chair staggered by their request. I asked them why they had come to me. "Because we believe you have influence. You are one of those people who have a way of getting what they want."

I thanked them for the compliment but I was much too busy to start on a fund-raising campaign, and in such haste. I asked if they had any figures, any books with them. No. I said I must have a financial statement before I could act. They thereupon left and promised to return in a couple of hours. When they brought their statement I saw that the position was desperate. "You will help us?" asked Miss Compton. It is hard to resist the tearful appeal of a pretty woman. "I have one improbable idea on which you must place no reliance. You shall know the result by tomorrow afternoon," I said. Two thousand pounds in little more than twelve hours! I would not have set myself the task had I not had a great admiration for Mrs. Compton. She had contributed much, at considerable cost, to the cultural life of the city.

My idea required that the next morning I should catch the 8.25 train to London. There was one man I must see. Would he be in town and if so, would he see me? This man was Sir Jesse Boot, our

---

* How different it would have been forty years later when the Nottingham Corporation spent £200,000 building a splendid Playhouse with a cylindrical auditorium, providing both a "picture frame" and "open stage". It is supported by government and municipal subsidies, amounting to £80,000 p.a. It stands on a site where, a boy of ten, I made my first public appearance, playing a pianoforte solo at a diploma distribution.

local Maecenas. I rang up his solicitor, Mr. Huntsman, who acted for him in his benefactions. Was Sir Jesse in London? Yes, he was going there the very next morning to see him at his house in Smith Square. "Will you give me five minutes of your appointed time with him?" I asked, and briefly explained my mission. Huntsman, a man of culture, later the city's first Lord Mayor, was an ardent supporter of the theatre and he responded to my appeal immediately. "But it's on your own head!" he assured me.

He had reason to warn me. The boy who since the age of thirteen had built up the vast business of Boots Cash Chemists and was now a millionaire, crippled by arthritis, had been a most generous donor. With a magnificent gesture he gave to his native city a quarter of a million pounds "to commemorate seventy years of a happy life". This was only one of many benefactions. Today a generously planned University, a fine boulevard, a swimming pool and two pleasure parks represent his munificence. A warm-hearted man, his hand was always in his pocket. "But why don't you go to the other millionaires in the town?" he complained to supplicants. "Because you are always generous, Sir Jesse," they replied. "Ay, I'm a bit of a fool that way!" he retorted, and wrote a cheque. He responded so often that his family got alarmed. His wife became somewhat of a watch-dog. The successful petitioner had to by-pass her these latter days.

I already knew Sir Jesse. He had bought some of my poems for calendars when I was a youth. Denholm Davis, the artist, found him fretful when painting his portrait and got me to go and chat with him. I played tennis with his son and daughters.* John, his only son, who succeeded to the peerage conferred on his father, died without male issue. Sir Jesse was a stern Nonconformist. The theatre was anathema to him but I thought I had found a chink in the Nonconformist armour.

The next morning, in London, Huntsman finished his business and announced my presence. When I entered the room Sir Jesse gave me a gruff greeting and bade me be seated. He was in his high invalid's chair, with his back to the curtained windows of a room into which the murky light of the London day penetrated. The

* Fifty years later I often dined with one of them, Dorothy (The Hon. Mrs. Bruce) in her Roman villa on the ancient Appian Way, in Rome.

85

height of his chair and the lowness of mine increased the sense of inequality with which the interview began. Enthroned, Jove-like, he looked down on me with Olympian detachment.

I began frankly. "I have come, Sir Jesse, to ask you for two thousand pounds." There was nothing new to him in this, the prey of audacious beggars, but my second sentence was novel to him. "I want it for a theatre." Briefly I outlined my need. I met with a blank refusal. He had already given far too much to Nottingham. He knew nothing about theatres. He never went inside one. He disliked them. No!

I had expected this. It was a preliminary round. I then developed my real argument. He had given large sums with the sole desire of raising the social and moral life of the city. He had planned a university and pleasure park. But a university was restricted in its service, and pleasure parks could be enjoyed only in summer. What of the life of thousands in the long winter nights, when some form of entertainment was essential? Mrs. Compton's theatre, situated in the heart of a working-class district, was performing a social service. The best drama, the most wholesome plays, were being provided for the masses, a counter-attraction to the public-houses.

Sir Jesse was not insensible to my argument. A few questions followed. Would this sum be sufficient and be well spent? Why did not others give as he had given? I replied that the sum I asked for would guarantee at least one more year, which meant a fresh chance. Others had not given because they always awaited the example of one public-spirited man.

There was a momentous silence. I thought of the actors in the theatre at Nottingham, of the curtain that might fall for the last time. Sir Jesse raised his hand with difficulty to pull at a cord attached to the lapel of his coat. His secretary came in. "My cheque book," he said briefly. The book could not be found at once. I counted the moments in heartbeats. If Lady Boot came in! At last it was found and he wrote his name with the painful effort of a chained Prometheus. "I give this to you," he said, "on the condition that nothing is said about it. I want no thanks, not even a letter of acknowledgment. The whole thing will be dismissed from my mind. There you are—I hope it will do all you wish. Good day, young man."

86

I left the room and the presence of this rare soul happier than if I had obtained the cheque for myself. I informed the astonished Huntsman, who had provided this opportunity, then I walked across St. James's Park. Big Ben struck the noon hour as I left The Mall. In my club post-office I sent off a one-word telegram that released a flood of joy in the hearts of the anxious company. The word was *Eureka*.

The theatre survived for two more years after that postponement of sentence. It died ultimately from the trouble to which repertory theatres are prone, an inability, without subsidy, to meet expenses.

III

Sometimes when I went to London I lunched with Alfred Noyes in his apartment in Cadogan Gardens. He was now about forty, powerfully built with a strong-jawed face. No one would have suspected him of being a poet. He looked too robust. I was not surprised to see an oar hanging on the wall of his study. He had rowed at Henley in the Exeter College boat. He published in 1902 his first book of poems, *The Loom of Years*, while at Oxford. It was widely acclaimed. George Meredith and W. B. Yeats wrote him complimentary letters. On leaving Oxford he took rooms in a cottage on Bagshot Heath, intent on completing an epic poem on Drake. Blustery gales swept the open heath, which might have been a haunt of highwaymen. One night the first line of his poem *The Highwayman* came to him. "The wind was a torrent of darkness among the gusty trees." In two days he finished the poem. It appeared in *Blackwood's Magazine* and carried his fame throughout the English-speaking world. It was recited everywhere, anthologised and filmed. An American composer, Deems Taylor, wrote a highly popular cantata on it.

The Highwayman was not a flash in the pan. Noyes followed this up with three books of poems that had a big sale. The first sold fifty-three thousand copies, the second thirty-five, the third forty-six. He was probably the only living poet who could make a living out of writing verse. This brought upon him the envy and derision of his less successful contemporaries. When someone at the Poetry

Bookshop, haunt of the 'Georgian' school, asked, "Have you any of Alfred Noyes's works ?" the assistant replied, in an icy voice, "It is possible. We are broadminded." As is so often the case in the literary world, to sell is to be damned. The pigmy poets were full of bile.

Noyes's fame was firmly sealed with *The Forest of Wild Thyme*, his third book. Sir Beerbohm Tree purchased the dramatic rights proposing to make a play of it. He thought it better than *The Blue Bird* and *Peter Pan*, both of which he had rejected! An American producer, interested, listened to Noyes reading the script. For one scene Coleridge Taylor had composed some beautiful music for the religious atmosphere in which it closed. The producer was not impressed. Removing a cigar he had been chewing, he interrupted. "Yeah! I'd cut that out, I'd put in a leg show there." It happened to be Beerbohm Tree's favourite scene.*

At the age of twenty-seven Noyes married an American girl. "We had my pen and £50 a year between us," he said. He made his first lecture tour in the U.S. in 1911. Being an excellent reader of his own verse, he drew enthusiastic audiences. His poems were clear, forceful, musical to the ear, and had a story to tell. The "highbrows" derided him. He was excluded from the popular "Georgian Poetry" books. Once when I mentioned Noyes's name to Eddie Marsh he exclaimed in his petulant treble voice: "But you don't read him ?" This banishment preyed on Noyes's nerves though his star shone brightly.

A few months before the First World War he was appointed Professor of English Literature at Princeton University where his lectures were very popular among the undergraduates. Two of these were Scott Fitzgerald and Edmund Wilson. He stayed at Princeton until America joined the War. Returning to London he took a small flat at 85 Cadogan Gardens and became a neighbour of Philip Gibbs and Arnold Bennett. From time to time he made lecture tours in the U.S.A. He held the Princeton professorship until 1923. It was in New York in 1920 that we became acquainted. After my return to Nottingham I was frequently his guest when I visited London.

Noyes had every reason to be content with his achievement. He was in the *Encyclopaedia Britannica* at forty-two but he allowed the young, ebullient Sitwells, Edith, Sacheverell and Osbert, "The

* *Two Worlds for Memory*, by Alfred Noyes (Sheed and Ward).

Sitwell Circus" as he called it, to get under his skin. He charged them with blatant vulgarity in pushing and advertising themselves. In turn they attacked like gadflies. I could never understand why he should have let himself be provoked. He was well-established.

At this time the leading critic was Edmund Gosse. His weekly column in the *Sunday Times* provided him with a powerful platform. He was also librarian at the House of Lords, which enabled him to conduct his correspondence on its heavy, cream-laid notepaper embossed with the Royal arms. Gosse was always careful to cultivate the right people. With small creative talent but a good critic, he occupied a dominant position. His autobiographical book *Father and Son*, the story of a religious crank and his nervous small boy, was always referred to as a masterpiece. Read today, one wonders about its réclame. He got it crowned by the *Académie Française*. He failed as a poet. Gosse was a scholar, he wrote with a clear, incisive style. Unhappily he slipped and came under a withering attack from Professor Churton Collins. It was a sensational collision. Collins's bold affront to the powerfully entrenched Gosse called up defenders. The great Lord Tennyson thundered from Olympus in defence of the Lords' Librarian. "Churton Collins is a louse on the locks of literature," he told the shaken Gosse, a sentence rich in alliteration but poor in taste.

At the time when Noyes began to attend Sir Edmund Gosse's soirées and lunches, given in his stately house, 17 Hanover Terrace, the critic was at the height of his prestige. He was regarded by the younger generation as the gateway to fame. He had great influence and dispensed much patronage. Those Chairs of English in foreign universities, even as far afield as Tokio, which provided comfortable salaries and dignified quarters to young needy poets, were attainable through the pundit of Hanover Terrace. At this time he was "The official British man of letters", as H. G. Wells described him. Alas for the whirligig of Time! Forty years later sacrilege was committed. A reviewer in the *Times Literary Supplement* (Oct. 13th, 1966), heading his article "Victorian Bore", wrote of him: "The librarianship of the House of Lords, the knighthood, the honorary degrees, the foreign decorations, all testify to his secure position in the Establishment of his time . . . Of his numerous books, nearly a

hundred, all but one are as solid and as dead as tombstones."
During Gosse's lifetime a queue formed to offer incense at the
Hanover Terrace shrine. Osbert Sitwell said that Gosse "had two
genuine, sincere, and perhaps not un-English affections—one for a
title, the other for an amateur". Gosse boasted that he knew personally nearly a hundred peers. When he gave a lecture the front seats
were occupied by duchesses. He obsequiously courted, if not in person
then by correspondence, all the eminent authors in England and
America. He also encouraged literary neophytes to gather at his
Afternoons, if properly conscious of the privilege extended to them.
Goethe at Weimar, and Gosse at Hanover Terrace.

Sometimes when I went to call on Noyes he had just returned from
one of the Afternoons. He always arrived home, it seemed to me, in a
state of nervous prostration, like some courtier returning from an
audience at the court of Louis XV. Gosse was a sleek, cosseted cat
with an unpredictable temper and formidable claws, and the scars he
left were visible. "He spent all his life saying disagreeable things about
other people, his father included," observed Lytton Strachey.

One of the causes of Noyes's agitation was the presence at Hanover
Terrace of the Sitwells. There was war between the hippopotamus
and the gadflies. Noyes thought Edith's and Osbert's poetry was
pretentious rubbish. They thought the same of Noyes's poetry, and
said so violently. Gosse enjoyed the contest, now encouraging, now
rebuking the combatants.

Noyes kept saying that it was unfortunate that I did not know
Gosse, he was so very influential, which was true. He would ask him
if he might present me. I gave him no encouragement to do what he
regarded as a friendly service to a literary aspirant. I have never been
a calculating bearer of incense. One day I found Noyes unusually
agitated. He had just returned from a public debate with Edith
Sitwell on the poetry of the old school and the new. Gosse had taken
the chair, "With the air of someone running a cockpit," said Noyes.
"Edith appeared regally dressed in a robe of purple, a gold laurel
wreath crowning her head. She was got up like a female Dante—
making the most of her unfortunate nose. She was deliberately rude
to me, as ever."

I asked whose side Gosse was on. "He's always very careful to

hide his opinion—he isn't going to quarrel with the Peerage,"
replied Noyes. "But when the debate was over he said to Edith as
we left the platform, 'Now come along, my dear. It's probable
that in his time people thought Shakespeare was mad.' "

I always enjoyed my visits to Noyes, and when he read to me the
poem he was working on and sought my opinion, I felt compli-
mented. Some of his lyrics had a haunting beauty, in the Tennysonian
tradition. He was happily married to his shy little American wife.
They had no children. They entertained quietly at Cadogan Gardens.

My friendship with Noyes was somewhat restricted by my absence
from London between 1920 and 1926, but we continued to meet from
time to time and we kept up a correspondence through those years.
I was just emerging as a novelist and he gave me warm encouragement. Always industrious, he had embarked upon his magnum opus,
The Torch Bearers, an epic work in three volumes, based on the life
stories of the great astronomers, of which he sent me the first volume
in March, 1922. During one of his American tours he had been invited to visit the great observatory on Mount Wilson, near Pasadena,
California, where a 100-inch telescope had just been installed. He was
the guest of the chief astronomer in charge of the project, who on the
night of his visit "made a remark that cost me ten years' work. He said
the poets had written too much about war. Was there not a subject
for a poem on another battle, the advancement towards knowledge ?"

This fired Noyes with the idea of an epic poem tracing the history
of astronomy down the ages to this latest great achievement on
Mount Wilson. He opened his epic with a description of the great
observatory, seen from Pasadena, where he was staying—

> At noon, upon the mountain's purple height,
> Above the pine-woods and the clouds it shone
> No larger than the small white dome of shell
> Left by the fledgling wren when wings are born.
> By night it joined the company of heaven
> And, with its constant light, became a star.

The completed work was a tour-de-force and was much acclaimed,
but it never got off the ground. Its brief vogue saddened Noyes. He
was unfortunate in his time. What he had failed to realise was that

the age of the epic was dead. Our present civilisation is too hurried in its interests, and shallow in its capacity, to understand or care for any poem that exceeds a hundred lines. Living in an age of universal mechanised slaughter, with science its handmaiden, the universities its laboratory, dehumanised by atomic bomb and germ warfare, the modern hero is pocket-sized, an automaton, a puppet of the daily Press, and debunked by the school of Stracheyan biography. The epic poem, like the three-volume novel, is dead for ever. *The Torch Bearers*, splendid though it is, has gone the way of other "master-pieces", Hardy's *The Dynasts* and Doughty's *The Dawn in Britain* (six volumes). Noyes attempted a work alien to the times. His obstinate belief in his epic kept him at his long labour. The last volume appeared eight years after the first, in 1930. Few remember the work.

In the middle of his task Noyes suffered the loss of his wife. She died suddenly while they were holidaying at St. Jean-de-Luz. In that same year I had lost my mother. The next year, in July, 1927, visiting him on my return from America, I condoled with him on his loss and we had a long discussion on death. He then gave me two shocks. "I've news for you. Next month I'm marrying a charming woman of some distinction," he said. He opened Burke's *Landed Gentry* and pointed to the name of his future wife. Mrs. Weld-Blundell was a beautiful young widow with one child. She had married her cousin who had been killed in the war. She belonged to one of the oldest Catholic families in England, the Welds, who had produced in the early nineteenth century Cardinal Thomas Weld, who gave Stonyhurst to the Jesuits and the Lulworth Castle estate to his brother.

Having given me details concerning his future wife, Noyes then informed me that he was joining the Roman Catholic Church. Perhaps I displayed some astonishment but he explained that he had been considering "going over" for some time. His apartment was opposite St. Mary's Catholic Church. He was receiving "instruction" there, so he could "go over" in a corporeal sense as well! There was a literary touch in this migration. "Would you believe it, the door of the Presbytery is opened by Joseph Conrad's cousin!" he said.

The newly-weds spent their honeymoon in Canada on a social lecture tour. They were the guests of the Governor-General of

Canada, the Governors of Manitoba and British Columbia. It was almost a Royal progress. On their return they took No. 13 Hanover Terrace, a few yards distant from Sir Edmund Gosse at No. 17. This proximity caused Barry Pain to remark on their new house. "It is of the kind that one sees but never gets. You have the ornamental water but is not dear Mr. Gosse also of Regent's Park? *Eau et Gosse à tous les étages*, as they say in the advertisements. Be careful!" Splendidly housed, Noyes gave elegant dinner parties. His muse seems to have died in Hanover Terrace, not from *l'eau* or *le gaz* but from *l'air trop distingué*.

After the announcement in Cadogan Gardens I did not see Noyes again until seventeen years later, during the Second World War. He was living in Santa Barbara, California. We met on a train going to Washington and picked up the old threads. Fate had been kind to him. He had children and his wife had had an extraordinary windfall. Shortly after marriage her uncle had succeeded to Lulworth Castle and all its contents. Among these were the famous Luttrell *Psalter* and the Bedford *Book of Hours*, Weld heirlooms. The new owner proposed selling these to provide estate duties but a legal point as to inheritance arose and it was determined that all the contents of Lulworth Castle were the property of Mrs. Noyes. The *Psalter* had been on loan to the British Museum for thirty-two years. There was a great outcry on the possibility of its leaving the country. The book was withdrawn from the Sotheby sale at the last hour with the statement that Mrs. Noyes had accepted the sum of £31,500 offered by the British Museum, a sum much lower than its value. The *Book of Hours* was not withdrawn, and for this the Museum paid the auction price of £33,000.

As common with proselytes, Noyes became an ardent Catholic. He entered into a controversy with the Anglican Bishop Barnes; with some justification since that iconoclastic cleric, a rich 'leftwinger' appointed by Ramsay MacDonald to the episcopal bench, had attacked the dogmas of the Virgin Birth and of the Eucharist, in which he did not believe. The bishop had been antagonistic towards Catholics. However, Noyes's stout defence of the Faith did not spare him an unpleasant collision with his adopted Church. It suspended a book he had written on Voltaire, thereby implying

93

the taint of heresy. The future Pope, Pius XII, intervened and an accord was arrived at, the Church accepting the book without alteration. This Galileonic touch badly shook Noyes, who was quite guiltless.

I did not see Noyes again after our meeting on the train. He died in 1958, aged seventy-eight. He had sold his London house and moved to the Isle of Wight. The new owner of 13 Hanover Terrace was the campaigning agnostic, H. G. Wells. Throughout the bombing of World War II he doggedly slept on the top floor. In these last years he was a deeply depressed man and at seventy-two contemplated suicide. He flitted from publisher to publisher, extorting sums his books no longer earned. For years he had inveighed against the stupidity of the human race, especially its politicians. He was now an unheeded Jeremiah, his public gone. The prophet of the New Age watched folly engulf the world. When I met him in New York in 1940 he seemed desperate and defeated. He had been denied his one remaining ambition, to be elected a Fellow of the Royal Society, for which scientifically as well as prophetically, he had sound qualifications. "The Society's obtuse behaviour still makes me angry," wrote Lord Snow, twenty years after his death. The end of Wells was tragic. He died slowly of cancer, aged eighty, forgotten by those who were living in the New World foretold by his constructive imagination. Fame is a wayward bitch that often devours its offspring.

Will anything of Noyes's work live ? The Georgians sniffed at him and derided him for being the slave of rhyme, rhythm and reason. In turn the disciples of T. S. Eliot crowded the temple of the Muse, according their new god a premature apotheosis. And now a still more "advanced" horde of versifiers strives desperately for originality. Its newly "liberated" Muse has no anatomy. Never has so much money been spent on publishing boneless verse of such inanity. It is unsafe to prophesy. In the raffle for immortality the winners are unpredictable. One day in a Sussex country town, as I passed a newly built Council school, I heard children's voices reciting in unison—

And still of a winter's night, they say, when the wind is in the trees,
When the moon is a ghostly galleon tossed upon cloudy seas,
When the road is a ribbon of moonlight over the purple moor,

94

A highwayman comes riding—
  Riding—riding—
A highwayman comes riding, up to the old inn-door.

I had last heard those lines chanted by thirty little Negroes in an
open-air school in Florida. You can never tell what jetsam will be
borne on the current of Time.*

IV

At one of the lunches given by Noyes at Cadogan Gardens in 1925
I met a guest, a vivacious young man of about my own age. It was not
our first meeting. On being introduced I saw that he had no recollec-
tion of me, which did not surprise me.

Late one night in 1919, coming out of the Café Royal into Piccadilly, I was about to take a taxi when a delicate-looking youth
stumbled against me. I did not know whether he had come out of the
Café, where I had been talking with Mark Gertler and a group of
artists presided over by Augustus John and his somewhat gipsy
entourage. The youth on the pavement was hatless and untidy. I
noticed he was flushed and perspiring. As my taxi came up he said to
me, indistinctly, "I'm very unwell, will you take me home?" At first
I thought he was drunk and then realised he really was unwell, as he
nearly collapsed before me. He was very thin, with the high colouring
of a consumptive. Parrot-nosed, he was sandy haired, perhaps about
twenty years of age. In the taxi he seemed to shrink to nothing and
slumped in the corner. I began to feel alarmed about his condition and
wondered whether I should seek a doctor. I asked him where he lived.
He answered inaudibly, so I repeated my question to which he
replied, "Forty-eight Grosvenor Street". The address surprised me.
It was one of the most fashionable streets in London. I surmised that
he was a footman or valet. During the ride he did not speak, but
twice, fearing he might be unconscious, I enquired if he was all
right. He responded with a monosyllabic "Yes", very faintly. When
we arrived in the deserted street I helped him out and paid off the
taxi. As we reached the railings, I turned to go down the area steps
with him whereupon he said "No—no!", fumbled in a pocket and

* *Collected Poems* by Alfred Noyes (Blackwood & Sons).

95

pulled out some keys on a ring. He selected one and gave it to me. I opened the large main door and we entered a hall, dimly lit from a chandelier high up in the well of the staircase. The light was sufficient to tell me that I was in a luxuriously furnished house. A soldier in a suit of armour stood by one wall. I gave the keys to the youth and turned to leave. "Please take me up to my room," he said. The thought of climbing to the servants' floor dismayed me, but I helped him up the stairs. On reaching the second floor, he steered me, still supporting him, to a door that he opened. He then fumbled at a switch and turned on some shaded lights, sufficient to reveal a large room with a massive canopied bed, a red leather settee and chairs, a mantelpiece, and a round library table with books and a Chinese vase full of flowers. On the walls were oil paintings. A crimson brocaded dressing-gown and silk pyjamas lay on the turned-down bed.

I put the youth on the settee. Was he drugged? Somehow I did not think so, though I had no experience of drugged persons. "Shall I ring for a servant?" I asked. "I want a drink," he muttered, not answering my question. There were bottles on a side table. "Whisky?" I asked. He nodded. I took the glass to him. He drank slowly and then lay back with closed eyes. By now I began to feel uncomfortable, and wanted to get away. Who was he? The carpets, the decorations, the quilted bed and furnishing all spoke of wealth. This could not be a servant's room.

He presently made an effort to get up. "I'll go to bed," he said almost inaudibly. He stooped and tried to untie his shoes. I untied them for him and ended by undressing him and getting him into his pyjamas. As he sat on the bedside, he suddenly said "Do you like that?" I turned to a table he indicated. On it was a pair of beautifully modelled hands. "They're mine, by Epstein," he said. If he had said by Rodin I should not have been surprised. I noticed over the mantelpiece a portrait of a young man with an elongated neck. "Is that you?" I asked. After a few moments he said, "Augustus John did it." He shut his eyes. I got him into bed and covered him up. He looked like a frail child with his thin, fresh-complexioned face on the pillow. I noticed now that his hair, falling over his brow, had an auburn tint. "Are you sure you wouldn't like me to call someone?" I repeated. He shook his head slowly, and his eyes closed. "I don't know your name," I said. His eyes half-opened, and in the dim light I thought they had a mocking glint. "I don't know yours! You're very kind," he murmured, closing his eyes again. I stood for a few moments looking down at him. He appeared to have gone to sleep. I picked up my hat, opened the heavy mahogany door and switched off the light. From the landing on which I stood I saw the marble hall below and the staircase. I began to descend. Suddenly I realised that if anyone saw me they might think I was a burglar and not believe my explanation. The strange youth might deny he had ever seen me, or be unconscious that he had. I soundlessly reached the hall, tiptoed across it, watched by the man in armour. It was dark by the door and I had difficulty in finding the right lock. Finally I opened the door, stepped out, and closed it behind me. Before me was Grosvenor Street, lamp-lit, deserted. I stood there for a few moments unable to believe all that had happened. I looked at my watch. It was a quarter to one. I began to walk to my lodgings.

The next day I tried to find out who lived at 48, Grosvenor Street. From a directory I discovered that it was the house of Viscount Tredegar. Turning to Debrett, I learned that he was the first Viscount and third Baron Tredegar. He had married Lady Katherine, daughter of the ninth Earl of Southesk. His seat was Tredegar Park, Monmouthshire. Obviously this could not be my mysterious youth but I found Viscount Tredegar had one son and one daughter. *Heir* The Hon. Evan Frederic Morgan, born July 13, 1893. I was surprised to learn he was twenty-six years of age, one year my junior. I did not then know that I had met one of the most extraordinary young men in the kingdom.

Now, six years later, introduced by Noyes to my fellow guest, Mr. Evan Morgan, I looked at him with considerable interest. Throughout lunch he talked vivaciously and wittily. I learned from Noyes that he had published a book of poems and my host must have told him that I also had published some books of verse for he began to discuss "our contemporaries".

In the drawing-room later I found an opportunity of taking him aside. "You don't remember meeting me before?" I asked. He did not. "I once took you home to Grosvenor Street and put you to bed," I said. He looked at me, incredulous. "It was about six years ago.

You had a large bedroom on the second floor, a crimson brocade dressing-gown, and on a side-table there was a model of your hands which you told me had been made by Epstein."

"My God—then you must have taken me home! Was I very drunk?"

"No. I never knew what was the matter with you. You were not drunk but you seemed ill. You asked me outside the Café Royal to take you home, which I did."

"How extraordinary!" he exclaimed, and laughed gaily. "Since you've been my Nannie you must come and dine, and meet my mother —who makes wonderful birds' nests. We're quite a bird family!"

Before I could recover from this astonishing, irrelevant information someone interrupted us.

I purposely was the last to leave in order to ask Noyes about him. "Oh, yes—he's a remarkable fellow. He's written quite a good poem about an eel. I'll lend you his book," he said.

He was indeed a remarkable fellow. I knew him well until he died twenty-four years later, aged fifty-five. He never ceased in all those years to astonish me, and everybody else. He could be eccentric and outrageous to a point of insanity and I was not surprised to hear one day that his sister had drowned herself. When he succeeded to the title he had an income of £60,000 a year and an estate of some 30,000 acres, so he was able to indulge every whim. Much of his income came from the family coal interests, but this did not prevent him from advocating the abolition of coal royalties. He was a figure straight out of the Italian Renaissance in his range of interests, a super-dilettante, a man of many gifts and parts, but unpredictable in his behaviour. When I met him at the Noyes lunch he had already played many roles. Educated at Eton and Christ Church, Oxford, he was gazetted in 1915 to the Welsh Guards. Delicate, he did not see active service and in the last two years of World War I he acted as private secretary of the Parliamentary Secretary to the Ministry of Labour, being then twenty-four. When Sir George Riddell, Lloyd George's Press adviser, represented the British Press at the Versailles Conference in 1919, he took Evan Morgan, a fellow Welshman, with him. Evan had resigned his commission. In Paris he indulged in one of those irresponsible acts that marked his conduct. He invited Lloyd George's secretary, Miss Stevenson and some other friends, to be his guests at a performance of *Samson and Delilah* at the Opera House. He was annoyed to find the best seats taken. He intimated to the French authorities that Lloyd George and some friends wished to attend the performance. On arrival Miss Stevenson found that the high dignitaries were expecting the Prime Minister, as well as his secretary and escort. They had the red carpet down for a ceremonious reception of the great statesman. With French tact they hid their indignation when they discovered the truth.

Soon after that Evan became a Roman Catholic. The Church offered the décor that appealed to his histrionic nature. As in all things, wholehearted for a time, he wished to become a priest, so he went to Rome and entered the Pontifical Beda College. He took a suite at the neighbouring Hotel Bernini, for entertaining purposes, and lodged his chauffeur and valet there. He sent the latter to the theological lectures in order to take notes and pass them on to him. He fell in love with an Italian youth. The Rector decided that this aristocratic collegian did not have a true vocation. It was a kind of Baron Corvo case again, except that this time the baronial connection was authentic. On rejection, Evan took an enormous sheaf of white lilies, carried under his black soutane, and deposited them at the foot of the Madonna in a neighbouring church. (Did he borrow this act from Duke Albrecht in *Giselle*?)

And so he left Rome sorrowing. But he was soon back again with a more resplendent plan. Passengers on the Continental Express at Victoria Station were astonished to see a young man running down the platform waving some papers and shouting, "Stop the train! Stop the train! I've papers for the Pope!" The train was halted and he boarded it with his suite. The Cardinal at Westminster had given him credentials. Soon he was established in Rome wearing the sixteenth-century costume of a Knight of the Cape and Sword, the trimmings of a Privy Chamberlain to the Pope, and an officer of the *Guardia Nobile*. His Rolls-Royce car, his retinue of Italian servants and his lively parties soon made his name known. He astonished the Roman nobles by arriving at their receptions nursing a Siamese ape.

Returning to England, vivacious and good-looking, there seemed no limit to his protean character. He took up painting and exhibited his work at the Paris Salon. He became a discerning collector of *objets d'art,* specialising in the Renaissance period, and he published several books of poems. He could play the violin and the piano creditably. He was a ready speaker. It was said that he was a favourite of Queen Mary who found him knowledgeable as a collector of bric-à-brac. Lytton Strachey when he met him in July, 1916, at one of Lady Ottoline Morrell's house-parties, on his twenty-third birth-day, was as deceived as I had been about his age. Morgan had been at Christ Church and came with a group of undergraduates, "a tall, bright-coloured youth with a parakeet nose and an assured manner, and the general appearance of a refined old woman", recorded Strachey. He was wrong about his height since he was of medium stature, and he was characteristically derogatory about the "old woman" appearance. Bright-coloured, with a parakeet nose, certainly, but Evan Morgan was always vividly alive with youthful enthusiasm.

Shortly after our meeting at Cadogan Gardens I received an invitation to dine at Grosvenor Street along with Noyes and his wife. There I met his affable mother. His father was not present. I learned that he was going blind. After dinner, when coffee had been served in the drawing-room, a footman opened a trestle near Lady Tredegar and put on it a large tray with an assortment of wools, straw, hair, cotton, twigs, moss and leaves. "You may think it peculiar," she said. "Some women like to do petit-point and needlework—it tries my eyes too much. This is more amusing." We inquired about the types of nests she made. "Large ones and small ones, some rough and some lined, for different birds. I've had all sorts of tenants!" she replied. "I plant the nests out in bushes and hidden places. Then I watch. It's better than fishing—getting bird tenants!" She laughed and demonstrated her work. Her fingers were very nimble. She achieved an astonishing verisimilitude. "Of course, I take my models from real life," she explained.

Later I was taken up to Evan's study-bedroom, which I recog-nised at once. But this time it had a number of bird cages, with a parrot, budgerigar, jackdaw, etc., a bewildering assortment. He opened the door of a cage and called out of it a small bird with glittering eyes and yellow beak. I thought it was a blackbird, sur-prisingly tame. It leapt up on to Evan's finger, and they kissed each other. "Say how-d'you-do to my friend," commanded Evan. Then to my amazement the bird said, clearly, "How d'you do ? I hope you are well." It was not a blackbird but a mynah. I was to learn later that my host was a considerable ornithologist. He could talk to his birds in a language they understood. Birds in cages were often part of his luggage. At lunch one day, some years later, at one of his country houses, a bird proceeded to walk down the long dining-table pecking at the plates of the guests. One lady gave a cry of alarm. Evan at the head of the table shouted, "Peter, go back to your cage!" The bird, a raven, looked at him then flew off and sat on the top of his cage.

Once, when I arrived at an hotel in Kansas City, the desk clerk, looking at my name and address when I signed the register, said, "Hey, we had another Britisher here a few days ago. A strange guy. He was travelling with a priest, a red-haired youth, a baby panther, two snakes, a mongoose and a couple of bird cages. My, he was an odd 'un. Said he was a Lord—an' he was! We objected to his animals but he said they all slept with him. That panther skeered us. He opened its mouth and put his hand in it to show it wouldn't bite. He was taking it to his private zoo in England."

"Was his name Tredegar—Lord Tredegar ?" I asked.

"Sure!—that's it, Tredegar." The clerk flipped over the cards of a file. "Yeah, there you are." He showed me the card. I was not surprised. Two years earlier he had succeeded his father as second Viscount and kept a menagerie at Tredegar Park. Once, his guest there, he took me to see the animals. He had a boxing kangaroo and invited us to try it. One rash member of the house party went into the compound and was so badly knocked about that he had to be rescued.

Some time after the Noyes lunch the volatile Evan contested Limehouse in the Unionist interest. It was a notoriously tough constituency and he tackled it with great spirit. He was not successful but was very popular. In 1930 he became Conservative candidate for Cardiff, where his family had many interests. He withdrew in favour of a National Labour candidate. Meanwhile he had been an Honorary Attaché at the British Legation in Copenhagen. Later he founded The Tredegar Memorial Lecture of the Royal Society of Literature and delivered the inaugural lecture, choosing John Donne as his subject. I was to hear this lecture elsewhere. In 1947 I was asked to take the chair for him at one of the Foyle Lunches at the Dorchester Hotel. His subject had been announced as "The Restoration Love Poets". I introduced him, naming his subject. Without any forewarning he got up and said he had been too busy to prepare his talk as announced. He pulled out the printed lecture he had given to the Society of Literature and bored the assembly by a wearisome reading of his paper on Donne, in whom the audience had little interest. Afterwards I expostulated with him for his nonchalant behaviour. It had no effect on him, always wilful.

He could be alarmingly *méchant*. An American guest at his town house pestered him with a request that he put on the peer's robes he had just worn at the coronation of King George VI, in order that he might make a colour cinephoto. He consented finally and told his guest to take him as he came downstairs. Evan duly appeared in all his regalia, wearing his coronet, ermine cape and crimson robe. Halfway down the stairs he opened his robe. He had nothing on underneath. Eccentric, perverse, unpredictable, arrogant, outrageous, he could also be a charming host, thoughtful and witty. At Tredegar Park he presided at a wonderful table of some twenty guests. He had a grand piano put in the Servants Hall so that they could dance after dinner. He was astonishingly well-informed on a hundred subjects. He was a great joiner of societies of all kinds. He was a Knight of Devotion of the Sovereign and Military Order of Malta, a Knight of St. John, a Knight of the Order of the Holy Sepulchre, a Knight of the Constantinian Order of St. George, a Knight of the Cape and Sword, a colonel of two regiments, a lieutenant of the Welsh Guards, and a major of the Royal Corps of Signals. He was the president of two hospital boards and a treasurer of the Prince of Wales Orthopaedic Hospital. With his love for birds and animals it was natural that he should be a Fellow of the Zoological Society (he had a private key for the Zoo in Regent's Park) and should be the honorary president of the People's Dispensary for Sick Animals of the Poor. He was also a Fellow of the Royal Society of Antiquarians, of the Royal Society of Literature, a Fellow of the Royal Historical Society (he restored a ruined Welsh castle), a governor of the Royal Agricultural Society of England and of Wales. The list went on. At Oxford he was the founder of the Celtic Society.

His interests embraced the Navy League and the Boy Scouts. Along with all these official, social and philanthropical interests, he had a vivid and unconventional private life. His attire was sometimes theatrical but always in good taste. He knew the night life of Paris, Rome, Berlin, Vienna and Budapest, 'milord' being well-known in the bars, cafés and night clubs. He indulged a jackdaw-passion for accumulating precious stones. On a rosary of rubies he had a minute ivory crucifix carved by Benvenuto Cellini. In his pockets he carried a small fortune of Fabergé's microscopic jewelled fantasies. Calling on him at the Hotel Lancaster in Paris one noon I found him just rising. On leaving with him I noticed he had left on the dressing-table four rings, a Fabergé gold cigarette-case studded with emeralds, a Cartier wrist-watch with gold bracelet, and tie-clip I much admired, made from a Venetian gold ducat. I said, "Shouldn't you lock them up—it's a great temptation for servants to steal." "Why should they? They're well tipped!" he cried airily, and walked out of the room.

He was a person of sudden whims, behaving as one who had never known any parental control or financial restrictions. Withal, there was an endearing side to his character. He would go to considerable trouble to be kind. One day in 1938 he called at my cottage at Henley-on-Thames, finding there two American ladies, my lunch guests. They confessed they had not yet seen Oxford, whereupon Evan said he would show them it. He drove us in his Rolls-Royce to Christ Church, where he had been an undergraduate. The great dining-hall was closed. He had it opened. He seemed to know the name and history of every portrait on its walls. Then he took us to the library in Peckwater Quad. It was closed. Again, he had it opened. Every object and painting was embellished by his comment. Then he took us to other colleges. For over two hours he was a tireless cicerone, very knowledgeable. Finally, he put the ladies on the train to London and drove me back to Pilgrim Cottage. He was always excellent, if sometimes startling company and a lavish host at Tredegar Park, his beautiful Inigo Jones seat.

Evan made two marriages which were failures. They never had any chance of success. He rejected all of Nancy Cunard's passionate overtures. His excursions in matrimony were inspired only by his desire to have a son and heir, in order to thwart the eventual inheritance to his title and estate by a cousin he disliked. He married in 1928, first, a daughter of Lord Alington. There was a spectacular wedding, celebrated by the Catholic Archbishop of Cardiff at the Brompton Oratory. The couple soon went their own ways until their union was terminated nine years later by the wife's death while holidaying in Budapest. His second marriage, two years afterwards, was to Princess Olga Dolgorouky. It was annulled after four years. There were no children of either marriage. Six years later Tredegar died, in April 1949, of lung cancer, aged fifty-five. His death was a shock to his many friends. Two years earlier when I had taken the chair for him at the Foyle Lunch he was his usual vivacious self, and a year before his death he was my guest during Henley Regatta As *The Times* observed in its obituary, "He was a man of many parts to whom the word *dilettante* may appropriately be applied." He was a Renaissance prince born out of his age.

Evan Morgan's uncle succeeded as the 5th Lord Tredegar. He died in 1954, having held the title for only five years. He was succeeded by his only son who died in 1962. On his death the barony became extinct, with a span of only thirteen years between Evan and his cousin as holders. Tredegar Park was sold and became a Catholic institution.

CHAPTER FIVE

Italian Excursion

I

ON MY RETURN to Nottingham in 1920 I was often at the home of my friend Jack Laing, but since I no longer stayed there I saw no more the ritual of morning prayers with the servants lined up, and Jack's solemn father droning the chosen reading of the Bible, after which we all reversed, went down on our knees and buried our faces in our hands over the leather chairs. The grim relationship between father and son had not changed a state of affairs that contrasted so strongly with the domestic felicity of the home in which I had passed my boyhood.

Returning to Jack's home I became aware of a growing shadow over it. His cheerful, rosy-cheeked mother, who acted as a buffer between father and son, was ailing and her illness became menacingly progressive. Mr. Laing, a prosperous wine merchant, the antithesis of Ruskin's doting father who had also derived his fortune from a similar source, had two elderly sisters. They seemed to have been somewhat adventurous. One, a spinster, rigid and forceful but not without charm, had settled in Geneva. She moved in the best circles of an exclusive community composed of descendants of French-Swiss-Italian commercial dynasties. It was Miss Laing's position in Geneva that had caused Jack to be sent to a Swiss tutor's establishment after leaving Tonbridge School. A Pastor Muller presided over some dozen boarders, a man for whom Jack retained a lifelong affection. Pastor Muller was a character, a disciplinarian whose rule was varied by an endearing eccentricity. He was a gourmet. His pupils were marvellously fed. Once a month he took them to a lakeside restaurant to eat *fondue*, a melted cheese flavoured with wine and brandy, to which he was addicted. Jack's mouth watered when he talked of the *fondues*.

Mr. Laing's other sister had been still more adventurous. An Italian fell in love with her. After an impetuous courtship he had proposed marriage. Her family disapproved. The Italian suitor, Antonio, had no social position, worse, he had no money. He was the proprietor of a small hydropathic establishment in Caramanico, a remote village in the Abruzzi mountains, snow-bound through the winter. Love triumphed and the pair went off to run the hydro. The elder sister paid them a visit from Geneva. "Barbaric! It's a wild, poverty-stricken, wolf-haunted village wholly out of touch with civilisation. How anyone can endure it I don't know. Primitive! Absolutely primitive!" said Miss Laing, used to every luxury provided by Swiss efficiency, describing her sister's home to me one day during a visit to the Laings. Even so, the marriage was a great success. In due time despite the hydro and its remedial waters, the wife became bed-ridden from arthritis. Antonio nursed her patiently through the years.

Mr. Laing was devoted to his sisters. In order to have a reliable report on the invalid in the Abruzzi he devised an ingenious plan by which he could keep himself informed and at the same time make his son's annual holiday something of an ordeal. He satisfied Jack's thirst for Italy by making it a condition that he should visit his aunt in Caramanico. He would provide the money, for second-class travel. This journey involved several nights of sitting up in the train, and the time was strictly allotted. Two days for the journey to Caramanico, with a three-day halt there, then two weeks free to visit whatever place Jack desired. It wasn't "The Golden Journey to Samarkand" but a journey to the Abruzzi.

In 1921 my friend proposed that we should have a summer holiday together, three weeks in all in the Italian Lakes and Switzerland. We would visit Lake Lugano, Lake Como and Lake Maggiore. For six days I should be left alone while Jack made the Caramanico call. The prospect excited me. Since a boy, I had dreamed of Italy, the land of Gibbon, Keats, Shelley, Byron, Browning, etc. We counted our pennies. Jack, a born economist and a precisionist, drew up a dazzling schedule. Leaving Nottingham early in the morning, sitting up in the train all night, we should be able to have coffee and crois-sants at 6 a.m. the next day in Bâle station. Then would follow

Lucerne and the tunnelled, spiralling journey of the St. Gotthard. We should reach Lugano on its lake in the early afternoon. What a delightful companion I had, scholarly, equable in temper, and a master-planner! Even Jack's idiosyncrasies were endearing. He was precise to a degree that provoked my mirth. Nothing for him was "about" or "perhaps". I was spontaneous and slapdash, he was calm and meticulous. He was the banker when we set out. Every detail went into his little book. When at the end of the tour he rendered me an account I noticed that the items debited often went into two decimal points.

Crossing the Channel I reflected how different had been my experience of it in the freezing winter of December, 1916, in a destroyer of the Dover Patrol that barred the German Fleet's egress, and on other crossings, again in winter, when I went out to France as a war correspondent and came back on a December day in 1918, my role finished. And here I was, the crossing made, in a comfortable French train. My last foreign train, bringing me from Cologne via Belgium and France, had no floors to its wrecked carriages, the track being visible below us. And now, unbelievably, I was bound for Italy, the land of which I had so long dreamed. Behind me was England, released from the trials and restrictions of war time, newly exuberant in victory, beginning an era that was regarded hopefully as the Bright Twenties.

When the train drew out of Calais station Jack rummaged in a satchel that held his travel equipment, compass, maps, guide-books, combination knife-fork-spoon-bottle-opener, foot powder and sun cream. He produced a small object made of leather, with a button-hole and a metal clip, and passed it to me. I asked what it was for. "It's most essential. Pastor Muller equipped us all with one for excursions. It's a *porte-chapeau*. When you go into museums and want your hands free for holding a catalogue and making notes, you fasten this to your coat button, and clip your hat to it, *Voilà!*" Singularly, Jack carried no camera, which I did. "It's a tourist mania—what do you do with all those bad photos when you've taken them—paste them in an album, bore your friends with them and then never look at them again. One of the world's great waste-pastimes!" he declared.

The afternoon light began to fade. How strange to be traversing in comfort those bloody battlefields of Northern France, Cambrai, St. Quentin, Laon, Rheims, where three years ago great armies had been locked in combat! The landscape still showed shell-blistered villages and trees. In darkness our train ran on towards unscarred Switzerland, and the passengers settled down for the night. I was too excited for sleep and at dawn went out into the corridor.

It was light when we reached Bâle and detrained in that international station. Why do I vividly remember down the years the diced red and white tablecloths, and waitresses with plaited flaxen hair who served coffee and rolls? In half an hour we boarded a neat Swiss train. We were out of France and in Switzerland and the next excitement was running in an electric train along the shores of Lake Lucerne. Later we plunged into the great tunnel under the St. Gotthard range, three spirals up and three spirals down, with intermittent darkness and blinding flashes of light, one of them showing the Devil's Bridge over a yawning chasm. In after years, on foot and by car, I took the road route cresting bleak Andermatt, topmost village of that rampart of mountains that shuts off sunny Italy from the rains and snows of northern Europe. After our last airy spiral, the tail end of the train visible from the front carriages, we emerged into blazing light at Airolo, above us the incredible blue of the Italian sky. The chill in the air vanished, the growing heat steamed the windows. We dropped to a plain of ochre-coloured houses, trailing vines, Lombardy poplars, ruined castles vertiginously perched, and the vowelled names of Swiss-Italy, Lavorgo, Bellinzona, and then, at 2 o'clock in the afternoon, our destination, Lugano, with its station high above the lake. Down precipitous silent streets we reached our modest hotel. We went up in a lift, walked along a corridor and entered a dark bedroom. The manager went forward and threw open two long *persiennes*, giving access to a balcony. *Bella vista!* he exclaimed, as the light flooded the room.*

* Alas, today those characteristic *persiennes* of Mediterranean dwellings, slatted and painted, have almost vanished. The roller blind has replaced them. To shut out the light this must be fully lowered; to let in the air, it must be raised, and admits the light. Today hotel and villa windows look like the façade of a factory with their unpainted roller blinds. Adapted to old windows, the roller boxes cut off a metre of light. I have seen, since 1960,

In those days Lugano had not been discovered by the tourist mob
and ruined by prosperity, its front roaring with traffic, its villas
demolished to give place to towering *appartements*, its streets blocked
with cars. In 1921, as with the French and Italian Rivieras, no one
came in the heat of June. Everything appeared shuttered. Lake water
lapped audibly. Boatmen dozed under dark ilex trees. Late one night
I heard singing below in the Piazza. I opened the shutters of our
room and went out on to the balcony and listened. Two voices came
up out of the darkness, accompanied by the playing of the fountain,
moon-bright. First one man's voice and then the other's, mellow,
liquid, full-throated tenor and baritone, they sang arias from *La
Traviata*. For half an hour we listened, entranced, then silence, and
only the persistent notes of the fountain. In the morning the concierge
said "I hope you were not disturbed by those men singing last night?"
"Disturbed! We were enthralled—who were they?" I replied. "A
couple of drunken boatmen. We had to go out and silence them."

Two days later we sailed down the lake and crossed over to
Cadenabbia on the shore of Lake Como. Our hotel faced the water.
The road by day and night was silent and deserted, not yet, as through
the crowded summers of later years, infested with motor-charabancs
and camera-laden tourists. We made excursions up and down the
lake, to the princely Villa d'Este outside Como, to the Villa Pliniana
with the well whose waters mysteriously rose and fell, a phenomenon
described by Pliny over eighteen centuries earlier, and by Shelley.

One day we made a venturesome excursion across the lake to
Monte San Primo. We climbed 6,000 feet to the summit and then
came down to Nesso on the shore, where a steamer called. We went
on board and sat in the little saloon. I became interested in a pair of
passengers who got on at the next port of call. One was a man of
about forty, spectacled, very thin and tall. He was dressed in an
open-necked shirt and white trousers, his panama hat stuffed into a
knapsack. A long red beard increased the bizarre effect of his atten-
uated figure. For a few moments I thought he was French or Spanish
until I heard him speak in English in a high squeaky voice to his
companion, a youth of about twenty who wore tight white trousers,

the picturesque façades of Italian palaces, villas and hotels ruined. But the
roller-blind costs less to maintain, so it is triumphant.

a blue shirt open to the navel, and red sandals on his bare feet. He had flirtatious eyes and flapped his hands as he vivaciously chatted.

We watched them, fascinated, like ornithologists who had spotted a pair of strange birds. This image must have been in my companion's mind. When they left the boat higher up the lake Jack observed, quietly, "They look like something out of La Fontaine, but I don't recall any fable of The Stork and the Jay."

I wondered who the elder man was. There was something unique about this limp figure with the waterfall beard and long skeletal hands. Jack's guess was a professor, mine, an artist. And the youth? "You can never tell at that age—he might grow into a Director of the National Gallery. There's something brainy about him, for all the flapdoodle," said Jack.

Five years later we identified the elder man. As will transpire, we were both wrong.

II

After Lake Como we proceeded to Milan and here my companion left me for his Caramanico excursion. At once I went to see Leonardo da Vinci's *The Last Supper*. It was very faint but lovely and I had not known how cleverly it was painted on the convent's blank end wall to give the illusion of three windows of an upper chamber. Over five hundred years old, the faded fresco was still a miracle of design and characterisation. I then went to the famous Brera Gallery, and to the cathedral, a huge white wedding cake outside and a sham within.

There was a very attractive girl in my hotel at Milan. She was Finnish, twenty-three, intelligent and self-possessed. We made excursions together. It was pleasant to have such a companion while awaiting Jack's return. Her face was a complete oval with silver hair brushed down over her brow. She had bright blue eyes. Vivacious, alert, her English was excellent. She told me that she was a daughter of a professor at Helsinki and was studying medicine. One day we went to an open-air lido. She was a magnificent swimmer with the body of a seal, velvety and supple. The briefness of her costume for those days added to the sensation she created with her lithe beauty. There was soon around her a swarm of excited young Italians whose ardent attentions she firmly repulsed. I was a poor swimmer. She played round me like a dolphin, sliding over me, under me, tantalising, full of laughter, throwing up sprays of water. One rash youth seized her ankle. In a second she had him by the hair, pulled him under, and held him there. He emerged, choking, scared, and made for the side. She was nowhere visible and then surfaced halfway down the pool, radiant with laughter. Once, as I playfully struggled with her, she seized my wrist with an iron grip. When she told me she was training to throw the javelin at the Olympic Games I did not wonder. She could have picked me up and thrown me. Nevertheless, she was warmly feminine, with a teasing allure. Her brown skin was sheer silk.

On the night before Jack's return, after dinner, we discussed music. It transpired that her father was a friend of Sibelius, the composer, and they often visited him. She had an album of photos, would I like to see them? We went to her room. It had a balcony that overlooked a garden court with a fountain. After she had shown me her photo album we sat on the balcony. The night was warm, scented with the flowers below. A moon came up over the tiled roofs. It was like a theatre set for *Romeo and Juliet*. When I left in the first light of dawn the simile was complete. We had known ecstasy. Our farewell was rather desperate.

Jack arrived back at midday from Caramanico and we left for Cannobio on Lake Maggiore. "I hope, dear boy, you have been able to amuse yourself?" he asked. I assured him I had, not mentioning my nocturnal adventure. There was an austere streak in his character that did not encourage confession.

Our Lake Maggiore visit was confined to three days. Crossing in a paddle steamer from Pallanza to Baveno, en route for the Simplon, we were struck by a violent squall coming from the mountains. Pandemonium broke out, with hysterical peasant women among the hencoops praying to the Madonna. A black night engulfed us, the wind screamed, the steamer was tossed about like an eggshell. It was incredible that within half an hour a heavenly day could be changed into a wave-lashed inferno.

We left Baveno the next morning and via the Simplon Tunnel traversed the long Rhone Valley and the shore of the Swiss lake until we reached Geneva. Our room had been booked by Pastor Muller in an hotel on the Quai du Mont Blanc. It had a magnificent view across the lake and we arrived to see sunset on the snowy massif of Mont Blanc. The next day we paid our respects to Pastor and Madame Muller. They were like a pair out of a French novel. He was leonine, with a long black coat and bow tie. One could picture him thundering from a Calvinist pulpit. Madame Muller, petite, was dressed in a black leg-of-mutton sleeve blouse, with highboned collar and flounced skirt. There was a hullabaloo of welcome, with much bowing, hand shaking and cries of joy. So the *cher garçon* had returned. How tall, how distingué, how full of health!

We lunched *en-famille* with ten demure youths at the table, one of them being the son of the house, Etienne. Poor youth, he was destined to be drowned in the lake six years later. The following day was the day of the *fondue*, of which the Pastor was a connoisseur. We drove in a landau to a quayside restaurant gay with a striped awning. The order for the *fondue* had been given, but before it was served there was a preliminary rite. Aperitifs were ordered, whereupon Pastor Muller took from his pocket a small book. "Before we eat I will read to you a little essay *De la Fondue*, from Brillat-Savarin's masterpiece *La Physiologie du Goût*. Perhaps you know it? *Non?*" He put on his pince-nez and solemnly read, beginning, *La fondue est originaire de la Suisse*, and ending, *dont le prélat se servit copieusement.** "And now a lesser prélat will serve you a *fondue!*" said Pastor Muller, closing his book solemnly and removing his pince-nez. It was as if he had just concluded reading the Lesson.

---

* La fondue est originaire de la Suisse. Ce n'est autre chose que des œufs brouillés au fromage, dans certaines proportions que le temps et l'expérience ont révélées. J'en donnerai la recette officielle. C'est un mets sain, savoureux, appétissant, de prompte confection, et pourtant toujours prêt à faire face à l'arrivée de quelques convives inattendus. Au reste, je n'en fais mention ici que pour ma satisfaction particulière, et parce que ce mot rappelle un fait dont les vieillards du district de Belley ont gardé le souvenir. Vers la fin du XVIIe siècle, un M. de Madot fut nommé à l'évêché de Belley, et y arrivait pour en prendre possession. Ceux qui étaient chargés de le recevoir et de lui faire les honneurs de son propre palais avaient préparé un festin digne de l'occasion, et avaient fait usage de toutes les ressources de la cuisine d'alors pour fêter l'arrivée de Monseigneur. Parmi les entremets brillait une ample *fondue*, dont le prélat se servit copieusement . . .

He made a sign, whereupon the waiter placed the well-heralded dish on the table. The appropriate wine was served. We tucked our napkins under our chins and began. There was a few moments' silence, broken by Jack. "*Epatant, cher Pastor!*" he cried, and we all chorused our agreement.

I remember down the years that lakeside lunch and my delightful host. All gone, their only son drowned, their villa demolished, and of that happy company I alone remain. Before saying farewell, at my request the Pastor gave me the recipe for *la fondue*—"*Telle qu'elle a été extraite des papiers de M. Trolliet, bailli de Moudon, au canton de Berne*". Thirty years after the lunch at Geneva I was able to please a renowned cook and gourmet, as well as novelist, Mrs. Belloc Lowndes, who came to lunch at my Pilgrim Cottage. She was surprised and delighted by the *fondue*.

III

One night, about 2 a.m., soon after my return from our holiday, while I was working on my novel, I heard a tap on the street door. Opening it I was astonished to see Jack standing there. The Laings lived some distance away and his presence at this time in the morning surprised me. "What on earth brings you?" I began, but as he stepped inside his grave face gave me the clue to his call. For a year his mother had been dying of cancer. He had come to me a few minutes after her death. I walked back home with him through the quiet lamplit streets. I realised this was the close of an era in his life. The bright, tranquillising spirit in a home where there was little accord between father and son had vanished. Within a year the widower, turned seventy, had married the housekeeper-nurse who had been brought in during the long illness. Jack moved out and set up his own establishment in a tall slim house on a high terrace of the Park that overlooked the Trent valley and the distant Charnwood Forest. Here he lived, scholar and confirmed bachelor, surrounded by the art collection of his maternal grandfather, a dilettante and one-time Master of the Honourable Company of Skinners, whose lavish annual banquets in the Company's Hall, Jack, also a Skinner, attended.

Events soon carried us into separate channels in the ensuing years but I never failed to pay him an annual visit. He was a perfect host. He had a rare quality. He was one of those whose mind and conversation always extended one's knowledge. We sat up until late hours talking of countless subjects that interested us. He had a very good reference library, kept in his top-floor den. If I had doubts about a date, a place, a name, or some facts of geography, art, archaeology, astronomy, literature, he would dash upstairs and come back loaded with books relevant to the subject under discussion. Sometimes I was almost barricaded in my chair by these volumes.

IV

Shortly before departure on the Italian holiday two clouds gathered on the horizon. My unfortunate brother, with a wife and two daughters, had undergone his third operation. Forty years of age, he became an invalid for the rest of his life. I came to his assistance. Now my mother caused me anxiety. My return to Nottingham had given her deep joy. I had uprooted her when I went to my first journalistic post in Liverpool. On my moving to London she was stranded again and lived in uncomfortable lodgings in Nottingham, until she found the tiny house we now inhabited. There was always in her mind a desire to return to the house to which we had moved on my father's death. We had now emerged from those dire days when, a boy of fifteen, I had been her sole support. There had never been a moment when her spirit failed her. For twenty years a semi-invalid, nothing had impaired her gallant nature. She was now approaching her seventieth year and was still lovely to behold, with her alert blue eyes, abundant hair and rosy complexion. She possessed an almost riotous sense of humour. We called one another by names of absurd invention that kept strangers wondering about our sanity. We maintained our invented dialogue rich with key words beyond common interpretation. There was the nickname I gave her, Lady Pelican Pouch. Troubled by chronic indigestion, her diet was a monotonous one of arrowroot and fish. I declared that a double chin was surely the result of so much fish-eating. Pelican-wise, she had developed a pouch, hence my nickname. She protested vigorously when I threatened to put her in my second novel, *Sails of Sunset*, which I did, since she dared me. In London I had observed the pelicans on the lake in St. James's Park. I bought a postcard of them and wrote on it—"Dear Elizabeth, We have not seen you for such a long time. Won't you visit us here, we have a spare nest. Your affectionate cousins, Alice and Peter Pelican." The postman, delivering it, asked "Is this right, Mrs. Roberts? It's for a Lady Pelican Pouch?" "Quite right, it's from my ridiculous son," replied my mother. We lived on those terms.

Before I left for my Italian holiday the condition of my mother began to cause me deep anxiety. There was a strange, persistent pain. The specialist was grave but would not commit himself. Weeks passed and the shadow grew. Books went unread, sleep was broken. My first car, bought with the intention of happy outings, could not be used. We still hoped that all would be well. With some misgivings I left on my holiday. Back home, I received disturbing news. My mother's condition was worse. Another consultation was held. A stage had been reached where surgery became inevitable. The end of Jack's mother haunted me. The irony of it! The dreams of a boy who had scribbled, ambitious to become an author in easy circumstances, if not famous, were coming true. I was in a position to give my mother a better, untroubled life. And now this. Success, money, did anything matter faced with a threat to the dearest person in my life? I had a lady friend who was a skilled surgeon, and to ensure every chance another surgeon was engaged with her to perform an operation. A few days before I took my mother into the nursing-home my artist friend, Denholm Davis, came of his own free will to draw her portrait. The result was masterly. "Your mother is a sheer delight to sketch," he said, and the delight went into his lines.

I saw my mother on the evening before the operation, expecting a trying ordeal. But there she was, very tranquil, sitting up, pink-cheeked and blue-eyed as ever. She was quite philosophical about it. "You are all doing your best, I'm sure," she said. Marvellous old Pelican!

On the morning of the operation, waiting by my office telephone, I looked out on a street filled with healthy, hurrying folk who meant little to me. One hour, two hours, I tried to concentrate on my work. Surely they would not keep me waiting if—the bell rang and I could hardly believe the news. It was not cancer. She would live.

I now made a plan to give a fairy-tale ending to our drama. I knew my mother's heart was set on that little house with the laburnum tree to which we had retreated on my father's death thirteen years ago. I went to the house and explained to a stranger what I wanted and was prepared to pay for. I must have told my story well for I achieved my purpose. Weeks went by, weeks of visits and growing strength. Was I being properly looked after, getting enough rest, etc. What was I doing? I told her, but on one thing I was silent.

These were secret busy days. I visited shops, measured and planned. The little house was in a commotion with plumber, plasterers, painters, paperhangers and furnishers. Two more articles, sold in America, financed the work. The windows were soon gay with curtains, the floors soft with carpets, the doors white with paint. I advertised for a housekeeper. Those were the days when they were not as rare and costly as orchids. From a dozen interviews I selected a cheerful youngish Irish woman. Then I went to the doctors and got their permission to take my mother home. My car hummed along and I could not help thinking it was singing with my own heart.

"Would you like to have a look at the old house, it's on our way?" I asked. "Oh, yes!" she replied. So we turned into the Grove and, arriving, very slowly we walked down the narrow path. "I wonder who lives in it now? How nicely it's kept!" said my mother. "Let's see," I replied. The housekeeper, primed for our coming, opened the door. "Does Lady Pelican Pouch live here?" I asked. "Yes, Mr. Roberts. Please come in," she answered, all smiles. We went in.

V

It was strange to be back in the little house where once our lodger, Mr. Hartley, occupying the front room, had given me Latin lessons, and whose rent, erratically paid by him, helped my mother and me, striving to live on an office boy's eighteen shillings a week. In my attic room, in sheer desperation I had written in my diary, on May 18th, 1908, my sixteenth birthday, the vow that by May, 1927, the half-way of my life, I would have saved £10,000. It was now 1921. I had £4,000 in hand. Six years to go for another £6,000! I still had faith in my resolution.

Mr. Hartley's room was now my study. There, in the small hours of the morning, returned from the *Journal*, I laboured to complete *Scissors*. It was natural that something of my Latin tutor's home, the vicarage of his brother at Rempstone, where I had spent such happy hours working in the garden and browsing in the study of the vicar on holiday, should have gone into it, the name changed to Renstone.

Towards the middle of 1922 I finished my novel, had it typed and sent to a literary agent. I waited hopefully, like a fisherman, for a publisher to bite.

VI

My chief, Sir Charles Starmer, was a dynamic character. He was intensely ambitious and year after year he increased his newspaper holdings. Hitherto he had satisfied himself with provincial papers, but in 1921 he became engrossed in a new project. He added a London morning newspaper to his provincial ones. He had met and joined forces with the son of Lord Cowdray, the millionaire oil tycoon. They formed a company to purchase the *Westminster Gazette*, a long-established evening paper. Like the Liberal Party, which it had nobly supported, it was in a decline. Sir Charles and his partner converted it into a morning paper. From the beginning of this venture I had a fear that my chief might seek to recruit me for its staff. I was pessimistic about the chances of the *Westminster Gazette* as a morning newspaper. The morning market was already supplied by *The Times*, *Chronicle*, *Telegraph*, *Daily News*, *Mail*, *Mirror* and the booming *Daily Express*. It seemed to me that it would have been wiser to have revitalised the old *Westminster Gazette* as an evening paper, but I kept this opinion to myself, aware of Sir Charles's intense enthusiasm for his first London enterprise.

The old paper had always had a high literary standard, but it had grown moribund and was clogged with faddy intellectuals. A bluestocking ran its literary page. She specialised in Greek conundrums and classical anagrams. A special light green paper had to be supplied for her to write on. There were other oddities in other departments. Its editor for thirty years had been J. A. Spender, the leading Liberal journalist, very able and distinguished but now, sixty, tired, and disillusioned. I used to see him in the Reform Club when I lunched there with Sir Philip Gibbs. There was a little coterie, consisting of H. G. Wells, Arnold Bennett, and a few ex-Liberal Cabinet ministers, that used to settle in a corner of the coffee-room after lunch. They discussed everything but chiefly the wickedness of Lloyd George who had split the Liberal Party, of which he was once the prize boy, and who had sent into the wilderness its revered leader, H. H. Asquith. In this after-lunch gathering Spender was the Solon, Wells the Herodotus and Bennett the Themistocles, all of whom regarded the renegade Lloyd George as Alcibiades. Bennett apart, they had the sad air of "Has Beens".

Spender, always informed, persuasive and benign, had been carried over, from mingled deference and prestige, as a consultant-contributor of the new *Westminster Gazette*. A lively acting editor was brought in from Starmer's Birmingham paper. Spender felt alien to these energetic newcomers.

The new paper began publication in October, 1921, with a flourish of trumpets. It was a creditable and serious paper. It ran a serial, *Mr. Prohack*, by Arnold Bennett, and later, two by me. It was thought this might help to build up its circulation. Other newspapers were running serials as binders to hold their readers.

One day Sir Charles, attending a business conference in Nottingham, came up into my room, as was his habit on such occasions. He walked about and chatted genially. Presently he said, "My boy, I may send you to the Washington Conference for the *Westminster*—you'd like that ?"

His statement took me by surprise and I hardly knew what to answer, but without waiting for my reaction he said, "I'll let you know about it later," whereupon he left.

The more I thought of his proposal the less I liked it for several reasons. I had only been back from America eighteen months. I had it in my mind to make another lecture tour in the autumn of 1924 if he agreed. I was labouring on *Scissors* which I was determined to finish, I knew very little about the proposed Washington Conference. I would have to do considerable research to prepare myself for the task. There was one other factor, the strongest in my dislike of the idea. I was resolved not to revert to being a special correspondent, losing my editorial chair, and being sent all over the world for the *Westminster Gazette.*

I waited anxiously for a further communication from Sir Charles, considering whether I was yet in a position to make a stand against his proposal. But no word came and I began to think it was one of Sir Charles's sudden ideas. of which he was prodigal. Later I learned what had occurred behind the scenes concerning the Washington Conference coverage for the *Westminster Gazette.* The first idea, initiated by Spender, was to commission Arnold Bennett, who did not want to go. Wells and Spender pressed him. Cautious when asked about his terms, Bennett said he would accept whatever Wells was getting from his paper. He made enquiries and learned that Wells was to receive a fee of £3,500. For this sum he was to write articles totalling 30,000 words. In view of the work involved, the loss of time for writing a novel and doing remunerative journalism, Bennett did not find the proposal attractive and finally turned it down. It seemed that Sir Charles had then thought of sending me. I should have cost nothing! But Spender demurred. They should send a "big gun" to Washington. In the end Spender went.

I heaved a sigh of relief but I was not wholly reassured. When suggesting the Washington trip Sir Charles had said to me, "You know, my boy, you're being wasted here!" It sounded an ominous note. I was determined not to be moved to the *Westminster Gazette.* I had no faith in its future.

The Washington Conference was the brain child of the United States Government. On August 11th, 1921, America invited the four principal powers, Great Britain, France, Italy and Japan, to attend a conference on the limitation of armaments, in connection with which Pacific and Far Eastern questions would also be discussed. The leading figures at this conference were the American Secretary of State, Charles E. Hughes, a lawyer of tremendous prestige and great personal charm, and A. J. Balfour, representing the British Empire. These two statesmen acted in whole-hearted co-operation. The Conference began its session on November 12th, 1921, with a speech by Hughes that had an overwhelming effect. "The core of the difficulty," he said, "is to be found in the competition of naval programmes and in order appropriately to limit naval armament, competition in its production must be abandoned . . . There is only one adequate way out and that is to end it now." This bold initiative set the tone of the conference and fired the imagination of the world.

The Five Power Treaty was signed on February 6th, 1922. Like so many noble resolutions it was slowly abrogated and was dead before the outbreak of war in 1939. One thing the treaty did not attempt to deal with, deeming it of small importance, it reported that with regard to aircraft: "It was not at present practicable to impose any effective limitations upon the numbers or characteristics of aircraft, either commercial or military." The conference could not foresee that within twenty-five years aircraft and the nuclear bomb were to make naval power of secondary importance.

The Steinway Grand Piano.

Count Armand de la Rochefoucauld and the author at Quebec.

My Mother, aged 70.
By Denholm Davis.

CHAPTER SIX

Breakdown

I

EDITING A LIBERAL newspaper I was naturally interested in politics. From boyhood I had been an ardent Liberal. When Lloyd George split the party I remained with the body loyal to Asquith. In the spring of 1921 I went to a meeting of what was known as the Grasmere Group. A number of ardent Liberals had banded themselves together under the chairmanship of Professor Ramsey Muir. Their purpose was to promote a progressive policy. It consisted of distinguished young Liberals, among them Maynard Keynes, famous for his book, *The Economic Consequences of the Peace*, a shattering exposure of the folly of reparations as enunciated in the Treaty of Versailles, Walter Layton (later Lord Layton) a leading economist, William Beveridge (later Lord Beveridge) the future architect of the plan for the Welfare State, D. Simon (Lord Simon), later a Lord Mayor of Manchester, and Philip Guedalla, the essayist and historian. We gathered that spring in a house at Ambleside in the Lake District. Every day we discussed the future Liberal charter. Our chairman, Ramsey Muir, was the founder of the Liberal Summer School. He was a man of about fifty, who had recently forsaken a professorship to enter politics. He had had a brilliant career at Balliol College. A Gladstonian, somewhat depressingly earnest, he had changed courses too late. The mantle of the professor still clung to him. He was elected to the House of Commons in 1923 but was in it for less than a year. He had not the requisite mental agility to succeed in politics. He was a dull, good man but voters prefer a bright, slick one. He produced, in two volumes, *A Short History of the British Commonwealth*, which subsequent events rendered obsolete.

The brilliant member of the group was Philip Guedalla. He was a dazzling speaker. His career had begun at Rugby with notable contributions to the school magazine. At Balliol College he took two Firsts and became President of the Oxford Union. His *bons-mots* were famous. Before he left Oxford he published two books of verse. In 1932, aged forty-three, he made his mark as a historian with *The Queen and Mr. Gladstone.* He had already established himself as a brilliant scholarly essayist and as the wittiest speaker of the day, but he failed to get into the House of Commons. He looked "foreign", being born in a Spanish-Jewish family, but what really frightened the electors were his coruscating speeches. He was too obviously "brainy" and smart. His brilliance also defeated him in his attempt to become a successful barrister. Norman Birkett put his finger on the cause of his failure. "I used to see him at luncheon at the Inner Temple Hall and for ten years he persisted at the Bar but without any success worth talking about. Then, like so many others, he had to make the great decision whether to continue or to seek some other way of making a living and he left the Bar. It is one of the fascinating questions why men succeed or fail at the Bar. Guedalla, with every gift, was brilliant in speech, highly intelligent, industrious, and yet he failed. My own view is that he was *too* clever and gave the impression of being a little superior to the ordinary run of men."

He was thirty-two, three years my senior, when I met him at Ambleside, already famous enough to have been caricatured by Max Beerbohm, whose victims constituted a kind of Who's Who of the era. He was easily the best speaker present. A student of public speech, I was captivated by his technique. He was forceful, witty and well-informed. In subsequent years it was sometimes my fate to find myself speaking at the same functions. He was always formidable, in complete command of his audience. Because of my admiration I treasured a compliment he paid me on one occasion. I liked to recall it against visitations of doubt and despondency. He came up to me after he had been overwhelmingly excellent and congratulated me on my own contribution, saying: "I never know whether I prefer to precede you or to follow you—you're such a high jumper." It was generous coming from a master. In a few years he was well-established as a biographer. Some critics accused him of being a disciple of Lytton Strachey, who then led the field, but "he was more conscientious and scholarly" as the *Dictionary of National Biography* observed. *Wellington,* his last biographical work, sets the standard of his quality. His death in 1944, aged fifty-five, took from the public scene a brilliant figure. Guedalla was a war victim as much as if he had fallen on the field. He became at fifty-three a Squadron-Leader in the Royal Air Force in order to write, at official request, a survey of the war in the Middle East. During one of his many journeys he contracted the disease from which he died.

II

I had been a year in my editorial chair when there was a surprising development, something I had not sought. I was selected as the prospective Free Liberal parliamentary candidate for the East Nottingham constituency. The term "free" denoted those who had remained faithful to the former Prime Minister, H. H. Asquith, whom Lloyd George had dethroned during the war.

It was impossible not to admire Lloyd George, even while one distrusted him. His courage, resource, and indomitable spirit had pulled England out of threatened defeat and carried her to victory. A demagogue of unrivalled skill, he was a wizard with the crowd. He had great wit and a genius for a phrase, which sometimes embodied scurrility. The charm of his personality was so great that his critics feared to become his guests. Like my war-correspondent colleague, Philip Gibbs, who detested "the murderous old man in Downing Street", they went there to breakfast at his invitation and came away chloroformed by charm. After the war, ungratefully discarded by the Tories he had carried, he founded a break-away Liberal Party and filled his campaign chest by the sale of honours. He went down to defeat and left the old Liberal Party in ruins. A remnant, among them Churchill, tried to keep the old banner flying. The opportunists went over to the rising Labour Party where second-rate politicians got first-rate prizes.*

* Such as Sir William Jowitt, K.C., who became the Labour Government's Lord Chancellor in 1929. His defection from the Liberals aroused bitter criticism. "He did it in the wrong way," said Churchill. "If he had come to me I could have explained to him the technique of tergiversation."

Sir Jesse Boot, a staunch Liberal of the old school, remained an Asquithian. For some years he had financed the *Nottingham Journal*. Now old, and retiring from the local scene, the paper passed under the Starmer control. I had by this time some reputation as a speaker but I had never contemplated a political career. I was an author and wished to remain an author, but ambition and vanity often deflect a man from his chosen course. With the Starmer backing I seemed a likely lad for unseating the Conservative member for East Nottingham, Sir John Rees, a retired Indian Civil Servant. He had held the seat for some years with a comfortable majority, but he was stuffy and cocksure. Possibly the local Liberals thought I was snappy and cocksure. I was unanimously adopted as Liberal candidate. Thus I added one burden to another. Evasively, I failed to consider what I should do if I was elected. M.P.s had minute salaries. I had no trade union to finance me, I had no private fortune behind me. It would be difficult to retain my editorship in Nottingham and sit in the House of Commons. When I mentioned the problem to Sir Charles he slapped me on the back and said cheerily, "My boy, we'll deal with that when you're in!" Neither he nor I had any doubt that I should get in.

There was no prospect of a General Election for some time. I addressed a couple of meetings a week, opened bazaars, attended garden fêtes, following all the vote-catching techniques. There were signs that the sitting member, at first indifferent, became nervous. An absentee member, he began to visit the constituency more frequently. Brash, I soon ran into trouble. There was a new Licensing Bill, proposing to restrict the opening hours of public houses. Questioned on this, I said I was not in favour of it. I did not see why a man should not be able to get a drink when he wanted one. Thereupon a Liberal-Nonconformist city councillor sitting on my platform walked off it, outraged. He was a worthy man but a teetotaller, a shining light in a body of temperance reformers who bore the banners of The Ancient Order of Rechabites and the Band of Hope. "You've lost some of the chapel vote," said my party agent. But my lively editorial assistant reported "It's brought you a wallop of votes." I fear that I did quite a lot of treading on the toes of cranks but my meetings were crowded and enthusiastic.

III

Meanwhile I waited anxiously to learn the fate of my novel *Scissors*. The weeks passed. It was steadily rejected. Ten publishers read it. Some of them thought it "very promising". It is the experience of most beginners. Well, one day I would laugh at all those hesitant publishers. "Never Take No For An Answer". Then fate gave me a ball to play, for this is a story of cricket, almost a religion in the British order of things.

We had a local Maecenas, the son of a very prosperous Jewish furniture dealer whose fortune was built on hire-purchase sales. He created a chain of stores, and became a millionaire. He had a son Julien, who, socially ambitious, had a passion for cricket. Julien bought a stately Hall and added a small theatre, but the apple of his eye was his cricket field. He formed a private eleven, entertained liberally, was well-liked and soon achieved knighthood. The son of the furniture dealer steadily mounted the social ladder. Sir Julien Cahn's Eleven carried his name afield.

I was sometimes his guest, and thus I met the world-famous South African cricketer, G. A. Faulkner. He was a prodigious bowler whom Sir Julien had acquired on a South African cricket tour.* Sir Julien persuaded Faulkner and his charming young wife to settle in England. He put him on the firm's payroll with a nominal position and furnished a nice house for him in a suburb of Nottingham, within view of the Trent Bridge cricket ground.

All went well for a time and then Faulkner, the star of Sir Julien's eleven, a big, powerfully built fellow, got restless. He felt he was too much in Sir Julien's pocket. He became irritable. To friction with his employer was added domestic trouble. One day, without warning, his dainty little wife packed her bags and fled back to sunny South Africa. He rang me up and implored me to come to dinner. There I was told of his wife's desertion.

* Faulkner in *Wisden* is credited seven times with records. In 1910–11, for South Africa against England at Johannesburg, 125 runs and 5 wickets for 120. In the same year at Melbourne, 204 runs, at Adelaide, 115 runs. In 1912, South Africa against England at Manchester, 122 runs. In one season he achieved the cricketers' "double" of scoring over a 1,000 runs and taking over 100 wickets.

Later, I learned there had been trouble over another lady. I learned something else, more surprising. He was taking lessons from a correspondence college of authorship. Tired of cricket, he thought he would take up authorship. He had bought a large dictionary and paid £12 down for a course in writing. Writing what, I asked. He did not know. He showed me a few articles. They were childish. He had not the slightest idea of composition. There was something tragic in this great fellow, world-famous in handling a cricket ball, hoping to be a successful author. I picked up a book of stories by de Maupassant. "The course editor tells me to study him— he's one of the world's great writers. I've read him. I think it's punk!" said Faulkner. "Now Sax Rohmer's another dish—have you read him?" "I couldn't!" I replied. Very gently I tried to disillusion him. I told him that with all my literary experience my novel had been turned down ten times. "Good God—you! Don't you know any publishers?" "No." "Look, I've played cricket with a fellow who's in a publishing firm. I'll give you a line. Try him."

Thus it was I came to call on Sydney Pawling, a director of Heinemann Ltd. I felt a slight connection with the firm. They had published the first novel of one Nottingham lad a few years back, *The White Peacock*, by D. H. Lawrence. Now another presented himself. It was Pawling who had spotted Lawrence. He received me very affably in a back sitting-room in their office in Bedford Street. He listened patiently to my "sales" talk. I told him what I had already done. Finally I asked: "Do you think I sound like a young man who could write a novel?" He blinked at that question and said: "Well, I should think it's quite likely that you can. Send it for us to read." "Oh, no!" I replied, "that won't do! I want you to say now that you will publish it." He laughed at my proposition. "My dear young man, we've never done anything like that!" "You've never met a Cecil Roberts before," I retorted, full of the egotism of youth. "Show a little courage for once and take a chance!"

By this time there was an element of comedy in our conversation. "Have a glass of sherry," he said, taking a bottle out of a cabinet. He began to talk about Aubrey Faulkner. "A nice fellow. Give him my regards." Then, our interview ending, as I rose to leave he put a hand on my shoulder. "I should hate to disappoint you and I've a feeling we shall publish your novel—but do let us see what we're taking!" As I went down the staircase I had a feeling that I had found a publisher. I walked over to my literary agent, "I think I've placed *Scissors*." I told him of the interview. "Send him the manuscript."

Six weeks passed. I was so pressed with engagements that I had not noticed the absence of news from the publisher. Then one day in a pile of letters on my desk I found one from Heinemann, with the familiar windmill trade-sign on the back flap. I hesitated a few moments before opening the momentous envelope. They were pleased to inform me that they would like to publish *Scissors*. They were in touch with my agent and an agreement would be submitted.

That evening I went to call on Faulkner to give him the news and to thank him. I found him very agitated. He was leaving for London the next day. He had had a scene with Cahn. He was through with him. "I want you to have all my books. The maid will bring them round tomorrow." I asked where he was going and when he was moving the furniture. "To London," he replied. "The furniture's not mine, it's all Cahn's. He'll have it back."

Two days later the maid left a large parcel at my house. I opened it. It contained not only books but, to my amazement, a dozen cricket balls, all with silver mounts commemorating famous feats of bowling. There was a note with the package. "Please keep these souvenirs until I find somewhere to lay my head. I'll let you know later."

I never heard from him again and I assumed he had returned to South Africa. A few years passed and then one day his name appeared in the newspapers. It transpired that a School of Cricket run by Faulkner in London had failed. I was distressed to read that the poor fellow had committed suicide. For some time the cricket balls rolled about in a drawer. Finally, their shields tarnished, I gave them to keen cricketing friends.

It was destined that my novel *Scissors* should be linked with two suicides. Of which more in the course of my story.

IV

Before we had moved to our new home I was compelled to make a painful decision. I was now under such heavy pressure of work that it became impossible for me to find time for practising on my grand piano. One cannot achieve any proficiency at the keyboard with less than two hours' daily practice. When, forty-seven years later I met Artur Rubinstein in Rome, vigorously concertising across Europe at eighty years of age, I asked how much practice he did. He replied: "One hour every day with my right hand, eating chocolates with my left. One hour with my left hand, eating chocolates with my right. Then one hour with both hands and no chocolates". "Do you get any practice when you're touring?" I asked. "Yes. One hour fingering on my left thigh, and then one hour on my right. People who sit near me in the plane think I'm a lunatic. Who knows?"

Fortunately my Steinway found a good home, where it was available to me. My friend Jack bought it. He could not play. He attached a pianola to the instrument, so it got plenty of exercise.

V

The spring of 1922 found me heavily engaged. There is no respite in the editing of a newspaper. Like the captain of a ship at sea one cannot relax. I nursed my constituency ceaselessly. By now I had little doubt that I could win the seat at the next General Election. On the top of all this there had been the strain of finishing my novel, and of the illnesses of my brother and my mother. Through overwork my sleep began to be affected. One day at my office I had a disconcerting experience; while dictating, my mind suddenly became blank. It was as if the current had been switched off. Never before had I had such an experience. I was always fluent in speech and composition and quick in the despatch of business. I dismissed my typist, got up and paced my room. Obviously my brain was tired and I was not getting enough sleep. I was young, on the verge of thirty. Even so, I had had a warning. I must slow up. Within ten minutes I had recovered. I called in my typist and resumed dictation as easily as was customary. That evening I spoke at a public dinner. Everyone thought I was in good form.

One of the letters I had dealt with that afternoon came from a man very much in the public eye because of a book he had written called *The Great Illusion*. His name was Norman Angell.

Flying Horse Hotel. April 29, 1922.
Dear Mr. Roberts,

I am staying in Nottingham until Wednesday evening and I should like to take the opportunity of making your acquaintance and having a few moments chat. Are you likely to have ten minutes free during the day time of Monday, Tuesday or Wednesday—my evenings are taken up. I have nothing specific to see you about so if it is not convenient just now, put me off.

Yours very sincerely,
Norman Angell.

P.S. I feel like offering you an article on "Nottingham, U.S.A. v Nottingham, England." The U.S.A. Nottingham of, I suppose, thirty thousand population, is, in the material and mechanical conveniences, as much beyond this city, as this city is beyond Timbuctoo. Why? We English started the steam business. Why have we fallen behind? The Nottingham hotels (for e.g.) are . . . . ! I am just back from America.

I answered at once that I should be very happy to see him. I had heard that he had been selected as Labour candidate for the Rushcliffe Division of Nottinghamshire. It explained his presence in the city. Aged fifty, he already had a distinguished career behind him. Educated at a French lycée and Geneva University, at nineteen this small frail youth ran off to America and became a cowboy, engaged in driving cattle in and out of Texas across the Mexican border. He stayed in America for seven years, taking to journalism, working on the *San Francisco Chronicle* and the St. Louis *Globe*. In 1898 he returned to Europe, and in Paris acted as correspondent for several American papers. The next year he was appointed editor of the renowned *Galignani's Express*, a Paris English daily with a wide circulation. Later, having gained a controlling interest, he offered it to Northcliffe, who made a counter-offer, that Angell should become the editor of the *Continental Daily Mail* he was planning. Angell accepted the offer and edited it for several years with great success. His wide knowledge of continental affairs resulted in the birth of an idea which he embodied in a small book entitled *Europe's Optical Illusion*. It fell stillborn from the press. He induced Massingham, the influential editor of the *Nation*, to read it. He was impressed and devoted two pages to a review. A weekly called *Public Opinion* also took up the book, now reissued as *The Great Illusion*.

E
129

When a youth I had followed the controversy the book provoked. Angell began a tireless propaganda for his momentous theme. Fifty copies of his book were sent to the most eminent men in the land, with little result, but Lord Esher, impressed, sent out two hundred copies to political leaders. One of these was Sir Edward Grey, the Foreign Secretary. He made a speech at a Guildhall banquet where he spoke at great length commending Angell's original thesis. A revised edition was a best-seller and Angell became a figure of fame, clad in the mantle of a prophet. A Europe that felt a growing apprehension of the march of events turned eagerly to Angell's comforting theory. His theme was that with the complex fabric of society and all its international ramifications, war could not be made to pay as in the past. The victor would be as disastrously involved as the vanquished. It was a theme that found wide endorsement though there were some sceptics who thought it fallacious. It was not to be regarded as a pacifist doctrine but as a logical one based on financial more than on moral grounds.

The 1914–18 war demonstrated the fallacy of *The Great Illusion*, but Angell, tenacious and mentally adroit, would not admit defeat. Mankind one day would learn the economic lesson. He was able to point to a Europe prostrate after the Great War. He attended the Peace Conference in Paris, and despaired of the Treaty of Versailles, which he found savage and economically unworkable. He turned to practical ameliorative work and served with the Fight the Famine Fund. He also turned to active politics, joined with Ramsay MacDonald in founding the Union of Democratic Control, wrote and lectured extensively in the United States and, returning home sought, as a member of the Labour Party, a seat in the House of Commons. It was this political phase of his career that had brought him to Nottingham.

He came to see me in response to my invitation. When he was shown into my office I was astonished to find he was a midget. He did not come up to my shoulder. It was difficult to believe how he could ever have been a cowboy for he was delicately built, his frailty emphasised by his pale face and soft, modulated voice, There was an air of shyness in his manner, though, as I learned later, this was deceptive for he proved a tough fighter on the platform.

Our conversation was amiable and long. Before Angell departed I said that as a fellow candidate I realised his handicap in having no local newspaper sympathetic to his party. I made him an offer. Although we stood for the Liberal interest I would see that his speeches were adequately reported and I would place at his disposal a column once a week for his exclusive and unedited use. He accepted my offer.* When he left I told him I should always be very glad to see him. I could not foresee that twenty years would elapse before we met again, and then in America where both of us were conducting British propaganda during the Second War. He then seemed frailer than ever, being seventy years of age, but he was still a forceful and adept speaker. He was now a world figure, much respected and liked, carrying the halo of being a winner, in 1933, of the Nobel Peace Prize. He had no illusions about the nature of the Nazi menace.

Angell was defeated in the Rushcliffe contest but got elected in 1929 when he unseated the Conservative member at Bradford. He retired from the House and was knighted two years later. He was not really a House of Commons man. For the rest of his life he devoted himself to social causes. He was ninety when he went to America on another lecture tour, his subject, "Education in a Nuclear Age." He was ninety-four when he died in 1967.

VI

Over three years had elapsed since the end of the war. The League of Nations, with its Covenant, the hope of the world, founded on President Wilson's Fourteenth Point, had been established in 1920 in Geneva. There sprang up in England a society, The League of Nations Union, to support the aims of the Covenant. Its enthusiastic and influential membership was headed by Lord Robert Cecil,

---

* "I had the support of all parties when I fought Nottingham. A sort of manifesto urging my election was signed by, among others, Arnold Bennett, Canon Barnes, Noel Buxton, Edward Carpenter, G. Lowes Dickinson, Hamilton Fyffe, G. P. Gooch, Austin Harrison, J. A. Hobson, Dean Inge, Jerome K. Jerome, J. M. Keynes, Lord Loreburn, H. W. Massingham, Sir George Paish, Cecil Roberts, Arnold Rowntree, Bertrand Russell, Graham Wallas. Among those who came and spoke for me were Sidney Webb, G. B. Shaw, R. H. Tawney."—Norman Angell in *After All*.

who commanded more respect, with his probity, flawless character, devotion to public service, and aristocratic descent, than any other man in the Empire. All the political parties endorsed the work of the Union. To oppose it, and they had no mind to oppose it, would have been to lose the votes of the great body of citizens filled with the hope of establishing at last the brotherhood of man.

As a parliamentary candidate I, of course, put the League in my programme. My opponent dragged his feet. His scepticism had received some endorsement, for, in November, 1919, the U.S. Senate refused ratification of the Treaty of Versailles, and thereby the Covenant was rejected. President Wilson had fought a vain battle. Stunned by the repudiation of his signature on the treaty, he suffered a paralytic stroke, lingering on until his death four years later.

Despite America's refusal to join the League, the other signatories went ahead, Russia aloof. A site was chosen above the lake at Geneva, plans were drawn for a gigantic headquarters, the list of officials grew and grew. Britain's bright faith in Wilson's repudiated offspring remained. The new world seemed to be born. The future looked promising.

VII

On June 2nd, 1922, a sub-editor entered my room with a press telegram. I read it and re-read it, dazed. My Conservative opponent, Sir John Rees, had fallen from a train and been killed. The cause of his death remained a mystery. It was surmised that on going to the lavatory he had opened the wrong door. A writ was issued for a by-election. I was suddenly plunged into an electoral campaign. The Conservatives hurriedly found a candidate, a Mr. Houfton, a stranger to the city. It looked as if my success was assured. I had gained much ground from having assiduously coached the constituency. I was a local-born candidate, now well-known, with my own paper behind me. Sir John had not been in favour of the League, I was. I therefore wrote to Lord Robert Cecil, President of the League of Nations Union, asking him to come and speak on my behalf. I received the following reply, written in his own hand. He declined the invitation. His reason was incontestable.

Chelwood Gate, East Grinstead,
June 10, 1922.

Dear Mr. Roberts,

Many thanks for your letter. The question you raise is difficult. You are the Liberal candidate and you ask me to come and speak for you not as such but because you are a strong advocate of the League of Nations. If the late member were your opponent that would be defensible. He had openly declared himself hostile to the League and could not have complained if its advocates took up the challenge. But you do not say that your present or prospective opponent is likely to adopt the same line. If then I were to bring the League into the fight should I not be making it a party question—which would be very undesirable if it can be avoided? If you were unconnected with any party the case would be different.

I do not remind you of the convention by which ex-Cabinet ministers do not speak at by-elections partly because the circumstances you put forward are special and partly because though I have always acted on it, I am not sure how far others have done.

With very many kind regards,
Yours very truly,
Robert Cecil.

In feverish haste we pulled our organisation together. Ceaselessly busy addressing meetings in the constituency and editing my paper, my day went on until 2 a.m. when I left my office. One fine morning, while canvassing, my mind suddenly went blank. I did not know who I was or where I was. I learned later that a friend took me home, where I began to make a speech, delirious. A specialist was brought in by my doctor who forbade my candidature being continued. My unfortunate election committee, at this late hour, gallantly proposed to continue with an absentee candidate, but the doctors would not hear of it since it might involve a serious strain if I were elected. It was a bitter blow, the first real check in my career. I had set my heart on winning the seat. At this late hour an unknown London journalist was brought in to stand in my stead. The Conservative candidate won the by-election.

At the beginning of July I was able to go away to convalesce. A complete rest from all business was considered essential. Once more my devoted old friend William Kiddier came to my help. My mind turned inevitably to Italy. He arranged for my friend Duncan Macpherson to accompany me to Rapallo. Two famous Englishmen, Max Beerbohm and Gordon Craig, were living near Rapallo, in adjacent villas overlooking the Mediterranean. I carried a letter of introduction to Max Beerbohm from Heinemann. My friend was armed with a letter to Craig, whose theatre designs he admired ardently, being an architect. So with a congenial companion I arrived one evening and went to an hotel near the old fortress on the shore. From the balcony of our room we looked down on a garden full of exotic flowers. Before us was the mountain-side with villas and cypresses. A crescent moon hung over the ravine. That evening we posted our letters of introduction to Max and Craig.

We soon received replies. I was invited to lunch at the Villino Chiaro. My friend was invited by Gordon Craig to lunch at his villa near by. On the morrow towards noon we set off along the Provincial Road, out of Rapallo, past the sea-coast village of Zoagli, to keep our separate appointments. In about half an hour, arriving at the Villino Chiaro I rang a bell and ascended some steps. A maid met me and escorted me up more steps on to a wide marble terrace built over the house where Max greeted me. My host was dressed in a flawless double-breasted shantung suit, a gardenia in his buttonhole, a straw hat rakishly set on his head. He was very elegant in appearance, a spruce, middle-aged little man with pink cheeks and round china-blue eyes. He showed me his study, a minute blue-washed room isolated on the long wide terrace. Its open door looked on a great expanse of sea and sky. Before us there was a magnificent panorama of the bay as far as the castle and church-crowned peninsula of Portofino. The little study seemed like the charthouse of a ship, full of books instead of maps.

When the gong sounded for lunch Mrs. Beerbohm, frail and composed, joined us. Just before we left the terrace I leaned to stroke a cat and was rewarded by a vicious scratch. Blood flowed freely. Mrs. Beerbohm, very concerned and apologetic, bound my hand with her handkerchief. They both denounced the wretched animal. "Scratchy is very unfriendly," said Max, shooing it away. The name seemed appropriate. I wondered why they kept a cat with such a propensity. But it transpired that I had misheard its name. Years later I learned from a letter written by Max to Lytton Strachey that, to mark his admiration for the author of *Eminent Victorians*, the cat had been called "Strachey", not "Scratchy"!

The hour at the table was a feast of wit. In vain did Mrs. Beerbohm reprove Max for being maliciously flippant. He neatly assassinated some contemporary reputations. For some reason unknown to me he detested Kipling. During lunch he repeatedly pressed on me the wine decanter. Rejecting it, I had one of those inspirations when we say the thing that usually comes too late. The decanter recalled Max's essay on Swinburne with its story of the single bottle of pale ale allowed the poet by his keeper-friend, Watts-Dunton, at The Pines, Putney. I declined the decanter quoting Max's superb comment on the once-Bacchic Swinburne. I had had, I said, "the ultimate allowance of one who had erst clashed cymbals in Naxos". "Bless you! I shall love you forever for that!" cried Max, raising his glass.

I did not tell him, apropos of his famous essay "The Pines, Putney", in which he described Swinburne's last days, what Alfred Noyes had told me of his visit to Swinburne. He said that Max's description was clever and amusing but a complete caricature of the poet and his home. In actuality Swinburne had great dignity and composure, and despite his deafness was alert and talked brilliantly. "The Pines" was not a musty Victorian nest, as Max made out.

Regaining the terrace, Max discoursed enchantingly, poking fun at his contemporaries. "But they work and I don't—so I'm less of a target, I suppose." As we sat talking under a sun-umbrella on that blazing July day I recalled to mind how precisely one hundred years ago, on July 8th, 1822, Shelley had been drowned only a few miles down the coast. Max's innocent blue eyes gazed at me a little reproachfully as I mentioned this and then he said, "How clever but morbid of you to recall that!" We were silent for a few moments gazing upon the smiling expanse of sea and sky so different from that day when Shelley, in fulfilment of a prophecy in his memorial poem to Keats, was "borne darkly, fearfully afar".

As we talked the sun began to slant upon the mountain side. I bade Max goodbye. We had begun a friendship that was to last forty years. I little knew that one day I should be instrumental in organising the placing of a memorial plaque on the wall of the villa where he had lived so long.

I crossed the road to the Villa Reggio, to collect my friend who was visiting Gordon Craig. Like a sheik, robed in a loose white burnous, Craig greeted me. Isadora Duncan's ex-lover was tall and strikingly handsome, with a leonine head, and a grand panache worthy of Ellen Terry, his mother. He was "theatre" in every sense.

Max was a very playful neighbour of Gordon Craig. Soon after our visit he published a collection of his theatre notices covering the years 1898–1910, when he had succeeded Bernard Shaw as dramatic critic of the *Saturday Review*. In his first article Max had provocatively declared "I am not fond of the theatre. In drama I take, unfortunately, neither emotional nor intellectual pleasure,"—which all his reviews contradicted. Collecting these for publication, Max wished to dedicate the volume to his neighbour Edward Gordon Craig. So he sent the following letter across the road.*

My dear Ted,
    Will you accept the dedication of a book of mine? Don't bother to write. Just give a verbal answer, yes or no, to the bearer of this. As your house is within a stone's throw of mine, you may wonder "Why does he write? Why doesn't he come round and ask me by word of mouth?" My answer is that it is difficult for so good-natured a fellow as you to refuse anything to a friend pleading *in propria persona*. My faltering voice, my appealing gaze, would move you to say yes, and have done with it.
                                                                                    Max.

VIII

Now, for the first time in my life, in the heat of these days of July, 1922, I had the opportunity of practising *dolce far niente*. We slept, ate, bathed, talked and dined al fresco in the hotel garden. I was recovering from the shock of the past weeks, the deep disappointment born of a serious check to my ambitious plans. All the time in this lovely seaside town, with the adjacent delights of Santa Margherita and Portofino, I was storing up impressions to be used later when I came to write my third novel, *The Love Rack*. In the second week we

* *Around the Theatre*, by Max Beerbohm. (Hart-Davis.)

moved to Levanto, one of those secluded crevices on the rocky Italian Riviera where there is no through road and the precipitous mountains shut out the world. Levanto was a favourite retreat of well-to-do Italians who, about June, arrived here with children looking like a garland of Correggio's cherubs.

On a rock jutting out to sea stood an old fortress, with a battlemented tower. A local Englishman named Smith, stranded in Levanto for twenty years, told me it was for sale. I visited it, a deserted stronghold with walls ten feet thick. It was a relic of the time when raiding Saracens were the terror of the coast. Now the old castle, with a history of assaults and murders, reared its rugged keep above the little town. It was for sale for two hundred pounds. A medieval castle, picturesquely situated on its own high rock overlooking a Mediterranean bay, with battlements, dungeon, powder rooms and cannon embrasures, for two hundred pounds! Mr. Smith's information set me dreaming. To live in a castle in sunshine, to write there, to . . . No. I must not become another impecunious, stranded Englishman, suspiciously marking the level on the *pension* wine bottle. The castle was bought later by Mussolini—alias "Mr. Smith" by name to the cautious resident English, since it was dangerous for foreigners to be heard talking of him.

At this stage Italy was in a state of turmoil which ended in the March on Rome and Mussolini's seizure of power. The Government had fallen, the old parties were utterly discredited, either by corruption or inefficiency. The wild experiments of Socialism had ended in frightful deficits in national and municipal resources. Mussolini's black-shirted Fascists came into bloody conflict with the labour unions. It was every blackguard's opportunity. The rise of the Socialist blacksmith was characteristic of a land of *condottieri*. Mussolini met violence with violence. Resolute, with a spineless dwarf-king on a shaky throne, he seemed a lifebuoy in a raging sea, offering salvation.

In remote Levanto this turmoil scarcely touched us. Each day passed in a dream under the blue sky. The sea was warm. We bathed or dozed. I contemplated the physical beauty of the young Italians; the vivid golden girls, slender and black-eyed, the youths like tawny gods such as had camped by Agamemnon's ships near the plain of Troy in that epic morning of the classical world. I was invited out to dine on terraces of beautiful villas, while the vermilion sunset faded leaving a lemon-green sky. One evening I found myself in cosmopolitan company; Cortot, the pianist, La Argentina, the dancer, Princess Colonna, the fabulously rich but simple American, Mrs. Duke, an admiral of the Italian Navy, the president of the Fiat company, Tetrazzini, the opera star, and my host's daughters, famous for their beauty in Turin society. As we took coffee on the terrace, from a peasant's garden below came the strumming of a guitar. The bay was now a crescent of glistening lights, brightest where the small Casino stood reflected in the dark sea.

IX

At the end of my visit to Levanto my friend had to return to England. My health had greatly improved. There were rumours of great events in the air. I decided to go on to Florence, a few hours away, attracted not only by its renown but also because it seemed a storm centre. Levanto was full of stories of things happening down the line. The day I left a railway strike was declared. It failed owing to action by the Fascists. My train arrived twelve hours late. It was manned by an admiral as the engine-driver, a naval lieutenant as a stoker, together with an armed guard of Fascists. At Pisa there was a tremendous ovation for two hundred of the black-shirted brotherhood who had just come in from Leghorn, where there had been desperate street fighting. At Empoli there was an outburst of shooting and we had to lie on the floor of our compartment to avoid bullets whistling overhead. At the end of the week the Fascists were everywhere triumphant. *A Roma!* was now heard on the lips of excited young men, but Mussolini bided his hour.

I stayed four days in Florence and paused overnight in Bologna, en route to Venice. My advent coincided with a tremendous tumult. I witnessed the ugliness of the political passions that swayed mobs of hysterical young men. There had been murder in the narrow streets and under the arched galleries. Youths in black shirts hunted Communists in white or red shirts. In the late afternoon I saw an unpleasant assault upon a woman. She was dressed in white and some young Fascists, their anger stifling any sense of chivalry, pelted her with bags of soot. She was chased by the hooting crowd until she

138

took refuge in a tobacconist's shop. The headquarters of the Socialists was wrecked. If a man openly declared his opposition to the Fascist *credo* he was seized and dosed with a pint of castor oil. He emerged later a weak figure of ridicule. Some died of the treatment. That evening a chanting flood of blackshirts marched to the Piazza, and there I learned the reason of this triumphant hysteria. Mussolini appeared on a balcony. Squat, bullet-headed, with blazing black eyes, he ranted before the delirious, cheering multitude. Thirty years later in that same Piazza at Bologna I saw another mob frenziedly acclaim the new Sindaco, elected by the Communists who had swept the municipal polls.

In Venice I was met by my friend Jack who had arrived overnight. From that first moment when I emerged from the railway station and stepped into a gondola that bore me down the palace-bordered Grand Canal, by pavements thronged with cafés humming with life, with everywhere a drift of music, I knew that my heart had been captured as no other place, not even Rome, was ever to capture it.

The Venice of 1922 had not yet become a maelstrom of tourists. There was no causeway across the isolating Lagoon to bring in the international motor-coaches. The automobile had not evoked a huge garage in Venice. The motor-launch with its phut-phut of petrol engines had not shattered the centuries-old silence. The Piazza, called by Napoleon Europe's drawing-room, was still an oasis where Guardi might have painted, Casanova have made an assignation, or Goldoni have read his new play to a few friends gathered at Florian's. Day after day I moved in a dream, enchanted by the changing colours of the lagoons, the magnificence of palaces, the little marble bridges over countless canals leading from vista to vista of crumbling mottled palaces and leaning belfries.

We stayed at an hotel on the Riva, fronting the great lagoon that ran south to the fishing port of Chioggia. My friend had taken a room whose splendour made me apprehensive of its cost. It was an immense room, the high ceiling coffered with timbers lined with gold, the walls hung with tapestries, the floor a lake of shining marble, the whole lit by a gigantic chandelier of Venetian glass. Two Gothic windows looked on a lagoon thronged with vessels. Our beds might have come out of a picture by Carpaccio. We were housed like princes in a fabled city. "What does all this cost ?" I asked. My friend laughed. "Dear boy, you can sleep unperturbed. It's less than what we paid for our room in Cadenabbia last year. A fellow pupil at Pastor Muller's is now assistant manager here, and look what he's done for us!"

The wonder of it all was enhanced when I learned that in the room on the corner George Sand and Alfred de Musset had spent their 'honeymoon'.

We had a week of ecstasy. One day, sailing down the lagoon to Chioggia, the small fishing port on the southern end of the Lido, I saw a Venice that has now almost vanished. I was just in time to see the vegetable and fruit boats that set forth at sundown, a mass of coloured sails reflected in the glassy lagoon. They sailed in silence through the night, to reach at dawn the market on the Rialto. Graceful, windborne, sail-borne, there was no ghastly phut-phut of a petrol engine to break the hushed beauty of the starlit night. To my companion's astonishment I arranged to go back to Venice as a member of a crew, sitting among a pile of yellow melons and purple aubergines during that soundless passage down the lagoon. A lemon moon rose out of the Adriatic, a crimson sunset faded over the Euganean Hills.

How smooth the water rippling at our painted prow, how vast the sails, rainbow-hued above us, how warm the silent evening aglow about us! Looking upon those sails, tempted as the artist in words is ever tempted to name an experience, I said, quietly, "Sails of Sunset!" And at that moment, though I did not realise it then, I had found the title and theme of my next novel.

When I left, at early dawn, the fruit and fish market on the Rialto, where Shylock had transacted business, and the brash Antonio had insulted him—"Many a time and oft in the Rialto you have rated me about my moneys and my usances"—I carried with me a present of peaches and grapes from Mario and Sandro, the youths who had kept a hand on the tiller while their father dozed in a bower of fruit baskets. I quietly entered our hotel bedroom. The risen sun was blazing but the shuttered room was dark. My friend woke. He had returned last evening by steamer, leaving his crazy friend to sail overnight down the lagoon. We opened the shutters, and ate the

peaches. "Jack, I've got my second novel!" I exclaimed. He looked
at me, wondering. "I found it out there, over the lagoons, sailing
from Chioggia—Sails of Sunset—Sails of Sunset," I repeated,
walking over the marble floor, under a Murano glass chandelier.
He looked at me, calm as ever, quite certain I was a little fey. Who
else would want to journey all night in a dirty vegetable barge?

One week was too short a time to even skim the riches of Venice. I
vowed I would return, I could not foresee that I was to visit and
explore this incomparable city for the next forty years of my life and
still not exhaust its riches or suffer any disenchantment.

CHAPTER SEVEN

Scissors, *Naples, Corfu*

RESTORED TO HEALTH, I returned to my editorial chair at Nottingham but I was not the same person. My breakdown had left a shadowy threat over me. It had never occurred to me that I was not inexhaustible. I was thirty, an age when the body and mind renew themselves after a night's sleep, when all things desired seem attainable. I had arrived at a day of assessment. I had to plan my future anew. Was I still to attempt the ambitious flight into politics, with high office as its allure? The candidature for East Nottingham was still open to me.

In two months of convalescence I had had time to consider my circumstances. Factors I had ignored in my entry into the political arena presented themselves. It had seemed to me that either from vanity or ambition, perhaps both, I had changed courses. Since the age of fifteen my one ambition had been to become an author. I had pressed on to that goal by way of being a journalist, war correspondent and editor. Suddenly I had been lured into politics. My facility on the platform had brought this about. Was it really what I wanted, and if so, had I the qualifications? I now doubted whether I had the stamina. To this was added a doubt whether I had the mental flexibility. The endless pressure to placate, to compromise, to suppress, to exaggerate, had become growingly distasteful to me. I began to see that the Liberal Party had no future. The terms of the contest had changed. The Labour Party had arisen, controlled and financed by the trade unions. It was aggressive, with no intention of compromise, marching to a head-on collision with the Conservatives. It by-passed the Liberal Party, contemptuous of its waning power. Lloyd George, with the adroit manipulation of his political war chest, and his "coupon" candidates, had split the Liberals in twain, one half being cynically opportunist, the "L.G. rabble" as we called it, the other, the old Asquithian half, conscientious, but impotent to capture the support of the electorate.

In the first year of my candidature when I attended the Liberal Conference at Ambleside, I had returned dismayed. The party seemed to me to be on the way to extinction. Moderate policies had no appeal where the adversaries were resolutely Blue or Red. Gladstone had become a joke and Asquith an obsolescent figure. Labour marched behind the handsome Ramsay MacDonald, an oddly aristocratic-looking leader who had not yet lapsed into a somewhat gaga figure lost in a fog of words.

To my own uneasiness over the state of my party, and my lack of physical toughness as revealed by my breakdown, were added other misgivings. I began to discern the fallacy of the principle of democracy. It had never worked with the ancient Greeks, who invented it; they destroyed themselves with political factions. The majority vote as a means to power too often resulted in the bribery of the electorate, by promises unfulfilled or, if fulfilled, economically unsound. It seemed to me that a democracy must inevitably vote itself into bankruptcy. Sociologists inform us that of every hundred persons thirty are thrifty, and seventy thriftless. The majority will consistently vote to spend what the minority possesses, spurred on by cupidity and envy. We have seen this in Great Britain where, threatened by the weapon of the strike, the two chief parties, Conservative and Labour, have succumbed to uneconomic policies, to supporting a state-subsidised standard of living beyond the economic resources of our over-populated island, increasingly threatened with bankruptcy and appalling taxation. In the early Twenties, so bright and promising in many aspects, I saw ominous clouds on the horizon. I became apprehensive of an electoral system that seemed bound to lead to disaster. If I courted Brown's vote I must go one better than my opponent, the economic consequences ignored. Frankly, I do not know what is the alternative to this failure of democracy. We are a kindly people not given to dictatorships and violence. The frenzy of the French Revolution with its murders, the bull-throated menaces of a Mussolini, finally hung upside down by his gullible supporters, the blood-glut of the maniacal Hitler, driven to suicide, the purges and forced labour camps of the Russian doctrinaires, are all outside our compromising nature. We can only hope that the tolerance and good humour of the English character will find a solution, without producing a dictatorship whether by an individual or by labour unions exerting blackmail on the public. But in the Nineteen-Twenties it seemed to me that democracy began to write its own death warrant.

Obviously, with these reservations, I was not an ideal candidate. Apart from misgivings arising from political doubts and the state of my health, I was aware of another drawback. The Conservative or Liberal candidate was invariably a man of independent means. The Labour candidate was maintained by the union sponsoring him. I had no private means, no sponsor. I could not, if elected, have retained my editorship. I had no intention of becoming a political hack. I was not a barrister who could find membership of the House of Commons a remunerative asset. I might, if elected, have walked into a cul-de-sac.

Weighing these things, I returned from convalescence resolved that I would not stand again. I discussed with the chairman of the party who should take my place. The unknown London journalist who had been hurriedly brought in on my breakdown had made no impression on the constituency. I was still convinced that it could be won for the Liberal cause if a suitable candidate were found. However, for the time being, no action was taken about finding my successor.

The autumn after my return I began to think about the novel I planned to write, to follow the publication next year of *Scissors*. I had found in Venice the germ of a story; *Sails of Sunset*, suggested by my memorable nocturnal journey in the fruit boat down the lagoon to the Rialto. It would be an Italian story based on the fishing fleet at Chioggia. This little port had two claims to fame. Eleonora Duse had first appeared on the stage there, aged four. Goldoni had written one of his liveliest plays about the notoriously quarrelsome natives of whom he made fun in *Le Baruffe Chiozzotte*. The port's history went back into antiquity. It had gallantly withstood the Genoese navy when it besieged Venice.

Chioggia was not really an island in the Venetian lagoon. It was a peninsula of the mainland across which a canal had been cut. A drawbridge saved the town from complete isolation. The little port had once occupied a strategic position in the defence of the lagoons. It stood by a deep sea-channel at the mouth of a break in the twenty-mile littoral of the Lido, the sandy bar that held back the Adriatic Sea from the inland lagoons that protected Venice. A large fishing fleet was based on Chioggia. Its breed of sailors had been the backbone of the powerful Venetian navy.

I immersed myself in the history of Venice. I obtained a set of navigation charts of the northern Adriatic. I believed that at the end of three months I could have navigated a boat between the shoals that had constituted the defences of Venice. It was strange to walk at 2 a.m., from my editor's desk, through the empty streets to my study, where I embarked on a painted *barca* with russet or crimson sails, or sat in a café on the Vena Canal crowded with disputatious Chioggians, as in a scene from Goldoni's lively play. Sometimes, absorbed in this dream-life, I wrote until the lamplight on my desk was dissolved in the growing dawn. "You have not heard a word I've said to you, and you don't know what you are eating!" complained my mother. How could I? I was sailing my Venetian craft down the canal of "The Seven Dead Men", in the crimson sunset staining the silken water. Much of my life has been lived in that other-world more real than reality.

II

I spent some of my weekends in London, combining business and pleasure. The war seemed forgotten. London had few scars to show, or buildings to repair. Almost everyone was flush with the paper money that the Government blithely printed. Gold had disappeared, mostly into the American coffers. Relaxed Britain indulged in a whirl of gaiety and prosperity. Income Tax had been reduced from six shillings to four. The cost of living had fallen. Ladies still went to Court with three feathers in their hair and two chauffeurs for each limousine. The theatres were packed, the night-clubs booming despite rumblings from the coalfields. The Russian Ballet was back with a magnificent production in 1922 of *The Sleeping Princess*,

Bakst's last creation, for he died not long after. It was a full-length ballet, a stupendous spectacle in four acts, with Tchaikowsky's music and choreographed by Serge Grigoriev, as Massine was no longer with the company. It was danced by Lopokova, Tchernicheva, Idzikowsky, Woidzikowsky, all established favourites. Diaghilev lavished large sums on it, presenting such a spectacle as London had never seen. I had the great luck to be a guest in a box on the night of January 5th. It happened that the beloved *Maestro* Cecchetti, who had taught so many of the great ones their steps, was celebrating, aged seventy-two, his fiftieth anniversary as a dancer. He had played The Fairy Carabosse in the first production of *The Sleeping Princess* at St. Petersburg in 1890. Diaghilev invited him to dance the part again on his anniversary. Cecchetti responded and gave a wonderful performance. He had a tremendous reception and the curtain fell with him buried in bouquets and presents sent by Diaghilev, the company and the balletomanes. We all dined later at the Savoy. It was a night to remember. Alas, the ballet was not a commercial success and after little more than a hundred performances it was taken off, greatly to Diaghilev's distress. "This is the last relic of the great days of St. Petersburg," he said. "You will never again see such a perfect *ensemble* and décor."

Social life had now reverted to its pre-war gaiety. It recovered from the long agony of the struggle by land and sea against Germany. Perhaps the bright young things were not so bright since Lady Diana Manners had led them in pre-war days. In November, 1923, now Lady Duff Cooper, she sailed for New York, to make a spectacular success as the Nun in *The Miracle*, Reinhardt's dramatic triumph. Although she did not know it, I felt a personal interest in her career. I had first seen her crossing the hall with her mother and sister at Belvoir Castle in 1905. I was a small boy with a group of tourists looking down from a gallery, and from that moment I "adopted" her as a sister, not knowing she was going to be one of the most beautiful, talked-of women in England. We were born in the same year and this enabled me to follow a sort of Plutarchian parallel life, on very different levels!

London in the mid-Twenties was enlivened by the three Sitwells Osbert, Sacheverell and Edith, an aristocratic trio who were relentless producers of themselves. I was carried along one afternoon in June, 1923, to the Aeolian Hall in Bond Street, where they put on *Façade*, a bizarre concoction not devoid of buffoonery, in which, from behind a curtain, Edith declaimed through a megaphone her verses, which seemed to me affected nonsense.

> The stars in their apiaries,
> Sylphs in their aviaries . . . .

"Doesn't she mean 'ovaries'?" asked a ribald friend.

There were catcalls and a near riot towards the conclusion, with an indignant young man named Noël Coward walking out, thereby starting a feud that was to last thirty years. Another young man had provided the accompanying music. His name was William Walton. The world was to hear from this composer, with increasing fame. The audience was so infuriated that Edith was persuaded not to leave until it had gone. I found it all rather amusing. The audience was a mixture of Socialites, sniffy Bloomsburyites, snobs, gossip writers and the "arty" section of Chelsea.

The Sitwell brothers were then living in a house in Carlyle Square. I had been taken to a party there by a friend. It was my first close-up sight of them. They were affable and excellent hosts. Edith, with a long nose, had a Gothic-gargoyle look which she and young Cecil Beaton with his camera cleverly exploited. Her sad pallid face was made an asset.

Façade gained a lot of publicity for "The Sitwell Circus" and henceforth they were never out of the limelight. It was about this time that their father, Sir George Sitwell, the baronet of Renishaw whom Osbert turned into such a derisory figure, called on me. He was doing research for a book on the history of his family. Some of his ancestors had lived in and near Nottingham. I was glad to help him a little and he wrote an excellent book. I found it difficult to identify this intelligent, courtly gentleman with the caricature drawn by his son.

All these oddities and gaieties did not mask a change in the visual face of London life. Chesterfield House, where Johnson had vainly sought patronage, was the first to disappear; then followed the demolition of Grosvenor House, taken over in the war years by the

Ministry of Food; and Dorchester House, built in the Italian Renaissance style. All three were magnificent mansions. I had been in each of them and soon they were no more. The carriage horse had vanished from the streets. A lady in a landau with a groom on the box-seat was almost a museum piece. The old world was dead.

Little by little the Sunday morning parade in Hyde Park with riders in the Row, had wilted. As late as 1918 it had been a spectacle, though the top hat and the tail-coat had gone and ladies no more appeared in "creations". The motor-car brought the vogue of excursions to the country. One Sunday morning I hired a hack. I was soon put to shame by Don Roberto Cunninghame Graham, as he was known, riding like an hidalgo, black sombrero-hatted, superbly mounted with a Mexican saddle and Spanish boots. I saluted him diffidently, and being a great gentleman he pretended not to be aware of my mount.*

The riders grew fewer and fewer, the parade less and less dressy. There was a shrinkage in hospitality. Red druggets were no longer visible in front of the houses in Prince's Gate, and Queen's Gate and the fashionable squares. Butlers were becoming extinct. The survivors were somewhat shabby and doddering objects. At a tea-party I heard a dowager tell a frightening story about a neighbour's house. "Yes— they've converted it into bed-sitting rooms. And there's nothing one can do about it! A row of milk bottles on the front porch!"

The most popular figure in this time of transition was Edward, Prince of Wales. Everyone was afraid that the handsome fellow would break his neck riding at hunt steeplechases. And when, and whom, would he marry? The beautiful mother of Mrs. Dudley Ward came to see me, to ask if I could do anything in the Press to stop the

---

* Robert Cunninghame Graham (1852–1936). Known as 'Don Roberto'. A Scottish laird, descended from Robert II, legitimate uncrowned King of Scotland. M.P., suspended from the House for saying "Damn". He joined John Burns, the dockers' strike leader, in a riot in Trafalgar Square and went to prison with him. He was at home in Argentina and Mexico. In 1914–18 he bought remounts in Argentina for the British Government. A great figure there, a town was named after him. When he died in Buenos Aires he was given an official funeral. The city erected a monument to his memory. He was an excellent speaker and author, a great horseman, handsome, slight in figure, with much panache. "A grand seigneur born out of his time," said Joseph Conrad.

gossip about the Prince and her daughter. "We love to have him visit us, he's such a dear boy—but all this scandal! What can we do?" she asked. "Nothing," I replied. "Just let it wear itself out." It did.

Wars that break up the old order push the top classes down and bring the bottom up. Money began to go into pockets that never had had any, from pockets that formerly had. Servants were no longer obtainable for a pound a week, working ten hours a day, running up and down four flights of stairs. Clerks on starvation wages, working from nine to seven with one half-day a week, vanished. Miners were not willing to lie on their backs in the bowels of the earth for thirty shillings a week. The Duke of Northumberland, with an income of one hundred thousand pounds a year, might be very clever in argument with Mr. Cook, the miners' ill-educated, somewhat hysterical leader, but a better sense of values had come out of the rat-infested trenches, and smart argument rang hollow. There was unrest abroad. An increased gaiety rubbed shoulders with increased discontent. A Labour Government took office, went out and in again, ending in a coalition. All this happened within a space of ten years.

We suffered from the General Strike that had convulsed the country. The Bright Twenties could not foresee what was to come. By June, 1926, over one million men were unemployed. This rose to two millions in June, 1930, and nearly three millions in June, 1931. Unemployment pay, an inadequate "dole", rotted the character of the recipients, and no politician had the ability to organise this vast cohort and employ it in useful national work.

Some of the great houses kept up a show with maids instead of footmen, one gardener instead of four. The liveried flunkeys who had delighted Mr. Henry James, the visiting American novelist, never came back from the war. Waitresses served in the exclusive clubs, now less exclusive.* The Londonderrys held political parties on the grand scale in their Park Lane mansion, with Mr. Ramsay MacDonald, the lad from Lossiemouth, now Prime Minister, taking in the Marchioness to dinner. To make this social elevation more

* "All the great chairs and lounges and sofas are filled with men having afternoon tea—lolling back with their laps filled with magazines, journals and fresh Mudie books, while amiable flunkies in knee-breeches present them the divinest salvers of tea and buttered toast."—Henry James, at the Athenæum Club in 1877.

creditable it was rumoured that the Premier was the illegitimate son of a Scottish baron. He was indeed noble-looking.

Lady Cunard ("Emerald") gave lavish literary-political lunch parties and was visible, in her box at Covent Garden, supporting her *grand ami*, Sir Thomas Beecham. The Glasgows at Moncorvo House still put down the red drugget and somehow found ten footmen to serve champagne to three hundred guests. I went to what was their last grand flourish, a fancy dress ball. My photo album shows costume groups, Nancy Mitford, Oliver Messel, Robert Peel, and myself in an ambassador's court uniform! It was all very jolly but there were rumblings of the economic volcano. Mr. and Mrs. Sidney Webb, not yet in the peerage, were compiling their gloomy statistics of the homeless and hungry. Mr. Churchill, now out of office and favour, was bricklaying and doing freelance journalism. It was a Barmecide feast with pound notes thick as the leaves that fall in Vallombrosa.

Prices began to rise at the close of the decade. I was horrified when in 1927 my Mrs. Brown, who cleaned my London apartment, asked five shillings for the half-day. I had not got adjusted to the new era, recalling our 1906 "char", who lived in sin with a miner and often carried a black eye as a mark of affection. She arrived at 8 a.m. and worked tirelessly until six, for two shillings and sixpence. For many it had been a bad old world and few were sorry to see it go. At the beginning of the decade twopence procured a ride on a bus from Piccadilly Circus to Marble Arch. My club lunch was half-a-crown. Looking back from the apprehensive overtaxed Seventies, how bright were some aspects of the Twenties! We thought the nightmare of war was gone for ever. England was to be "a land fit for heroes to live in". We could not know that fifty years later one would have to be a hero to live in it. Messrs. Ford, Morris and Austin gave us a car for little more than one hundred pounds. We gaily journeyed forth; and there was always Charlie Chaplin, a genius of the silent film, in that cosy place of oblivion, the cinema.

III

In April, 1923, *Scissors*, on which all my hopes were founded, was published. I experienced the thrill of opening the parcel containing

Heinemann's six copies for the author and placing one of these in my mother's hands. I was more fortunate than another young Nottingham author, D. H. Lawrence, who twelve years earlier had also placed his first novel, *The White Peacock*, in his mother's hands. She was dying and scarcely knew what it was. Heinemann's advance of £50 was used to pay the doctor's bills and funeral expenses. I had received no "advance on royalties".

Breathlessly, I awaited the reviews. In the Twenties they gave much space to book reviews. Advertising rates being low, publishers freely spent money announcing their new books, and this financed the cost of pages devoted to reviewing them. Reviewers could spread themselves. Well-known writers were prominently featured as critics. What Arnold Bennett said of a new book was headline-news and he drew a princely sum for saying it.

It is a miracle, all the chances considered, for anyone to get a book published. Each year thousands of manuscripts are hopefully submitted. One well-known publishing house stated that it accepted only ten to twenty new writers out of two to three thousand aspirants each year. Such is the first gamble of authorship. My own reception by the critics was generous. I received thirty-four reviews of which only three were "bad", the others encouraging, some laudatory. What heartened me most were letters from Israel Zangwill, Joseph Conrad, Arnold Bennett, Max Beerbohm, John Masefield, John Drinkwater, Holbrook Jackson, and Alfred Noyes, all Field Marshals of letters, complimenting the new recruit. "Although I was most impressed by the beginning," wrote Zangwill, "with its new local colour and the musical writing one expects from a poet, still the whole is extremely vivid and shows no small gift for the absorption, comprehension and the transcription of the tragic realities amid which we move . . . I did not like the title when I saw it advertised, as it suggested a flippancy which did not seem characteristic of you, but of course one gets accustomed to the name and its attractive owner, one of the nicest boys in fiction." From the Villino Chiaro came Max Beerbohm's salute: "So here is *Scissors*, most welcome, most engaging, and a charmer indeed, full of effervescent youth." And from John Masefield: "I was wholly absorbed by it. Beautifully written, delicate, moving, a fateful panorama."

But Clement Shorter, another power in the literary world, who wrote a famous Book Page in the *Sphere*, gave me a cold douche to reduce any swollen head. He thought it lamentable that I should have so much success so young. "Never has there been an age when young writers so easily . . . Thackeray, Meredith, Hardy, Kipling were all in the thirties when success had come to them, although Dickens had won fame in his twenties, but then, Cecil Roberts is no Dickens. It is a good first novel but will he last as a novelist? Probably he will go on to other things." I was commended and I was reproved. It seemed my offence was to win success while I was in my twenties. In this Shorter was wrong. I had just reached thirty-one, so in the age-sense I qualified for the Thackeray, Meredith, Hardy bracket! The thing that pleased me most about Shorter's review was that he used almost his whole page for it, heading it with a photograph. Was I going to last? This was the question I was asking myself. The answer lay in Time. Forty-five years later, I wrote a preface for the reset twenty-second reprint of *Scissors*. I had added twenty-three novels to its company through those years. Shorter could not know that I would be writing his Book Page in the *Sphere* within seven years!

It might be thought I had made a good start. The future looked rosy, the day of liberation from my editorial chair seemed not too far distant. I was received on visits to my publisher with some warmth, as though I were one of the family. Pawling had passed me on to the managing director, a young dynamic little man called Charles Evans. He had begun life as a Council schoolteacher and was now one of the foremost publishers of the day. Our relationship became extremely cordial. He was delighted to learn I had another novel near completion. So here I was, a boy's dream had come true.

Coolly considered, the triumph was not as bright as it looked. Young authors learn with surprise how small the basis of an opening success can be. The public imagines the author has made thousands of pounds. Actually, he is fortunate if he has made three hundred. My novel was reprinted three times in the first six months, and reached a sale of eight thousand copies. Evans was jubilant. "Only eight thousand?" I asked. Evans pointed out to me that any publisher was happy to sell two thousand copies of a first novel; it covered his costs. A sale of five thousand was excellent, eight thousand extra-ordinary. My tiro's royalty of 10 per cent, rising to 12½ per cent, brought in, on a novel priced at 7s. 6d. about £400 gross. What price success? It seemed rather small for a labour covering two years. I could not, like Sir Hall Caine, the Manx novelist, see myself living in a castle and riding in a Rolls-Royce car. It did not seem as if this was the road to easy independence. A footballer did better.

It was pointed out to me that I had done very well indeed. I had found a good publisher, I had run into three impressions in six months. I had become a promising property. In 1903 Arnold Bennett, at the age of thirty-six, sold only 1,500 copies of *Leonora*. In 1907 he had to borrow £50 from his agent, Pinker, to finance his marriage. The next year he begged Pinker to send him £10. This was the year he published *The Old Wives' Tale*, his masterpiece, for which he received an advance of £150. It established his reputation but only brought him £180 in the first year. For nine years Pinker advanced him £50 a month, on which he lived and wrote. His total indebtedness grew to £3,000. When in 1927 I visited him in his stately house in Cadogan Square he had, in addition to the town house with five servants, a country house with four gardeners and, for a while, a yacht with a crew of five. Success had flooded in at last. His income was £40,000 that year. From novel writing? Not at all. "A solemn thought," he wrote in his *Journal*, towards the end of his life, "I have never had what I call a sale. If I have made money by my pen it is in point of the fact that I produce as much as H. G. Wells and three times as much as other people." The secret of his fortune was prolific journalism and a very successful play. The growing film market by-passed him. He failed as a dramatist after one great and one mediocre success.

Within twelve months the return from *Scissors* had increased. It had sold 12,000 copies, bringing in £500 at 12½ per cent royalty. An American edition earned £400, and five translations, £300, a total of £1,200. But from this were deducted British and American income-tax, two agents' fees, typing bill, a total of £400, leaving me with a net of £800. It was not a fortune but I felt encouraged to go on. Had the book brought in £100 I should have gone on. Writing was my life. I was born that way.

I had dedicated my novel to Harry Cunningham Brodie, the cicerone of my London advent. With characteristic kindness he arranged a lunch party at the Reform Club to celebrate its publication. On a sunny June day fourteen guests sat at a table in the Reform Club that overlooked the green lawns and trees of Carlton House Gardens. Friends, old and new, were gathered there. The menu was worthy of Harry, a perfectionist who delighted in dispensing hospitality. There were caviare and lobster and Aylesbury duck and a soufflé. The toast to the book's success was drunk in champagne. I was the youngest present, the oldest was Sir Alfred Mond, a luminary of the Liberal party in the triumphant days when its Premiers and Cabinet ministers had haunted this club. Their life-sized portraits in oils still hung in the rooms and corridors.

There was, of course, among my friends, Charles Prescott, the Robert de Montesquieu of my London scene, heir to a baronetcy, immaculate, serene, high-voiced, Harry's intimate friend and gentle bully; he was unusually complimentary. I smiled inwardly recalling that day, six years earlier when I was Harry's guest for the first time in this club, and, looking me over, Prescott had enquired of him: "And what does your young friend do?" Well, he knew now. Also present was my old chief of my Ministry of Munitions days, Sir Burton Chadwick, now a Parliamentary Private Secretary, and busy founding the Company of Master Mariners. And present, too, was my stalwart backer from boyhood, leonine-headed old William Kiddier, enjoying this celebration possibly more than I. For a moment I felt myself detached from the festive scene. I observed it, a little incredulous that I should be its cause.

I told myself "It will never again be like this—whatever you do in the coming years. This is the peak, with the morning at your feet." I was right, it was.

IV

I had completed the writing of *Sails of Sunset* by July, 1923, and decided that I must return to Venice to check my manuscript on the spot. I went there at the beginning of August, having arranged to join my friend Jack Laing in Rome when he returned from his annual visit to his aunt in Caramanico. Venice, hot, crowded, was as enchanting as ever.

In the middle of August I went on to Rome. It put a spell upon me. "One day I'll come and live here," I said, and tourist-fashion threw a coin in the Fountain of Trevi, to ensure my return. "That's about the seventh city you swear you're going to live in. You'll have to have a long life!" commented Jack.

After five days we left for Naples. I was particularly eager to visit the Museum. "I hope it's art and not pornography," said Jack, "I refuse to ask them to open the Pompeiian brothel for you." I denied any such desire. There was something I specially wanted to fulfil. "Dear boy, you are a great fulfiller. When you were sixteen, you wanted to sleep in Wordsworth's bed at Grasmere, and you did. What is it now?" he asked. I explained. In the Museum at Naples there was a bronze statue called "Narcissus". It had been excavated at Pompeii, and was of Greek origin. When I was a small boy my father showed me a copy of it in the museum at Nottingham. "It's not really a Narcissus at all," he told me. "It's Dionysus, the Roman Bacchus, the god of wine. There's a goat skin hanging over his shoulder and he's crowned with vine leaves. He's looking down, with one finger upraised. Gladstone used to have a copy of this statue on his desk. He thought the youth was warning him to meditate before he did anything rash. Gladstone was wrong about that. The young god had a panther as a pet, and he's really admonishing it. The panther's missing now. Look at the sandals, one has a thick block of lead under it which tilts the statue. It wasn't designed like that. It probably stood on a marble plinth—the present base is Pompeiian, not Greek. Some Roman soldier may have looted it when the Romans invaded Greece and he just wrenched it off its plinth, pulling the lead socket away with the statue."

A few days later I went back to look at it. It seemed as if the statue wanted to speak to me. It was my first encounter with the fabulous world of Greek art. "Narcissus" gave me an idea for my first novel. A young English couple were honeymooning in Naples. One day in an antiquarian's shop they saw a copy of the statue. "I'd love to have that—isn't it beautiful!" cried young Mrs. Dean. Her husband replied, playfully: "Well, if you'll present me with a real Narcissus, I'll buy it for you," which he did. When their son was born, in whimsy they called him "John Narcissus" which caused a lot of mirth when he went to school. He was soon nicknamed "Scissors". "That's why, my dear Jack, I want to go to the museum, not to see a Pompeiian brothel. And after that I want to go to Pompeii and see the place where Narcissus was excavated," I explained.

We found the original in the Pompeiian room of the National Museum. It was all that I expected. My father, as usual, had his facts correct. So to Pompeii we went, on such a sunny, blue-skied morning of August, 1923, as was that other morning in August, A.D. 79, a few hours before the eruption of Vesuvius utterly destroyed it. We found a good guide and after a general survey of that silent, awe-inspiring town, I told him I wanted to go to Region VII, Section 12, to see No. 21 in the street of the Augustali, where the statue had been found eighteen hundred years after it had been buried under volcanic ashes. We found the house, situated in the centre of the city. It appeared to have been an aristocrat's dwelling with a colonnaded atrium where the statue had stood. Was it the house of a Roman general, who had been in Athens and who had looted "Narcissus" from its Greek home? One could only surmise. Generals are apt to do things like that. Napoleon was a super-thief. What a long journey through Time the original Narcissus had taken, from the Praxitelean era of Greece 350 B.C., to Roman Pompeii, A.D. 79, to be buried there for eighteen hundred years in ashes before it saw again the bright Italian day!

"Now are you 'fulfilled', dear boy?" asked Jack, as we left Pompeii. I was fulfilled, to over-brimming, and could find no words.

But I had not finished with "Narcissus". Like young Mrs. Dean in my story, I coveted the statue. We obtained the name of an Italian professor of sculpture who was renowned for making copies for museums. We went to his workshop and there we found a superb "Narcissus", faithful in every detail even to the green patina that all those centuries in Vesuvian ashes had given the bronze. The price was modest. The professor would send it by ship, crated, for £12! And Jack, who had deprecatingly come with his crazy friend, found the statue so irresistible that he commissioned one also.

Ten weeks elapsed, then one wet November morning the crate

arrived at my home. When it was opened and all the straw packing was undone, I lifted the heavy bronze up into the light of day. I placed Narcissus on my writing desk and I swear he brought something of the bright Pompeiian day into the room. I called in my mother to admire the statue. She contemplated it for a few moments, and then said "Yes, it's very lovely—but isn't it rather rude?"

I saw her objection, and perhaps the professor in Naples had anticipated it. I took out of an envelope a portable fig-leaf which neatly fitted Narcissus. "I thought it was a little too naked!" said my mother, now wholly approving my acquisition.

V

In that summer of 1923 the Conference of Ambassadors, at the request of the Council of the League of Nations, appointed a commission to define the Albania-Greek frontier, a long-disputed matter. On August 27th, 1923, one of the commissioners, the much respected Italian General Tellini, and three members of his staff, were murdered by a person, or persons, unknown, on Greek soil, near the Albanian frontier.

On August 29th the Italian Government sent an ultimatum to the Greek Government. Mussolini, supported alike by Fascists and anti-Fascists, was able to show a strong hand. The ultimatum in its demands had an ominous similarity to that sent to Serbia by the Austrian Government, following the assassination of the Archduke Francis Ferdinand at Sarajevo on June 28th, 1914, which started the First World War.

The Italian terms were humiliating. The demands were: (1) A full apology by Greece. (2) A solemn funeral service in the Catholic Cathedral in Athens in homage to the victims. (3) The Italian flag, hoisted by an Italian squadron off Phaleron, to be saluted by Greek battleships flying the Greek flag, the salute not being returned by the Italian squadron until its departure at sunset the same day. (4) Greece to carry out within five days a strict enquiry, with the assistance of the Italian Military Attaché. (5) All persons guilty to be sentenced to death and Greece to pay Italy within five days 50 million lire (£500,000) as a penalty. (6) Military honours to be paid to the victims on embarkation of their bodies.

A reply was demanded within twenty-four hours. It will be observed that No. 5 almost prejudged the verdict of the enquiry.

The Greek Government accepted within the time limit the demands made in Nos. 1, 2, 3 and 6. It rejected Nos. 4 and 5 as "outraging the honour and violating the sovereignty of the State". If the Italian Government was unwilling to recognise the satisfaction offered as adequate the Greek Government would appeal to the League of Nations and accept its decisions.

The Italian reaction was quick and violent. Here was a heaven-sent opportunity. At a naval conference in Rome a month earlier the Italian Minister of Marine had deplored the decline of Italian naval prestige in the Mediterranean, *Mare Nostrum*. Mussolini, the March on Rome not a year old, saw the chance to increase his prestige as a man of action. Within an hour of receiving the Greek reply he ordered the occupation of Corfu and some adjacent Greek islands. He thereby by-passed the League of Nations as a court of appeal. On August 31st an Italian squadron entered Corfu harbour. "Its commander demanded the hoisting of the white flag over the citadel. When compliance with this demand was delayed, he proceeded to bombard the citadel, which was obsolete as a fortress and was at that time being used to house Greek and Armenian refugees from Turkey. Fifteen of these unfortunate people were killed and many more wounded by the Italian shell-fire, after which troops were landed and Corfu was subject to Italian military occupation."* The Italians deliriously acclaimed Mussolini. Duce! Duce! Duce! they screamed when he appeared on the balcony of the Palazzo Venezia. There was some irony in the Greek appeal to the League of Nations. In May, 1919, the Greeks, ignoring the League, had declared war on Turkey, with disastrous results; hence the refugees in the bombarded Corfu citadel.

Immediately on receipt of the Greek reply, with its suggestion of the League acting as an arbitrator, the Italian representative on the Council of the League denied its competence to deal with the dispute.

* *Survey of International Affairs*, 1920–23, by Arnold Toynbee. (Oxford University Press.)

It was a matter, he said, to be judged by the Conference of Ambassadors on whose Court Italy would sit as one of the three judges, but with no Greek member! Mussolini let it be known that this was his unalterable view and if the League intervened he would occupy Corfu indefinitely.

Lord Robert Cecil, the British representative at the League, and the Swedish representative, supported by a few other countries, insisted that the League take action even if it entailed sanctions. There was no support from France, always lukewarm towards the League. She had no desire to lose Italian support over her occupation of the Ruhr in January that year. She endorsed the ultimatum to the Greeks. The League surrendered to the Italian demands and passed the case to the Conference of Ambassadors. There was some weakness in Britain's support for the League. She was not eager for a collision with Italy. Her Navy in the Mediterranean was unprepared, as it was to be twice again, when Italy defied the League and massacred the Abyssinians, and when Eden embarked on his ill-starred attack, in collusion with the French, on Suez in 1956.

The Corfu affair should have made it plain that without the United States, Russia and Germany as members, the League was impotent. Later, Japan flouted the League over its occupation of Manchuria in 1931.

The Ambassadors' Conference, now seized of the case, Greece accepted its competence. Pending the verdict of a commission appointed by the Conference to make a judicial enquiry into the frontier murders, the Greek Government deposited £500,000 with the Swiss National Bank.

The commission of enquiry was despatched on September 17th. It reported on the 22nd "that it could not formulate a firm, definite and unanimous opinion on the responsibilities in connection with the outrage of August 27th". It failed to discover the perpetrators of the crime or their nationality. Nevertheless, on September the 26th the Ambassadors' Conference instructed the Swiss Bank to pay to the Italian Government the Greek deposit of £500,000! Corfu was evacuated the next day.

It was a flagrant miscarriage of justice for Greece, a triumph of blackmail for Mussolini, and an ineradicable stain on the prestige of the League. The invasion of Manchuria was to follow, then Abyssinia, then in a disastrous concatenation of lawlessness, Hitler's annexation of Austria and the Sudetenland.

My friend and I were in Rome during the Corfu incident. The excitement was intense. Italy became bellicose overnight and Mussolini now assumed the role, heavy-jawed, posturing, arrogant, that he maintained for the next twenty years. The scene in Rome was somewhat frightening. When the bodies of General Tellini and his companions arrived there was mass hysteria. We were glad to leave the overcharged atmosphere. Lord Robert Cecil's activity at the League of Nations, demanding its direct action in procuring a settlement, filled the Italians with rage against the British.*

When news of the decision of the Ambassadors' Conference came into my office I was deeply perturbed. I called in my assistant, showed him the telegram and said: "We can regard the League as impotent. *Mene, mene, tekel, upharsin.* Here are the seeds of another world war. Mussolini has set the pattern of successful brigandage."

For myself the League was dead. Its demise saddened me but the reality could not be ignored; it was a house of straw. There followed the Abyssinian War and the futile sanctions against Italy. In June, 1935, there was a Peace Ballot in England. It was supposed to be a plebiscite of the nation's opinion. It had the backing of the venerable Lord Robert Cecil, whose sincerity was beyond question. Behind the ballot was a strange collection of idealists, pacifists and cranks, with the politicians giving their lip-service since it was a vote-catcher. The questions put to the public were: "Do you favour reductions in armaments by international agreement? Do you consider that if a

* I wrote a letter to *The Times*, (Oct. 9th, 1923): "Returning to England after some time spent in Italy during the Corfu crisis one is conscious that the public has roughly two opinions. First, that the League of Nations is utterly discredited. Second, that the decision of the Conference of Ambassadors bears no relation to justice . . . Allowing for the Latin temperament, the amazing scenes enacted in Rome on the day when the bodies of the four murdered soldiers were received showed that the Italians had lost all sense of proportion. The extravagant preparations, the amazing apotheosis accorded by the Press, which magnified the unfortunate soldiers into heroes of gigantic proportions who had fought desperately to the last breath for the honour of assaulted Italy, and the complete paralysis of traffic and business, gave new meaning to Byron's 'butchered to make a Roman holiday'."

nation is attacked other nations should unite to make the aggressor stop, by: (1) Economic and non-military measures. (2) If necessary, military measures?"

Twelve million persons filled in the forms. Naturally, three-quarters said "Yes". It was an exercise in sheer idiocy. Meanwhile, Mussolini and Hitler were panting to go. Mussolini was gathering troops to invade Abyssinia, Hitler had walked out of the League and was forming the Luftwaffe. Baldwin and MacDonald held hands in a Cabinet that had no policy except avoidance of any commitments. And this time it could not "pass the buck" to an Ambassadors' Conference. As Churchill incessantly warned, with few to listen, we were shuffling towards the *Götterdämmerung* of Sunday, September 3rd, 1939.

CHAPTER EIGHT

Churchill and Bracken

I

I HAD RETURNED from Italy only a few days when I received a telephone call from my chief, Sir Charles Starmer. A death had created a by-election in West Leicester. It was a strong Labour seat. Winston Churchill was going to contest it as a Liberal. "There's no local Liberal paper. I've told Churchill we will run a special edition for Leicester so that he gets press coverage. His agent will come to see you," said Sir Charles.

I promised that I would do everything in my power. Here was a chance to serve my political hero. Churchill was at a low ebb of fortune. Everywhere he was maliciously pursued as the culprit of the Dardanelles disaster. In vain had the report of a Commission of Enquiry cleared Churchill and put the blame on the lethargic Asquith and his vacillating Cabinet. The failure of this great conception had been due chiefly to Lord Fisher at the Admiralty, who had suddenly shown cold feet for the enterprise, and to Admiral de Robeck, in charge of the fleet operations in the Narrows at the Dardanelles, who, frightened by the loss of three old battleships, had lacked the spirit to press the attack. Subsequent information has confirmed that Churchill's brilliantly conceived enterprise to force the Dardanelles and open a Balkan front would probably have succeeded. It would have shortened the war and have saved thousands of lives lost in the military assault on the Gallipoli peninsula. We know now that the Turks were on the point of withdrawal. The Commission's report had little effect on the British public. The Dardanelles had been a failure. Churchill remained the culprit in its eyes. Lloyd George had shown courage in bringing him back from the

Western Front, where he had gone to serve in the Army, and making him Minister of Munitions, but it was an office that carried no Cabinet rank. There was organised opposition among the Tories. When the Coalition was broken up at the Carlton Club meeting in 1922, Churchill found himself in the wilderness. Under the colourless Bonar Law the mediocrities moved in, Baldwin, Wood (Halifax), Neville Chamberlain and Joynson-Hicks. They were solid, they were dreary, and suspicious of the bright intellects of men like Birkenhead and Churchill. They had never forgiven a scion of the House of Marlborough for his desertion to the Liberal camp. Even more antagonistic was the Labour Party. To Churchill communism and socialism were the same thing, and wholly detestable. He had committed unpardonable sins. He was not only the author of the Dardanelles fiasco, but he was the avowed enemy of the Labour Party. He was an aristocrat, he played polo. Had he played cricket all might have been well but polo was an aristocrat's foible. Also, he had never been forgiven for his threat against the munition workers who struck in July, 1918. He told them, bluntly, that the alternative to war-work was military service. With swollen wages loading their pockets the threat was effective. The strike collapsed. Again, always magnanimous in victory, he was in favour of sending food ships to Hamburg for the starving Germans. Churchill discovered that he was badly out of step. The mood was to hang the Kaiser, not take pity on the Germans, who had innovated poison gas, the bombing of open towns and the murder of sailors and civilians by German submarines. Again, in his hatred of the Russian Revolution, Churchill was a prime mover to help, with military stores, the White Russians who, under Kolchak and Denikin, were leading exiled officers against the Red Army. By this gesture he made recognition of our debt to the Czarist armies that had taken pressure off the Western Front.

In the General Election that followed the end of the Coalition Churchill lost his seat at Dundee. During the campaign he fell ill, undergoing an operation for appendicitis. With Lloyd George in the wilderness, Asquith discredited, he seemed to belong to no one. As he succinctly put it, he was now "without an office, without a seat, without a party, and without an appendix".

But Churchill was never a man to lose heart, or time. With a box of paints he took himself in the early months of 1923 to convalesce on the French Riviera. It provided him with the bright colours he loved. He took with him also, for the final touches, a work on which he had been engaged for three years, the first volume of *The World Crisis*. The pen had ever been his support and his solace. Had he never entered politics he would have entered the front rank of writers. Not as a novelist, for his first and only venture into fiction, *Savrola*, revealed that he had no gift for that genre. It was a lesson immediately learned. But he was a born journalist, whether in the field of adventure or at the desk, as *The River War* proved. Next, with a pious excursion in family history, the excellent *Life* of his father Lord Randolph, he showed a true gift for biography. It may be he lacked depth and sometimes the detached impartiality essential to accurate assessment of events, but he had the wide sweep, the sense of drama, and an eloquence in his prose style that few of his rivals in this field could approach and none surpass. It is amusing to observe that when he came to write what is considered by many his *magnum opus*, the grandiloquent and forceful *Life of Marlborough*, his great ancestor, a task undertaken to sweep away the calumny that had gathered about the great soldier's life, Churchill made a spirited attack upon the veracity of Macaulay's treatment of Marlborough. In doing so he borrowed the forceful style of that master and blended it with the assured sweep of Gibbon.

Churchill had no private means to speak of. The rewards of office were intermittent and not large. He had inherited very little. The millions of his adventurous American grandfather, Mr. Jerome of New York, had melted away leaving his pretty, spirited mother a plucked heiress. He had gained an early notoriety, always cashable in Fleet Street. He needed money always. A passion for polo is not conducive to economy. So journalism was the answer and, in the early years, and the later disastrous ones, he did not hesitate to importune editors. He must live by his pen. "After all I am a member of your profession," he wrote to the Editor of the *Strand Magazine*. "I've never had any money except what my pen has brought me." Sometimes his financial position was acute. Churchill and Birkenhead were plungers. One evening, dining together, the subject of their debts came up. Birkenhead asked Winston how much he owed. He told him. "Phew! my lad," cried Birkenhead, blowing out his cigar smoke after an excellent dinner in Eccleston Square, "that's nothing! I owe three times as much!" Their ends were very different. One died financially embarrassed, with no visible means of support, the other a millionaire, matching another octogenarian best-seller, Somerset Maugham, both marshals of the written word. But those days of affluence were far off.

In 1922 the *Strand Magazine* paid Churchill £500 for two articles and £400 for coloured illustrations of his paintings. "Would £1,000 be reasonable?" he asked, having proposed another contribution. He was coming up from Chartwell. "Pray would it be convenient to you to call and see me at noon on Friday?" The editor called and had a long session in a small room at the top of 28 Hyde Park Gate. "These were times when he apparently needed money urgently," recorded Reginald Pound, who had succeeded Reeves Shaw as editor of the *Strand Magazine*. "Shaw told me that he had more than once drawn cheques at Churchill's urgent request and sent them to him by hand." In his letters submitting articles, Churchill courteously asked for payment—"if possible by Monday morning."*

In April 1923, Churchill published the first volume of the work that was to run to five before his task was completed. This was *The World Crisis*. He was formidably equipped, with his periods in office, to write a comprehensive history of the four momentous war years of 1914–18. He had been a member of Asquith's Cabinet when ominous war clouds gathered and Germany was aggressively building her fleet. First Lord of the Admiralty, he was in unique possession of all the facts. An artist in words he did not jump into his history of events. The first volume was a preliminary survey that ended with 1914. It was forceful, comprehensive and eloquent—perhaps too eloquent, for Churchill loved the set-piece. He occasionally over-dramatised the presentation, with himself the *régisseur*. "I have been immersed in Winston's brilliant Autobiography, disguised as a history of the universe," commented Lord Balfour after reading *The World Crisis*.

It was, rightly, an immediate success. Churchill received from his publisher an advance payment of £4,000 and the prodigious royalty of $33\frac{1}{3}$ per cent. Hardy, Wells, Bennett and Galsworthy never

* *The Strand Magazine*, by Reginald Pound. (Heinemann Ltd.)

bettered this in the heyday of their long writing careers. For the second volume, published in October, 1923, he received a £5,000 advance on the same royalty terms. In the first six months after publication 12,000 copies of the first volume, and 14,000 of the second were sold, bringing him in, within a year, about £15,000 gross, exclusive of American royalties, on which he had drawn an advance of £3,500. With the first two volumes successfully launched the financial bogy was banished. Churchill, the booming author, displaced Churchill the discredited politician. The fear that he might have to sell his beloved Chartwell was dispelled. He was able to embark on its reconstruction and enlargement, thereby adding bricklaying to his talents. Considering his active public life, his industry was phenomenal. The pen seldom rested in his hand.

But the life of a man of letters was not sufficient. Late in 1923 Churchill directed his energy towards regaining a seat in the House of Commons, a thing vital to his public career, which he had no intention of dropping. He was determined not to be bogged down as a political failure. He was now forty-nine years of age and possessed the most vigorous mind and truculent spirit in the country. His position was curious. He was a man without a party. The Tories repudiated him. He did not like Lloyd George's new brand of Liberalism. He knew that Asquith, a man of splendid principles and always helpful and loyal to his assistants, was a discredited and spent force.

For the time being Churchill retained his connection with the Coalition Liberals. In one thing he firmly believed, and advocated, a renewed coalition of Conservatives and Liberals to fight the menace of a Socialist government. He never wavered in his opposition to the growing political power of the Labour Party. In turn this party saw in him its most dangerous enemy. It sought to blot him out. There was a singular aspect to this antagonism. No man, even considering Lloyd George, had been more instrumental in passing legislation to alleviate the lot of the working classes. He was moved by the poverty he saw around him when he joined Asquith's Government in 1908. He would do something about it. "Why have I always been kept safe, within a hair's breath of death, except to do something like this? I'm not going to live long," he said. Possibly Lord Randolph's early death haunted him. Yet he had forty history-making years in front

166

of him. He had joined forces with Lloyd George, starting an enduring friendship between a fiery Radical and an aristocrat's son born in a ducal palace. He supported a Miners' Eight Hour Bill. He established Labour Exchanges, calling in a young Oxford sociologist, William Beveridge, whom, thirty-five years later, during the Second World War, when he was Prime Minister of the Coalition Government, he called on to plan the Welfare State that should come with the peace. He did all the spade work for the Unemployment Insurance Bill. Well might those industrious Fabian Socialists, the Webbs, complain he had taken the wind out of their sails. Beatrice Webb wrote in her Diary (1910): "L.G. and Winston have practically taken the limelight not merely from their own colleagues but from the Labour Party." In the public view Lloyd George was the fiercest assailant of the House of Lords, but Churchill's assault was equally vigorous. In 1910 he wrote a memorandum to the Prime Minister stating: "The time has come for the abolition of the House of Lords." He strongly supported the epoch-making legislation that established Old Age Pensions. As Home Secretary he visited the prisons and made enlightened reforms, which could in no way be attributed to vote-catching. General William Booth of the Salvation Army was received by him and he listened patiently to a homily on behalf of the prisoners. It ended with a long prayer for the Home Secretary's conversion. Churchill kneeled with his exhorter, and they parted with mutual respect.

As early as 1910 Churchill was in favour of Home Rule and said he would become Chief Secretary for Ireland instead of Home Secretary if he could satisfy his ambition to bring in a Bill conferring it. Eleven years later he laboured as a Cabinet minister to bring about a treaty. After signing it, the Irish leader, Collins, the forerunner of the Irish Free State, sent a message saying, "Tell Winston we could never have done anything without him."

It was singular that with such a record in social service Churchill met with venomous opposition from the Socialists. True, he did nothing to mitigate their venom. He saw in the members of the Labour Party the half-brothers of the detestable Communists who had brought down Russia in bloody ruin. It was perhaps quixotic but characteristic that when at last a relatively safe seat in Manchester was offered him in the late summer of 1923 he declined it. He deliberately chose to fight West Leicester, a Socialist stronghold, with an extremely formidable opponent. It was a temperamental constituency and had thrown out its member Ramsay MacDonald, incensed by his pacifism during the First World War.

II

A few days after the telephone call from Sir Charles Starmer I was informed that a Mr. Brendan Bracken, "Mr. Churchill's secretary", was below, asking to see me. An astonishing apparition was shown into my room, a tall youth who looked like a golliwog. His head was covered with a thick thatch of reddish curls. In manner he was very self-assured. I concluded that he was a political helper employed by the Liberal Party organisation, and could hardly call himself Churchill's secretary, a role fulfilled by the celebrated "Eddie" Marsh. I was in error. I should have remembered that the high-voiced, precise "Eddie", who had first introduced me to his chief in the Ministry of Munitions, in 1917, was a civil servant and was only associated with Churchill when he held ministerial office. By the code of the Civil Service "Eddie" could not serve Churchill in a political capacity. But who was this assertive golliwog, Brendan Bracken? How closely was he associated with Churchill, and in what capacity? He soon defined his sphere. He was not a political agent. Churchill had appointed him to take charge of the campaign in West Leicester as his personal assistant.

After a few minutes my doubtfulness vanished. This youth certainly knew what he wanted. There was a moment when he was so peremptory that I had to remind him that a captain on a ship does not take orders from the crew or the passengers, and that I was in control of the *Nottingham Journal*. He accepted the definition at once. Before he departed we had achieved a degree of mutual respect. I was aware of a strong, downright personality. This lad was tough. Ignorant of his story, I felt he had fought every inch of his way. Sturdy, unabashed, he struck me as rather like some young captain commanding a phalanx, one of that faithful band with whom Alexander the Great had made the conquest of the world.

We agreed on our campaign. I would appoint special reporters to cover all of Churchill's meetings. We would have a convoy of trucks to take the *Journal* early to Leicester each morning. Finally, before Bracken departed, I asked if he would like me to go to Leicester to address some meetings. "We should be delighted. You must dine with us after. Mr. Churchill and I will be staying at the Grand Hotel," he said.

When he left I felt as if a gale had blown over me. What an extraordinary fellow! Where had Winston found him and where had he come from? He had none of the hall-marks of the typical public school–university product. Neither his accent nor his manner gave me any clue. There was, of course, at his age, nothing to be learned from the usual reference books. He had not yet appeared in *Who's Who*. I began to make some enquiries, with no results. Finally I called up the editor of the *Westminster Gazette*. He had never heard of Brendan Bracken. He said he would ask their parliamentary correspondent and call me later. That evening I was still in the dark. Their House of Commons man had never heard of Brendan Bracken, neither had the Liberal headquarters.

Three days later the electoral campaign opened. I went to Leicester to address meetings in the constituency. It was very obvious that the campaign would be a rowdy one. We were in a hot-bed of Labour. Churchill's opponent, Pethick Lawrence, was formidable, though, like him, a stranger to the constituency. "He's an odd bird. He's jumped the family nest!" said Bracken as we sat at dinner in the Grand Hotel. "So did I!" said Winston, swallowing an oyster. "We won't hold that up against him. I don't believe there's a single thing in this world on which we could agree but I respect him. He's a phenomenon—he's slippery but honest, a born crank."

I went to hear Pethick Lawrence. He was a good, quiet speaker, persuasive and somewhat unctuous with universal goodwill. All would be well under socialism; less work, more wages, pensions for all, no army, no offensive weapons, sweet reason and peace flourishing in the universal brotherhood of man. It seemed that the British Government had an infallible gift for wickedness, greed, tyranny, corruption and sheer wrong-headedness. The whole social order must be overthrown and a reign of Pure Reason established. "Would you get rid of our splendid Navy, that saved us?" asked a man in the audience. "Sit down, silly ass!" "Throw him out!" "A Tory stooge!" they cried. The candidate calmed the meeting. "It is a proper question, and I will answer the gentleman," he said blandly. "Yes, sir. I would abolish the Navy, the Army, the Air Force, every tank, every gun, every rifle. I would re-employ the generals and admirals in constructive, not destructive work. We would spend our money abolishing slums, on providing food, education and social amenities. We would abolish poverty and the parasites who live on the wealth the workers create." There was loud applause.

No doubt he believed every word he said. It was remarkable considering his background. Educated at Eton, he had been Captain of the Oppidans, the most exclusive circle of the most privileged boys in the Kingdom. He had had a brilliant career at Cambridge where he had been a President of the Union and a Fellow of Trinity College. He had been called to the Bar, where he gained a good practice. But he had always been a protester. He championed the Boers during the South African War. He had been a prominent advocate of Votes for Women. He had opposed the First World War and had served a nine-months' prison sentence for conspiracy in connection with one of the militant demonstrations for Women's suffrage. There was nothing dishonourable, if perverse, in all this.

I was to encounter him thirty-three years later. One day I was riding on a street-car in Vienna when I saw a frail, little old man, obviously English, board the car at one of its stops. He took a seat next to me and I recognised him. He was now Lord Pethick-Lawrence, a Privy Councillor and Labour Peer. In the interim he had been Financial Secretary to the Treasury and Secretary of State for India. I spoke to him, reminding him of the West Leicester contest in 1923. I found that, like myself, he was attending the P.E.N. Congress. He was now eighty-five years of age, quick-minded. Perhaps he felt he should explain his presence on a street-car. "I simply can't afford taxis," he said. He was on his way back to his hotel and seemed glad to talk. "Let's get off and have a coffee," he said, when the street-car halted by the Stadtpark.

There was a large open-air restaurant with an orchestra playing in a bower of flowers. We found a table and over coffee reviewed the eventful years since 1923. Churchill's name came up. "Yes, a most remarkable fellow, most remarkable but always wrongheaded," he said. "I imagine that is Winston's idea of you!" I commented. He laughed. "Yes—yes—but he is always a great gentleman and we owe him much."

We parted cordially after an agreeable hour spent in a delightful setting. He gave no sign of his great age. He had still six more years to live. In stature, alertness and longevity and many of his views, he reminded me of another Labour candidate I had met in 1922, Norman Angell.

III

I was soon aware that addressing the electors of West Leicester on behalf of Churchill was a tempestuous affair. Hatred of him was aflame. His spirited opposition to Bolshevism, with which he allied the Labour doctrine, made him a particular enemy of the party's supporters. They followed him from meeting to meeting like a swarm of hornets. No insults were too gross to hurl at him, and, of course, the Dardanelles fiasco, regarded as his particular crime, was always brought up. I heard him speak on four occasions. The halls were packed. The opposition was determined to shout him down. He was always admirably self-controlled and good-tempered, and he never failed to quell the opposition and get a hearing. But the atmosphere was turbulent and exhausting. "The worst election I think I've ever been in," he commented.

All this apart, there was an undisguisable defect in Churchill's position. If elected he would be an isolated figure. The old Liberal Party, despite a patched-up truce between the Asquith and Lloyd George factions, was virtually defunct. Churchill's theme, the need of a coalition between Liberals and Conservatives to avert the menace of a Socialist takeover, carried no conviction since everyone knew that he was ostracised by the Conservatives. Within two months of this by-election Baldwin's Conservative Government was swept out of office and a Labour one took over. The outlook for our candidate, even if successful, was bleak.

Speaking on Churchill's behalf was a thankless business. I rather enjoyed the stormy atmosphere but I was building sand castles. Often, just when I had the audience in hand, I was abruptly swept away by the arrival of the candidate, to a storm of catcalls and cheering. He was the man they had all come to see and hear. Whatever their feelings about him he was a dynamic figure. He had made history and he belonged to one of the great families of England, for which the British public never quite loses its affection. I stopped speaking immediately on the advent of Churchill. It was his custom, order having been restored, with the formal courtesy that always marked him, to turn to the speaker of the moment and say, "Pray, continue!" (Neither in speech nor correspondence did he use "Please", it was always "Pray".) Apart from the essential custom of giving way at once to the candidate, the figure of the evening, it would have been impossible to continue. There was nothing else but to withdraw immediately.

He was wonderful to watch. He would spread his delicate white hands over his waistcoat and smilingly wait for complete silence. Then he would begin and continue his argument quite unruffled by noisy opposition. He had flashes of wit. To an abusive fellow he retorted, "You wouldn't dare talk to your wife like that!" The audience was convulsed in laughter. He was often naughtily humorous at the expense of the Labour leader. "Now, that aristocratic figure from Lossiemouth, Mr. Ramsay MacDonald, has told us—nay, lost in a fog of verbosity, can anyone say what he intended to tell us?"

This exhibition of a sense of humour, of innate puckishness both in the spoken and the written word puzzled me. I had been told he was devoid of any sense of humour. One evening, dining, I related what I thought was an extremely funny incident at one of our meetings. My story fell absolutely flat. There was an awful silence. Churchill picked up his wine glass. "Um," he grunted, drank, and put it down. I looked across the table at Bracken. He opened his eyes a little as if to say, "Well, now you know. Don't try that again!" Some twenty years later at a dinner party given by Churchill's host in Miami, Florida, I heard a guest tell him a story. It had a similar flat reception, though everyone else laughed. Then there was the episode at Eaton Hall, where he was a member of the Duke of Westminster's house-party for the Aintree Grand National Steeplechase. To entertain his guests "Bendor", as the Duke was known to his friends, had engaged an Italian conjurer who was also an adept pickpocket. One of his acts was relieving his victims of their possessions. Churchill went up and, wary, held on to his cigar case, to discover that the conjurer had somehow relieved him of his braces so that he had to hold up his trousers, and lost his wallet. He was furious with "Bendor" and threatened to leave the house. This deficiency in humour was the more singular because, as the world learned, he was a master of derisive humour in his speech, as in the famous "some chicken, some neck" retort to Pétain. And Washington had a story of how, during a visit to the White House, Roosevelt precipitously wheeled himself into the Prime Minister's bedroom and caught him emerging naked from his bathroom. Churchill checked Roosevelt's apology for this unceremonious intrusion. "Don't apologise, Franklin, don't apologise! The British Government has nothing to hide."

Recalling these examples of Churchill's sense of humour with some later experiences of him when he had grown into a growly but genial Old King Cole, who called for his brandy and his cigar, I was never able to define the springs of his mirth. My knowledge of him was intermittent. I learned from intimate friends of his that he had a delight in some humorous things, as witness his considerable knowledge of famous music-hall songs, but others said he possessed no sense of humour in anything that concerned him personally and was very quick to resent any witticism that seemed to infringe his personal dignity. Here again the evidence seems contradictory. During the Leicester campaign I never saw him lose his temper or good-humour in face of the most outrageous provocation.

It was during one of these after-meeting dinners that the incident of the watch-chain occurred.* Even in those days these chains were going out of fashion but Churchill clung to his. I remarked that we had both had the misfortune to lose our fathers when young, he at twenty, I at fifteen, and that, like him, I revered the memory of mine. "But you have been able to enshrine his memory by writing a

---

* See *The Growing Boy*. Ch. I.iv. Having observed the "dog-chain" Churchill was wearing, I remarked that my father had worn a similar watch-chain. He lifted up his, saying, "And this was worn by my father."

masterpiece about him," I said. This reference to his *Life* of his father pleased him. "It is a great grief for a boy to lose his mother, it is a tragedy for him to lose his father," he observed. And yet he had never received from his parents the warm affection that I had. I was about to ask him his opinion of Freud's theory of parental relationship. Chatter about the Œdipus complex, which Freud regarded as his greatest discovery, was very much in the air. During my recent visit to the U.S.A. I had found the Americans, always avid of a new cult, wallowing in psychoanalysis and rushing to lie prone on the psychiatrist's somewhat expensive couch, and there to release their *libido*. I suspected that Churchill's rejection of the Freudian thesis would be downright. Unfortunately, as I was about to put the question someone joined the table and the chance was lost.*

IV

I now had an opportunity, following my particular interest in public speaking, to hear and study Churchill's technique. I had only heard him once, when he came to Nottingham in 1906. He was then thirty-two, an Under-Secretary of State for the Colonies. But to me, aged fourteen, he was something more than the audacious youngest member of the Government. He was an author. I had devoured *The River War*. He had just had a resounding success with his *Lord Randolph Churchill*. Distantly, in a fog-filled hall, I saw him, boyish, chubby, then the Liberals' darling. I soon detected something a little wrong with his speech, and was startled to find that this aristocratic scion sometimes dropped his aitches (". . . and at 'ome . . ."). Years later I discovered that someone else had noted his speech defects. He had trouble with his 's's'. H. G. Wells had used this to caricature him in *Men Like Gods*. "There was some slight impediment in his speech, the little brother of a lisp, against which his voice beat gutturally. His first few sentences had an effect of being jerked out by unsteady efforts."

The packed audience had noticed nothing of this. The bold,

* Freud wrote in *The Interpretation of Dreams*: "It is the fate of all of us, perhaps, to direct our first sexual impulses towards our mother and our first hatred and our first murderous wish against our father."

174

bright boy, who had walked over from the Conservative camp into the Liberal, was too glamorous for finical appraisal. Within ten minutes he was in buoyant control of the audience. Now at Leicester, seventeen years later, I noticed how he had turned a defect into an asset. Like a steeplechase rider approaching the high fence, he "reined in" before going for it. He had become a master of "the pause", of making his audience wait expectantly, and then delivering the great cannonade of his prepared sentence. It was art, perhaps artfulness, disguised as hesitant simplicity. His printed speeches, alas, provide no evidence of that masterful timing. He also developed the art of repetition "And I would say . . . and I would say . . . as I have said on former occasions . . . and will continue to say on future ones . . ." Thus he kept his audience waiting to know what it was he had said, would now say, and would repeat in future. He also had at hand his endearing chuckle. It was not so much a chuckle as a sucking in of his breath in boyish delight. "Isn't that a good one!" he seemed to ask.

There was no opportunity in the Leicester campaign for an exhibition of the Churchillian technique at its best. There could be no set pieces in these stormy meetings where he was baited and interrupted outrageously. Even so, there were vehement passages that silenced the enemy and evoked applause.

One evening, during supper, Bracken came in late. A telegram had arrived from Asquith. "What has he to say?" asked Churchill, swallowing an oyster. Bracken read out a long telegram. It was a strong recommendation of the candidate to the electorate, wishing him success in a triumphant Liberal cause.

"H'm!" murmured Churchill, and swallowed another oyster. Then getting up and pacing the room, as he rubbed his wet fingers on a napkin, "Well, very nice of the old gentleman, but should we use it? He can't do us any good!" It was probably a true estimate. Bracken demurred. "Very well, use it," said Churchill, resuming his seat at the table.*

* It would be wrong to create the impression that Churchill had small regard for his old chief, Asquith, who, in 1908, creating the most progressive government England has ever known, gave the thirty-four-year-old Churchill his first seat in a Cabinet of all talents. But in 1923, Asquith, suffering discredit, and aged, had retired into the shadows. Churchill's position was

Two nights before election day there was a canvass of the probable poll. We were badly down. It was a time when Labour was riding the flood that would take them into office within a few months. The result of the canvass cannot have been a surprise to Churchill. He sat quiet while Bracken read out the figures, then pushed back his chair from the table. He had had a very hard evening and looked tired. He said nothing for a few minutes. Then he looked at us. "So—they don't want me. Very well! One day they will want me!" he said, almost truculently. He drew up his chair and resumed his dinner.

The air was charged with drama. What next? He was a man without a seat, without a party, and—perhaps Lloyd George apart, who was ageing—the most brilliant politician in the country. Would he retire to his study and go on with the next volume of *The World Crisis*? Clearly for him the times were out of joint, his future clouded. On the verge of fifty, reviled and rejected, he might well have decided that the pen offered more than the platform. He could become the comfortable squire of Chartwell Manor. When I hinted at this to Brendan Bracken his reply was forceful. "Not on your life! He'll always bounce back."

He lost West Leicester. Pethick Lawrence's majority was 4,398. When I came to say goodbye to Churchill I was sad, for him and for myself. It seemed the termination of my contact with one whom I deeply admired. In the course of this by-election I had seen him in different aspects, and close-up. The nearer view enlarged my veneration for the man who had fascinated me since boyhood. I was sad to think that it was unlikely that I should ever again have any association with him, however remote. I could not foresee at that moment of farewell how soon, and in what changed circumstances, I was to meet him again.

V

For me the second most interesting person in the by-election was Churchill's assistant, Brendan Bracken. It would not be an exaggeration to say that this red-headed youth, the general in command of the curious. He had enjoyed a long friendship with Lloyd George, who, after the Dardanelles tragedy, boldly recalled him to office. Lloyd George was the man who had demolished Asquith. Churchill was a realist.

campaign, stunned everybody. Nine years my junior, he gave a salutary shock to my self-esteem. An editor at twenty-eight of one of the oldest newspapers in the kingdom, the author of several books, a journalist and war correspondent who had been in the midst of great events and met a variety of famous people, who had been selected as a parliamentary candidate and had toured the United States as a celebrity, it would have been false modesty for me not to pride myself on having got somewhere after starting from nothing. I was not conceited. I had an innate fundamental humility. The Wordsworthian admonition was ever in my ear—"Getting and spending, we lay waste our powers; little we see in Nature that is ours." Sometimes rising from my desk in the quiet of the night-time I would go out into our little garden and look at the Universe above me, to read upon the heavens suffused with stars the awesome enigma of Creation. If there was any complacency in me the figure made by Brendan Bracken would have challenged it. For he was a dominant young man, dwarfed not even by Churchill, with whom he appeared to have considerable influence. He primed him, he arranged his day, he handled the Press, and the inevitable cohort that Churchill drew about him, variously useful or sycophantic. The professional election agent, supplied by headquarters, was reduced to a nonentity by this golliwog-giant of twenty-two. Nothing slipped in his hands.

Who on earth was he, where had he come from, how had he established himself so firmly with Churchill, never a man to suffer direction? There was something bizarre, something inexplicable about Bracken's early background. I was hardly any wiser about him after the election than before. I talked with a friend of mine, a young member of Parliament. He knew little more than the Press Gallery representative of the *Westminster Gazette*. "He's a mystery boy," he said. "No one seems certain where he comes from. He appears to have no relations. Some hint that he's Winston's illegitimate son, perhaps to explain the extraordinary hold he has over him. That's sheer nonsense, of course. A Dublin friend of mine says he's the son of an Irish monumental stonemason, and that as a boy he emigrated to Australia. Bracken says he went to school in Sydney, but he has no Australian accent. The story is he returned to England with a small fortune at seventeen. How do you make a fortune at seventeen?

I don't know how he found Churchill or Churchill found him."

Bracken was colossally self-assured. I soon lost my touch of jealousy towards a younger rival and came to admire him. He fitted no known category, either by birth or education. His speech was classless, his manner, without polish, was compelling but agreeable. He was full of humour, a ready conversationalist and he always proved to know more than one expected. After the campaign we parted on cordial terms and he was ever quick to render me a service when I went to him. In my first essay in autobiography, *Half Way*, published in 1931, eight years after our first meeting, describing the West Leicester election, I ventured on a prophecy concerning him:

"This is not the last of him. If ever Churchill embarks upon a dictatorship, following the abject incompetency of the House of Commons as a governing instrument, I shall look for Bracken among the Dictator's aides-de-camp."

The years of Churchill's supremacy during the Second World War did not belie that prophecy. Bracken was successively his Parliamentary Private Secretary, Minister of Information and First Lord of the Admiralty.

We can follow the astonishing story to the end, crowned with success. *The Times* published a four-column obituary. It did nothing to clear the mystery surrounding his early years. It described him as "ebullient, full-blooded, energetic, highly intelligent. Success was written all over him." But *The Times* complimentary obituary was written by someone ignorant of the true facts, or kindly in suppression of them. They are indeed hard to come by, for Bracken was a "romancer", and ordered all his papers to be destroyed at his death. The true story of his life is probably even more amazing than the legend he created about himself. He was born in very modest circumstances, the son of a monumental stonemason in Tullamore, Co. Offaly. The dynamic of his life came largely from the remarriage of his mother to a Tipperary builder. He seems to have resented her marriage. He ran away from a Jesuit college when fourteen. Rebellious, he wished to emigrate, as do so many poor Irish boys who dream of making a fortune abroad. Undoubtedly his mother was glad to ship her son to Australia. He carried with him a letter to a priest, a family connection in a small town there.

He worked for a short time on a sheep farm. Not liking this he moved to Sydney where he found work as a teacher, although he had no qualifications and little education, but he had quick wits and was a voracious reader. He also did some journalism for a diocesan Catholic paper. At this time he was a devout Catholic with a great admiration for Cardinal Newman. When the First World War ended Bracken sailed for England. He was nineteen. Armed with a cheque book he proceeded to enter himself at Sedbergh School, lying about his age. His finances were mysterious. A boy in Sydney seemed unlikely to have made a "pile" after only four years in Australia. He romanced later about a non-existent uncle there who had left him a chain of shops. After two terms at Sedbergh he became a master at Liverpool Collegiate School. He astonished his colleagues by holding forth in the masters' common-room on every subject. After a short time there he became games master at a Bishops Stortford school. He retained his affection for Sedbergh and later became Chairman of its Board of Governors, built it a fine library and left his books to it.

Bracken had arrived from Australia with one great asset, a letter of introduction to Sir Sydney Colvin, Keeper of Prints and Drawings at the British Museum, who opened all doors for him, taken by his sharp mind and vivid personality. He met the powerful J. L. Garvin, editor of the *Observer* and Oliver Locker Lampson, owner of the *Empire Review*. They introduced him to Churchill, who was about to contest West Leicester. Bracken offered to work for him and thus he appeared in my office in October, 1923, aged twenty-two. He soon found backing to start an illustrated weekly, *English Life*, together with Robert Lutyens, son of the famous architect. He had also established himself with Messrs Eyre and Spottiswoode, the printers of the Authorised Version of the Bible and the Prayer Book. He revealed an interest in finance as well as politics, and had the assistance of an experienced financier, Sir Henry Strakosch, chairman of *The Economist*, whom he eventually succeeded in that position.

In 1926 the owner of the *Financial News* discussed with me the possibility of adding a general news section to this journal, proposing that I should edit it. I was not happy about this idea, moreover I had no wish to re-enter journalism from which I had now retired, having launched myself as a novelist. I called on Bracken to consult him. He gave me a warm welcome and a downright opinion. "Leave it alone!" he said. I left it alone. In 1928 he formed a holding company, Financial Newspaper Proprietors, which took over the *Financial News*. I wondered whether I had unconsciously given him a tip! His company also acquired the *Investors' Chronicle*, a half-share of *The Economist*, and the controlling interest of the *Liverpool Journal of Commerce*. Within two years of the acquisition of the *Financial News* it declared a dividend of 115 per cent!

Bracken marched on. His association with Eyre and Spottiswoode grew. He became a director of that company. During the fanatical battle over the revision of the Prayer Book, he was asked his opinion. "What do I think of the Prayer Book? My dear sir, we print it!" he replied. He was now a most faithful supporter of Churchill who in turn advanced his assistant. In 1929 he entered the House of Commons. He soon impressed the critical Press Gallery with his aplomb. Members found him truculent and formidable in debate. As the country under Baldwin and Chamberlain drifted into the Second World War, scornful of Churchill's warnings, Bracken, twenty-seven years younger, never wavered in support of his derided chief.

A Liverpool interest demonstrated his adventurous nature and his readiness to serve a friend. In 1927 he heard of a revived proposal to build a Roman Catholic cathedral in Liverpool. He wrote to Professor Reilly, holder of the Chair of Architecture in Liverpool University, stating that, if Sir Edwin Lutyens was made architect, he would contribute a large sum to the building fund. Lutyens was appointed in 1928. He created a grandiose plan, costing some millions, that was never carried out. His death, the Second World War, and rising costs, required a much curtailed plan. The cathedral, from another architect's design, was finally completed in 1967. This was only one case in which Bracken played the role of an *éminence grise*.

His financial interests widened. To his chairmanships and director-ships he added the chairmanship of the powerful Union Corporation of South Africa, one of Strakosch's promotions. Vivid, forceful, tireless, by the age of forty-five he was an influential figure. It was no surprise when Churchill went to the Admiralty as First Lord on the outbreak of war, returning to the post he had held on the outbreak of the First World War, that he took the faithful Bracken with him. When Churchill became Prime Minister in 1940 he made Bracken his Private Parliamentary Secretary. He was also appointed a Privy Councillor, and in the summer of 1941 he became Minister of Information. His was a difficult post but he succeeded in maintaining excellent relations with the Press. Once again I was in association with him, engaged in propaganda in U.S.A. He held this appointment to the end of the war, when he became, briefly, First Lord of the Admiralty, still under Churchill. In 1952 he was created a Viscount and three years later a Trustee of the National Gallery. But his glorious day was ending. He learned that he was stricken with cancer and retired from the public scene to await the end.

He had established himself in a beautiful house in North Street, Westminster, where, always a booklover, he had collected a choice library. A bachelor, a vivid conversationalist, widely read, a stealthy benefactor, a lover of a good cigar and a glass of wine, he liked to play the host, but he kept members of his family at arms' length, a breach deepened by the fact that he had become a renegade Catholic, and was evasive about his origin. A brief entry which he had contributed to Debrett's *Peerage* recorded no ancestry, no relations, no collaterals, no heir. At the end he was attended devotedly by his friend, Sir Patrick Hennessy. A remarkable volume of tributes was published when he died, painfully and prematurely, in 1958, aged fifty-seven.

VI

Some two months after I had said goodbye to Winston Churchill and Brendan Bracken at West Leicester a pleasant footnote was added to the brief story of the election campaign there. It ran:

> 2 Sussex Gardens, W.4.
> Jan. 3rd, 1924.

Dear Mr. Cecil Roberts,
    I have not until now found an opportunity to thank you for the energetic and cordial support which you gave me during the

recent election. We had every disadvantage to contend with: no local press; no organisation; universally interrupted meetings. In these circumstances the special efforts of the *Nottingham Journal* were invaluable, but I have to thank you in addition for your own personal assistance and encouragement, of which I am most sensible.

Yours very truly,
Winston S. Churchill.

CHAPTER NINE

A Singular Letter

I

ONE DAY IN 1921, during the Nottingham Assizes, I went into Court with one of my reporters to listen to a case in which I was interested. A tall, lean young barrister was addressing the jury on behalf of the defendant. His manner was smooth and he exuded goodwill but most notable of all was his mellifluous voice. If it had been a 'cello the great Pablo Casals could not have played it more ravishingly. I tried not to be seduced by this persuasive advocate. Resisting, I became aware of another quality he possessed. He supported his argument with a most adroit marshalling of his points. There seemed no flaw in his smooth logic. I was not at all surprised when the jury returned within twenty minutes to announce a verdict of Not Guilty. I decided that if ever I found myself in the dock on a serious charge this was the counsel I would seek to defend me.

A student of public speaking, I was so fascinated by this adept barrister that, learning he would be appearing in another case on the morrow, I returned. His advocacy was just as beguiling. His voice had a caressing quality, so persuasive that it moved one to effortless acquiescence. When the Court rose I asked a solicitor I knew to introduce me. Thus I came to meet Norman Birkett.* On that day we began a rare friendship which lasted until his death forty years later.

At the time of our meeting he was verging on forty, fair, sandy-haired. As an undergraduate he had been a President of the Cambridge

* Lord Birkett (1883–1962), M.P., 1923–24, 1929–31; K.C., 1924; High Court Judge and Knight, 1941; Judge, Nuremberg Tribunal, 1945–6; P.C. 1947; Lord Justice of Appeal 1950–57; Baron, 1958.

Union. He was a contemporary of Rupert Brooke, with whom he had appeared in the *Granta*, his article on one page, Brooke's poem overleaf. He told me that in an open contest for a prize given by the University for the reading of a passage of English verse or prose, "Brooke walked in from Grantchester, the mud on his boots, stood up in turn, and swept us all away."*

Birkett's father kept a draper's store at Ulverston, Lancashire, on the edge of the Lake District. He was a devout Wesleyan Methodist and had made a sacrifice to send his son to Cambridge, thereby relinquishing all hope that he would enter the family business. Instead he was to have an education that would equip him more fully for entering the Wesleyan Methodist ministry. Young Birkett had already proved himself to be a fluent local preacher. The father's pious hopes were shattered. At Cambridge, in a wider world, Birkett found he had no "call" for the Ministry. His thoughts began to turn to the Bar. There was a somewhat harrowing discussion with his father who, deeply disappointed, accepted gracefully his son's change of view. Soon he had every reason to be proud of him. When ex-President Theodore Roosevelt visited Cambridge to receive an honorary degree it fell to young Birkett to propose the election of the distinguished guest to an honorary membership of the Union. It was a good beginning for a future President of the Union who, one day, would be President of The Pilgrims, the Anglo-American Society.

So instead of going into the pulpit Norman Birkett set his course for the Courts of Justice. On leaving Cambridge he formed a connection with the Cadburys of Bournville, taking a secretarial post. Subsequently he went to the Birmingham Bar and on the Midland Circuit. This was in 1913. He soon attracted notice, but it was at the Nottingham Assizes in 1918 that he first gained publicity. An Army captain was charged with abducting a girl under fifteen, whom Birkett described as "fast, forward, frivolous, romantic, adventurous, a confessed liar, and lured by khaki". The judge summed up heavily

* Christopher Hassall in his *Rupert Brooke* has a slightly different version. "Throughout May (1909) as the time of Tripos drew near, Brooke was more than ever beset with distractions. One of them was the Winchester Reading Prize, a competition held in the Senate House. Brooke entered it, reading aloud Keats's *Ode to a Nightingale,* but could not prevail against the sonorities of Dalton declaiming Milton."

against the captain. Birkett's appeal to the jury resulted in his acquittal. There was an outburst of cheering in Court when the jury's verdict was given. The judge expressed a sense of outrage but Birkett had won the day.

In the General Election that year he ran for Parliament as a Liberal in the Birmingham area, and emerged bottom of the poll. In 1920 he made two momentous decisions. He married a young lady on the Bournville staff and "lived happily ever after" as the fairy tales run. He moved to London, going into chambers in Temple Court. He took a great risk and it paid.

II

In the autumn of 1923, when Parliament had reassembled, Baldwin, the Conservative Prime Minister, became increasingly unhappy about Britain's Free Trade policy. He was bound by an undertaking given by his predecessor not to change the fiscal policy and introduce Protection during the life of that Parliament. Baldwin therefore, wishing to raise the Protectionist flag, decided to dissolve Parliament and go to the country. Thus in the middle of November a General Election was announced. The Liberals of East Nottingham were caught unprepared.

Early that summer I had been asked whether I would stand for my former constituency. After the previous year's breakdown, I was aware that I had neither the stamina nor the taste for a political career. I declined the proposal to become again a candidate in any future contest. The local Liberal Committee had delayed finding my successor and thus on the eve of a General Election it was without a candidate. I suggested that Norman Birkett should be invited to stand. Owing to his appearances at the Nottingham Assizes he was not unknown in the constituency. He was approached and there was a last-hour adoption. Polling day was December 6th. We had barely recovered from the West Leicester campaign when we found ourselves plunged into the East Nottingham contest. With such a candidate as Birkett I was convinced we could unseat the Conservative member, a local mining engineer who had a majority of over 4,000 votes. With only a fortnight in hand Birkett moved in with his charming young wife. The *Nottingham Journal* was at hand to reinforce the campaign.

Birkett's fluency and personality at once began to make an impression. At 11 p.m., on December 6th when the votes had been counted, he was M.P. for East Nottingham with a majority of 1,436.

It was characteristic of his generosity of spirit, on thanking me for my help, for him to say: "You know, in a way I regard this as your seat, you'd done all the spade-work, and when you want it, I'll stand down." But I was out of that field for ever.

III

After the excitement of the elections I closed the year of 1923 by sitting down to my desk and doing something for my own private career. On Christmas Day I began my third novel, *The Love Rack*, which occupied me until the end of May, 1924.

Meanwhile the *Westminster Gazette* serialised *Sails of Sunset*, which was published at the end of its run both in England and the U.S.A. For the serial rights I received £500, and for second serial rights £300. It passed through three editions in a year.

I had been somewhat nervous about this second venture. A first novel is usually easy to write. It draws on autobiographical material, but a second novel is a test of invention and imagination. Moreover, I was apprehensive of a critical backlash. First novels are generally hailed as "promising". "We look forward to even better work", say the critics. My fears were allayed. It was well received.

Financially considered the result was gratifying. In its first year the novel brought me in from various sources, including four translations, a net, after commissions and income tax, of £1,500. This sum went straight into what I called my Author's Independence Fund. In the next forty years *Sails of Sunset* sailed through sixteen reprints.

My third venture *The Love Rack*, written in five months, so smoothly did it run, I held back. I wanted to look at it detachedly after a time. A third novel is the real critical test. The first writes itself, the second derives some momentum from its predecessor.

Once over, twice over, the third hurdle tests staying power. "If you can go over with the third then most likely you're a born novelist and will stay in the field," said Philip Gibbs when I mentioned my fears. He had just taken his highest hurdle with the phenomenal success of *The Middle of the Road*. After my third effort had been in storage for three months I looked at it again, re-wrote some passages and sent it to the typist. When towards the end of 1924 I sent the novel to my agent he informed me soon afterwards that the *Daily Express* had bought the serial rights for the following spring.

I had received from my American lecture agent repeated invitations to make another tour. On sounding my chief, Sir Charles, always accommodating, he agreed for me to take leave and make a tour in the last three months of the year. This time I was to be sent into the deep South, through the Cotton Belt and well over the Mason-Dixon Line, down to New Orleans.*

IV

In that year, 1924, I made frequent weekend trips to London, keeping in touch with my friends there. I looked critically at Sir Charles's new venture, the *Westminster Gazette*. It appeared to me to be a doubtful enterprise. Its circulation was not rising rapidly enough, but hope was still strong. The years of the Twenties were full of excitement and of a sense of adventure, but the political scene was troubled. After the Tory dismissal of Lloyd George, the man who had saved England, the entrenched mediocrities assumed power. Bonar Law, Baldwin and Ramsay MacDonald—"The Boneless Wonder" Churchill called him—gyrated in and out of office. The

---

* The Mason-Dixon Line is, today, a loosely used term to denote an imaginary division between the northern and southern States. The actual Line was created by two English surveyors, Mason and Dixon, 1763–8, to settle a bitter dispute between the English Colonists over the territorial claims between the Penns, proprietors of Pennsylvania, and the Baltimores, proprietors of Maryland. The Line agreed on was marked by milestones brought from England. But in 1768 the Line ran only 233 miles westward, from the Atlantic Coast to the Potomac, the hinterland being sparsely occupied.

Great War won, we were too exuberant to heed the storm-clouds gathering. For the young this was a bright new world. Some of the old cramping conventions had been shattered. There were dazzling figures on the scene. It was the era of the new automobile, of aircraft, of the cinema and radio. Charlie Chaplin dominated the silent films with *The Kid* and, later, *The Gold Rush*. A strange little contraption appeared on sale. It consisted of a mounted "whisker" with which you tickled a crystal. This detector picked up invisible waves in the atmosphere. The tiny instrument had headphones attached. Suddenly the outside world was inside the house. Few realised the immensity of this invention; a potent force, the radio, would change our civilisation. As its vogue spread the newspapers grew nervous about their monopoly of news. In 1923 they boycotted the B.B.C. programmes. I printed them. I did not have any such fears. Newspapers would be consulted for radio programmes. In 1924 I made a broadcast and received a letter from the Managing Director of the British Broadcasting Company. It carried a double compliment. He wished to tell me he had enjoyed my "Talk" and also to say that he and his wife had just read *Sails of Sunset* with much pleasure. The letter was signed J. C. W. Reith. It was my first sight of the name of the Napoleon who would later build up the British Broadcasting Corporation into a great national institution.

It was a decade of many surprises. Tutankhamen's tomb had been discovered, crammed with incredible treasures. Mussolini had marched on Rome. It was the age of freedom and the barriers of convention were down. We were free to travel, as once Shelley, Byron, Browning, Ruskin and connoisseurs of art and architecture had been free to travel through France, Italy, Germany, Austria, and anywhere that fancy took them. There were no currency controls choking the spread of culture. The Twenties as I experienced them were full of gaiety, adventure, surprises and achievements. More and more I longed to be living in London. The Russian Ballet had returned, with new triumphs, but Massine had gone. Its brightest star Nijinsky, peremptorily dismissed by Diaghilev, had begun that sad journey into the shadows. One day he appeared naked in the vestibule of his hotel, another day he threw his dinner out of the window. He was nursed devotedly by his wife through a long twilight but all hopes proved vain and at last the flame of his spirit was extinguished. But the legend of him has lived on. His was still a vivid presence when, forty years later, I dined in Rome with his widow, Romola Nijinsky and his sister, Bronislava Nijinsky; his spirit dominated our conversation.

V

In those early Twenties I was frequently the guest of a delightful couple, Beresford Chancellor and his wife. I had met him in 1919 when we both worked with the Civil Liabilities Commission. A scholar, he was a distinguished authority on the history and topography of eighteenth- and nineteenth-century London, with a dozen excellent books to his credit. He possessed adequate private means, and so could be painstaking in his researches. I had first been the Chancellors' guest at a delightful country house they owned at Wargrave-on-Thames. Later they moved to Onslow Gardens, living in one of those tall, porticoed houses whose fronts and backs look on the lawns and trees of the enclosed gardens which are such a pleasant feature of Victorian South Kensington.

In the Second World War many of these houses were taken over for housing East End refugees from the bombings. They were soon reduced to a slummy state and never quite recovered their former prosperous elegance. When eventually they were evacuated and redecorated the earlier owners could not afford to live in them. There were no servants to service them and a great number of these houses were divided into flats or tiers of bedsitting-rooms, with an itinerant and bohemian population. In the Twenties, when I was a guest of the Chancellors, these houses were generally staffed by a butler, a couple of maids and a cook. The Chancellors' house was run by two parlourmaids, old retainers, well trained, a cook and scullery maid. Occasionally there was a hired butler for parties. Only Beresford and his wife and son lived in this large house. Their elder son Richard, who had played in the Harrow Eleven at the Eton and Harrow match at Lord's, had been killed in the war. Mrs. Chancellor was like a bit of Dresden china, very frail, lovely and always beautifully dressed. She had a faint, high-pitched voice, and almost fluted when she spoke. They were a most devoted couple and perfect hosts. They travelled a great deal, intelligently. I always felt fortunate in having such a delightful couple for friends.

One evening at a dinner party at their house one of the guests asked: "Do you get a lot of 'fan' mail? Do you answer them? I'd love to read one!" she exclaimed. "He's an offer of marriage by every post!" said Beresford, mischievously.

"As you've asked the question, my answer is, I do, and I'm vain enough to be pleased by the fact," I replied, laughing. "I answer them all. Since they take the trouble to write to me the least I can do is to thank them. Most of the letters are very pleasant, a few are rather silly, and occasionally there's a conundrum. I've one in my pocket now—it's a month old and I've not answered it yet."

"With that build up, you artful old fellow, you've just got to read us that letter! We're all agog," said Beresford. I promised to read it during coffee in the drawing-room. I had not replied to the letter because it seemed as mysterious as it was stupid. What kind of a compliment could I derive from someone who had not even troubled to get my name right? And it contained an odd proposition that I had no interest in investigating. The letter was written on a sheet of notepaper that had been obtained from an American banking agency in Pall Mall. The writing was bold and hasty. Upstairs in the drawing-room I read it.

> Dear Mr. Robert Cecil or Cecil Roberts,
>   Some friends have spoken to me about your courage and cleverness, so I am taking the great liberty of writing to you to ask if you won't come and talk to me as soon as possible about collaborating with me upon a work which I've planned, and which can only be done by someone who has thought deeply and worked hard and has courage. Being an American myself, and hearing that you have more courage than any man that I've encountered in London, I take the bold step of asking you to consider it with me. I don't mention the names of the mutual acquaintances, for I don't wish them to feel in any way implicated or responsible for me. Hoping you will come to London soon. Please don't mention this to anyone.

The name at the foot of the letter I found indecipherable. America, being a "melting pot", is a land of some curious names to English ears. The heading of the notepaper had been crossed out and the address of a house in Ennismore Gardens had been substituted, with a telephone number. I had decided that the letter was from a crank.

When I read the letter everyone wanted to see it. "That's a woman's writing!" declared Mrs. Chancellor. "A beautiful young woman with a romantic mind and very annoyed at your churlishness in not answering!"

"Now, my boy, you go to the telephone and call up that number, and find out who's living there. That's the first step. We've got to solve this mystery," cried Beresford. "Come along!"

We went down from the drawing-room to the telephone. I called the number. A man's voice answered. I said I wished to know who lived in the house.

"This is the house of Colonel M—," said a voice, obviously a butler's.

"May I ask if you have an American gentleman or lady staying with you? Someone has written to me from your house and I cannot make out the name."

"We have an American lady staying here, sir, Miss Lange."

"Is she in, may I speak to her?" I gave my name.

"A moment, sir, I will ask her to come."

I told Beresford, agog at my elbow, that the letter-writer was an American—a Miss Lange. Presently an excited voice came over the telephone. I was involved in a conversation and finally I promised to call on her the next day at five. My hosts were jubilant. Of course it was the beginning of a romance. I replied that I feared a white-haired spinster of sixty with a moral-propagating play or a new religion incubated in San Francisco.

At five o'clock the next day, calling at Ennismore Gardens, I was ushered by a butler into a small library. While I waited I surveyed its contents. Magazines on the table spoke of travel and wide interests. I was looking at one of these magazines when I heard a step and turned. Into the room, holding out her hand came a very beautiful young woman of about twenty-four. She was very slim, with a high complexion and blue eyes of great clarity. Her fair hair had a flush of gold, her mouth was exquisitely shaped. Tallish, she was a sylph who might have stepped out of a rout of Aphrodite's maidens.

Mercifully her voice had not a transatlantic twang. It was low and mellow. I was overwhelmed by an enchanting vision as she held out her hand and greeted me. Her first words were an embarrassed apology. She feared her letter must have seemed very strange and bold. It had been written on an impulse.

I apologised for my delay in replying. We sat down and she began to talk about a play she was writing. It sounded nonsense to me, on a theme of divorce! But I promised to read it. I said that frankly I was incapable of collaborating with anyone. When could we meet again, to discuss it, she asked. I explained that I had to return to Nottingham on the morrow to edit my paper. And then, reluctant to think I should not see her again, I made a suggestion. Next week I was coming to London to attend the Private View of the Royal Academy Summer Exhibition. Would she like to go to it? She clapped her hands in ecstasy. "But how wonderful!" she cried. And so it was arranged.

When I told the Chancellors that the writer of the mysterious letter was quite the most beautiful girl in London, they were incredulous. "We'll believe she isn't a wizened old frump when we see her!" declared Beresford. I asked if they were attending the Academy Private View. They were. "Then you'll see her. I'm taking her to it," I said, triumphantly. "And she'll steal the show!"

That is precisely what she did. In 1922 the sensation of the year was the discovery of the tomb of Tutankhamen by Lord Carnarvon and Howard Carter. In due time the splendours of the Pharaoh's tomb appeared in the illustrated papers. They created a vogue. When on the appointed day in May, 1924, I called at Ennismore Gardens to collect my companion I was overwhelmed by the spectacle she made. She was dressed à la Tutankhamen's girl-wife; on her brow a gold filigree emblem of the winged Horus. The sheen of her green lamé dress, tightly swathing the slimmest of figures, had the iridescence of an Egyptian beetle. Her fair hair had been tightly pulled up to emphasise the proud loveliness of her poised head and superb neck. I was a little frightened by her almost outrageous beauty. She laughed merrily as I surveyed her. "Do you approve?" she asked. It was a quite superfluous question. When we went up the steps at Burlington House all the Press cameras clicked. They never ceased clicking. As we walked through the rooms there was a silence of astonishment in our wake. I encountered the Beresford Chancellors and I introduced her. They were overwhelmed. She was as vivacious in conversation as she was beautiful. Someone came up we both knew. It was Sir Harold Bowden, from Nottingham, the handsome magnate of Raleigh Cycle fame. Later I asked her, "Was that how you heard of a 'Mr. Robert Cecil or Cecil Roberts, a man of courage and cleverness'?" "Yes, I was staying with them and they talked about you," she replied. When I took her home she asked me if she had looked all right. It had been the happiest day of her life. "Almost, but there's one thing missing, my lovely child. You should have carried a label since you aren't in the catalogue. 'Exhibit No. 1. Miss Myra Lange'," I said. The remark brought me my first kiss.

And so it began, an ecstatic, tantalising, baffling *Embarquement pour Cythère*. I saw her again and again. She became the lodestar of my London. Alas, my editorial duties entailed much absence. At weekends we went to art exhibitions, concerts, theatres. We sauntered in Green Park. One Sunday morning I took her to the Chapel Royal in St. James's Palace. I felt it would interest an American. It had formed part of Henry VIII's palace, with a ceiling attributed to Holbein. Here Charles I had received Holy Communion on the morning of his execution in 1649. Queen Victoria had been married here in 1840 and also King George V, when Duke of York, in 1893.

Myra drew all eyes, and still more attention when she dropped a prayer book with a resounding bang. The rose-leaf loveliness of her colouring when she blushed with embarrassment as I retrieved it! So May passed, and June, and the cones of the chestnut trees wasted away in the warmth of summer days. Little by little I learned more about her. She had been travelling in Europe with her widowed mother; Paris, Rome, Baden-Baden, Stockholm. She was of Scandinavian stock, which accounted for her translucent fairness, but born in America. Her mother had gone home to Washington and she had remained behind to promote her mission. What mission? She wanted to be useful, to help humanity. Her play, for instance, was written to alter the cruel divorce laws. The play in which I was to collaborate. I killed that idea. The play was impossible. I teased her. "My dear girl, you're goofy!" I said. She laughed merrily. "I know you don't believe in me, but you'll see!"

She had boundless good nature. I learned of one of her excursions in "usefulness". She had joined a "social uplift" society working in the East End of London. Not wishing to appear fashionably dressed, she put on an attire that she thought would be in keeping with her mission. But she overdid it. "People jeered and the children swarmed after me and said dreadful things!" she told me, her eyes dancing with laughter. "I was a guy!"

I was soon aware of her many admirers, suitors far better equipped than I was. She dealt with them peremptorily, indifferent to their titles, their money, their cars. They were plainly disgusted that I should have preference. With a few she held court, among them, usually older, Sir Harold Bowden, the Duke of Sutherland (Geordie), Sir Thomas Lipton ("Tommy"). They plied her with boxes of choco- lates and mountains of bouquets. She had a special liking for Sir Thomas Lipton, an "old darling", a bachelor, old enough to be her grandfather! He merited the description. England's greatest grocer and tea dealer, who had risen from a Liverpool errand boy to be a millionaire yachtsman and the friend of King Edward, was avuncular and courteous. Myra took me to lunch with him at his large suburban house. Some twenty guests were waited on by coolies from Ceylon, dressed in white, with dark brown faces, lacquered black hair and bare brown feet. Sir Thomas was a perfect host.

It would seem that Myra had ample means, I never sought to find out how ample. She dressed well but was simple in her tastes. She was considerate to my pocket. I discovered that she was a paying guest at Ennismore Gardens. Quick, intelligent, in some things she was ingenuous. She believed in the goodwill of everyone. She refused to acknowledge the existence of sickness and evil, character- istic of a Christian Scientist, without being one. My friends were captivated by her beauty and an eagerness for life that was almost childish. But a few of them, while liking her, thought she was too much of a bird of paradise for the needs of the common day. She made no secret of the fact that she was in love with me, and I recipro- cated. I had the first call upon her. She refused everything that inter- fered with our companionship.

I was aware of insurmountable obstacles to marriage. I had not the means to support her in the style she merited. My sense of independence never tolerated a thought of marrying for money, or subjecting myself to its dominance. It was impossible to imagine her content with provincial life. There was another thing that deterred me. I was conscious of an indefinable sense of mystery about her although outwardly she had the simplest and frankest of natures. I knew nothing of her background.

The weeks ran on, our idyll unbroken. She was lovely in a hundred ways, and always of the most equable temper. Some of my friends began to be critical of me for hesitating. "Here's one of the loveliest girls on earth in love with you, and you do nothing!" They had, of course, no knowledge of the problem that marriage entailed. There would always be a court of admirers in her wake. There would be no quiet, essential to an author's life. I began to discern something else. There was an instability in her nature. Ingenuous, she was caught up in sudden enthusiasm for odd causes. There had been the slumming phase. She now astonished me by saying that while I was lecturing in the United States she would spend the time in Geneva. Why Geneva? She was joining a group that was working with the League of Nations to procure the emancipation of Turkish women. They must change the outrageous Moslem marriage laws. Turkish women must have the rights of civil marriage. "We're going to organise a Turkish Women's Freedom League and hold a protest meeting in Carnegie Hall, New York. You men must be made to do something about it!" I stared at her in amazement. "My dear girl, why bother yourself about Turkish women? What about Indian women, Egyptian women, Chinese women?" I asked.

"You men are reactionary. The outrageous divorce laws must be changed. Darling, you must see it, you must help!" she cried.

Our arguments never got anywhere. She was always good-humoured but obstinately earnest. First her enthusiasm had been for collaborating with me on a play about divorce, then for charity work in the East End, now it was Turkish women's liberation. I wondered what next. When I told a much-travelled friend about this he said, "My dear fellow, America's full of purposeful rich women, do-gooders, looking for a cause. If it isn't Turkish women in the harem it will be stopping foot-binding in China. Their energy's terrific, and they ruthlessly divorce their unco-operative husbands." When I relayed this to Myra she rippled with laughter.

She would be back in London when I returned in the New Year. On our last night together we went to see a play at the Criterion Theatre that had had a sensational first night. It was *Fata Morgana* by a Hungarian dramatist. It was SEX in capital letters rearing its head again, very deftly and romantically. London was having its fill of this. Tallulah Bankhead was weaving her spell, husky-voiced, with an exotic hot-house allure. *Fata Morgana* gave us the male counterpart with the slim, tawny-haired Tom Douglas, an American, in the leading role.

The curtain rose on a youth doing his homework, seated at a lamplit table in a Hungarian farmhouse. The family had gone off to a dance. There was an eerie stillness broken only by the barking of a dog. A knock on the door. He goes to open it, and temptation walks in, in the form of his uncle's young wife. Some muddle of telegrams had brought her too late for the dance. We now see the protagonists. He is disarmingly young, the bloom of innocence and adolescence about him, a lock of fair hair falling over his brow. He wears a loose white shirt, open to the navel, tucked into skin-tight cream breeches that end in shining top boots. He sports a bright sash. At the moment it escapes attention that this is no attire for the student son of a farmer. He is dressed more for the role of Duke Albrecht in the *Giselle* ballet. His aunt (Jeanne de Casalis), pretty, sophisticated, is ready for adventure. The boy, scared, enchanted, is ripe for seduction. The drama proceeds in the hot, still night of the farmhouse. When on a following evening the final curtain falls, the student is back at the lamplit table, the light-hearted aunt has departed for Budapest with her lumpy husband. For her an incident is closed. For the boy at the table ecstasy has taken wing. He monotonously repeats the text he tries to learn. Then slowly under the burden of emotion the flaxen head, with its rebellious lock, sinks into his arms on the table while he is shaken with sobs. The acting of Tom Douglas was flawless. He held the audience entranced. All London talked of him. The play ran to packed houses for a year.

Myra and I came out into Piccadilly Circus very emotional, like everybody else. I took her home in a taxi, and our parting was somewhat desperate. She would write from Geneva, I from the United States.

CHAPTER TEN

Texas via Quebec

I

IN 1924 THERE was a British Empire Exhibition in London.* It would be a melancholy experience visiting it now and seeing how much of that Empire has vanished in a quarter of a century. The Canadian section was exceedingly impressive. It displayed the vastness, the uncountable resources of the North American continent. It gave much publicity to its scenic richness. There was a particularly beautiful panorama of the Gulf of St. Lawrence and the great river with Quebec and Montreal situated on it. When I came to plan my second lecture tour of the United States for the autumn of 1924 I decided to select a new route of entry. So on October 2nd I sailed on the *Carmania*, again from Liverpool, but this time for Quebec. From there I would go on to Montreal, then, via Lakes Champlain and St. George, to Albany, the capital of New York State, and thence by boat down the River Hudson to New York. I had been told that the autumn tints of the forests were sheer gold in the wonderland of a North American Indian summer.

It happened that as I boarded the *Carmania* my departure was not to go unnoticed. I had been connected with journalism in Liverpool. The Press cameras flashed but I was a lesser diversion on that October afternoon. At the dockside a motor-bus had disgorged some shawl-clad girls who seemed in a state of excitement. Could it be an emigration of Lancashire mill-girls? There emerged with them two young

* It was at the state opening of this Exhibition in April, 1924, that Elgar's *Land of Hope and Glory* was performed. He conducted the massed choirs and bands before an audience of 10,000. Elgar, having composed what he thought was suitable as a national song, invited A. C. Benson to write some words for it, which he did instantly, thus collaborating in what has become almost a national anthem.

men. They would have been notable anywhere, and they seemed the object of noisy enthusiasm from their feminine escort. They were very young, of medium height, and singularly dressed. They wore black billycock hats, mackintoshes with bright plaid linings, grey cloth-top boots, and yellow chamois gloves. They carried knobbly cane walking sticks. From the deck I watched this singular pair ascend the gangway to the noisy acclamation of the mill girls. Who could they be, and why this excited escort on the dockside? Film stars? Somehow they did not fit this category.

I went below to attend to my baggage. When I came up to watch the liner being warped out I saw them again, waving to the girls on the quay, whose farewell grew more and more vociferous until we had slipped out of hearing. I did not see my singular fellow passengers again that evening but the next morning they were on the promenade deck. One of them carried a large reflex camera. I saw they were about twenty or so, vivacious in manner. Presently we became acquainted. They were French, en route to Quebec and Montreal, then south to Texas. We exchanged names. They were a pair of French aristocrats. One of them had a resounding name, Count Armand de La Rochefoucauld. He was just twenty-one. His friend, the Viscount François de Deservillers, was a little older. You could not have had anything more French in name. They both spoke a fair English. They invited me down to their stateroom. The baggage and apparatus that overflowed into every corner suggested that they were embarking on a big game shooting expedition. It was news to me that there was any big game in Texas. Perhaps, since there were Red Indians in Texas, there were bison? "Oh no, not game—cotton!" said Armand, grinning. "I have inherited a cotton ranch. I go to see it!"

Little by little an astonishing story emerged. One of Armand's relations had died leaving him a cotton plantation in Texas. In order that he might have some knowledge concerning his inheritance he had worked for a month in a Lancashire cotton mill, where he had been joined by his friend François. The presence of two good-looking young French aristocrats had caused not a little commotion among the mill girls, with whom they had not been lacking in gallantry. Hence the motorbus excursion to Liverpool to celebrate their departure.

Within two days we were firm friends. I was the veteran of the party, not only because I was ten years their senior but also because I had already visited America. Needless to say, we caused much speculation among the other passengers. Armand had at once been taken for a young actor, possibly of the Comédie Française, en route to Hollywood, and the tall Englishman was probably his agent. Armand's checks, François' Fair Isle pullover and my astrakhan collar made us a bizarre trio. The second day out something arising out of our singularity came to my ears. I rushed to the boys' state-room and announced the news. "They are calling us 'The Three Mad Musketeers'!" I cried. "Then it is very necessary we do not disappoint them!" replied Armand. On the fourth day out we had made them speechless. At noon that day Armand had emerged with bowler hat, black cravat with a pearl larger than a pea, yellow cash-mere waistcoat, white spats and a hickory stick. François wore a vented shooting jacket and a beret. I was more sober in "plus-fours", golfing knickerbockers which the Prince of Wales had made fashionable. Soon Armand's sense of humour, courtesy and French accent had made him a popular fellow. He had discovered two pretty girls, sisters. They were Americans travelling with their parents to New York after a European tour, Mr. and Mrs. Townsend Wain-wright. This family were most hospitable to me later.

The journey up the Gulf of St. Lawrence was magnificent. The clear October sun touched to golden flame the woods of maple, larch and sumac. In the mid-winter of 1920 I had approached New York via the Hudson. Now in the late autumn of 1924 I approached the American continent via Belle Isle, past the mysterious high coast of Labrador, and then up the great St. Lawrence River to Quebec.

Soon after we had berthed we found ourselves in a palatial hotel, the Château Frontenac, at one end of the Dufferin Terrace where the high citadel commands the confluence of the St. Lawrence and the Saguenay. But if we were in Canada it seemed as if we were also in France, as I soon had reason to know. The Press descended upon us. Had I been under any illusion that I was the visiting "celebrity" it was soon dispelled. The names of my companions dazzled the reporters from *Le Soleil*. "*Deux Nobles Français à Québec. Le Carmania, arrivé ce matin, avait à son bord le Comte Armand de La*

Rochefoucauld et le Vicomte de Deservillers et un auteur anglais." At
the bottom of a column devoted to the pedigrees of my companions
un auteur anglais had a dozen lines. "*Les deux jeunes gens ont fait la
traversée avec M. Cecil Roberts, journaliste et nouvelliste de réputation.
Bien que très jeune, il a déjà publié quelques ouvrages tels que 'Scissors'
et 'Sails of Sunset'.*"

Plainly in such exalted company I was an "also ran". I had achieved
Who's Who but not the *Almanac de Gotha.* I was not to rank as an
independent celebrity until I parted from my friends in Montreal for
a later reunion in New York.

Little by little I learned much more about my endearing companions. Armand, descended from the line of the Ducs de La
Rochefoucauld, including the famous author of the *Maxims,* was,
it transpired, half Polish. His mother was born Princess Radziwill,
of the princely family that had spread itself across Europe since it
came out of Lithuania in the sixteenth century. Armand's father was
the Duc de La Rochefoucauld-Doudeauville, President of the French
Jockey Club. His married sisters were the Princesse Sixte de Bourbon-
Parme, and the Duchesse de Mouchy. An uncle was the Duc de
Bisaccia, another, Prince Léon Radziwill. His elder brother was the
Vicomte Sosthènes de La Rochefoucauld. As I subsequently remarked
to Armand, his young head would have been very ripe for the
guillotine during the French Revolution.

Trailing such clouds of glory, my *deux nobles Français,* with me
courteously included, were swept into a series of receptions—by the
Governor of the Province at the Residency, magnificently situated
above the cove where Wolfe landed to scale the Heights of Abraham,
by the Prime Minister, the Chief Justice, the Speaker, and the President of Laval University. Since I was the fluent one and my friends
were tongue-tied, it was I who had to make a reply in response to an
address of welcome from the assembled students of the university.
But I began to wilt. "This won't do!" I protested. "Too much
handshaking, drinking, eating, talking—altogether too much celebrity.
We must flee, *mes enfants.*" "But it's you. You've brought on all this!"
protested Armand. "Not at all," I retorted. "Look, at the Press. After a
column devoted to your pedigrees, which reads like a potted history
of France, I occupy a dozen lines. And the women, of course, mob

200

The author, aged 32.
By Kahlil Gibran.

'Tall, suave, honey-voiced, he hypnotized the audience with his adroit British propaganda. It was like watching a cobra swallowing its prey.'

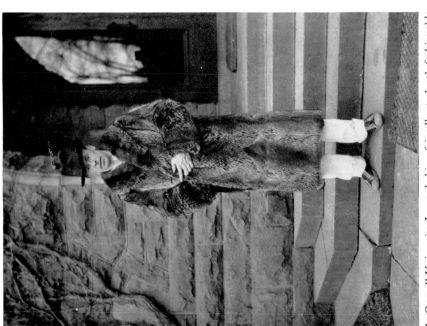

At Cornell University I was clad in a friendly student's fashionable racoon overcoat.

you—two such rich, handsome, well-born, *ravissant* young—."
A well-aimed cushion stopped me. We agreed to leave for Montreal.
On departure I had my revenge. The editor of *Le Soleil* had asked
me to write my impressions of Quebec. In the train to Montreal I
handed the boys a copy of that morning's paper. My article occupied
a column. It was headed *La Cité Serène*. I had let myself go, especially
in the closing paragraph.

> Gardienne resplendissante des trésors de l'Ouest, sirène
> chantant l'effusion de ta force virile, je t'écoute avec attention
> surabondante espérant—comme—jadis, le vieil Ulysse passer
> devant toi en toute sécurité. Mes yeux, vraiment, ne sauraient
> contempler plus grande beauté, ni meilleur enchantement.
> O belle cité, je laisse à d'autres d'imaginer le récit de contes
> merveilleux! Toi, ô cité sirène de l'Est, tu offres au cœur
> de l'homme tout ce qu'il peut contenir de joie et d'amour, car
> c'est dans tes murs que l'on goûte le repos d'une intégrale
> félicité!"

They read it through. *"Formidable!"* said Armand. I felt I had
got even; a column of my own.

It had been an error to imagine that we should have a quieter life
in Montreal, but here I was on somewhat more British ground and my
two friends were not the star turns. After three days of lavish entertainment I took a night-train to Albany. Armand and François
proceeded to Niagara Falls, from which they would journey to our
rendezvous in New York. In Montreal Lord Atholstan, the owner of
the influential *Montreal Star*, proudly conducted me over his splendid
newspaper plant. Discussing Canada's industrial relations with the
United States, I asked him whether America's Prohibition was likely
to be adopted by the Province of Quebec. There were accusations
that the Province was doing a roaring trade in bootlegging, as the term
went. "We are not as mad as that—the whole experiment is insane
and will crash. Meanwhile our Province made a profit in the liquor
trade last year of six million dollars. The tourist traffic of thirsty
Americans from the States into Montreal, Quebec and our summer
resorts suggests we are meeting a public need!" he replied, with a
twinkle in his eye.

New York is four hundred miles due south of Montreal. This route provides a wonderful excursion through a golden landscape. You enter the United States at the top of the ribbon-like Lake Champlain. One side of the lake is in Vermont. The railway line hugs the shore of New York State, with the Adirondack Mountains for background. You soon touch Lake St. George at Fort Ticonderoga. It had been the scene of a long and costly struggle, first between the French colonists and the English, and then between the English and the American revolutionaries, the campaign covering twenty years.

My sleeping car deposited me at Albany just as the town was waking to breakfast. The streets were almost empty. The splendour of the buildings filled me with wonder. The State House and the Education Office had "a glory that was Greece", with long columned façades and majestic pediments and friezes. There were moments when I wondered whether by error my train had discharged me into a reconstructed Athens. A few months earlier I had not heard of Albany—a name that carried for me an echo of Byron's, Macaulay's and Gladstone's lodgings in a recess off Piccadilly. Albany's splendour was due to the fact that it was the capital of New York State.

A young giant in a lumberjack's diced shirt offered his services as a cicerone. "You're the first Britisher I've met," he said agreeably. The more I saw that morning, the more I wondered. How did a town of one hundred thousand inhabitants come to build in such colossal style? The Capitol had cost five million pounds. The State Library had a million books. Where did all the money come from? "Mostly from the taxpayers down in New York City, I guess," replied my guide, "but Albany ain't a parasite. This place makes 90 per cent of the linen collars Americans put round their necks, and unlike me, boy, they're much given to them chokers." He rolled himself a cigarette. On a street corner he saw a café opening. "Have a coffee?" I had a coffee, and learned a lot more history. He was of Swedish stock. He had just come down by boat from Lake Erie. He noticed my surprise, Erie was some four hundred miles away. "This place is an entry port for the Hudson. The Erie canal brings me in here. And I've a girl here," he added.

He stayed with me until my Hudson River steamer left. He insisted on carrying my portmanteau on to the boat. The siren hooted. "Nice to know you, boy. Come again," he said, giving me such a handshake that I winced. He stood on the wharf waving until we glided out of sight. Something for Armand and François, I reflected. They had had a Lancashire mill-girls' send off, I a Lake Erie lumberjack's.

I never left the deck of that comfortable old boat as we sailed downstream between mountain and forests all blazing with autumn foliage. We passed the blue Catskills, and Sleepy Hollow with its legend of Rip Van Winkle, then the red battlemented heights of West Point, the fir-mantled Beacon Mountain, and finally, in the evening glow I saw the panorama of New York, scintillating with lights.

II

Glass at the Lecture Bureau was all smiles on my arrival. He produced a list of bookings. "You're sold out—haven't a spare date. You see we've not forgotten you!" I scanned the list. It was formidable. I jumped from New York and Montreal to Chicago, from Minnesota to Texas. Much of it was new ground in the deep South, San Antonio, Houston, Waco, Dallas, New Orleans.

"Montreal—I've just come from there!" I said.

"Too bad, but we have to pick up when and where we can," replied Glass, seeing my dismay. I looked at the fees. In nine weeks I should earn nearly $8,000 gross. But the travelling involved was prodigious. For the first two weeks I was in and out of New York, reading my poems and lecturing on the European situation.

The Press soon found me at my hotel. There was a General Election in England. Would Baldwin get in? Would Churchill get back? Was he finished? It was surprising how interest in Churchill had precedence over the fate of Baldwin, Ramsay MacDonald and Lloyd George. Seen from America he was *still* the outstanding figure in England. I ventured a prophecy. "Churchill will come back sooner or later. You can't keep him down. He's the floating kidney in our political body." The Press loved that. "Churchill, floating kidney, won't sink," ran a newspaper headline. "British novelist backs kidney-Churchill," etc. The kidney simile was not mine. It had appeared years back in a derogatory leader in the *Morning Post*. I had turned an insult into a compliment. My venture into prophecy was a happy one. Baldwin headed a new Conservative Government. He did a thing that took everybody's breath, including Churchill's. On November 24th he made him Chancellor of the Exchequer, whereupon Winston put on the robes of office once worn by his father Lord Randolph, which his mother, now dead, had carefully preserved for her son through thirty years. When a small boy he had said—"My father's Chancellor of the Exchequer and that's what I'm going to be too!" Most stunned of all, somewhat rebellious, were the Conservative rank and file who could not forgive his apostasy and the Dardanelles tragedy.

I had been a week in New York when Armand and François arrived. I had expected they would go to one of the leading hotels. Instead they went to an obscure lodging in the lower and cheap end of the city, in Greenwich Village. They called on me and explained. Thereby began a fairy tale that had elements of tragedy and pathos. They had gone to stay with three friends, young Russians. These were the Princes David, Serge and Alexis Mdivani. Their father, General Mdivani, had had an adventurous career. He was a Persian, married to a Polish-Georgian woman. With his brother Bodany he was educated in Russia, joined the Russian Army, became an A.D.C. to the Czar and eventually was appointed Governor of Georgia. His brother's career was equally adventurous but ended disastrously. He became a Communist and a henchman of Stalin, who ultimately liquidated him. The Mdivanis had five children; three boys and two girls, Rousadana and Nina. When the Russian Revolution broke out the Mdivanis lost their estates, were penniless, and in danger of their lives. The family fled to Constantinople and arrived finally in Paris after hair-raising adventures across Europe. En route one of the boys even turned bootblack outside an hotel.

Madame Mdivani, shrewd, saw that her sons' futures lay in the United States. Young, handsome, taking the status of Georgian princes, they embarked. Well-educated, polished in their manners, they arrived in New York full of zestful enterprise. At the time that I met two of the brothers they were scraping a living in menial positions. They had a·small apartment in a brownstone rooming house with squeaky stairs and shabbily furnished. Here Armand and François had found them, with a few pathetic mementoes of former wealth—old leather trunks, Vuitton portmanteaux, and some photographs of family groups on their country estate.

The reunion of these young men had a warmth derived from memories of their Paris. It was in keeping with the kindly nature of Armand and François that they resolutely refused to install themselves in an expensive hotel. They lived in this shabby apartment because, as Armand explained to me—"The poor boys, they have not the clothes or the money to visit us at a de luxe hotel. We can be happier here together." I think that, in addition to unfailing tact and good nature, there was the spice of novelty for them in this grim setting.

I never ceased to wonder at the courage with which these exiled Russians who had enjoyed considerable wealth faced the hardships of a new, alien life. One day Mrs. Dorothy Caruso, the widow of the tenor, gave Armand a box at the Metropolitan Opera House. He wished the Mdivani boys to join our party—but had they the necessary dress clothes? Out of the wreckage they had somehow retained these and joined us, immaculately dressed, with a sangfroid that never betrayed their strained circumstances. Out of office hours they cooked and cleaned their apartment. But this was not to be for long. Great adventures awaited them.

III

I was much entertained in New York, an exhilarating city that I came to love. It is a well-dressed window looking out across the Atlantic towards Europe, from which it is never quite detached. It has problems difficult to solve; the ferment of Negroes striving for social equality, with wrongs that went back to the slave plantations of the South; the population of Jews, so large that people seeking jobs thought it wise to state "Christian" in their advertisements. It is a bewildering jungle. The various civilisations of the world seem to have been thrown into a cocktail-shaker and poured out in a kaleidoscopic mélange. An elevator shot me up to a banking tycoon's fifteenth-floor apartment with a stupendous view of steel and glass canyons thronged with traffic. An English butler in tails served afternoon tea in a room with a Tudor fireplace imported from a Somerset manor house. "Yes, we've a colour problem," said my hostess and called me over to a window. I looked down on a waiting limousine. Presently a fat, flamboyantly dressed Negress emerged, accompanied by another. They crossed the pavement to the car. A white chauffeur opened the door for them and then went to the wheel. The car glided away. "Those two women are cooks, one is ours. Once a week they hire that automobile to drive round Central Park," explained my hostess. "Well, what would you? This is a free country!"

We were bright young men and the hospitality of New York kept us out of our beds until the small hours. Before I began my tour Armand took me to lunch with the Duc de Richelieu, a near relation. He was a man of about fifty who had settled in New York where he earned a living as a statist, being consulted by leading Wall Street firms. I could not help marvelling that the bearer of such a historic title should be working in the United States, but he had American blood in his veins. His ducal father had married an American, born Alice Heine, who, still living, had had a remarkable matrimonial career. Her husband died after five years of marriage. She then married, fourteen years later, Prince Albert of Monaco, from whom she was separated thirteen years later. So this adventurous American girl, who married a French duke at seventeen, was the mother of my host, and the ex-wife of the Prince of Monaco! Her son Armand had also married an American, Eleanor Wise of Baltimore. The duke gave us lunch at the New York Yacht Club, an old house, possibly a former ship-captain's, which had a curved verandah. It overlooked the mouth of the Hudson River. Our host told us that he had given away his French château to the University of Paris. "I could never live there, too large, too draughty—no, not after this ghastly World War has shattered our old civilisation!" Could anything be more bizarre than to be lunching with a mathematical Duc de Richelieu, related to the great Cardinal that once ruled France, who, half-American, married to an American, now entertained us in New York, by virtue of the fact that his sister had married a La Rochefoucauld? "A nice old boy, isn't he?" said Armand when we left. "And what a good lunch!"

Before I departed, the ever alert Mr. Glass arranged for me to be the guest of the Dutch Treat Club. It was a lunch affair held in a vast room crammed with journalists, theatrical people and bohemians. I took Armand and François along with me. Our fame or notoriety had preceded us. In order to live up to the expectations of Americans who regard Europeans as odd, we had walked down Fifth Avenue wearing white spats and carrying canes. "I think, *mon cher*, we should have had monocles!" said Armand. The Club's invitation card, that bore my name announced "Also the Dolly Sisters". They were a young pair of vaudeville artistes, Rose and Jenny, Hungarian twins of international fame, whose conquests were not wholly before the footlights. They knew that fame is fleeting but diamonds are for ever. Among the tycoons they had scalped was Mr. Gordon Selfridge, who had made a sensation by founding Selfridge's store in Oxford Street, London, and giving tremendous parties at Lansdowne House, which he had rented from the Marquess of Lansdowne.

I was kissed on both cheeks by the Dolly Sisters at the close of my remarks, and the badge of the club, a huge plaster medal, was hung round my neck. "Mr. Roberts appeared yesterday at the Dutch Treat Club in a marvellous white waistcoat and white spats," reported the *Herald Tribune*. "He brought with him his friend Count de La Roche-foucauld because he was afraid to go down Fifth Avenue alone."

The speaker who followed me was Irvin Cobb, America's wittiest writer, on whom the mantle of Mark Twain had fallen. "Our friend," he said, "seems surprised that we New Yorkers should all turn round to look at his spats, but our wonder is based on a reason he cannot appreciate. We do not turn round because they are white, but to see if their wearer can possibly be a Christian! Still," he added, in the uproar that ensued, "I think he is the most likeable young Englishman, *without adenoids*, I have yet met."

IV

The *New York Times Book Review* asked me to sit for my portrait to an artist I had not heard of, with the curious name of Kahlil Gibran. I went to a studio apartment house in the bohemian down-town section of New York, Greenwich Village. Gibran was a slight, swarthy little man around forty, sickly looking. While he drew me he talked quietly. There was a veil of sadness over him. It was later that I learned his history. He was born in 1883 at Bechari, a small village in sight of the cedars of Lebanon. His father was a shepherd. His mother, the daughter of a Maronite priest, had one son, Peter, by a previous marriage. By her second marriage she had two daughters and a son, Kahlil. Peter had emigrated to the United States and in 1894 persuaded his mother and the children to join him in Boston. They left the father behind in Lebanon. In Boston the Gibran family lived in a poor Lebanese community. Peter worked in a store. Young Kahlil went to a local school where his talent for drawing attracted attention. Peter, the family support, sent his delicate half-brother back to Beirut where he entered a Maronite school and with his shepherd father made mountain trips. After four years, his health restored, he returned to Boston.

In 1903 Peter, the breadwinner, died, and three months later, the mother. Kahlil was left with his two sisters who, nearly destitute, sewed for a living. At this time, a boy of twenty, he found a benefactor, an idealistic young social worker named Mary Haskell who saw genius in him. She decided to send him to study in Paris, denying herself to make him an allowance of $75 monthly.

At this time he was in love with a girl, Micheline, who followed him to Paris but refused to become his mistress. He was three years in Paris. He studied at the Ecole des Beaux Arts and came to know Rodin. He drew portraits of Debussy, Rostand, Sarah Bernhardt, and Rodin, who said of him: "I know no one else in whom drawing and poetry are so linked together as to make him a new Blake." Young Gibran was now writing verses of a mystical nature. After visits to Brussels and London he returned to America in 1910. Throughout this time Mary Haskell denied herself to support her protégé. Gibran proposed to her, ten years her junior. She asked him if he was a virgin and getting no assurance she refused him. A year before I sat for him, a book of his, *The Prophet*, mystical verses illustrated with Blake-like drawings, had considerable success and reached fifty editions. He followed this with other works and something of a cult grew from them.

Unfortunately Gibran lost his savings through unwise property investments but Edgar Speyer, the German banker friend of Asquith, who had been driven out of England and deprived of his baronetcy, during the anti-German war-mania, came to Gibran's aid. His advice enabled the artist to regain much of his fortune. When he died of consumption in 1934 he left some $60,000.

After providing for his surviving sister, he bequeathed the royalties from his books to the poor of his native village. He left his furniture and many of his drawings to his benefactor Mary Haskell, now married, who to the end looked after him. He directed that his body should be taken to Lebanon. By now he had a considerable fame as prophet and artist. A large cortège followed his body from Bechari to the ruined Maronite monastery at Mar Saarkis where, at his request, he was buried in a tomb bearing the inscription *O Beato Solitudine*.

Such was the strange and gifted man, the seer-artist-poet, to whom I sat for a few days before starting my tour.

V

It was time for me to depart. I did not see the Mdivanis again. I need not have been anxious about their fate. In the next ten years they achieved spectacular success not in the stock but in the marriage market. Their matrimonial adventures kept their names in the headlines. Handsome Alexis, married, the fabulous Woolworth heiress, Barbara Hutton. It was the first of her innumerable marriages, but after three years she divorced him. In 1926 David became the film actress Mae Murray's fourth husband. In 1930 Serge married the movie siren, Pola Negri. None of these spectacular marriages endured. It was said that Prince Alexis on being cast off received a consolation prize of one million dollars and a pension of one hundred thousand a year. Their honeymoon in Venice created a sensation. They bought the old Abbazia San Gregorio at the mouth of the Grand Canal, opened a blank wall on the Madonna della Salute side and put in three windows. The Venetians thought it an outrage, though the alteration gave to dark rooms one of the finest views in the world. The windows looked across the Canal to the Piazzetta and the noble façade of the Doges' Palace, facing the lagoon. The Abbazia, with its fine water gate and galleried courtyard had a grave defect. Prince Nicholas of Rumania, who bought it later, told me one day in Madrid that he could not go on living there. It had a ghost, a hooded nun who haunted the gallery. No servants would stay.

The divorced Alexis, with too much money in his pocket, bought high-powered cars, in one of which he killed himself, aged twenty-seven. Serge was killed playing polo, aged thirty-two, a millionaire who had struck oil in California. The younger sister, Rousadana, a struggling artist in Paris, ran off with Sert, the Spanish artist who created the great murals in Vich Cathedral and in the Rockefeller Plaza building. He married her, divorcing his wife Misia, the famous mondaine. Rousadana died young, of consumption. Her sister, Princess Nina, married Denis Conan Doyle, a son of the creator of Sherlock Holmes. The Mdivani story has plenty of light and shade.

The Wainwrights with their two pretty daughters, who had been on our boat from Liverpool to Quebec, had a delightful house at Milton Point, Rye, on the Sound, a short distance from New York. They invited me for a weekend. My host had a brother, Colonel Jonathan Wainwright who was a member of the House of Representatives. He had been Assistant Secretary of War in President Harding's Government. He came of an old colonial family and had fought in three wars. He was an eminent lawyer, the owner of a show place in Rye. We discussed the European situation. One evening he said: "I would like you to meet President Coolidge. Would you come to Washington as my guest if I arranged it?" I told him that at the close of my tour I should indeed be honoured to meet the President.

VI

My tour took me from the icy air of Montreal, through country rich with the colours of the Indian summer, via Chicago, south through Indiana, Kentucky, Tennessee, Alabama, and in ever-increasing warmth to New Orleans, palm-girt and sultry on the sub-tropical Gulf of Mexico.

This time I did not stay in Chicago in an hotel but with the friends of a former visit, the Higbees, father, mother and daughter, of Evanston, a suburb of Chicago, with a large university where I lectured. The family virtually adopted me. I breakfasted to the singing of canaries in a sunny glassed-in loggia.

One day they took me to see a freak settlement, Zion City, on the shore of Lake Michigan. It was a miserable collection of wooden houses where the remnants of the Prophet Dowie's disciples dragged out a poverty-stricken existence. The soil of America seems fertile for religious cranks but in this case the Prophet Dowie, founder of the Christian Catholic Apostolic Church, was born in Edinburgh in 1847 and reached America via Australia. He anticipated Mary Baker Eddy's Christian Scientists. Imbued with belief in healing by prayer, he founded, in Melbourne, The Divine Healing Association of Australia and New Zealand. He then sought a richer soil in America, and in 1896 established The Christian Apostolic Church, appointing himself the first "Apostle". Soon he had a hundred thousand converts and the money poured in. He built a great temple in Zion City. This settlement covered ten square miles on the shore of Lake Michigan. He made a missionising visit to London but was mobbed. Later, charged with embezzlement and polygamy, he was deposed. Insane, struck with paralysis, he died in Zion City in 1907. "The City of God" was now a collection of tumbledown shacks. Its revenue, since the disciples had faded away, was derived from fining motorists who exceeded ten miles an hour. "We must drive through cautiously," said my host. Huge placards proclaimed that we were now in "God's city where no man may swear, drink or gamble". Poster after poster announced the various hells for unbelievers. The Main Street was a long avenue of half-derelict shanties from which hungry-looking disciples peered out. A placard announced that "The white-robed choir of five hundred sings daily in the Tabernacle". I wanted to hear the choir but apparently it no longer functioned. Part of the Tabernacle had collapsed. Was it one of these disciples who, after a lecture, pursued me into my railway coach to admonish me, declaring that my "precious gift of the tongue" should be devoted to higher service in spreading the good news that, by salvation, of the Dowie brand, "millions now living will never die".

In Chicago a friend made me an honorary member of the Athletic Club where I swam in a pool on the top floor, in water unchanged for a year, being electrically purified. It was here, not in Zion City, that I ran into sin. A number of members, to defeat Prohibition, had set up their own bar, with bar-tender and a store of liquor, in a private room. A member took me there. I encountered the jovial Chief Justice of the State of Illinois. As he lived in Evanston district he kindly offered to drive me home. On leaving he embarrassed me with a present of a bottle of whisky, placed in the boot of his car along with his own supply. Nearing the Dearborn River bridge whistles began to blow. "Step on it, boy!" cried the Chief Justice to his Negro chauffeur. Fearful of hoodlums, I enquired if we were in any danger. "Well, we'll spend the night in a lock-up if these Prohibition officers find the liquor in our trunk!" he answered. "Surely as Chief Justice they wouldn't arrest you?" I asked, somewhat alarmed. "We're still in city limits—my jurisdiction runs for the state, not the city," he replied. Presently we shot over the bridge. "Well, that's all right. Now I'm in my own territory," said my host. That bottle of whisky was an embarrassment to the Higbees. They were law-abiding Prohibitionists and it was a problem what to do with the incriminating bottle. It was emptied in the bathroom and the label was washed off.

In Chicago I had engagements to speak at the weekly lunch of the Executives Club, and the Rotary Club. The former had eight hundred members who had to qualify by being company directors. In the next twenty years I returned again and again. It was an important and well-informed audience. It provided one of the best platforms in the country on which to present the British view in international affairs. This being Chicago there was naturally a strong and suspicious anti-British element. The *Chicago Tribune* called me a "smooth British operator". "Cecil Roberts is here. Tall, suave, honey-voiced, he hypnotised the audience with his adroit British propaganda. It was like watching a cobra swallowing its prey." The *Daily News* was kinder: "He is making a host of friends during his Chicago visit." "O wad some Pow'r . . ." Burns's wish was fulfilled in these Press reports but I often wondered which of the Protean figures I really was. More often I was filled with mirth rather than indignation. Americans are a kindly folk but I did jib on reading: "He has a tremendous intellectual equipment but morally is as slick as a Casanova"—this after a kind reception from a university Faculty Club.

From Chicago in a great blizzard, I found myself within twenty-four hours in sub-tropical New Orleans on the Gulf of Mexico. What a dilapidated listless city it was, a dustbin place after the orderly North. It looked as if the tide of prosperity had gone out for ever. The drive from the station to my hotel revealed a littered labyrinth of buildings, dusty, studded with withered palms. Americans profess a love for New Orleans, it reminds them of Europe. Once it was a city of splendour and wealth where the old planters had lived in luxury. Thackeray had drawn material from here. It had also been a city of horrors where more than five thousand slaves were auctioned off, chained and branded, each year. Something of ancient beauty was visible, too, when I drove out along a palm-girt boulevard bordered by villas with green lawns and semi-tropical gardens on my way to lecture at Tulane University.

The next day I witnessed a demonstration with a touch of comedy. Three mounted policemen led a procession of white boys dressed in white, and black boys dressed in brown, blowing bugles and banging drums. Down broad Canal Street they marched, preceded by a baby elephant on a dray decorated with flowers. A banner announced that the baby elephant, brought from India, was going to the city's zoo. The black boys, not to be outdone by the white boys, carried a banner declaring that "Loyal coloured citizens" had subscribed towards the civic elephant. Indifferent to all this fuss the baby elephant munched its straw.

Obviously I saw New Orleans under poor conditions, after the summer heat and a long drought. On a hundred-mile curve of the Mississippi Sound lay the Riviera of the Gulf of Mexico. Little piers jutted out to sea, white villas amid "live" oaks and palms, had gardens of magnolias, oleanders, and crimson poinsettias. Fleets of anchored sailing boats were glimpsed from my train. It was a shore of lotus eaters, with a crushed-shell or tarvia road bordering the yacht-crowded Gulf.

On the evening of my departure for Houston, Texas, where Armand and François awaited me, I received a telegram. It was from

Howard Phillips. He was coming from California on business connected with the family orange estates, en route to his home in Orlando, Florida. The hotel announced him and there he was, four years older, without the violin I had heard in Smith Dormitory, Harvard, but the same dark youth. While he took a shower after days in the train he told me how, learning I was in the United States, he had wired my agent for my schedule, found the date I was in New Orleans and had jumped the Santa Fé express that ran via New Orleans to Florida. *"Et voilà!*, dear good Limey with the clipped speech!" he cried out of the shower. I delayed my departure. We had only twenty-four hours together before he went east and I went west, but the twain had met.

Two days later I arrived in Houston, the cottonopolis of the South, destined to be the town where almost forty-five years later the National Aeronautics and Space Administration watched on the television screen Armstrong and Aldrin walk on the moon. I asked in the hotel if they happened to know the telephone number of the two young Frenchmen who—"Say, you mean the Cotton Counts? Sure! They drive an Oakland with white wire wheels and have all the girls crazy!" Half an hour later they were in my hotel and I was carried off. They had acquired a house and a coloured cook out of New Orleans who spoke French. "The life, *mon cher* Cecil, ees it not marvellous?" cried Armand, as we glided along a palm-fringed boulevard out to their verandahed house. François confessed that he had ceased to pine for Paris. At lunch a party of ten represented France, Belgium, Britain, Russia, Rumania, Italy and Germany, all drawn to Houston for various reasons.

Armand liked Texas so much that he stayed in Houston for a year working in a cotton agent's office to learn the business. The State produced five million bales a year. "I'd like to add a few bales," he said. My visit was too hurried. I left with regret. There was a parting gift from Armand, appropriately a volume of *The Maxims of La Rochefoucauld*, in which he had written, handsomely quoting his namesake—" 'Dans la vie prendre toujours le mieux et le meilleur'— Voilà pourquois j'ai pris Cecil Roberts."

Texas never ceased to surprise me. Dallas is its smart city, of phenomenal growth. One morning I saw a crowd carrying a boy of

214

fifteen shoulder-high. The traffic halted for the procession. The city's crack baseball player? "No, sir! That boy shot a nigger for insulting his sister. He's been bailed out for fifty dollars. This is a law-abiding city, sir!" Some forty years later a friend came into my New York hotel and astonished me by saying that President Kennedy had been shot in Dallas. "By a Negro?" I asked. No, a White.

One day I passed a queue outside a Fort Worth church. A very popular preacher? "Very, you have to book your seat. The parson was acquitted of murder last month. He shot dead the Mayor. Previously he was charged with arson—firing his church and collecting the insurance money. He was acquitted."

In the hotel there I saw a magnificent figure in naval uniform, gold epaulettes, breast covered with medals, sword swinging. An admiral? He went out, mounted a horse and led three hundred Shriners of the Order of Stamboul, clad in Turkish plush breeches and tarbooshes, gathered for a conference. More astonishing, at Montgomery, Alabama, I saw two hundred men clad in white nightgowns and hoods with eye-slits ride down Main Street. In the sky glowed a red electric cross. They were members of the Ku Klux Klan. They lynched Negroes, tarred and feathered unfaithful husbands, defied the law and swayed elections.

At Baylor University, in Waco, I was the guest of Professor Armstrong. He specialised in Browning and collected Browning manuscripts. These are housed in a splendid large library with forty-six stained glass windows illustrating Browning's poems. As I entered the lecture hall to give a reading of my poems Dr. Armstrong said, gently, "Could you bring in a little about Browning in Venice as a footnote to your charming poem about him?" So I described an eighteenth-century Venetian palace and reconstructed *A Toccata of Galuppi's*. After all, Galuppi lived in Venice until 1785, and Byron and Browning both lived in palaces on the Grand Canal, in 1818 and 1889. I had never a more alert audience. "Students, faculty members and townspeople jammed the lecture hall, which was lined with listeners who stood during one hour and a half, enthralled. He made Byron and Browning walk," recorded the local paper.

Two years after my visit Professor Armstrong invited me to breakfast at the Savoy Hotel, London, to meet sixty Baylor students who had visited places in Italy mentioned in *The Ring and the Book*! His enterprise did not end there. He raised a fund to enable the university's representatives to attend a special service in Westminster Abbey and lay flowers on the poet's grave on each birthday.

When I arrived in San Antonio news of the Baylor lecture must have reached my audience there. "Give us that Browning poem you gave at Baylor!" shouted a member of the audience when I had finished my lecture. So again I made brave Galuppi play his *Toccata* "stately at the clavichord". Where in England could that happen, I asked myself. Footnote in the *San Antonio News*: "He ate a typically English breakfast of tea, marmalade and toast."

I had had splendid audiences in Houston, Denton, Dallas, Fort Worth, Austin and San Antonio. All these places had fine hotels, theatres, auditoriums and shops. But on the whole the Texan landscape is as monotonous as the Sahara. One can travel in a straight line for eight hundred miles over a vast plain. Texas supported five million inhabitants and could support a hundred million without overcrowding. It is larger than Germany or France. There are Arctic conditions in the Upper Panhandle and Mediterranean warmth in the Lower Grande and on the Gulf coast.

I started North, picking up engagements in the Carolinas and Maryland. My last lecture was at the University Museum in Philadelphia, the one on "Byron in Venice". How different the audience and climate! The city was white under snow, the temperature eight below freezing. Gone were the palms and green savannahs of the South. The audience, elderly, sedate, sophisticated, was in strong contrast to the eager, young and demonstrative audiences of the South. During the reception after the lecture a man shook my hand warmly and said "May I ask you a question?" I expected something about my lecture, but no. "May I have the name of your tailor? I'm going to London in the Spring." I asked the Curator of the Museum how it was I had been engaged to lecture on Byron. "Well, when I got your agent's syllabus with 'Byron in Venice' I couldn't resist. I'm a fanatic on anything about the poet. You see, my name's Byron—but I'm in no way related, and this is also the centenary year of his death at Missolonghi!"

The Phillips home, Orlando, Florida.

Pino Orioli, Frieda and D. H. Lawrence on the Ponte Santa Trinità, Florence.

Count Armand de la Rochefoucauld.

CHAPTER ELEVEN

Coolidge and Churchill

I

I HAD NO sooner arrived back in New York than I received a message
from Colonel Wainwright who had arranged for President Coolidge
to receive me. I left at once and was met by my host who had a small
lunch party for me consisting of some Senators and Representatives
of Congress. I gave some thought as to why my host had arranged
for me to be received by the President. I was, of course, very sensible
of the honour accorded to me but, doubtless, there was a purpose
behind it, and since Colonel Wainwright had taken the greatest
interest in my views concerning the War Debts I surmised that my
invitation to the White House was related to this embittered controversy. I was not a politician, I was not a financier, I was in no
sense connected with the British Government, but at thirty-two I
was not devoid of experience. I might be a young man worth seeing.
Possibly Colonel Wainwright had advised the President in this sense.
It was to pick my brains, not to pay me a compliment, that I was to
be received at the White House.

I knew a little concerning President Coolidge, and took pains to
enlarge my knowledge. He was a grim, cool little man. He had not
been originally elected President. He was the Vice-President when
the sudden death of Harding made him his successor. He had already
a considerable reputation as the former Governor of Massachusetts.
He increased this by his firm handling, in September, 1919, of the
Boston police strike. He called out the State guard and took over the
police department. He refused to reinstate the policemen who had
struck to compel permission to join the powerful American Federation of Labour. He told Gompers, the tyrannous president of the
Federation, "There is no right to strike against the public safety by

217

anybody, anywhere, at any time." Goliath crumpled before this little Vermont David. When warned that his action might defeat him in any future election, he retorted: "It does not matter." Taciturn, wary, he was no public glamour-boy or popularity-hunter. "We need more of the office desk and less of the show window in politics," he said.

When the news of President Harding's death came very early on the morning of August 3rd, 1923, Coolidge was in his father's simple house at Plymouth, Vermont. The father, a justice of the peace, administered the oath to his son, the 29th President. He left by the first train to Washington. He was fifty-one, unknown outside the United States. In the 1924 presidential election, almost without effort, he was elected President, overwhelmingly, such was the trust in his shrewd common sense and character. Though opposed to the League of Nations, he advocated American membership of the World Court, but the Senate defeated him. He proved a stern economist. He reduced taxes, thrift was his passion, silence his strength. There was a favourite story that on returning from church his wife had asked him what the sermon was about. "Sin," he replied. "And what did he say?" "He was agin it," replied her husband, known as Silent Cal. Probably an apocryphal story but characteristic. There was nothing glamorous about him and he gave no clue to the fact that he was a man of some culture. A fine Italian scholar, he worked during his honeymoon on a translation of Dante's *Inferno*, a task which probably enabled him to remain taciturn on such a festive occasion. I was warned that he would ask questions and say nothing. He was known to be very critical of the Allies in their failure to settle their debts with America. To suggestions of a general cancellation he turned a deaf ear. He wanted full payment. "They hired the money, didn't they?" He was the creator of the image of "Uncle Shylock". The argument grew more and more acrimonious.

There were grave faults on both sides, slyness, stupidity and a lack of foresight. In my tour I was astonished at the venom the War Debts question evoked. Finland was paying her small debt to the United States. Her example was held up as a reproof to us. "Little Finland pays, why don't you?" With nearly all the gold of the world in her coffers, from profits made out of the war during the years she had kept out of it, the American attitude seemed outrageous to her allies. In the event her policy was to prove disastrous, leading to financial collapse in Europe, and in U.S.A. to the crazy speculation that produced the disastrous Wall Street crash of 1929.

In December, 1924, when I went to the White House, the War Debt controversy was at its bitterest. We, for our part, acted unwisely in threatening debt repudiation. At the close of the war the European allies owed the United States ten thousand million dollars, four thousand million of this being the British debt. Our allies owed us seven thousand, Russia being our largest debtor. In 1920 Britain proposed a general cancellation. We should lose some 7,000 million dollars but receive a cancellation of our American debt. The United States would not agree. They would be the heaviest losers since they were owed the most. The British offer appeared to them as an attempt to pass the buck. There was a deadlock. In August, 1922, the Prime Minister, Lloyd George, made another proposal in what was termed the Balfour Note, namely, that Britain would seek to collect no more from her debtors, ally or enemy, than the U.S. collected from Britain. "A worthy statement," commented Churchill, but again the U.S. thought it an attempt to put them in bad light. They said "No". In December, 1922, Britain made another move. She sent a mission under the new Chancellor of the Exchequer, Mr. Baldwin. To sweeten the approach Britain paid one hundred million dollars on account. It was a token payment in respect to the interest on the debt. The Baldwin mission provisionally agreed to pay the whole of the debt, $4,600m. "We seek a settlement that will secure for America payment to the last cent," said Baldwin. We agreed to pay £32m. in the first year, rising to £37m. in the last, over a period of sixty-two years. The rate of interest was reduced from $4\frac{1}{2}\%$ to $3\frac{1}{2}\%$. Baldwin returned like a conquering hero, but Britain, including the Prime Minister, was aghast. There was a cabinet crisis. Maynard Keynes telegraphed from New York that he hoped Britain would refuse the American terms. "They are as much at our mercy as we are at France's." Baldwin advised acceptance. We had put a halter round our necks from which it was difficult to extract ourselves. A leading New York banker told me that America would have accepted $2\frac{1}{2}\%$ instead of $3\frac{1}{2}\%$. "Your Baldwin's no poker player!"

"The enforcement of this high-priced settlement became a factor in the economic collapse which was presently to overwhelm the word, to prevent its recovery and inflame its hatreds," observed Churchill. In June, 1923, Britain made the first agreed payment. Churchill deplored this burden which he inherited on becoming Chancellor of the Exchequer in November, 1924, being still wholly in favour of the Balfour Note.

It was at this moment of international tension that I was drawn into the vortex. I had my own views about the debt settlement. We should have maintained a policy of deferment until we had arrived at a settlement with France, Russia and Germany. The French were incensed by what they considered our precipitate action. As it was we did not keep our undertaking. We stopped payments after 1933. We should have stood by the Balfour Note. We began too early to attempt payment. On the other hand there should have been no support for a threat of debt repudiation. It would have paid us to wait. America is always some years behind the sound policy she ultimately adopts. She is a larger and looser democracy, with all the delaying tactics involved in reaching a solution.

To me it was clear that, although I might think along these lines, being wholly against repudiation and also against precipitate settlement, I must tread warily. It might be, of course, that the President would not raise the subject. I decided to follow the custom with Royalty and wait for him to open any discussion. Would he discuss the debt? I was, officially, nobody. Why should he want to see me? I had an idea. I might be a suitable cat's-paw. Already I was under scrutiny. Sir Esmé Howard, our ambassador, rang up and invited me to lunch that noon. I accepted the invitation. It looked as if I had put my head in a noose.

It was a beautiful sharp, sunny December morning when Colonel Wainwright took me across to the administration annex of the White House. Our appointment was for ten o'clock. We were received by the personal secretary of the President. He shattered the serenity I sought to show. He looked hard at me, just in from the cold air. "Ah! What a boy's rosy face! That nice English pinkness!" he exclaimed with embarrassing frankness. Before the deep colour his remark had provoked died away we were ushered in to the President. Colonel Wainwright made the introduction and then immediately withdrew. I was invited to take a seat.

I found myself looking across a flat-topped desk at a quiet, sandy-haired man of medium height. His mouth was thin and compressed, but in his somewhat difficult smile there was a geniality that belied the mouth. Rumour had lied for I found him neither cold nor taciturn. His first statement was: "You don't look your age. You've got around a lot in a short time!" I then saw that he had a typed sheet in front of him with my name at the top. He began to talk easily, asking me how I found American audiences. "Yes, we are good listeners, perhaps it would be better if we thought more for ourselves," he said. His manner was relaxed, his speech slow. I formed the opinion that he was a man who would never know panic, or allow decisions to be made for him.

He began to ask me about the new government that had just come into power in England. "What is your opinion of Mr. Baldwin?" he asked. I had my opinion of our new Prime Minister which was not very favourable but I kept it to myself. "I have really no knowledge of him, sir—I've never seen him," I said. "Is he popular?" Again I hedged. I could have said that he was adversely criticised for the debt settlement he had made here in Washington. "Will the Government last—it's a five-year period, isn't it?" "Yes. I think it will stay the course." "And Lloyd George and the Liberals—what of them?" "My opinion is they are out for ever. The Labour Party has stolen their slogans. The contest henceforth will be between it and the Conservatives, each driven to outbid the other," I replied.

He looked at me keenly. "You've been a Liberal candidate, haven't you?" he asked. "Yes, Mr. President." "Will you be again?" "No." "Why not? Giving up politics for writing?" he asked, smiling. His dossier on me must be detailed, I thought. I began to wonder what he was leading to. As we talked I became more aware of the large, well-lighted room in which we sat. The Stars and Stripes stood on a pole near his wide flat desk which had portraits that I assumed were of his wife and of two boys. He had lost the younger one, aged sixteen, five months ago, which explained his black tie. A large bow window behind him looked out on to the sloping grounds before the White House. In the middle of the lawn lay the tennis court on which Theodore Roosevelt had played so strenuously during his term of office.

There was a long pause, I felt he was weighing me up. He half-turned in his chair. "You told an audience in Chicago you don't believe democracy will work. Why do you think that, Mr. Roberts —from experience or philosophy?" Having asked this he sat back in his chair. Before I could answer his secretary came in with some papers. He motioned him to go out, so it was not an arranged thing to get rid of me.

"From a little of each, Mr. President," I replied. "The Greeks invented democracy. It didn't work—it led to chaos. Of every hundred persons, thirty are, by effort, thrifty. Seventy are thriftless. The majority will vote to tax the minority until they are both bankrupt. Every election is a bribery contest for the votes of the majority."

"Do you think democracy works here?"

"Yes, at present. You have a fat margin to cut. Enormous natural reserves. In Europe there are no margins today. Taxation is increasingly destructive. We shall grow more socialist under pressure of the democratic electoral system and deplete our assets. There will be crisis after crisis."

"Is that why you think Europe cannot pay its debts to us?"

"It can pay but at a disastrous cost," I answered. "England has begun to pay."

"You think she shouldn't?" he asked, looking at me keenly.

"I do not say that—you have rejected a general cancellation. I can understand that, from your point of view—"

"Unlike Mr. Churchill?"

"Mr. Churchill is a pragmatist—like yourself, if I may say so, Mr. President. He will put up a fight. It would not be good policy to press him—that is us, too hard."

He compressed his thin lips, shifted the ruler on his desk, and said, very quietly: "Mr. Roberts, we have no intention of pressing you, but we like a debtor to consider his debt is valid and not talk of repudiation. It aggravates our public."

"And makes difficulty for you, Mr. President, as a policy maker?"

"I think that is a reasonable assumption," he replied, slowly.

He toyed with the ruler again, and looked at the clock on his desk. "The League of Nations—have you faith in it?" he asked.

"No, no longer."

"Why not?"

"You have killed it. With you out, the Russians out, and Germany excluded, it is mortally wounded, particularly after the Corfu affair."

"That is not the opinion of you English, generally?"

"No, Mr. President. In a Europe decimated by war, President Wilson lit a flame of hope that will not be quenched easily."

"We repudiated the League, afraid of unlimited involvement in Europe's quarrels, but you shouldn't write us off entirely. We believe in limitation of armaments, perhaps some form of a World Court that could exercise a moral influence, without definite physical commitment," he said.*

He then began to talk of the British settlement, and of the proposed French debt settlement, a vexed question. France, in July, 1923, had opened direct negotiations with America for the funding of her debt, but no settlement had been reached. In this present month, Churchill, growing increasingly apprehensive of French action, had officially announced that he would expect any country making a funding agreement with America to come to terms, *pari passu*, with Great Britain. He requested France to observe the principle of the Balfour Note. This had put the fat in the fire, and angry senators in Congress denounced Britain and told her to mind her own business. It was at this moment of the imbroglio with America, Britain and France that I found myself listening to the President.

"I can quite understand England's insistence upon a *pari passu* debt settlement with France. Mr. Churchill should not be alarmed by any French pourparlers with us. Speaking personally and privately, I would rather we did not endanger such unity as still exists among us."

The significance of this statement was at once obvious to me. I knew now why I had been brought to the White House. I had not raised the matter of the French pourparlers, knowing how inflamed the situation was. The President of his own accord had commented on it, very significantly, as I thought. I said nothing when he ceased

* The President proceeded with this intention. But in January, 1926, Congress, which seemed to have accepted his proposal for American participation in a World Court, and for progressive limitation of armaments, added so many reservations that the Powers rejected them. The President made no further attempt to forward his policy.

speaking. He touched a bell. He expressed a hope that I had had a pleasant "and profitable" tour. A secretary came in and gave him a folder. It contained a large photograph. He signed it. "To Cecil Roberts. With Kind Regards of Calvin Coolidge, December 14, 1924." He rose, gave me the photograph and moved from his desk. "It has been a pleasure to talk with you. Thank you for the visit," he said affably. He walked with me to the door and shook my hand warmly.

Colonel Wainwright was waiting for me. "I'm now taking you across to the State Department to call on Charles Evans Hughes, our Secretary of State. Do you know you've been half an hour with the President?"

In the taxi I gave him the gist of our conversation but I omitted what seemed to me the most valuable part of it, something that explained my reception. I never saw President Coolidge again. When the Republican Party sought to nominate him in 1927 for President he said: "I do not choose to run for President in 1928." He was resolute against all attempts to draft him. In this decision he was fortunate, or wise. Did he foresee the financial débâcle of October, 1929, which engulfed President Hoover, his unlucky successor? He had retired at the height of his reputation. He wrote his autobiography. He died nine years later, aged sixty.

II

I was glad to meet Charles Evans Hughes, the Secretary of State. I had a deep respect for him. I had missed seeing him as Chairman of the Washington Conference in 1921, to which my chief, Sir Charles Starmer, had once thought of sending me on behalf of the *Westminster Gazette*. A great lawyer, a Justice of the Supreme Court, a much respected Governor of New York State, he ran for the Presidency against Woodrow Wilson and came near to defeating him. A renowned speaker, a firm friend of Great Britain, he gave me a lucid explanation of America's refusal to join the League of Nations. "The League is based on a wrong assumption, that peace can be maintained by economic pressure and military force. There is no path to peace except by the will of peoples, and the way to peace is through agreement not economic pressure or force," he had said. But he supported America's joining a World Court—in which, like his President, his hopes would be defeated. He was renowned for his enlightened views and his judicial impartiality. He eventually became a judge of the Permanent Court of International Justice.

We traversed, it seemed, a mile of marble corridors in the State Department and were ushered into the Secretary of State's office. Tall, bearded, he had a splendid presence and a warm voice and manner. One felt at once in his presence an Olympian air, serene and open. Our talk was general. He was much interested in learning how I felt about American audiences compared with British. "Of course ours are not homogeneous like yours, we have so many divergent racial origins. But I'm sure you found us eager and friendly." I told him this was so, but that I wondered why they thought all Englishmen were devoid of humour. "Most of my Press notices talk of my 'clipped speech'," I said. "Is that because we don't drawl? And they say I have a vivid sense of humour despite the fact that I am an Englishman. After all, we created *Punch*!"

Mr. Hughes laughed. "Yes, we have an *idée fixe* about the Englishman's lack of humour but Americans do find *Punch* a problem! It has a passion for jokes about curates and charwomen. You in turn must wonder at our passion for slapstick, bums, stars, physical violence—as in the Keystone Cops Fire Brigade films—but we are a very physically active people. We haven't yet bred your Tired Tims and Weary Willies. Our bums are apt to be obstreperous."

Twice we made a gesture to leave but were detained. As always, the conversation touched on the return of Winston Churchill to office. "Why is everybody so surprised?" asked Mr. Hughes. "You can't expect the sun to remain in permanent eclipse. We admire him but are always a little apprehensive; he will be so vigorous—but then he's half an American!"

I said goodbye to Colonel Wainwright. I never saw him again, although he lived into vigorous old age. In the taxi on my way to the British Embassy I thought over what I should tell our ambassador. I knew that I had been asked to lunch in order to be interrogated. He would want to be told everything.

I arrived promptly and was ushered into a small sitting-room.

Presently Sir Esmé Howard came in and greeted me. He was a handsome figure, fitting the role of a stage ambassador, perfectly dressed and groomed. He had a fine, sensitive face and silvering hair. He looked the aristocrat he was, a kinsman of the Duke of Norfolk. He was widely experienced from his many posts, and was now fulfilling his last, the apex of the diplomatic career. He was about sixty, alert.

He asked me to be seated. I had seen the President, and naturally he was interested in what had happened, if I felt inclined to tell him. He smiled kindly, a finger of his delicate white hand playing with the gold watch chain on his double-breasted grey waistcoat.

"I will tell you everything, sir," I replied. "I am breaking a promise. The President asked me, at the beginning, to treat all that was said as private—yet, he must know that you would ask me what had occurred!"

Sir Esmé nodded. "If you feel you would rather not—" he began to say. I interrupted him. "I feel certain the President expects me to do just what I am doing. Why should he invite me to the White House? I've been taken there by one of his Congressmen. Politically I'm a nonentity. I'm convinced I'm being used."

"In what way?"

"If what was said to me had been said to you, and it had created a rumpus, it would be difficult for him to say that you, an ambassador, had incorrectly reported him. But journalists are accused of faulty reporting, even invention, every day."

"Did the President say anything that might create a rumpus—about what?" asked Sir Esmé.

"May I ask a question first. Do you consider him antagonistic to us?"

"No, not really. I think he is a realist, cool-minded. He is anxious to sustain a reputation he has made as a stern economist, the taxpayers' watchdog," replied Sir Esmé. "He is opinionated, and perhaps Europe is unlucky in having to bargain with such a President. But it would be quite wrong to accuse him of being antagonistic to us. He is just very pro-American. Did he say anything that suggests my view of him is wrong?"

"No," I answered, and thereupon gave him as full a report as I could. He seized at once on two statements by the President.

226

"He said he has no intention of pressing us over the debt settle-
ments, and that he could understand our insistence upon a *pari passu*
settlement with France and on her adhering to the Balfour Note?"

"Yes."

"That is very important. May I cable this to the Chancellor?"

"Yes—I believe that, without responsibility, it is what the President wants the Chancellor to know. But, Sir Esmé, it's my head that
will be in the noose!"

He asked me just what I meant. I answered that if the Chancellor
reported this information too bluntly there might be a reaction and
Congress might want to know whether the President had really said
this. The mischief-makers would be busy. The President might say I
had misinterpreted his remarks. Journalistic history was full of such
cases.

Sir Esmé was silent for a few moments. "I think you may be a
little too apprehensive. I think the Chancellor will use the information warily," said Sir Esmé. "Do you give me permission to cable
what you tell me, fully?" I told him that I agreed. Sir Esmé looked
at his watch. "We will go in to lunch. After lunch I will ask you to
write out, as clearly as you can recall, the President's statement, for
me to cable the Chancellor."

We went into the drawing-room where I was introduced to Lady
Isabella Howard. There were no other guests. I looked at her with
particular interest. She was very pale and very delicate, surprisingly
so for the mother of five sons. Four of these, carried, with English
Christian names, those of Camillo, Carlo, Dominic, and Sigismundo.
Their respective ages ran from twelve to twenty years. Their names
gave a clue to the romantic line of their mother, for Isabella Maria
Giovanna Teresa Gioacchina Giustiniani-Bandini Howard was the
daughter of the Earl of Newburgh, strange as it might seem. In Italy
the earl had been also Prince Giustiniani-Bandini. Lady Isabella's
brother Charles, the 9th earl, and prince, had married the daughter
of the Prince of Trabia. In a few more years, as if to counterbalance
the heavy Italian element, Sir Esmé was to become Lord Howard of
Penrith.

I wanted to ask Lady Isabella about the Giustiniani-Bandini
line. It was a famous Venetian family dating from the fifteenth

century. One of them in 1443 was Procurator of St. Mark's, a scholar who translated Plutarch's *Lives* into Italian. He also was a writer of songs, and some of these were so popular that they were known simply as Giustiniani. His son in 1485 was a member of the dreaded Council of Ten and wrote a history of Venice. There was a Genoese branch that produced bishops and scholars. One, Agostino (1470), a bishop, became a pensioner of Francis I. He was the first to occupy a Chair of Arabic and Hebrew in the University of Paris, and was a friend of Erasmus and Sir Thomas More.

I knew a little, too little, about this astonishing family with Venetian roots. Now here was the wife of our Ambassador, descended from a family whose history reached back to Venice and Genoa in the fifteenth century. Lady Isabella must be a mine of history. Alas, after coffee had been served I was taken away by Sir Esmé to draft the cable to Churchill.

As soon as I had left the Embassy I went back to my room and spent two hours writing a précis of the events of this momentous day. It was to be both an *aide-mémoire* and a safeguard for myself. The next morning I returned to New York and prepared for my departure on the *Aurania*, a Christmas sailing.

On making a settlement with my agent the tour had proved quite profitable. I had also sold to an American magazine four articles. I had written for the Starmer syndicate twelve articles on U.S.A., and four for the *Sphere*. My novel *Sails of Sunset* had appeared in the American best-seller lists. Incessant travelling, lecturing, press interviews, radio talks and hospitality had pressed me hard but the atmosphere of the United States is exhilarating and youth's natural resilience overcomes fatigue.

Before sailing I wrote to Winston Churchill informing him that I should be in England at the end of the year. On my arrival a letter awaited me from Eddie Marsh, who was back as personal secretary to his old chief.

> Treasury Chambers
> Whitehall, S.W.
> Dec. 28, 1924

Dear Roberts,
   (I assume you are the Cecil Roberts I know!)
Mr. Churchill asks me to thank you for your letter and to say

he would be very glad to see you here on Friday next, the 2nd, at 4. I'm afraid I shan't see you myself as I'm going away tomorrow. All good wishes for 1925.

Yours sincerely,

E. Marsh.

My passage home was pleasant, the sea was calm. There was only one jarring note in the Christmas air that prevailed. At our table there sat a small elderly man with an irascible temper. I could find in him no distinction of mind or person. He was always seeking to impress us with his importance. He was a financier, travelling with his valet. He informed us that he was an intimate friend of Lord Beaverbrook with whom he frequently played bridge. He was contemptuous of everybody and everything. He had never before sailed in a "second-rate liner" and never would again. His table manners were atrocious. He complained loudly of the food, which was good, and abused the stewards. Our dislike was mutual. There was a delightful young American couple making their first trip to Europe. The wife was very pretty and bright. He embarrassed her with his attentions and snubbed the husband. He told them he had never heard of me, and he knew everyone in the literary world, and that I was just an over-dressed, provincial counter-jumper! One day on deck he looked at my cap and said: "I suppose you've never bought a hat at Lock's?" He was unlucky in his gibe. I took off my cap and showed him the maker's name. It was from Lock's, St. James's Street. One evening after a frightful scene at table, when, in digging into a Stilton cheese, he had scattered pieces all over us, swearing, I went to the head steward and asked to change my table. Thereafter the fellow never spoke to me, which was a relief. When disembarking at Liverpool I caught a glimpse of the valet, herding his employer's numerous pieces. The poor pallid little man looked as if he had had the life beaten out of him.

III

I went directly home to Nottingham, and two days later to London for my interview with the Chancellor. I was shown into a small room at the Treasury in Whitehall. As I waited for Churchill I thought of the singularity of the occasion, of the variable fortune of this stormy petrel of the political world. He had touched the heights and depths. When last I had seen him, fourteen months ago at Leicester, it was after his second electoral defeat, to which he was soon to add a third. He remained in the political wilderness. Many acute observers had written him off. A realist, he foresaw the Liberal Party had no future, broke the last links, but did not go over immediately to the Conservatives, by whom he was regarded with deep suspicion. They remembered his apostasy in 1906, his partnership with Lloyd George in his Tory-baiting campaigns, the Dardanelles disaster. Only two months ago he had at last won a seat as member for Epping, standing as an Independent. And now Baldwin, forming his Government, had made him Chancellor of the Exchequer. There was a story current that Churchill had misunderstood the Prime Minister and thought at first he was being offered the minor post of Chancellor of the Duchy of Lancaster, once held by him, instead of the Exchequer. No wonder he was stunned, as was the country.

Churchill came into the room, carrying a dossier, shook me warmly by the hand and seated himself at a table. I congratulated him on his good fortune since those grim days at Leicester. "Yes, I'm being given a chance to hang myself!" he observed impishly. He asked me about my tour, opened the dossier containing the ambassador's communication and then questioned me acutely about my interview with President Coolidge. When I had finished he sat back, joined the finger tips of his white hands and said: "The gist of it all is, I gather, that we should say little and mark time?"

"Yes, sir."

"H'm. Is Coolidge afraid of Congress? He doesn't strike me as that kind of man, nor do our reports."

"I am sure he is not, sir, but I think he is adroit and persistent, and well-intentioned towards us. He favours a cooling off period but must keep the Republicans behind him."

The Chancellor was silent a few moments, made a note and closed the dossier. Then he stood up and held out his hand. "Thank you. You have been helpful." He escorted me to the door and said goodbye.

I had written on December 31st a letter to *The Times*. It appeared unabridged, a column long, on January 5th, three days after I had seen the Chancellor. A communication had appeared, from their Washington correspondent, on the French debt settlement question. This had given me my opportunity. Soon after my letter appeared I received a note from Eddie Marsh. The Chancellor wished me to know that he had read it with much interest. At the end of the month the British and the French reopened negotiations. The latter asked for a definition of our position. After having reached a settlement with us the French proceeded to make a settlement with America. The storm over priority of payment was dead.

The subsequent history of the War Debts is an involved and sorry one. We eventually dropped our payments to U.S.A., saying we could no longer sustain them. We did not expressly repudiate our debt but in effect we did. It brought on us a frightful Nemesis when again, in the Second World War, we wanted American help. We then had to pay cash on the barrel and transport the munitions in our own vulnerable ships. It was not worth the saving of the thirty-five million pounds a year we had undertaken to pay following Baldwin's mission, for almost frivolous expenditure elsewhere.

Our repudiation gave a firm basis to American Isolationism in the following World War, and entailed the ruinous sale of our large American assets to raise money for the purchase of war material. But all this is a story for another day.

CHAPTER TWELVE

Beaverbrook, Shaw, Greene

I

WHILE I WAS in the United States I received a letter from Tom Douglas, the young American actor who was having a great success in London with *Fata Morgana*, the Hungarian play which I had seen with Myra before leaving for my lecture tour. Douglas wrote to me saying he had greatly enjoyed my novel *Scissors* and wondered whether I could make a play out of it for him. I had never thought that this novel would make a play, but after reading his letter I realised that my young hero might have the elements of a Douglas role. I was naturally pleased by his suggestion though well aware of the disaster that usually overtakes the novel turned into a play.

After the interview with Winston Churchill at the Treasury, where I had found him buoyant and affable, I rang up Tom Douglas at his apartment in Bruton Street. By good fortune he was in. He was most cordial and asked whether I could lunch with him at his rooms on the morrow. He was sure that in *Scissors* he had just the role he was seeking.

I arrived exactly at noon the next day and was received by a smart young valet in a blacktailed coat. The apartment was luxuriously furnished. Evidently Douglas was spending his earnings. The valet apologised for my host's absence but he would be returning shortly. I took a seat and looked through some magazines. Five minutes, ten minutes, fifteen minutes, twenty minutes and no Mr. Douglas. I am fastidiously punctual. Yesterday Churchill had not kept me waiting a minute. I repressed my annoyance, recalling the comment of a friend: "Never ask theatre people to dine. They always keep you

232

waiting. It is part of the build-up. They turn up with a rush and deluge you with apologies."

It was nearly one o'clock when at last Douglas arrived, profusely apologising. He was certainly, off-stage as on, a glamorous young man, slim, fresh-faced, with flashing teeth and a heavy lock of blond hair falling over his brow. His voice was pleasant, perhaps enhanced by his slight American accent. He was so apologetic that my annoyance vanished. He captivated me with a confession. "I'm late because of a hold-up at the hairdresser's. I've had to have my hair dyed again—this gold blond's a fake!" he said, laughing. He offered me a drink. "Do you mind if we eat now and talk about *Scissors*? I have to leave for a matinée at two. I've asked you today because I just couldn't wait to talk to you about it. It's been a great success, hasn't it? Tell me, is it autobiographical—was there such a person as Scissors?"

"Like most first novels it's partly autobiographical, except the tragic ending."

"Of course, or you wouldn't be here!" he cried. A champagne cork popped behind me and the valet filled our glasses. We began to talk about dramatising the book. I confessed that I was not very hopeful, novels were always troublesome to turn into plays. There were serious obstacles, the school scenes, the death of Scissors in the plane crash, etc.

"Oh, you can't kill him, no!" cried Douglas. "But you can select, build him up, and of course I've got to find Muriel in my arms at the curtain. It's got such glorious stuff, the boy's great!"

He turned to the valet and asked him to bring *Scissors* from his desk. When it came its pages were marked by slips of paper. "Here's all the bits I like. I can feel it all so intensely," he said.

The lunch was excellent. We talked on. I had to damp his enthusiasm, seeing a dozen difficulties. I told him that I would try but that it would be six months at least before I could produce a version. I had a paper to edit, I was in the middle of a new novel. He said he would wait but I must do it for him. "You won't let anyone else have it; you will talk to my agent?" he asked. I promised him the first option if ever it got to that stage. We parted very cordially.

Outside there was a Rolls-Royce with a chauffeur waiting to take him to the theatre. I reflected on how many years it took an author to get to the Rolls-Royce standard, if ever. Of course it was all part of the actor's façade. No one cared a damn whether an author arrived on foot, a taxi beyond his pocket. Authors are never expected to live by their writing; all their friends expect free copies, and the libraries lend one out two hundred times having paid a few shillings for it. Well, any man who writes a book hoping to make money by it should have his head examined. Authors mostly survive out of egotism; a book is something that has to explode inside them. Tom Douglas kindly offered me a lift, which I declined. As I watched him go, without envy, so luxuriously, so triumphantly, with London at his feet, pretty girls, suitors and hostesses in line, I reflected on the fate of so many of these successful children of Thespis. Rocket-like they soar, scintillate and crash.

I never saw Douglas again. Four months elapsed before I could turn to writing the play. I simply could not find a sequence or a satisfactory end. Finally I abandoned the attempt. Perhaps it might develop later in my mind. Then I heard that *Fata Morgana* was off and Tom Douglas had left England. He did not appear to have repeated that early success. Forty-five years later I learned from a friend who knew him that he had become one of the most successful interior decorators in California. Unknowingly he had planted a seed, in the capricious manner in which inspiration works. Within a year I had written not the play he wanted, but a light comedy that was produced the following year.

After these London interviews I returned to Nottingham to resume my editorship. On the Atlantic crossing I had surveyed my present position. I had written two novels, published with some success in England and in America. I had made two remunerative lecture tours and was pressed to undertake a third. Before departing on my lecture tour I had written my third novel, *The Love Rack*. This I now dedicated to Armand and François—"Souvenir de Québec à Texas." Two days before sailing for home I learned that it had been bought for serialisation by the *Daily Express*. All this might be considered success but could I keep it up? At thirty-two the flood of youth begins to recede. I was never physically strong, sustained by an ardour that pressed heavily upon my highly-strung temperament.

My newspaper editorship was an incessant strain. As a novelist I had now created my own business but public taste was fickle and I was not of a disposition to woo it. I wrote what I wanted to write, not what I thought it would like. I must not throw off one set of fetters for another.

On my return home, all this went through my mind. I had thrice burnt my boats, with justification. My aim had always been independence. I had never intended to remain in journalism, an arduous profession requiring incessant vitality. I reviewed my financial position. I had saved seven thousand pounds, not a fortune but sufficient, living as I was on five hundred a year, to give me a good basis for my gamble. The needs of an author are small. All he requires is food, clothes, a quiet room and freedom to embark on his adventure. Anything else is extraneous. I made my decision. I would edit the *Journal* for another year and then cut the painter. I made no mention to anyone of my decision, not even to my mother who had faced too many crises in her life. She had never lacked faith in my most startling moves, since when, an office boy, I had walked out of a "safe" municipal job with no more resources than my unquenchable ambition.

Back at the *Journal* office I received a warm welcome from my staff, well-informed of my American tour through the articles I had syndicated. One of my first engagements was to give the Byron Centenary Lecture, in the old City Hall, soon to be demolished and replaced by a new neo-classic Council House with a noble peristyle facing the great Square. The Duke of Portland took the chair. The local ties with Byron had always been strong. There had been his noble speech in the House of Lords on behalf of the Nottingham Luddites, the stocking-frame wreckers who feared for their livelihood. Byron's ridicule had checked the savage punishment, the hangings, the transportations. The one home he had loved, Newstead Abbey, nearby in the Sherwood Forest, seemed haunted still with his presence. His body on return from Missolonghi had halted for some hours in the city until it was taken for burial a few miles out of it. The ghost of a little lame boy walked in the streets up by the Castle.

A few days later Fate took a hand in my destiny. My chief, Sir

Charles Starmer, now engrossed in the promotion of the *Westminster Gazette* as a morning newspaper, telephoned that he wished to see me in London about an important proposition. Three days later he greeted me in his usual boisterous manner. He asked me about my tour, saying he had read my article with great interest. "However did you scoop the President ?" he asked, his eyes twinkling. I told him there had been no "scoop". I had been called to the White House through no effort of mine. "Well, well!" he said, pacing the room, "Very good, my boy, very good! What I want to talk to you about is this. I've always felt you were wasted in Nottingham. We've a wonderful paper here and I've a very good offer for you. I'll make you assistant-editor, at fifteen hundred a year. How old are you ?"

"Thirty-two."

"Well, did anyone at your age ever have an offer like that ?"

"Yes, Sir Charles—Delane of *The Times*. He was its editor at twenty-four."

He stopped walking, sat down at his desk, and laughed. "Delane! You would know that! Now, I'd like you here next month. How's that ?" he asked.

I looked at his eager, kind face. He had forced upon me a quick decision. I had always been grateful for his faith in me, for his consideration in every way. I was not wholly surprised by his proposition. Ever since that suggestion of sending me to the Washington Conference I had felt that one day I might be involved in one of his decisions, but the suddenness of the present proposal overwhelmed me. The position and the salary would be jumped at by any young journalist. I knew it was useless to ask for time to consider his offer. Like all tycoons he moved swiftly and you were expendable. Not for one moment did he think I would show any hesitation. I sat silent for a while. "Well, what about it ?" he asked, almost gleefully, like a father who had given his boy a surprising present.

"Sir Charles, you've precipitated a decision I've been considering," I said. "I've been five years on the *Journal*. I'm naturally very grateful for your offer. But I've decided that I want to quit journalism. I want to devote my time to my own writing."

He looked at me amazed. His knuckles whitened over a ruler he gripped. "You can't be serious! Do you realise what I've offered you? There are a hundred men in Fleet Street who'd give their eyes for the job!" he cried with a note of impatient incredulity. "Now, don't be silly, my boy. You can't make a living writing books!"

"I think I can, sir. I've made over a thousand pounds out of each of my books. But if I didn't I would still want to write for myself, to be free. Perhaps there's an element of vanity in it. On a newspaper there's nothing permanent to show for one's effort. The brilliant article you write today is wrapping up fish tomorrow."

"I suppose that's witty but it's nonsense!" he said curtly.

"There's another reason, Sir Charles. I'm not prepared to play second fiddle. I've been an editor. I couldn't be an assistant editor."

He looked at me hard. Then he stood up, terminating the discussion. "Look, my boy, I'm not going to argue with you. Go home and think it over for forty-eight hours," he said, linking his arm in mine and walking me to the door. "And don't be a fool!" he said, a fatherly kindness in his eyes as he shook my hand.

I went back to Nottingham. This was the biggest crisis in my life. What I had been contemplating had overtaken me too quickly, I faced a sudden reality. Only ten years ago, desperate to get on a newspaper, I had given my services under the subterfuge of "a gentleman pupil", and here I was declining the assistant editorship of a London morning newspaper! The rejection of a secondary role was not based on any dislike of the editor. He was an able man. I liked him and he had shown me much kindness. I had another reason besides my desire for freedom in rejecting the offer, a reason I felt I could not give Sir Charles since it would have been too wounding. I had never believed the *Westminster Gazette* would succeed. I felt that all Liberal London newspapers were doomed with the party they supported. Already the *Gazette* was encountering heavy seas. I feared its excellence would not save it. But the really determining factor in my decision was that I wanted to be free at all costs. I felt that it was better to fail in doing what I wanted to do than to succeed in what I did not want to do.

After forty-eight hours had elapsed I wrote to Sir Charles informing him that while I greatly appreciated his offer I was unwilling to accept it. I had edited the *Journal* for five years at the end of March. If he wished I would remain for another year or resign at any time earlier to suit his plans. There was an immediate reply. After expressing his appreciation of my work and his regret that I would not join the *Westminster Gazette*, he said he would accept my early resignation. He would give me a bonus of a year's salary. Despite his words of appreciation and his characteristic generosity I knew that I had hurt him. I was unhappy about this for I owed him much. He was right, I felt, in making a sudden end of the business.

My guess concerning the *Westminster Gazette* was fulfilled. It failed three years later and was incorporated with the *Daily News*, which in turn failed and was incorporated with the *Daily Chronicle*, which also sank after a gallant struggle. It was a heavy blow for Sir Charles when the *Westminster Gazette* failed, despite the Cowdray millions behind it. His whole heart had been in this new enterprise.

I saw him for the last time in 1934. I met a Fleet Street friend who told me that he was going to a cocktail party in Tufton Street, Westminster. "It's at Sir Charles Starmer's. He's married the widow of the Dean of Norwich. Come along, I know he'll be glad to see you. He always says nice things about you." So, hesitatingly, I went. I received a cordial welcome, the old warm manner was there and he seemed in good spirits, but I noticed how worn and grey he was. There was a moment when he drew me aside. "Well, you were right, my boy. You're doing very well, I hear." "I wish I had been wrong, Sir Charles," I replied. He smiled, pressed his hand on my shoulder and then turned to another guest He died two years later, aged sixty-three, while acting as Mayor of Darlington.

The news of my resignation was something of a bombshell. There was a farewell meeting with the staff and a presentation. I said good-bye with some sadness. We had been a very happy team.

II

Meanwhile there had been a singular episode as mysterious as it was unpleasant. The *Daily Express* had bought for serialisation my novel *The Love Rack*. It was the story of a young violinist. The scene was set at Portofino on the Italian Riviera. The *Express* paid £500 for the serial rights. There was considerable publicity about it spread over the preceding weeks. The first instalment, a whole page, appeared on March 18th, 1925. When the third instalment had appeared I received an urgent call from the literary editor. Something very serious had arisen, he wished to see me at once. I asked what it was about. He said he did not wish to discuss it on the telephone. I promised to see him the next day. During the ensuing twenty-four hours I racked my mind for the cause behind the summons. Had I slipped into a libel? Reviewing my novel I could not think of any such possibility. After all, as an editor I was well-versed in the laws of libel.

When I arrived at the Fleet Street office I found the literary editor, a youngish man, in an extraordinary state of nerves. The perspiration beaded on his brow. When he had closed his door without any form of greeting, he asked, "Have you done anything to upset Lord Beaverbrook?" Utterly astonished by the question, I replied, "Lord Beaverbrook! I've never met him. I've never seen him or had anything to do with him."

He moistened his lips, recovering somewhat and asked me to sit down. He began his story. "Yesterday morning Lord Beaverbrook rang me up. He was furious. He said he would not have your name in the *Express*. I was to stop the serial at once. I told him that it had already run three instalments and the reaction was already very good. To stop it would cause a great sensation and upset our readers. He wanted to know how I got your story. I told him through an agent. I'd read it. It was a very good story and you were a rising young novelist. A serial of yours had already appeared in the *Westminster Gazette* with much success. Heinemann's were publishing the book later."

"What reason did Lord Beaverbrook give you for stopping the serial?" I asked.

"He didn't give any."

"But you asked him?"

"No, I didn't. You don't ask Beaverbrook questions," he said grimly. "Are you sure you haven't done anything to upset him—written something sometime?"

"I am quite sure. I've never met him, seen him or written a line about him. There's no allusion to him in my novel, neither directly nor by inference. Are you stopping the serial?" I asked.

"Not at present. I've just sent tomorrow's instalment to press—but I don't know. Anything may happen yet."

"You've had no definite order to stop it—since the first outburst?"

"No—no, but—it's all a mystery to me," he replied.

"And to me. But I'm not going to lose any sleep over it. You know Fleet Street. If his lordship wants to create a sensation and advertise me, well and good. He'd have to give some explanation."

The literary editor stared at me. I felt sorry for him. His job might be in danger. "I don't think anything's going to happen," I continued. "As you told him, you can't stop a serial that's already running. But I would like you to find out what it's all about."

When I left him he escorted me into the corridor. "Thanks for calling," he said, as I entered the lift.

I lunched at my club preoccupied by this odd business. I went over all possible ways in which I could have enraged Lord Beaverbrook. For a week he must have seen the publicity build-up in his paper. Why this late outburst? Why any outburst? Beaverbrook had a reputation for being unpredictable. "The Beaver" they called him, and there was no liking in the epithet. Then, still cogitating, two things occurred to me. They both seemed fantastic. When I was in the Ministry of Munitions eight years earlier a Major Hills, an M.P. in the Government, hearing me speak at a meeting said to me that I was the kind of young man his friend Lord Beaverbrook would be interested in. I thanked him and he gave me a letter of introduction, couched in warm terms. I did not present the letter. I had no wish to be one of the Beaver's young men. Had the non-presentation of the letter annoyed him? It seemed too unlikely a cause, moreover, he may never have heard of Major Hills's kind interest on my behalf. The second query in my mind, searching for the cause of offence, concerned that unpleasant fellow on the *Aurania*, who boasted that he was a bridge-playing crony of his lordship. Again, I dismissed such a possibility.

A week passed. Every morning a fresh instalment appeared, nor was it relegated to an obscure page. My name was still prominent under the title. The story ran its full length of about a month. I had no word from the literary editor. The matter faded from my mind. Six months after the termination of the serial my publishers, Messrs

Heinemann, issued *The Love Rack* in book form. It was my third novel and they had high hopes for it.

A few days before publication I received a letter from Charles Evans, the managing director, saying that he would like to see me over an unpleasant incident in connection with my novel. Again! There seemed to be a hoodoo on the book. I called on him. He was a genial little man who had begun life as a council school teacher, had changed horses, and by sheer ability had worked up to a directorship in one of the best publishing firms in the kingdom. Our relations were always cordial.

As soon as I was seated in his room he said: "Have you ever done anything to upset Lord Beaverbrook?" He must have seen how startled I was. "Before I answer your question, I'd like to know why you ask," I replied. He picked up a sheet of printed paper and passed it to me. "There's the advertisement drawn up for our autumn publishing list. You will see your book has a prominent place. When our advertisement manager sent it to the *Daily Express* he was staggered at being told that they could not accept any advertisment that had your name in it! What's behind it all?"

"This is the second time I've been asked if I've upset Lord Beaverbrook," I replied. I then told him the story of the *Express* affair. At the end of it I asked what he was going to do about it.

"My dear fellow," he answered, "I've already done it. I've told the *Express* people that if this advertisement doesn't go in exactly as we've written it they will never have another Heinemann advertisement!"

It appeared, unaltered. I confess that I was shaken by this fresh evidence of a vendetta against me. It was a serious thing for a young man at the beginning of his career to find himself threatened with extinction by a powerful man. Thinking it all over, I decided to consult Brendan Bracken. He had his finger on the pulse of Fleet Street, but it chanced the same evening that I encountered Norman Birkett. I had implicit faith in his judgment. When I had finished and he had questioned me, he said: "My advice is that you do nothing. He has been twice defeated. He did not dare to stop the serial, and your publisher stood up to him. If he makes a third move we can think again."

"Shall I write to him and ask what it is all about?"

"No, you would get no satisfactory answer. These fellows think they are omnipotent and not to be questioned."

So I did nothing and what had begun as a threat ended as a farce. Seven years later I went to see a play by Somerset Maugham called *For Services Rendered*, at the Globe Theatre. It was a clever but mischievous portrayal of a soldier whose courage had won him the Victoria Cross but whose character was detestable. It was also an overt slander of the Army, with a pacifist undertone then becoming fashionable, leading up to that notorious encouragement of Hitler by the young men of the Oxford Union, who passed a resolution declaring that they would not fight for King and Country, and who then went out and gallantly died. I felt so enraged by the subtle poison of Maugham's play that on reaching home I sat down and wrote a scathing denunciation of it. It was beyond midnight when I had finished and I went out to post the article immediately. It was only when I returned that I realised what a stupid thing I had done. I had sent it to the *Daily Express*! Of course it would not appear. To my amazement it did, two mornings later, monopolising the leader page, my name and title of article in bold type. Reginald Pound was now literary editor. Poor fellow! I waited for a telephone call from the *Daily Express* but when it came it was from the editor, Beverley Baxter. "I think your article's very good. Look, we've got an idea. Will you visit the plays now running as our guest-critic? Write what you think of them. Say exactly what you like."

I was about to ask Baxter if he had consulted Lord Beaverbrook when I recalled a warning of my father's, "Never poke a lion." It would be a much neater revenge to spread myself in his paper. Perhaps Baxter, who had begun life as a piano-tuner, had the right touch with his fellow Canadian. He was one of the Beaver's "brilliant boys", the acting editor of Fleet Street's most successful newspaper. He was an energetic, burly fellow, a "glad-hander", with a volatile pen. He eventually won a seat in the House of Commons and got a knighthood. I agreed to write the articles. "Good!" he said. "Select your plays and we'll send you the tickets."

I reviewed nine plays and not a line was cut. One, a musical comedy at Drury Lane, was dying. I thought it excellent and said so. The review saved it. When the last of the articles had appeared Baxter asked me to call. "We like your work. What about being our dramatic critic?" he asked. "Thank you, no," I replied, "I'm not putting any halter round my neck." "No?" he echoed, astonished. "You don't need money?" "Not in that way. I'm a free man." He looked at me with a measuring eye. "I suppose you feel you're on the up and up!" he commented, a little acidly. "Perhaps, but I'm not starting on the down and down!" I replied gaily. A sub-editor and a typist had come into the littered den. He gave a loud laugh, thrust out his fat hand and shook mine in dismissal. "Good luck!" he cried. He was certainly one of the up-and-up boys of Fleet Street but he ended his life writing a gossip column, and died of exhaustion.

St. John Ervine became book critic for the *Express*. He reviewed in it a novel of mine very favourably. Again not a growl from the Beaver. The drama, or farce, now moves forward another twenty years. One day my friend Lord Iliffe, another Fleet Street magnate, while wintering in Nassau, received a cable from his son Langton. He had just seen near Roquebrune, on the French Riviera, the Villa Egerton. It was a lovely house, splendidly situated, with terraced gardens going down to the beach and a view towards Monte Carlo. It was for sale, furniture included, at a bargain price. Should he buy it? Lord Iliffe cabled his assent. I was living then in Alassio, where I had bought a property. As soon as Lord Iliffe took possession of his villa he invited me over to see it. It was within two hours' drive and I was often the guest of "Tod", as he was affectionately called, and of Charlotte, his wife. Such was the setting for the last scene in the Beaverbrook drama. I was again lunching there and talking to Lady Iliffe in the built-on salon, whose windows surveyed the rocky coastline, when I saw coming down the hall stairs from the higher road level, three figures, those of a small elderly man, an elderly lady, and a young man in the rear. I recognised the oldest of the trio at once though I had never before seen him. It was Lord Beaverbrook. He was exactly like Low's famous caricature, a gnome with a large head on a small body. Iliffe went forward to greet his guests and brought them to us. The lady was Beaverbrook's lifelong friend, Lady Dunn, a widow whom he would shortly marry. She had a lovely face and a kind, warm manner. The young man's name I did not hear. I wondered who he was. He seemed very subdued.

I now had an opportunity of examining the man who had tried to ruin me in my young arduous years. The first impression was of his insignificance, though the lack of height and figure was dispelled somewhat by the massive broad brow, the alert eyes and the strong jaw that gave a bull-dog contour to his grey wide-mouthed face. He was well-groomed. His small feet were encased in finicky but expensive boots with buttoned cloth tops. Though his manner was assured there was a certain furtiveness about him. He was a cool watcher, lizard-like. From all I had heard and from his behaviour towards me I had no reason to like him, but I tried to assess him without prejudice or being influenced by hostile report.

We went into lunch. The party was small, the conversation easy and pleasant except for one thing. Whenever that young man accompanying Beaverbrook said something he was contradicted by him. It became clear that their relationship was not that of a friend, but that of employer and employee. In a discussion that arose the young man, addressed by our host in a kindly attempt to bring him into the conversation, expressed a modest opinion. Immediately he was snubbed by Lord Beaverbrook. "What nonsense! You've no idea what you're talking about!" he growled. There was a painful moment and then Lady Dunn spoke. "Max, behave yourself! I won't have you bullying the poor boy!" she exclaimed. He looked at her and a faint smile appeared on his face. "Very well—I'll keep my mouth shut. But nonsense is nonsense," he said quietly. The conversation began to flow again but there was a slight uneasiness in the air. When his lordship opened his mouth again, which he soon did, he became quite jocular.

After lunch, when we went on to the terrace, he spoke to me. "What a beautiful position—are you visiting or do you live here?" he asked.

"I'm a lunch guest. I live along this coast, at Alassio, over the Italian frontier," I replied.

"Mr. Cecil Roberts is the novelist, you know," explained Lady Iliffe.

Here was my opportunity. I could have said: "You once published a novel of mine as a serial in your paper. You wanted to stop it. Your literary editor told me you were in a great rage about it. I've always wondered why. Perhaps you will tell me?" But I did not say this. My name had rung no bell. He looked at me calmly and said politely, "Oh, yes."

After a time we walked under the pergola. There was a moment when he was detached. I was near. Now was my chance to take him aside and tackle him. Again I refrained. I was a luncheon guest, like him. It would have been discourteous to the Iliffes to create any unpleasantness.

When the Beaverbrook party departed I remained behind. Lady Dunn's reproof came up. "I'm so glad she spoke—that poor boy, how awful he was to him!" said Lady Iliffe. I asked who he was. "He's sort of companion-whipping boy, poor devil!" said Tod. Before leaving I told him my story and the temptation I had resisted.

"You don't surprise me at all," said Tod. "He's quite inscrutable. He's a genius, of course, great gifts, great administrative ability, but you never know where you are with him. Even Churchill's afraid of him."

"Churchill! I can't imagine him afraid of anybody," I said.

"Well, he's afraid of Max—he's had to be wary. All their lives there's been a sort of love-hate between them. Now they're softening in old age," said Tod.

Driving home, my thoughts were much upon this singular man who had so briefly but menacingly stepped into my life when I was fighting for recognition. I was not the only one he had sought to crush. Compton Mackenzie fell foul of him but there was a reason. Mackenzie's name was banned from the *Daily Express* because he had not cancelled engagements in Poland in order to obey Beaverbrook's command to lunch with him. "Does the fellow think Warsaw's of more importance to him?" growled the Press Lord.* The Churchill relationship too, had been very stormy. Beaverbrook's behaviour to his friend Winston had not excluded denigration and treachery. In 1932, when Reginald Pound was on the *Daily Express*, he attended a conference on editorial matters at Cherkley, Beaverbrook's country house. In the course of a discussion Pound suggested Churchill as a contributor on politics. "Churchill! Why Churchill? He's a busted flush!" exclaimed Beaverbrook. Years later, in 1942, during the war,

* *Octave Seven, 1931–38*, by Compton Mackenzie (Chatto & Windus).

when he had broken with the Government after rendering the country notable service, Beaverbrook told Ernest Bevin, the Minister of Labour, that Churchill was on the way out. It was at a time when the Prime Minister was under severe pressure in Parliament owing to an accumulation of disasters. Beaverbrook offered to make Bevin the Prime Minister in Winston's place! Indignant, Bevin went off and told Churchill, who refused to believe him. Bevin could not understand the thraldom in which Churchill was held by his "friend". "He's like a man who's married to a whore. He knows she's a whore but he loves her just the same," commented Bevin.

There is another account of this incident other than Bevin's. the *Times Literary Supplement*, in a review of a book by G. Thomson, Beaverbrook's confidential secretary, alluding to "that complex Press Lord who was part evangelist, part ruthless man of action, with his switched-on rages, his sudden charm and his unpredictability," asked: "Why did Beaverbrook, Churchill's staunch and valued friend, resign from the Government in that dark February of 1942?" Mr. Thomson believes the reason was a temperamental antipathy to Ernest Bevin, who would not allow Beaverbrook to be the sole dictator of war material production . . . ."That such a thing could happen in one of the blackest weeks of the war, without any explosion from Churchill, underlines our need to understand far more than we do about the motives of resignation."

The harlot simile used by Bevin was not original. It had been used by Prime Minister Baldwin eleven years before, during a phase of the relentless Beaverbrook-Baldwin feud. For a long time Beaverbrook, together with another powerful press lord, Rothermere, had sought to drive Baldwin out of office. The feud came to a head in March, 1931, when Baldwin spoke at a Queen's Hall meeting in support of Duff Cooper, who was contesting the Westminster Division. Baldwin made a direct reference to the press lords, this time attacking their personalities. The culminating point was a sentence that is now part of political history. He said: "What the proprietorship of these papers is aiming at is power, but power without responsibility—the prerogative of the harlot throughout the ages." Lady Duff Cooper was in the audience. "I saw the blasé reporters, scribbling semi-consciously, jump out of their skins to a man," she recollected. It was a deadly sentence. It broke the power of Beaverbrook and Rothermere as political dictators. "It was generally believed," wrote Harold Macmillan in his Memoirs, "that the words were given to Baldwin by his cousin Rudyard Kipling. They are certainly worthy of him."

Beaverbrook never forgave Baldwin. Out of his grave he attacked the other dead man in a posthumously published article on their respective roles during the abdication of Edward VIII in 1936. He drew a portrait of Baldwin as the villain of the drama:

> "The King found Baldwin something of a bore and he suffered from his flow of unwanted information. Under the surface air of geniality he was a thoroughly good hater. He also hated me most intensely. He was a man of pretences. When he had friends in his library he would walk round picking volumes from the shelves and reading out passages with appropriate comments. This gave a pleasant impression of culture though I doubt if he was really a deep-read man. But he had another use for his library. He would frequently retire there to make a careful study of State papers, or so he would explain. But when he had safely locked the door he would stretch himself in an armchair by the fire, with a detective story, until he fell peacefully asleep."

One asks how Beaverbrook got past the locked door to witness this scene.

III

After leaving the *Journal* it was both strange and exhilarating to find myself a free man for the first time in my life. In two months, I should be thirty-three, with some capital, rowing my own boat. I also had a publisher's contract that gave me an advance of £500 on each of three new novels. I had another lecture tour booked. Since I no longer kept nocturnal hours or had to exercise the ceaseless vigil that editing a newspaper entailed, I was able to rise fresh each morning and go to my desk. I could now indulge my habit of watching a sunrise, a sunset and the calm magnificence of the moon sailing through the heavens. When, years later, I bought a terraced home on the Mediterranean coast, one of my great joys was to see the red disk of the sun come up out of the sea, or the full moon throw a silver path from horizon to shore.

247

Within three weeks of retirement I had planned my fourth novel, and early in June began *Little Mrs. Manington*. It seemed to write itself. It was the story of a Texan girl, enchanting but impulsive, who married a rising young English politician and with her imprudence almost wrecked his career. My tour through Texas had given me the background for the opening chapters. And while I worked on this novel there was a celebration to be held. My mother having achieved the age of seventy, blue-eyed and rosy-cheeked, qualified for an Old Age Pension. We had much fun over this. It was five shillings a week! She put on her best dress and went to the Post Office to draw it. The event was celebrated by a small tea-party. "I have never had a legacy in my life and it is nice to end my days with a private income, thanks to Lloyd George," she said, and put up his photograph on the mantelpiece. "I'm not so sure about L.G.," I remarked, "I believe the idea was started by Winston Churchill." "Then I'll put his up, too," declared my mother. She wanted to contribute her pension to the household expenses. I would not agree to this. "You go out and riot on your money!" I said.

IV

I planned to make a third lecture tour in U.S.A. in January, 1926, to coincide with the publication of *The Love Rack* there. I worked steadily on *Little Mrs. Manington*, which I finished in August, when I arranged to leave for Venice, Rome and Sicily. I would be joined by my friend Jack Laing via Rome when he came from his annual duty visit to his paralysed aunt in the wilds of the Abruzzi mountains. He would pick me up in September in Palermo. He suggested that we should then go on to Tunisia, new ground for both of us. Early in August I left for Venice. I had undertaken to act as a cicerone for three of my young friends who composed our "Four" at the Rowing Club. It had to be an economy trip for them. I therefore engaged rooms in the Pension Smith. It had the finest situation in Venice, overlooking the Piazza. The pension was on the top floor of a fifteenth-century building, with a zodiac-faced clock. Above, on the flat roof, two figures of Moors in bronze struck the hours on a great bell. Across the Piazza rose the arrow-like Campanile. The

Pension Smith had a terrace offering a stupendous view. Below was the great rectangular Piazza. The music of the various café orchestras floated up, and on three nights a week the municipal band gave concerts. To our immediate left was St. Mark's Basilica. On a terrace above the entrance stood the fabulous four bronze horses. They seemed almost within reach of us from the *pension*. Beyond St. Mark's was the palace of the Doges, with gothic arches above a long loggia. Our view extended down the Piazzetta to the mouth of the Grand Canal. No wonder that emerging on to the pension's terrace my companions gazed in stunned silence.

The owner of the pension was a character. Mrs. Smith was not English. She was German and had acquired her name by marrying a British soldier who remained behind in Italy at the end of the First World War. She was now a widow. The *pension* was packed by itinerant young Germans clad in little but brief lederhosen and open shirts who, at that time, unable to find employment at home, were wandering all over Europe. Penniless, armed with guitars, they sang for their supper to tourists who paid them to sing. Frau Schmidt, as they called her, sat at the head of the long table ladling out soup to these bronzed, flaxen-haired lads. There was a touch of Oliver Twist about their returning soup plates. They were lodged and boarded for the equivalent of four shillings a day. There were other guests— a professor from Florence with his two boys, and half a dozen Mädchen, variously German, Swedish and Dutch. There was one stranded English girl of eighteen who unwittingly put several thousand pounds into my pocket by providing me with some of her personal history which gave me a plot—a story for another part of this autobiography.

I had discovered the Pension Smith on an earlier visit through a German lad who had attached himself to us. He had a guitar and could sing folk songs in five languages. He told us that he was the son of a university professor in Munich, one of a family of ten brothers, seven of whom had perished in the war. He was full of music, laughter and puppy-dog affection. He became a sort of Figaro and court minstrel to Jack and myself. "I think he's an awful little liar," observed Jack, crushing any sentimentalism in me over his sad fate. When we refused to take him to England he cried, and tried to return the small gift we thrust on him. I think of him with gratitude, for he revealed to me the Pension Smith that in turn brought me the stranded girl who gave me a story.

I had only been in Venice three days when I was astonished by receiving a telegram from Myra, informing me that she would be arriving at the Danieli Hotel. Thus it was that my role of cicerone was curtailed. Myra, with some friends, stayed for a week. They were on their way to Vienna and Constantinople. It proved to be a delirious week. Never had she been more lovely and enchanting. She attracted attention everywhere and was a star turn at Florian's café, the noonday haunt of the smart set. She had a child's delight in everything I showed her. The weather was halcyon, the days brilliant, the nights soft and starlit. We were young, we were in Venice, we were in love. Forty years later, rummaging in a drawer, I came upon a photograph of us standing on the Ponte della Paglia by the Doges Palace. Out of the haze of years that bright day was poignantly recalled. It seemed significant that behind the balustrade on which we leaned was the Bridge of Sighs, "a palace and a prison on each hand". She was still deep in her campaign for the liberation of Turkish women. I teased her about her crusade. When the Venetians went to Constantinople in 1204 during the Fourth Crusade, they stole everything, including the four bronze horses. These were stolen again by Napoleon and restored by the Austrians. "I wonder what you girls will loot!" I said to them. Four years later I had to eat my words about the crusade for the emancipation of Turkish women. Under Mustapha Kemal they got female suffrage.

Myra and I rushed all over Venice in a fever of excitement. Lovely creature of evanescent moods, one moment there was laughter on her lips, another an air of sadness that puzzled me. She never spoke of her past and evaded any probing into it. I felt certain there was something withheld. After a breathless week she departed with her friends. Letters came frequently. They were excellent and glowed with her vivacity. Like so many Americans she thought there was an achievement, virtue even, in incessant travel. The letters flowed from Geneva, Paris, Vienna, Rome, Athens, Madrid. Now she was attending a conference in Brussels, now she was in New York organizing a meeting in Carnegie Hall for those Turkish women.

"Myra, you're crazy!" I had exclaimed as we sat in Green Park one June day. Her lovely eyes mocked me. "You never take me seriously!" she protested. A tiny boy came up and showed us a caterpillar in a matchbox. I talked with him until his nannie came up. "You love children, don't you? Why don't we marry?" she asked. "Because, my dear girl, you're too beautiful. I'd never be sure of you. You're too rich, too restless—too—" I paused. "Go on, professor! Psychoanalyse me!" she cried, mockingly. "You think I'm loopy. Well, so are you. We'd make a marvellous loopy pair!" "And have cross-eyed loopy children!" I retorted. She stood up, slipped her arm in mine and said: "Let's have tea at the Ritz. I love the room overlooking the Park," she said. "That's the dining room," I replied, rather shaken. "They don't serve tea there but we'll have it in the lounge." Two days later Myra left for Washington. All that was a year ago. And now after Venice, she was leaving for Constantinople. My somewhat neglected rowing companions returned to England. A week later I left for Rome, en route, to join my friend for our Tunisian excursion. I waited three weeks for him in Palermo. The British Consul was very hospitable and motored me about. The Greek temple at Segesta on the lonely mountainside left me stunned by its haunted desolation. You seemed to feel a heart beat in each honey-coloured column.

When my friend arrived he found I had been in bed a week with ptomaine poisoning. I made a great effort to get on the boat for the overnight journey to Tunis. The dawn approach to the city was ravishing. We glided towards the minarets, across a nacre and amethyst lagoon changing colour from the rising of the sun. A flight of pink-tipped flamingos passed overhead. Afar, on the upland that had been Carthage, gleamed the holy village of Sidi Bou Said. On a spot where now rose a slender lighthouse a Phoenician sentry had sighted the Roman galleys that had brought doom to Carthage.

Somehow, for all its brightness of white houses, noisy souks, minarets, arabesque patios and tinkling fountains, I found Tunis and the surrounding country eerie with memories of the long-dead Roman civilisation. Their temples crowning lonely hills, as at Dougga, their broken aqueducts striding across the deserted plain, the shell of Carthage, the vanity of human effort under the hand of

Time, were visible everywhere. I was conducted over ancient Carthage by a pale young French archaeologist, cultured, but surely consumptive, and sadder than the ruins about him. Unconsciously he fathered an idea allied to my obsession with Myra. I imagined a story set in a Tunisian scene. I, too, became an archaeologist, doomed, weighted down by a frustrated love affair. The devoted companion of my work was not free to marry me, tied irrevocably to a man she had long ceased to love. When I left the ruins that late afternoon, after saying goodbye to our gentle guide, the germ of a story, narrated in the diary of one, an archaeologist, to whom I gave the name of Russell Beresford, had already taken shape. I became the archaeologist, Myra his devoted companion. My letters to her from Palermo and Tunis, and her letters to me were a mine I could quarry. I bought every book I could that had been published by the French Archaeological Mission. I lunched and dined with the young members of it, alert, ardent, scholarly. My "Russell Beresford" and his *amie*, "Viola Burdett", began to have vivid entities. They walked with me through the Tunisian landscape. I would tell the story in the form of a diary left by the dead archaeologist, edited by his companion. Obsessions of this kind in the creation of an imaginative life are perhaps the greatest rewards of an author's life.

This was my first experience of North Africa, of the brown-skinned natives in their djellabas and slippers, the call of the imam from the minaret, the brass-workers in the souks, the narrow, climbing alleys, the oriental shops. I resisted buying a scarlet tarboosh but I went home with a green velvet djellaba, a red leather pouf, and a Kairouan carpet. I had yet to learn that these things never "go" in sombre England.

We hired a car and chauffeur to explore the country, especially Kairouan nearly a hundred miles south. Our companions on the dusty road were often donkeys and camels plodding in a string, under heavy burdens. For a time we drove alongside a Roman aqueduct running towards Carthage. We passed the mountains of the Sahara Atlas, the zinc mines that had worn out the lives of slaves. Before reaching Zaghouan we saw the first small salt lake and then La Mohamedia, a wretched village with the decayed palace of a Bey. We passed olive and orange groves, then under a lonely Roman

Arch of Triumph, by a mountain spur and alongside more salt marshes to the French colony of Enfidaville, once the granary of Tunisia. "Coiffeur pour Dames" said a sign over a shop, thus far had stretched the hand of Paris fashion. After the flat town with French schoolboys in *tabliers*, we came to the camp of the Oulas Said whose inhabitants, black-haired and lustrous-eyed, held out begging hands. We arrived at the vast plain of Kairouan. All along the route caravans were going south to the desert. They were Bedouins with camels and donkeys, returning from harvesting work in the north. They were wild-looking creatures, unkempt but smiling, the women very sturdy, carrying burdens, while the men sat on the donkeys. Then more cattle, goats, sheep and tribes of nomadic Arabs. Now the white houses and domes of Kairouan gleamed on the horizon. At last we came to the white-walled city. It was almost thirteen hundred years old, famous for its mosque, and the manufacture of carpets.

On emerging from our hotel after lunch, a dark, French-speaking Arab in shabby European clothes offered himself as a guide. No? Then perhaps two little Arab girls? No? Two Arab boys? No? Two fat French women? No? Two very strong Negro youths with two girls who would... No? He persisted, following and offering his wares. Jack turned on him. "J'aime, pour faire l'amour, une éléphant femelle ou une chamelle vierge. Vous en avez?" he asked. The wretch looked nonplussed. He fished in his ragged pocket and produced some post-cards of an unvarying nature. "I take them myself—much better. Now vanish!" said Jack. The tout vanished. The next tout was an Arab youth but his intentions were innocent. He gave us handbills announcing a camel-fight at six o'clock—"D'une brutalité prodigieuse, monsieur!"

Our first objective was the Great Mosque, in the old part of the town, the Medina, enclosed by a crenellated wall. The mosque was superb, built round a vast courtyard with a double pillared gallery. Inside, the roof of the prayer chamber, with its richly carpeted floor, was supported by two hundred columns of Roman origin. It had been desecrated by French soldiers in the Eighties and was now open to infidels. We removed our shoes and sat on the great carpet under the high dome. It was so quiet, so cool, with only the sound of a fountain in the courtyard about which white doves fluttered under an azure sky. That evening there was a very different scene. We went to see the Assouia, an Arab version of the Whirling Dervishes. A great din of tom-toms, men skewering themselves and dancing on red-hot embers.

During our tour I was troubled by a recurrence of the ptomaine poisoning contracted in Sicily. On our return to Tunis I became really ill again and a doctor was called in. After two weeks in bed, very shaken, we boarded a boat for Marseilles. My diet was troublesome. I eventually arrived home in a state of collapse. But my head was full of the story of Russell Beresford, and my portmanteau full of Tunisian notes, maps and guidebooks. I arrived home a wraith, haunted by my mother with a tablespoon, and that old panacea of my childhood, Scott's Emulsion of Cod Liver Oil.

On the financial front my condition was better. My third novel, *The Love Rack*, was published and doing well. With an advance on royalties of £500, the *Daily Express* serial rights £500, it had already earned £1,000, and there were American royalties to follow, but taxed in both the U.S.A. and the U.K. The novel was soon in a third edition. All this was encouraging, but the Beaverbrook threat to crush me, though abortive, left a bitter taste. I was to have other battles for survival in the literary cockpit, with the envious hooliganism success provokes, but this remained always the worst, being the first experience. Happily I was endowed from birth with an unquenchable spirit; with Browning I could say: "I was ever a fighter, so one fight more, the best and the last."

v

In November there were two notable events. The *Westminster Gazette* serialised my novel *Little Mrs. Manington*. Subsequently the *Daily Mirror* bought three of my novels. These were strokes of luck because I never wrote a novel intentionally for serialisation. When Compton Mackenzie sold one of his novels to the *Daily Mirror* he was "naturally handicapped from the reviewers' angle by having appeared serially". I suffered the same reaction, provoked by envy and highbrow snobbism. Charles Dickens had based his fame on serialisation. Thomas Hardy, Henry James, Conan Doyle, Joseph Conrad, Arnold Bennett, all were glad to have their novels serialised. Mackenzie expressed his indebtedness to the *Daily Mirror*'s literary editor, and I also, for he never mutilated my "copy" or "cut" without consultation.

The fees for these serials provided me with a fund that gave me artistic freedom. I did not have to do hackwork, or be subservient to a publisher. It enabled me to destroy a novel that I did not like on completion.

The other event was Bernard Shaw's visit to Nottingham. At that time the city had a flourishing Playgoers Club designed to help Mrs. Edward Compton in her efforts to establish a repertory theatre. From time to time the club induced some celebrity to address it. By some means its enthusiastic secretary succeeded in capturing a real lion. Bernard Shaw was then at the peak of his fame, having recently produced *Saint Joan*, by many considered his chief d'œuvre. He had been offered and had declined the Nobel Prize. Shaw's talk took place on an afternoon in the large drawing-room of one of the club's members. He had offered Shaw overnight hospitality but the dramatist declined, explaining that, a strict vegetarian, he did not stay in carnivorous households!

Our host, Mr. Fisk, presided over a gathering of about sixty. I was asked by the secretary to propose a vote of thanks. I had encountered Shaw on a platform only once before. It had been a memorable occasion. Holbrook Jackson had endeavoured to found a Federation of British Arts, on lines that anticipated the British Council. The meeting took place in the Aeolian Hall in Bond Street, London. On that occasion Shaw, the star performer, persistently *méchant*, had made fun of Jackson's project. When in turn I came to speak I made fun of Shaw's treachery, to the delight of the audience. Shaw showed some annoyance at a mouse that dared to bite the tail of a lion. In accepting the invitation to propose the vote of thanks on behalf of the Playgoers Club I thought it was highly improbable that he would remember me.

Somehow things went wrong that afternoon. Shaw had a cordial reception from a packed assembly. It was a memorable thing to see one of the most famous figures in the British Isles, as also in the United States, which he derided and refused to visit. When Shaw rose everyone anticipated a brilliant entertainment, but for some reason the performer was not on form. Every famous public figure has an off-day. It became apparent that this was one of Shaw's. He could not get into the swing of his verbal acrobatics and kept missing the trapeze. He said nothing worth while, but we laughed politely when we could. I think one of the causes of his unease was his position. He was one of those speakers who do best on a platform with an audience a little distant. The *causerie intime* was not his métier. Here he was jammed up against a mantelpiece with a row of provincial ladies almost on top of him. There was another perturbing circumstance. As he spoke he rested one hand on the high mantelpiece and slid it to and fro, quite oblivious of an anxiety he provoked in his audience. At the end of the mantelpiece there was a valuable Chinese vase. Each time G.B.S. moved his hand backwards it looked as if the vase would go crashing to the floor. This created a nervous tension. Finally our host got up and removed the vase from peril. Shaw noticed the intervention and made an ominous pause.

He was generous and spoke for three-quarters of an hour, making a graceful tribute to the amateur drama clubs though "they always expect to pay reduced royalties to me". He said nothing startling or outrageous, nor did he indulge in the Shavian witticisms of which he was such a master. At the close of his address we warmly applauded, but there was some disappointment. We had journeyed to Delphi and the Oracle had not spoken.

It was now that I committed a *faux pas*. Called on to propose the vote of thanks, which I did in complimentary terms, I took up his remarks and played with them. I was in good form and sat down to loud applause. While it sounded I realised that in my ebullience I had done an unpardonable thing; I had made a better speech than our guest. "You saved the afternoon with your vote of thanks," commented the secretary later. I replied that I had grossly misbehaved. I had danced on the coffin lid and deeply regretted my folly.

Perhaps I should not have gone with our host and the secretary in the limousine that took G.B.S. to the station immediately after the meeting, but I wished to pay him the courtesy of joining his escort. On the journey he talked to my two companions but deliberately ignored me. I was now certain that he had recognised me as the objectionable young man who had bitten his tail at the Aeolian Hall. What ill-luck to encounter me again! When his train drew out I believed that in my folly I had made him an enemy for life. I was mistaken. Shaw was a man of great generosity of spirit. Within four years I was to have proof of it.

VI

After the ptomaine poisoning in Sicily my health seriously deteriorated but I drove myself on, intent on finishing *The Diary of Russell Beresford* before I sailed for my American lecture tour. In December I collapsed and the doctors insisted on the cancellation of the tour and forbade any writing. I was now miserable from enforced inaction and became uncertain of my work. I felt I had arrived at a blank wall. My lecture agent took his loss very gallantly and suggested a tour in 1927.

Throughout my illness my mother nursed me assiduously but I had only just got on to my feet when I was stricken with influenza. While convalescent from this I received news that a light comedy of mine was to go into production in April. The rehearsals were to be held at Scunthorpe, preparatory to production at the Theatre Royal, Nottingham. Its producer, Hamilton Deane, was the proprietor of a touring repertory company. Before I departed for Scunthorpe my former editorial assistant informed me that they had on the *Journal* staff a youth, a Balliol graduate, who had come as a journalistic pupil. He said the young man would like to call on me. Myself once an unpaid pupil of that paper some ten years earlier, I was naturally interested in this recruit and invited him to call. He proved to be a tall, gangling youth of twenty-one. He had recently published a book of verse, *Babbling April*, which he presented to me. As I thanked him for his first offspring, I said: "I wonder if this is a presage. Young poets out of the cocoon often turn novelists—I have!" He shook his head, diffidently. He was shy at first. After all I was an ex-editor, the author of three published novels, and fairly well established. I suppose that in his eyes I represented success. I got him to talk, most intelligently, and after a pleasant hour he left. I expressed a hope that we should meet again We did not and I have it on my conscience that I was not more hospitable. He must have been lonely, coming recently from the vivid life of a university and now living in grim lodgings in a provincial city. Happily I had just recovered but my mother was now seriously ill. Years later I wondered whether I might have changed his reaction to Nottingham. When I got round to doing something about him it was too late, he had left and joined the staff of *The Times*.

Later my visitor's name came up again. I had called on Charles Evans at Heinemann's. A man of impetuous enthusiasm, he gave me a proof copy of a novel. "I believe we've got a winner! I want you to read it and tell me what you think." Evans was right. The book was *The Man Within*, Graham Greene's first novel. I wrote and endorsed his opinion. I added "He came to see me after I was on the *Journal*, three years ago. Do you think one Heinemann author led to another? After all, the old paper has started off Barrie, myself, and now young Greene."

The predictions were fulfilled, Greene's novel won immediate acclaim. It was felt a star was born. Like Barrie, Greene wrote an account of his descent on Nottingham in his story of an African tour.*

> It was late one evening when I drove into the Nottingham suburb from the station, round dark streets, down and down below the Castle rock and the municipal art gallery, with the rain breaking on the windows. I had a job, it excited and scared me. I was twenty-one and you couldn't talk of darkest Africa with any conviction when you had known Nottingham well; the dog sick on the mat, the tinned salmon for tea and the hot potato chips for supper carried into the sub-editors' room, ready salted in the strips of newspaper—if you had won the football sweep you paid for the lot. The fog came down in the morning and stayed till night. It wasn't a disagreeable fog, it lay heavy and black between the sun and the earth; there was no light but the air was clear. The municipal "tart" paced up and down by the largest cinema, old and haggard and used, her trade was spoilt; there were too many girls about who hadn't a

* *Journey Without Maps*, by Graham Greene. (Heinemann Ltd.)

proper sense of values, who would give you a good time in return for a fish tea. The trams creaked round the Market Place . . . In Nottingham I was instructed in Catholicism, travelling here and there by tram into new country with the fat priest who had once been an actor. (It was one of his greatest sacrifices to be unable to see a new play.) The tram clattered by the Post Office; "Now we come to the Immaculate Conception"; past the cinema; "Our Lady"; the theatre: a sad slanting look towards *The Private Secretary* (it was Christmas time). The cathedral was a dark place full of inferior statues. I was baptized on one foggy afternoon about four o'clock. I couldn't think of any name I particularly wanted, so I kept my old name. I was alone with the fat priest; it was all very quickly and formally done, while someone at a children's service muttered in another chapel. Then we shook hands and I went off to a salmon tea, the dog which had been sick again on the mat.

I had known that same loneliness in a strange lodging in a bleak city when I had gone to my first journalistic post in Liverpool. In his loneliness Greene fell into the hands of a "fat actor-priest". Possibly he was then a "mixed-up kid", fresh from a university where adolescents battle with life's problems, including spiritual ones. If I had been more hospitable to this lonely youth, would his personal history have been different and the tram-line catechism less influential? Perhaps it is a vain speculation and the mind was already set in the mould. I never saw Graham Greene again and retain a feeling that I failed in timely hospitality.

Greene's picture of Nottingham, derived from a mood, is rather a travesty. By general testimony it is one of the pleasantest, cleanest, well-situated cities in the kingdom and famous for its pretty girls whose standard of virtue is no lower than elsewhere. If the future novelist cultivated there, as well as his faith, a taste for fish and chips, he was in good company. Proust tells us how, returning from a call on some old servants, he came to a fair and was allured by a fish and chip potato stall. He bought some chips and walked home eating them with relish. If this is a low taste then I also have it. From boyhood upwards I found them irresistible.

Perhaps I am forgiven for my lack of hospitality. In another part of his story Greene narrates how a fellow passenger on the ship going out to West Africa told him of a literary club to which he went. "It was a change from bridge that club; they got really famous writers to talk to them. Chesterton had been and Cecil Roberts." So I was put in good company by my neglected visitor.

VII

In April I left for Scunthorpe and joined the Hamilton Deane Company, to begin rehearsal of my comedy. I soon discovered that I had made a mistake in letting Deane have it. His production was poor; they played their repertoire plays each evening and we had only six mornings for rehearsal. He took the lead in all his plays which were selected for the star roles they gave him. I went there with some misgivings, for my mother had fallen ill with influenza, doubtless contracted while nursing me, and her condition soon became serious. There were also rumours in the air of a miners' strike. Nevertheless I enjoyed my time with the company. A writer's job is the loneliest on earth. He sits at a desk hours on end, day after day, in communication with no one. In that sense I greatly missed the contacts of my former editorship and its daily conferences.

The members of the Deane company were young and gay. They were all ambitious for fame, undeterred by the presence in the company of some old stagers who, having made the essay, had failed. Two of the company were destined to have their hopes fulfilled within a few years. One, a young man named Kim Peacock, won fame and fortune on the television screen; the other, a mere girl, soon became a West End star. When at the first rehearsal she walked on the stage her beauty ravished me; complexion, eyes, voice and figure were exquisite, a Tennysonian virgin sweet and fair. She had only a few lines and was off-stage all too soon. I asked Deane who she was and where he had found her, why she was cast for such a brief role. He told me she was inexperienced, this being her first season. She was only twenty. Her stage name was Diana Wynyard. She was destined to become one of John Gielgud's leading ladies, a star until the day of her too early death at fifty-six. I immediately wrote more lines for her, to keep her on the stage. She might be unable to act but she was indeed something to look at.

A week passed very pleasantly. When I left, the company was going on tour with its repertoire. It would arrive at Nottingham on May 31st for the first night of my play. When I arrived home I found my mother seriously ill. Two days later, on May 3rd, there was the General Strike, in support of the miners. It was an attempt to paralyse the country and bring down the Government by a group of irresponsible Labour leaders who did not know exactly what they had embarked on or what they would do with victory. They foreshadowed the progressive decline by which the dominance of the Trade Unions would turn the House of Commons into a travesty of democracy. A good case for the miners was converted into an irresponsible adventure. All forms of transport ceased. Something in the nature of a civil war was threatened. An army of volunteers manned the national services and the threat of famine and revolution was averted. The newspapers ceased publication. Broadcasting was not yet a national medium and the public lacked news concerning the grave situation of the country. It was then that Winston Churchill, Chancellor of the Exchequer, revealed his organising genius. He took over the presses of the *Morning Post* and created an official newspaper called the *British Gazette*, which he edited. Its circulation soared. The strike collapsed on May 12th. It had been pronounced illegal and the Trades Union Congress was scared. Churchill then took a holiday. He went to look at the Pyramids and the Parthenon, had a talk with Mussolini in Rome, and came back to his beloved Chartwell to do a little bricklaying, and work on the final volumes of his war history, *The World Crisis*. The very substantial sums earned by this had enabled him to purchase his home. The complete work had nearly been misnamed *The Great Amphibian*, because the setting of the story was laid at sea as well as on land. Happily he was dissuaded from this ambiguous title by his American publisher and agreed to call it *The World Crisis*.

During my mother's illness I read to her the *British Gazette* and picked up what news I could by tickling the crystal of the wireless set. Her condition worsened and endocarditis set in. It was clear that she could not be present on the opening night of my play. The house was packed, the Mayor and Town Clerk attended, but I was aware that it owed this compliment to the fact I was a "local" author, and the Press was kind to a recent member of the profession. My pleasure in the event was marred by anxiety over my mother's condition. I had envisaged her sitting, triumphant, in the author's box with me.

During that week I persuaded the best producer in London to come and look at the play. This was Basil Dean, who had had such triumphs as *Hassan* and *The Constant Nymph*. His presence in the theatre almost paralysed the company, even Hamilton Deane was jittery. Dean's verdict was forthright. No. "Your dialogue's excellent," he said, "but the plot's too thin. I think you've got it in you. Let me see what you write next." But I had decided there should not be a next. The attempt to dramatise *Scissors* had warned me off. I would stick to my field—to my novels. They were more of a certainty. As it turned out Basil Dean did see my next, thirteen years later, when he was called in by impresario Jack Waller, for the West End production of *Spears Against Us*, a dramatisation of my novel.

My comedy *The Right to Kiss* ran round the provinces for a year. When it reached Liverpool I took my friend William Armstrong, the now famous director of the Playhouse, to see it. He sat silent until Diana Wynyard walked on. "Who's that?" he asked. He was impressed as I had been. Later he took her into his company and from it she was launched on London and fame. She had one drawback, she was "cold". When she went to Hollywood, Armstrong said: "I hope she'll have a roaring love affair and get seduced." She married twice. Both marriages were dissolved. She had great success on the London stage, and was awarded a C.B.E. She was always an adornment but, alas, fulfilled my Tennysonian simile in another way; to my mind she was "icily regular, splendidly null".

VIII

The cloud of anxiety over me lifted somewhat, when, early in June, my mother was convalescent. But illness had left her a wraith and I observed a listlessness that was unlike her bright nature. I became aware that she was being taken from me. She lost all sense of time and began to be harrowed by hallucinations. My presence availed nothing. My nights were broken until I was on the verge of breakdown. For two months I tried to deal with this state of affairs. I was warned that her decline would be prolonged. My doctor ordered me away for a rest. I reluctantly left for Venice after a goodbye that had not been comprehended.

There is a melancholy in the appreciation of all beauty and for me Venice, now, had another aspect. Its enchantment failed me, I became aware of its decline and decay. The gay company around me increased my discontent. At noon the tables of Florian's were filled with notables. I observed them as figures in a futile pageant, a note of despair sounding off, as in Browning's *Toccata*: "Here you come with your old music." The Italian contingent was led that year by the Countess Morosini, whose beauty had once enamoured the Kaiser Wilhelm. She ruled from the Morosini Palazzo on the Grand Canal, a Doge's cap enshrined in a corner of her salon. Her companion was the Princess de Polignac at whose musical soirées I had first heard young Artur Rubinstein play, a delight to be repeated for over forty years in various cities of Europe. The real sensation of the noonday was the advent of the death-pale, scarlet-cloaked Marchesa Casati, exotic as an Aubrey Beardsley drawing. She was preceded by a Negro page who led a doped panther with a gold collar and chain. It was sheer Tintoretto. She was destined to die in poverty years later in London, but now she made a sensational contribution to the pageantry of Venice.* In contrast was the elegant, handsome Robilant family, from the Palazzo Mocenigo on the Grand Canal, where Byron had kept a notoriously loose house.

Others prominent on the Piazza were the Counts Visconti, and another pair of brothers, English, Edward and Victor Cunard. The showpiece of the English contingent was Lady Diana Cooper, her beauty tantalisingly hidden under a large hat. She was accompanied by her gifted, stocky husband, a star of the English political firmament. Suddenly they vanished from the noon parade, having bought, of all things in Venice, a small Fiat car seen in a shop window, and in which they set off for Lake Garda. On the Piazza that year came another notable figure, the skeletal, negrophile Nancy Cunard. She was the cousin of Edward and Victor. I overcame my surprise at

---

* "The Marchesa was most eccentric. In 1913 she took me for a ride in her gondola, fantastically dressed, with a big macaw on her wrist and a little slave, holding two borzois, at the prow. When the gondola passed under the bridges we were clapped, cheered and laughed at."—Prince Alphonse Clary.

the African bracelets that rattled on her skinny arms. She had a strained beauty and a warm impetuosity. Michael Arlen had drawn her in his sensational novel *The Green Hat*, as also had Aldous Huxley. George Moore was devoted to her despite the fact that she quarrelled with her mother, adored by him. There had been an unrequited passion for Evan Morgan, a figure as bizarre as herself. She now had a little money. Her father, Sir Bache, had died, sadly alone, in an English country inn near Peterborough, hoping vainly that Lady Cunard would come back to him. He left £14,000 to Nancy. This sum enabled her to run a private printing press. Mercifully, her end was hidden from us. She was found penniless in a Paris gutter and expired alone in a French hospital. No relations attended her funeral. She had shocked them all beyond endurance, but they sent a six-foot wreath that seemed embarrassingly demonstrative in the almost empty church. I like to recall her as the sprite-like little girl I had seen in the Nevill Holt wood with her mother and George Moore, when my father had taken me on a Leicestershire bicycle tour in 1907, visiting my seventeenth-century ancestors.

Three weeks passed. I found I could take no pleasure in the scene, my mind elsewhere. Then one evening, as I sat in a friend's box at the Fenice Theatre, a voice spoke within me, clear, imperative. Hastily apologising to my friend, I rushed back to my hotel, packed, and caught the next train to London. The voice within me cried my name, and I knew it was my mother's. It proved to be no false call. On the evening before my return the mist had lifted and she had asked for me. The next morning my telegram had been received and she was told that I was coming home. On arrival I went at once to her room. She sat thin and worn, in her dressing-gown, the spirit visibly breaking through the flesh. She had no knowledge of how long I had been away. All her life and love flowed back in our moment of reunion. One of her hands was tight-closed and when I asked her what she had in it she just smiled. I opened her fingers. Crushed in them was my small photograph which they had not been able to take from her. "You have been a good son," she said softly. A few days later she died. So closed thirty-four years of our unbroken communion, of a comradeship that could never be replaced.

CHAPTER THIRTEEN

The Third Tour

I

IN OCTOBER, 1926, shortly after my loss, a friend of mine who was a lecturer at the University College rang me up. His wife was a bright little woman who often acted in amateur theatricals with my friend Jack Laing. He invited me to a small party they were giving. I told him that I felt in no mood to go to parties. "Oh, do come! It will do you good. I'll tell Jack to bring you along," he said. His wife then came to the telephone to persuade me. I agreed to go, reluctantly. I was leaving for Nice in a few days. I had found my home quite intolerable with memories and loneliness.

When I went I found at their home over a dozen friends assembled, some of them my host's colleagues. Presently more guests came in. One of them gave me a shock, a tall thin man with a long beard. I went over to Jack and said: "Have you seen who's arrived? Look over there!" He looked. "Good heavens! It's the stork from Lake Como!" he exclaimed. I sought my host and asked who was the thin fellow with the beard. He looked surprised. "My dear chap, surely you know! It's Lytton Strachey who wrote *Eminent Victorians*. He's visiting here. Come along, I'll introduce you." But, in the perverse manner of sherry parties, before my host got round to doing so, Strachey and his escort had disappeared. I was deeply disappointed.

Strachey's visit to Nottingham is recorded in letters which he wrote, abusing the city. He seems to have had a dreary time. The weather was bad and we learn he made no real attempt to see the town or its environs. He was often a malicious letter-writer, reckless and ill-informed. The letters from Nottingham are no exception. "It is the oddest, grimmest place in the world, with a certain hideous grandeur," he wrote. "Enormously large, it is grim and vast in a way I hardly expected . . . So far I've seen nothing in the shops, or out of them, to deserve more than passing attention."* In his opinion he seems to have been in accord with Graham Greene who had been there ten months earlier. Michael Holroyd in his monumental biography tells us that Strachey, who stayed with an old Cambridge friend, a lecturer at University College, "spent most of his time before a gas-fire reading Elizabethan books". Friends of his host came to tea but "they seemed a melancholy crew". One of these was Professor Weekley, whose wife, fourteen years earlier, had eloped with D. H. Lawrence, having known him for only six weeks. Strachey, meeting Weekley, called him "a pompous old ape". I knew the professor. The statement was a gross libel. Weekley had shown Lawrence much kindness when a student at University College. Later, when Lawrence sought his help in obtaining a better teaching post, he had asked him to lunch. From that meeting with Frieda, who tried within a few days to induce Lawrence to sleep with her while her husband was away, began the infatuation that led to the elopement. It was she who ran away with Lawrence. Throughout the ensuing fourteen years the professor had behaved with much dignity though the scandal had almost cost him his post at the College. To call the injured husband "a pompous ape" was yet another of Strachey's malicious, unfounded statements.

His judgment of Nottingham was equally ignorant and prejudiced. A city with 200,000 inhabitants could hardly be called "vast". Nor was "grim" the word for a place whose natural beauties had earned it the title of "Queen of the Midlands". As Defoe had remarked, there are few pleasanter cities in the kingdom, with its Castle rock, great open Market Place, terraced residential quarters, a hill-town sloping to the valley of the Trent.

I much regretted having had no opportunity of hearing Strachey talk. There is ample evidence that he was a brilliant conversationalist. As a letter-writer, albeit often venomous and double-faced, he ranks in the class in which Byron is pre-eminent. It may be that this is the

* *Lytton Strachey. Vol. II The Years of Achievement,* by Michael Holroyd. (Heinemann Ltd.)

Strachey that will outlive the brilliant but untrustworthy biographer, the "gamin" who threw a brick through the gothic windows of Victorian respectability.

II

I was now faced with the problem of my future. At thirty-four I was alone in the world and where I lay my head mattered to no one. The little home I had created was barren. I had considered, on resigning from my editorship, settling in London, the natural centre of my interests, but I dismissed the idea, then being unwilling to submit my mother to another uprooting, with life in a strange city. I decided to make no immediate change. Temperamental, prone to retrospection, I realised that work promised salvation. I therefore cabled my lecture agent to book for me the tour I had had to postpone last winter. Meanwhile, I left in the middle of October for the French Riviera, taking with me the unfinished *Diary of Russell Beresford*. I found a lodging in Nice, on the uncompleted west end of the Promenade des Anglais, on a top floor, with a terrace. I looked over the sunlit beauty of the Baie des Anges, the woody spur of Mont Boron, and the Maritime Alps. Alas, the change availed me nothing. A new despair fell on me and I could neither work nor sleep. I began to dislike the place. As I stood on my balcony looking down upon the brightly lit crescent-promenade, with its line of rococo hotels, how apt was the phrase of H. G. Wells about this "luminous eczema on the fringe of the sea"!

There was one tragi-comic episode in this unhappy time. The houseman who brought me my breakfast told me that each morning he saw from the bathroom window, at the back of the apartment, an almost naked woman wildly dancing over a plot near a large shed. "I think she must be crazy," he said. The next morning he called me into the bathroom and from the window I saw a middle-aged woman energetically dancing over the ground. Her movements were not ungainly but her figure, flimsily clad, was repellent. We wondered who the poor creature could be. One morning the houseman informed me that the eccentric dancer was the famous Isadora Duncan. It seemed that, being in low circumstances, she was living in a large house-studio she had bought in more prosperous times. She was now forty-eight years of age and had come to the close of a hectic career. Seven years earlier she had accepted the invitation of Lenin to open a school of dancing in Moscow. While there she married a half-mad young poet, Sergei Essenin, ten years her junior. The school failing, she left with him for the United States. There were difficulties in his entering the country. The immigration barrier passed, Isadora was soon in the news again. During a dance recital at the Symphony Hall in Boston on October 22nd, 1922, she created an uproar by waving a red scarf on the stage. The campaign against her became so intense that she left the United States vowing she would never return.

Her subsequent years were full of difficulties, financial and domestic. After stormy scenes her crazy husband shot himself. Her two children were drowned in the Seine. She was past dancing and her vogue was dead. Ten months after I had seen her pathetic exhibition outside her studio she came to a tragic end. One young lover having deserted her, she picked up another, a garage mechanic, "A Greek god," she avowed, in an Antibes café, and "dated" him. On the evening of September 14th, 1927, he called for her in his racing Bugatti. A friend, alarmed, begged him not to drive too fast. "Adieu, mes amis! Je vais à la gloire!" cried Isadora exuberantly, seating herself in the bucket seat. They had gone only a short distance when the end of her long silk scarf was caught up in the rear wheel. Her head was pulled down sharply and her neck was broken.

In fulfilment of her wish Isadora Duncan was cremated in Paris. A friend of mine went to the service. He arrived early in order to secure a seat in the chapel. To his amazement he found an immense crowd standing outside the gaunt crematorium. All Paris seemed to be there, waiting and whispering as a drizzle of rain fell steadily. The crowd was representative of every phase of Parisian life, from academicians to bohemian artists and café poets, from society duchesses to the poorest prostitutes. They all spoke of her as 'Isa' as if they had lost an intimate friend. It was impossible to enter the building. From the roof of the great block rose a chimney to which all eyes looked expectantly. Eventually there came out of it a steady column of smoke. The crowd watched in silence, until the last spiral vanished in the sullen sky. "I thought of a Papal Conclave," he wrote, "that I had witnessed in Rome, standing with a multitude in St. Peter's Square, awaiting the emission of smoke that would tell us a new Pope was elected. Now, a slow spiral informed us of the election of an Immortal."

After a month in Nice I returned to Nottingham to prepare for my lecture tour. With a desperate effort I finished *The Diary of Russell Beresford*, incorporating more letters from Myra who was now in Washington. I postponed any decision about my home and left my excellent housekeeper in charge of it and sailed on the *Samaria* for New York. Thus I spent a third Christmas in mid-Atlantic.

III

On arrival in New York I was rewarded by a brilliant morning as we proceeded up the Hudson River to the Cunard landing stage. I wondered if once again my lecture manager, the cheery Mr. Glass, would be at the dockside to meet me. Yes, there he was with his expansive smile. "Well! well! Welcome home!" he cried. He soon disposed of the Customs. "I've good news, you're sold out!" he informed me as soon as we were in the taxi. "And we've boosted your fee up to $200 and $250. Some of the old clients growled." "Where are you sending me?" I asked. "From Toronto to Texas, from Maine to Kansas. Heavy bookings around Chicago," he replied. My subjects were "What Europe is Thinking" and "The Art of the Novelist", so I covered two fields, the political and the literary.

We drew up at my hotel. I was glad to reach it. We had driven through snow-laden streets, ten degrees "below". Glass had only just left me in my room when the telephone rang. A bootlegger? No, it was a female voice. "Good morning, Mr. Roberts, this is your operator, Miss Worsheim speaking. Welcome to New York. I have a message for you." She delivered the message but she did not ring off. "May I give you a tip?" she asked seductively. "Yes?" What had I done wrong? "Buy Sears Roebuck, it's still rising. It jumped nine points yesterday." I thanked her and put down the receiver. This was another intimation of the stock-market boom that had smitten America. Everyone was gambling in shares.

I spent the New Year at Rye with my old friends the Wainwrights. Their son, Townsend, was home from Cornell University, a friendly youth who clad me in his racoon coat. These great fur coats, and hats with a feather stuck in their crown, were then the fashionable attire for college boys. He invited me to be his guest at Kappa Alpha fraternity house. "You've stayed at Harvard, come to Cornell. We're not in a swamp, we're on a mountain." I said I would if my schedule allowed it. Three days later I opened my tour at New Bedford. In four consecutive nights I slept there and in Boston, Buffalo and Detroit. In Detroit I occupied the room Hugh Walpole had just vacated. It was almost Box and Cox with British authors touring America. We English were very dominant in the literary world in those days, a phalanx headed by Galsworthy at the peak of his vogue. The "best-seller" lists were almost monopolised by us. Out of fourteen listed books nine or ten would be by British authors. In the next decade I was six times in the list, always in the company of my countrymen. The American writers had not yet dominated the field. Later a new consciousness of American authors, headed by Hemingway, Faulkner, Fitzgerald, Bromfield, and Steinbeck, caused us to be pushed off the scene. World War II saw the American writers take possession of their terrain and extend their conquests to Europe. Our monopoly was ended.

After Detroit I took a night train for New York and arrived in good time to lunch at Garden City with gigantic Russell Doubleday, my new publisher, and then went off to a select audience where I earned $200 just for reading my poems. The following evening the roles were reversed, I was a listener instead of a performer.

The Thomas Lamonts were again very hospitable to me. I was invited to dine and afterwards to listen to a lecture given by the famous Dr. Alfred Adler, Professor of Psychoanalysis in the Pedagogic Institute of Vienna. Psychoanalysis had become the rage in the States, following Dr. Freud's discovery of the "libido" and the "complex". None of us was normal. All of us lived with a buried consciousness, a "libido". This Latin word for lust had come into fashion. It accounted for the enigmatic smile on the face of Leonardo da Vinci's Mona Lisa. Leonardo suffered from a repression of the libido (beinahe verwirrende Libido verdrängung.). Tied to the fetish of his mother's lips he painted all women with a mysterious smile. Leonardo had been thwarted in childhood by being taken from his mother who had kissed him into erotic submission. "In the manner of all unfaithful mothers she took her little son in place of her husband and robbed him of part of his virility by maturing his erotic life too early," wrote Freud. In short, release your libido. You may discover you are suffering from an Œdipus complex. As Max Beerbohm commented: "A strange family the Œdipuses."

Freud, Jung and Adler were the prophets of this new science. A horde of psychiatrists moved into a new remunerative field. A wave of alcoholism, divorce, religious mania, stock-market hysteria and various other disorders afflicted the inhabitants of the United States, as if to match the hurricanes that swept that huge continent. There was a rush to the consulting rooms where troubled Americans lay on couches and unburdened themselves of their complexes, at considerable expense. The psychiatrists became as popular as the leech doctors of the eighteenth century. It was a new religion, with a confessional couch instead of a confessional box. In 1927 Hollywood sustained nineteen practitioners with fees ranging from fifty to five hundred dollars a sitting.

When I went to the Lamonts dinner on the evening of January 13th, 1927, I knew nothing of their guest of honour and lecturer, Professor Adler. On enquiry I learned that he had been a colleague of Freud, but differing, had broken away from the Freudian school. He was now on a lecture tour of the American universities. He spoke English fluently. After dinner he lectured in the salon to a large audience invited by our host. The company comprised the leaders in finance, society, art, music and literature in New York, for the Lamonts were influential and highly esteemed.

We listened and wondered. Dr. Adler revealed surprising facets of the human mind. It seemed that all of us lived with a buried consciousness, a libido which, suppressed, accounted for our curious behaviour. The elegant ladies and gentlemen in the audience looked at one another, more amused than alarmed. There were long intricate passages in the discourse. From time to time "case sheets" were revealed to us. One of these was startling. There had been a Viennese lady of fashion among the professor's patients, who was greatly troubled by the fact that she had ceased to enjoy sexual intercourse with her husband although she still loved him. The cause of this being obscure, she consulted our lecturer, who, after a time, got to the root of the trouble. The nape of the neck of her husband's young chauffeur induced a traumatic state that inhibited her natural sexual response. She had been quite unaware of this complex. On the professor's advice she procured the dismissal of the chauffeur. With his departure her neurosis disappeared. "The subconscious element latent in our psychosis will produce a psychosomatic malady," observed Dr. Adler. His discourse came to an end. There was enthusiastic applause for the savant. As we left the house, and the cars with their chauffeurs lined up for the guests, I could not help wondering how many of these Wall Street bankers present this evening would be curious about their chauffeurs' necks.

Some thirty years later there was a curious sequel to that evening. The novelist Francis Brett Young had died in South Africa and I wrote a letter of condolence to his wife. She thanked me and asked, "Why, over thirty years ago, at the Lamonts' dinner and lecture did you avoid us? You never spoke a word to us at dinner. Afterwards you sat aloof in a far corner of the salon and slipped away without greeting us. Francis and I were hurt. Why were you so proud?" The answer to this question was simple. I was not aware that the Brett Youngs, whom I had never met, were present. I should have been glad to talk with a colleague whom I greatly admired. And proud I have never been—"We ain't proud—Ma says it's sinful," I could say with Mrs. Kenwigs. It is singular that whereas I never experience a qualm on ascending a platform, I often suffer from nervousness amounting to panic whenever I enter a drawing-room and find myself in a group of strangers. I feel this so strongly that it often results in an involuntary exhibitionist reaction. "You're a born actor!" a friend would say, having witnessed one of these displays. He could not know that I had "put an antic disposition on", simply to mask my nervousness.

The Lamont dinner had overwhelmed me with its setting and its distinguished company. My host apart, I knew no one in this bright assembly. I was almost mute at dinner, and at the lecture sought an obscure corner. How gladly would I have responded to a greeting from another Englishman, particularly from the author of *My Brother Jonathan*. My right-hand neighbour at the table was Lady Ribblesdale, a woman of outstanding beauty, swanlike with her long neck and regal air. I think she found me a nonentity and unrewarding, for she talked most of the time with her other neighbour. I should have found her still more overwhelming had I known that she was the former Mrs. John Jacob Astor, a famous beauty and now the wife of the most spectacular nobleman in England, Lord Ribblesdale, the "ancestor" of Sargent's famous portrait. Fifteen years later she was to become one of my warmest friends. She was well-read and strikingly lovely to the very end of her long life.

After the Lamont dinner I immediately had to catch a sleeper to Baltimore where I was due to give a lecture at 9 a.m. the next day. It had been a momentous day for me. I had signed an agreement for Doubleday to publish me and in the afternoon I, too, had been "psychoanalysed", in a manner. The *New York World* had sent one of its most skilled writers, Harry Salpeter, to interview me. He was a little man with gimlet eyes, merciless in his questions. He was famous for the candour and incisiveness of his interviews, and some refused the ordeal. He had cross-examined monarchs and murderers with the same cool efficiency. Today he would have been a star performer on the television screen with those autopsies that give a vast audience a thrill.

Salpeter spent an hour dissecting me. I had been somewhat apprehensive of the result, but when his article appeared it was well-mannered, and accurate in detail. Under the heading "One of the most dynamic of English men", which struck a threatening note, he wrote: "The closest approach in a man to a steel spring is Cecil Roberts. Cecil Edric Mornington Roberts, as his full name indicates, is an Englishman. The name by which he is better known indicates the clipped, staccato character of the most American Englishman I have yet seen. He is tall, lithe, intense. Painfully thin, he gives the impression of being a condensed version of three vital men. His skin is drawn tightly over expressive features, and the gleam and glint of his eyes are as signals of volcanic vitality within, almost bespeaking at times impatience with draught-horse minds that cannot keep pace with him. He speaks with crystaline clearness, with economy, directness and force."

In two columns he analysed me. He did not like my views on democracy—what American could, since I had said: "Up to now democracy in pure form has not been tried in America. Because of its prosperity, which has made it, incidentally, the most hated nation in the world, America does not face yet the crisis that England does." (Read forty years later, was I so far out?)

Salpeter's acute mind underlined a doubt that was growing within me. Was it not better to do one thing well rather than two and put them in competition? "He reverses the case of the average English writer who comes here to lecture," he wrote. "He lectures better than he writes, perhaps because it would be impossible for anyone to write better than he lectures. From the dizzy height of thirty-five he can look back upon one lifetime of work and forward to another."

It was my habit to commune with myself in the bath and address myself in the mirror. Out of one's clothes one comes down to the naked truth. On the day that I read the Salpeter interview I had a long bathroom session with myself. "Dynamic," I said, letting more water into the bath. Wasn't that a mistake on my part? I recalled Max Beerbohm, who sat in the sun on his Rapallo terrace, did nothing, and watched his reputation grow. (Writing his Life many years later, Lord David Cecil told me that he found it very difficult—"There are such long periods in which Max did nothing!") Dynamism would have destroyed Max.

Salpeter said of me: "He lectures better than he writes." Again, wasn't this lecturing a mistake, basically a thing of vanity? You rushed all over a vast continent, worked your magic for two hours on an audience and at the end there was little to show for it, a few dollars, a few press cuttings and immense fatigue. There was little money in it, really. By sitting at home and quietly working one could earn twice as much with a quarter of the effort, and do something really creative.

I stood up, took a cold shower and stepped out of the bath. "Painfully thin"? I looked at myself in the long mirror. No, not so painfully, please. My tailor had misled lynx-eyed Mr. Salpeter.

"Skin tightly drawn over . . ." As I shaved, the mirror did not bear that out. Yes, when this tour was over I would cease to be dynamic, I would idle in the sun like Max, and be leisurely elegant as he was on his tiled terrace above the Mediterranean.

The morning after the Adler lecture, and before Salpeter's interview had reached me, I stepped out on the platform at Baltimore in the early morning. A kind, grey-haired professor from Goucher College was there to meet me and took me to an hotel where we breakfasted. In the taxi he said: "I think you'll find our young ladies—" "What!" I exclaimed, "I thought Goucher was a men's college! You're a sort of Vassar?" "No sir, smaller, and I would say mellower," he replied gently. After arriving at the college I had another shock. I was taken to the President's office. Someone produced a black gown for me. "Oh, no thank you!" I said. The Dame President looked at me like a fractious boy. "We expect all our lecturers to be gowned. Mr. John Cowper Powys always brings his own," she said firmly. Squashed, I submitted. Gowned, I followed the President in a procession to the platform. From it I looked upon tiers of solemn-faced young ladies, some five hundred of them. After a graceful introduction I rose and advanced, buried in my enormous gown. I tripped on it in front of the lectern. I lost my hands in it and had to shake it back to produce them. I felt like The Sorcerer's Apprentice. It suggested my opening lines, for before those calm young faces cruelly appraising me I grew desperate. "I hope you will not think me a necromancer. I am no Cagliostro. I am really a frightened mouse," I said. It brought down the house. The Dame President had to laugh. After that it was easy. I forgot for the time the subject of my lecture, "The Art of the Novelist". I recounted the overnight lecture at the Lamonts. The story of the chauffeur's nape was a wild success. "You see how we novelists find our themes. My next novel will be about the psychological adventures of a high-born Austrian princess. It will be both risqué and asterisky." I forgot the beastly gown under their warm encouragement. I was cheered when I left the platform. Later the President wrote to my agent: "He enchanted us. We shall never forget his lecture." So I was a necromancer after all. I had expected a letter of protest.

275

This, of course, was not my first appearance at a women's university. I had faced a thousand beautiful maidens at prestigious Vassar above the Hudson River. It might have been Cologne on the Rhine, and these the virgins led by St. Ursula as shown in Carpaccio's painting. I stayed on to help with a student production of *Romeo and Juliet*. I rehearsed Romeo, a beautiful peach-faced nymph of nineteen, ravishing in piebald hose, who said: "It's sure lovely to hear you, Mr. Roberts, but I just haven't got your vowels!"

IV

I did not stay in Baltimore—rows of red-brick houses with steps going up to the front door—I hurried on to Washington. I had a mission. Myra was living there with her mother. I had sent her a duplicate of the manuscript of *The Diary of Russell Beresford*, asking her to read it. I had used a number of her excellent letters. I asked her, if she had the slightest objection to my use of them, to tell me when I came to see her, and I would delete them.

I arrived in the afternoon and had a warm welcome. She was as lovely and vital as ever. I saw that some of her beauty was derived from her mother. She was dismayed when I said I must leave that evening by sleeper for New York. She had read the manuscript and was enthusiastic about the book. "I don't want a line deleted. But how did you find out?" she asked.

"Find out? What do you mean?"

"About me. Your heroine was not able to marry Beresford because she was a Catholic and couldn't get an annulment of her marriage."

I looked puzzled. She put her hands over mine, her eyes serious but with a mocking look. "My dear, I'm your Mrs. Burdett! I'm married, I'm a Catholic, and I haven't been able to get an annulment."

For a few moments I did not understand what she was saying. So this was the reason of my misgiving about her! But she had called herself Miss Lange. How could that be if she was married? She explained. When very young, impulsively, she had married. It had been a failure from the beginning and after a year of separation she had gone to Rome, accompanied by her mother, to obtain an annulment. All seemed to have gone well, it would go through, the lawyers said. She went next to Paris, where her mother left her, and then to London.

"But when I met you in London you called yourself Miss Lange."

"Yes, I anticipated the annulment and reverted to my maiden name. But an outcry had been made about an annulment granted to an American heiress married to a duke, and mine didn't go through. The whole thing was so prolonged, so costly and so futile. I wrote that play to publicise the injustice of it all."

"The play on which you wanted me to collaborate with you?" I asked.

"Yes. Isn't it all ridiculous and unfair! Of course my annulment may come through yet. The lawyers are still pressing my case. When I read this manuscript I felt certain you must have learned about my marriage."

"No, I had not, but somehow I have always suspected something," I replied. "Why didn't you tell me?"

"I was waiting for the annulment first."

"But you'd have committed bigamy!"

Myra looked at me wide-eyed. We began to argue. But you could not argue with Myra. She was as elusive as a figure-skater.

"I shall get free. You'll see. We women are going to change things!" she declared.

We dined with her mother. At eleven o'clock I left to catch my train for New York. I was quite dazed. It had been the most extraordinary twenty-four hours, the Adler lecture, Goucher College, Myra. I slept badly on the train, arriving early in New York. One wrote novels but the facts of life surpassed them.

Twenty-four hours later I was in Montreal where, after my lecture, a lady I did not know came up and said she was my cousin. If she had claimed that she was my wife I should not have been surprised in this upside-down world. But she proved that she was my cousin, and a very nice one, who had emigrated to Canada with her husband many years earlier. The next day I was in Toronto lecturing on "What Europe Is Thinking". I could not have told anyone lucidly what I was thinking.

Since autobiography permits a vista down the channel of Time I will complete the saga of Myra. She did not cease to give me shocks.

Six years after the Washington revelation I received one of those enormous Sunday editions of American newspapers, since then copied by our own. It had been sent to me anonymously. Puzzled, I searched for a review of one of my books. There was nothing, and then there leapt before me a full-page photogravure portrait of a beautiful young woman holding up a baby. It was Myra! The text underneath informed me that it was the portrait of the wife of Count S——, very popular in diplomatic circles, with her baby son. There had been no word of any marriage in her letters to me, and nothing about her having achieved an annulment of her former marriage.

A year later I was called up from the Dorchester Hotel in London. It was Myra, who informed me that she had arrived with her son and nurse. I must come to lunch. She had not changed. A bonny baby was brought in for inspection. A week later Myra left for Paris. Twelve years went by and the telephone rang in my cottage at Henley-on-Thames. Myra, in London, asked if she could come to lunch. She arrived with her son, a good-looking little boy and his tutor. I asked about her husband. "Oh, that's come to an end," she replied. "It was a mistake." The tutor, an Oxford undergraduate, engaged for the holiday, puzzled me by saying "Yes, Lady B——" several times. When he had gone out into the garden with the boy I said: "Myra, what's this Lady B—— stuff?" She looked at me innocent-eyed. "Oh, I married Sir John B—— last week." I knew Sir John. He was an eminent banker, a handsome old boy turned seventy. She had arrived in a Rolls-Royce, with chauffeur.

Again Myra disappeared. Ten years later, on the eve of sailing from New York, I heard someone call my name in the salon of the Ritz Hotel. It was Myra, robust and matronly, but her eyes were still crystally beautiful. She and Sir John were sailing for London on my boat! So we were six days together. Myra pretended to be very furtive, saying Sir John was jealous. He went to bed early, however, and then it would be safe for us to dance. I would have nothing of this nonsense, and old Sir John and I became quite cordial to each other. Then Sir John died, Myra died.

The memory of her is still with me, of a June day in Green Park when a child showed us a matchbox with a caterpillar in it, of wonderful days in Venice, of a dozen incidents and places that still have a radiance about them tinged with the sadness of vanished happiness.

V

On, on I went. Toronto, Detroit and then Chicago again with the Higbees carrying me off to their Evanston home, with the canaries singing in the sun-parlour at breakfast and a snow-bright, frozen world outside. It was my base for the next ten days while I lectured in and around Chicago. It was well that I was left no time to think. The rush of Chicago blotted out any introspection. The city had a menacing fascination, blizzard-struck on the verge of vast, frozen Lake Michigan, arctic in winter, broiled in summer. Chicago had been described as "the wickedest city in the world", and "a giant in a state of matted filth". During the fourteen years of Prohibition there were 703 gang murders arising directly from the drink traffic. In the year I visited it 275 persons were shot to death. But it was always hospitable to me. The Executives Club had become my platform. It provided a vital and influential audience. I went from the highly serious to the slightly comic, from addressing a Bankers' conference to the Medieval Club whose members played at being monks. Each had received a summons in red, green and blue Gothic script. We dined in pseudo-Tudor gloom at long tables lit by candles. We ate venison on wooden platters and drank mulled ale out of pewter tankards. It was all very solemn and idiosyncratic but enjoyable. Strange, how hard-headed Americans like to play at being fifteen!

The following evening I was invited to dine with the Vice-President of the United States, General Dawes, who lived in Evanston. He was a man who had gained fame as the people's advocate against the railroad tycoons. He was fifty-two when America entered the war in 1917. He volunteered and rose to be a Brigadier-General. A banker by profession, Coolidge appointed him chairman of the Allied Reparations Committee in 1923 and he found a financial solution that became known as the Dawes Plan, a famous achievement in European politics. In 1925 he shared the Nobel Prize with Sir Austen Chamberlain. Two years after I had been his guest he was appointed Ambassador Extraordinary to Great Britain. Such was my host. He was a warm-hearted man, rich in experience. We talked from nine until one in the morning. In contrast to the President he was an extrovert. He smoked a corn-cob pipe. He had a fine library. His favourite English poem was *The Shropshire Lad*, the whole of which he could recite. He was musical and had composed a "Melody in A minor" which he played at my request. In response I played the Chopin *Nocturne* also in A minor. I found that we both shared an ambition to visit Chopin's birthplace at Zelazowa Wola in Poland. How very singular that, seeing this birthplace two years later, I should be able to address a picture-postcard to him at the American Embassy in London and write on it the hackneyed bromide, "Wish you were here!"

Once more I set off on the trail, north to Minneapolis, south to Kansas City. The latter had a famous photographer who could charge five hundred dollars for a portrait. He invited me to sit. His studio was awesome with apparatus. It looked like the X-ray room in a hospital. He flooded it with Klieg lights. He spent an hour on me and I emerged perspiring and exhausted. The result was really wonderful. He had turned me into a Spanish Jew! It was art but it was not me. I have always been unphotogenic.

All the next night my train roared south. At breakfast I looked out on a prairie-like landscape at any moment expecting to see Red Indians. At noon I was at Muskegee. At four in the afternoon I detrained at Fayetteville in the State of Arkansas, pronounced Arkansaw. Fayetteville housed the State university with seven thousand students, to whom I was to lecture. On a hot sunny afternoon in February I was collected by a tall, thin professor in a cowboy hat, wearing a black string tie. He looked like a character out of a Mark Twain story. I was driven in a one-horse buggy through a dusty town to my hotel on the outskirts, near the professor's house. The hotel was built of wood, with a bar on one side of the reception room. There was a large plate-glass window looking on to a straggling street of telegraph poles. American telegraph poles are often bent and gnarled, just as they have come out of the forest. By the window there were five rocking chairs and three spittoons. The hotel keeper-cum-reception-clerk, in his shirt sleeves, with a green eyeshade, smoking a cigar, took my bag and conducted me up a squeaking staircase to an overheated room. It was bare but clean with an iron double bedstead and a side table holding a Gideon Bible. There was a rocking chair with the inseparable spittoon. "Ye're British, eh? Mah boy was there in the war. Sez you're nice folks when unstuffed. If you want anything, holler!"

I followed him downstairs to the waiting professor who had invited me home to an early dinner before my lecture. We arrived at a wooden chalet with a long, covered verandah on which there were rocking chairs. The professor's white-haired, spectacled wife greeted me. I must excuse her dress but she was helping to cook the dinner. There was a red sunset over the brown landscape. We sat in the rocking chairs. "You'll excuse me, I've a bit of foot trouble," said the professor, taking off his boots and resting his feet on the verandah rail. His wife brought us glasses of mint julep. "You'll have a fine audience tonight. Some of our faculty remember hearing you in Dallas three years ago. Our students aren't what you'd call Harvard Princeton material. They come from simple homes. We've been having a bit of trouble on the campus. Chamber of Commerce here complained our graduates couldn't write or count! Exaggerated, but I'm grieved to admit there was something in it. We've had to tighten up on degree-giving." I had long passed any ability to be surprised. Crossing the campus at Iowa University I had seen an impressive Greek temple. Above its front hung a banner. *The Pantorium*, it proclaimed. I asked what it meant. "Oh, that's an old lecture hall. It's now dedicated to pressing the students' pants!"

Four professors and their wives arrived for dinner. The food was excellent, cooked by my hostess and a coloured girl. After dinner, in the large auditorium of the university, I faced over a thousand students. After lecturing for an hour and a half on "What Europe Is Thinking" I was dismayed by my chairman saying that I would answer questions. These poured in on me for another hour. Most of them were surprisingly intelligent, belying all that I had been told about Arkansas being a "punk" State, a flourishing home of the Ku Klux Klan. What astonished me was the number of students who thought that America should have joined the League of Nations. When I left the platform I had been two and a half hours on my feet.

Nor was that the end. Having shaken hands for twenty minutes I was whisked off to a reception staged by the Faculty Club. More handshaking, more questions. It was past midnight when I reached my room where, in the corner of the ceiling, a horrifying, stupendous insect glared at me. As instructed, I hollered. A Negro youth came up. "Sure, sah, but it ain't nuthin', " he said, disappeared and returned with a whisk broom. I waited on the landing. Presently he appeared, grinning. "'E gone, sah!" "Where?" I asked. "Out of window, sah!" But had it gone? I had not heard the window opened. I undressed and got into bed, apprehensive.

The next day, Sunday, a young professor took me to lunch with some friends on a farm, a hundred miles out over a burnt-up plain near the Ozark mountains. It was the Wild West in the wild south. There were signs of astonishing luxury, a fleet of cars in the railed courtyard, fine china and glass on the table. There were sixteen guests at lunch. The women riders wore de luxe breeches and boots. They were pretty and well-dressed with a carefully achieved simplicity. I was not surprised to learn that this was a playboy ranch belonging to an oil magnate.

That night I entrained for Dallas, Texas, which I reached in the morning, but I went on to Denton, to the State College for Women where I was due to give a series of lectures. I spoke in a vast auditorium holding two thousand students of the ten thousand at the college. They were all housed in excellent brick dormitories built on ground where, fifty years earlier, the hooves of wild herds had thundered on the prairie. On one evening when I lectured we went to the auditorium without our overcoats and hats, the outdoor temperature being seventy degrees. While I spoke there was a strange external roar. A "Norther" had arrived from Alaska! When we went outside the temperature had fallen to thirty degrees and we had to wait for closed cars to take us away. The noise did not trouble the audience. They knew what it was. Apparently I had not shown any nervousness. "Like Keats, his diction is a joy forever," said the Press, reporting. What was Keats's diction like, I wondered—Cockney?

I spent a delightful week at Denton. I had a large sunny room where I could write my articles for the *Westminster Gazette* and correct the script of my new novel, *Sagusto*. One day I was driven some thirty miles to see another ranch. It was different from my last, though it had its luxuries, including an electric plant that supplied hot and cold air. It had a storm cellar against hurricanes. This ranch was small and had only one cowboy, genuine. It had originally been the cabin of a geologist who had struck oil. He had spent a hundred thousand dollars on the place as a memorial to his luck.

On leaving Denton I made a long trek. For the next thirty-five hours I was in the train going to Athens, Alabama. I came to enjoy these long journeys. Most of the trains had club cars at the end. Here I talked to everyone, in all walks of life. It was a continuous illustration of the vagaries of fate, its fickle justice, its patternless disappointments and rewards. They all had a story to tell, and they all sought some kind of sympathy or admiration, the foolish more than the wise. Often they were on strange errands, obstinate with hope or sustained by illusions. Here one could possess oneself, read and rest, free from telephone calls and lecture committees. At 7 a.m., the next day I rose to a lesson in geography, with echoes from one's reading; at Memphis we were crossing the American Nile, the wide, brown Mississippi, Mark Twain's river just as much as the Nile was Cleopatra's. Then came Decatur and, in the afternoon my destination, Athens, which unlike Nashville, had no copy, despite its name, of the Parthenon.

That same evening, while dressing for dinner, preceding my lecture, I saw a train slide by at the bottom of my host's garden. It carried a long sign "The Seminole Florida Express". Florida, where my young friend Howard Phillips lived, whom I had last seen in New Orleans three years ago. There was a gap of five days before my next lecture engagement in South Carolina. I asked my host about the Florida train. Yes, it ran through Athens each evening and reached Jacksonville in Florida the next morning. There was a connection that would get me to Orlando, the Phillips' town at noon. It was now or never. I sent a telegram and left Athens the following evening. At noon the next day I was being motored through a subtropical town to a large colonial-pattern house with a columned portico overlooking one of Orlando's twenty lakes. The temperature was seventy-five. I lunched with the family in a room with the electric light on and the blinds drawn to keep out the sun, which could be tiresome. That evening Howard took me to the greyhound racing under enormous arc lights. A huge crowd ate popcorn, drank Coca-Cola and cheered its favourite hounds. The colours, the vitality of it all on a February summer evening!

Orlando was surely the Garden of Eden, with broad tree-lined streets, houses bowered in palms and rose gardens, pellucid lakes encircled by red-brick promenades, shady with oaks hung with Spanish moss and orange groves from which blew a scented wind, for these trees blossomed and gave their fruit simultaneously. To their perfume was added that of camphor and eucalyptus trees. Flowers were in full bloom; scarlet poinsettias, the "flame vine", which trailed its blossoms of fire over walls and pergolas; hedges of yellow-tongued hibiscus. It might have been Tahiti, Bali or Honolulu.

My host owned great orange plantations with miles on miles of groves. The fruit hung like golden globes amid the dark metallic leaves and white blossom. I was taken to see the site of a future plantation of 10,000 acres. It was to have houses, school, shops, a railway station and a large fruit-packing factory. We stopped by a little lake, with a sandy shore and a cabin surrounded by pine trees. "Look, Cecil, I'll give you this lake and a little orange grove," said Howard. "Then you can come out each winter and write here!" I had the utmost difficulty in refusing to become a Florida orange-grower.

We played tennis at night on a floodlit court, we visited Daytona Beach soon to be famous for its twenty-three-mile long automobile sand track on which one day in 1935 Malcolm Campbell would create, with his Bluebird, a record of 276 miles per hour. Too soon the three days in paradise ended. I entrained, almost tearful, the recipient of so much kindness. Twenty-four hours later a new host, the President of Coker College at Hartsville in South Carolina, took me off the train. There was now a bite in the air, though poinsettias and hibiscus flowered in the gardens. Before the lecture that evening the President gave a dinner and I recall it because I met Mrs. Gay, aged eighty-four and lively as her name. She had come to America in a boat that had taken seven weeks to make the crossing and she had had to carry her own food and linen!

I rose the next day at 5 a.m. to make a train connection, and ten hours later arrived at Raleigh, North Carolina, the State capital, named in 1787 in honour of Sir Walter Raleigh. Here my host at Harvard University in 1920 again entertained me. My train was five hours late owing to a blizzard. We had gone in a few hours from summer into deep winter. My friend was now a Representative in the State Legislature. I was taken to a debate in the Senate House and invited to sit beside the Speaker. A Bill was being discussed. A copy of it was given to me. I was startled to read: "A Bill for the Prevention of the Sale of Condoms in the State of North Carolina." A very ribald debate soon enlightened me as to the meaning of "condom"—a contraceptive. One honourable member accused another of being motivated "by impotent envy". My host gave a lunch for me at the Walter Raleigh Hotel. Had Sir Walter ever been in Raleigh, I asked. "Well, sir, it ain't been proved yet but we go on hoping some professor will link us up!" came the reply. Again a night train and the next morning I was in Maryland, then on again to Massachusetts, to rock-bound, snow-bound Maine, and other places that grew colder and colder. In Minneapolis, muffled up like an Eskimo, I sailed on an ice yacht, at a terrifying speed.

At the end of April I had concluded my lecture engagements, except for one that would keep me in America until mid-June. I had lectured early that month at Washington, and Jefferson College, a venerable institution founded in 1787, in Washington, Pennsylvania. At the conclusion of my lecture the President asked if it would be possible for me to make the Commencement Day Address there in June. This is the day when American universities close their academic year with the conferring of degrees. It was customary to invite some eminent person to make the address. Sensible of the compliment, I replied that I would delay my departure for England for this purpose. The intervening free period allowed me to do two very pleasant things, to fulfil my promise to young Townsend Wainwright to visit Cornell University, and to make a tour through Maryland and Virginia as the guest of my Evanston hosts, the Higbees.

In the beginning of May I arrived at Cornell University. It is wonderfully situated at Ithaca on a high plateau above Lake Cayuga in the mountainous part of New York State. I was entertained in

Wainwright's Fraternity Lodge, Kappa Alpha, that housed some forty undergraduates. It was presided over by a young man, Jervis Langdon, who was the great-nephew of Mark Twain. Twenty years of age, grave of mien, he was a perfect host. I had soon around me a coterie of youths ardent with the springtime of life. It was the springtime in every sense, for the woods in a 3,000-acre arboretum were bursting into leaf, and down on Lake Cayuga eight young giants were in training to take their boat to Henley Regatta. I was entertained by some of the professors and their wives and encountered Ford Madox Ford, watery-eyed, puffy, stout, a romancer, but a rewarding conversationalist. His merit apart as a writer, he had discerned the genius of D. H. Lawrence and put him on the road to fame.

It was a great relief to be under no burden of train-catching and lecturing. I had come for five days and stayed sixteen. I shed my years and refused to become avuncular. I startled them by proposing a run at midnight as I had at Harvard seven years earlier, and it became almost a nightly event. There was another evening event that almost became an institution. One day a youth loaded with books came into the Common Room, threw them down and said: "The Prof says Browning's a punk poet, and I agree. What stuff!" I was shocked by this affront to my cherished Browning, picked up the book and began to read. I gave them "A Toccata", "The Statue and the Bust", and "Fra Lippo Lippi". Soon I had an audience, the reading interrupted by supper. Within a week we had a nightly reading class of a score of lads sitting round in their pyjamas and slippers. I noticed that it was the "toughs" who melted first under the magic of Browning. I varied the reading with passages of Milton and Keats. Perhaps the favourite poem of all emerged on the night when I concluded with Spenser's "Prothalamion". Some of them went up to bed chanting "Sweet Thames, run softly till I end my song". "Gee!" said Hank, who later became a renowned neurologist, "I've just got to cross the Atlantic and see sweet Father Thames!"

On leaving Cornell I was collected by the Higbees, father, mother and daughter. A joyous quartet, we set off on our motor tour to Maryland and Virginia, smothered in dogwood, Richmond, Charlottesville, with the lovely University of Virginia, its lawns bordered with white Greek porticos recalling the groves of Academe, and two undergraduates, Edgar Allan Poe and Woodrow Wilson; then Jefferson's stately home, Monticello, the Blue Ridge Valley, the Sky Line Drive, Harper's Ferry, with the ghost of John Brown whose "soul goes marching on", the Shenandoah Valley, Frederick, recalling Francis Scott Key, author of "The Star-Spangled Banner", Annapolis Naval College, and Washington's Mount Vernon, standing superbly above the Potomac; it was glorious springtime all the way. Once we halted in a forest of white flowering dogwood for me to read the address I had written for the Commencement Day ceremony. We arrived at Washington and Jefferson College coming up from Maryland. The College was gay with students and their parents, with dances and dinner parties. The next morning I delivered my address in a packed hall. It was not an easy thing for me, on the verge of thirty-five, to give advice to these young "Twenty-Ones". I hoped they would get as much fun out of life, with some struggle to temper it, as I had. When it came to the actual conferment of degrees, I had a surprise. I was called up and gowned as an LL.D.

So ended my third American tour. That night I parted from my friends and left for Pittsburgh and New York. Two days later I boarded the *Minnesota*. I had chosen it for two reasons. It sailed up the Thames and docked at Tilbury. It was a new route for me. Also I thought it appropriate that, having been in the territory of Pocahontas, I should follow her route to England, which she was fated never to leave, for she died and was buried at Gravesend on the return journey to her native land.

CHAPTER FOURTEEN

French Excursion

I

I NOW HAD to replan my life, the Nottingham phase was ended. I decided to settle in London, which had always drawn me. I was fortunate in having a friend who had taken a house in Westbourne Park and was willing to let his first floor to me. This consisted of a large drawing-room, bedroom and kitchenette. It had a high ceiling, a marble mantelpiece and two long French windows. It was light and quiet. We shared a dining-room and a manservant. I reviewed my financial position. In May, 1908, on my sixteenth birthday, facing the calamity of my father's premature death, I had vowed that by May, 1927, I would have saved £10,000. It was a desperate Declaration of Independence, to be fulfilled halfway in the seventy years allotted by the Psalmist. And now, aged thirty-five, I had achieved it, easily. Nevertheless, I was not unaware of the mutability touching all human things, of *hubris*. An author has no command of permanence. He sails a frail bark on the treacherous seas of public favour. In comparison with most of my contemporaries I had been singularly fortunate. But I had been ceaselessly industrious.*

I returned to Nottingham and began the melancholy task of breaking up the old home. By the end of July I was installed in my new quarters. My novel *Sagusto* had just been published. Within a year it had sold 15,000 copies. I was now considered a "best-seller", an

---

* Arnold Bennett, aged thirty-five in 1902, had published three novels and was borrowing £600 a year from his literary agent. Six years later he received a £150 advance for his masterpiece *The Old Wives' Tale*. He owed his agent more than £3,000 in loans. Fame and fortune came in 1909–14, at the age of forty-two.

Château d'Esclimont.

Château d'Ermenonville.

We were young, we were in Venice, we were in love.

The gate of the Château de Rambouillet. With his cousins, Carmen and Elizabeth de La Rochefoucauld, Armand holds a broken bar.

idiotic epithet that hung round my neck like a millstone for the rest
of my life. The term provokes an overtone of envy on a basis of
abuse. No one ever calls a Ford car, or a Rolls-Royce a "best-seller".
The origin of my novel *Sagusto* was singular. One evening as I dined
in a restaurant in Venice I was fascinated by the appearance of an
extraordinary, middle-aged woman who sat in a corner, alone. My
curiosity must have provoked her, for she sent a waiter across to
tell me that if I continued to look at her she would box my ears!
I got up at once and crossed to her table and said: "Madam, I've
brought my ears for you to box." She laughed, asked me to sit down
and have a glass of wine with her. "You're English of course. I'm
Greek." She then told me a remarkable story. She was in Italy trying
to recruit a private army. She owned an island on the Adriatic coast
which the Yugoslavs had occupied and stolen from her. She had
already recruited about fifty of the Arditi, left over from D'Annun-
zio's adventure at Fiume.

When the time came to leave the restaurant and settle the bill,
she had lost her purse! Like a greenhorn I had been properly trapped.
I offered to pay it—she had dined well. No, she could not allow that
but I could lend her five hundred lire. I lent her it. She wrote down
my name and hotel on the back of the bill. She would send me the
money in the morning. She then called a gondola and went off.
I felt I should never see my money, and wondered how many she
had caught like that. And in retrospect she seemed slightly mad,
with her private army and island story.

The next morning at my hotel I was called by the concierge. A
youth in a white uniform had asked for me. He gave me an envelope
and said he was to wait for an answer. In the envelope was a five-
hundred-lire note. There was also a letter of thanks, and an invitation. Would I lunch on board her yacht next Friday at 1.30? I told
the messenger to say that I accepted with much pleasure. The notepaper bore the heading S.Y. *Bryseis*. Later I went to the mouth of
the Grand Canal and asked a gondolier at one of the private landing
stages if he knew which was the *Bryseis*. He pointed to a white yacht,
one of the largest in the lagoon. When I went to keep the lunch
appointment I was really excited. At the top of the gangway a smart
young steward met me. The deck seemed swarming with tough young

Italians. I was conducted down a companion way, along a corridor and ushered into a small cabin, a gentleman's toilette room. I hung up my hat, examined myself in the mirror and straightened my hair. As I stood opposite the porthole to my amazement I saw the façade of the Ducal Palace begin to glide by. I rushed to the door to discover I was locked in. Was she kidnapping me for her army?

The rest of the story is banal. In panic I had pushed the door instead of opening it towards me. The yacht was not going to sea, it was swinging at anchor on the tide. I was one of ten guests for lunch, which was excellent. My hostess was charming. I left the yacht that afternoon with the story of my next novel: a young army officer, unemployed, is kidnapped, captains the hired army, recovers the lady's island, and—etc., etc., etc. I never learned where the island was, its name, or whether she recovered it. I heard later that she was Russian-born, the widow of a rich Greek shipowner.

After settling into my London apartment I was in Venice by the middle of August. I returned to London via the Dolomites at the end of September, in time for the publication of *The Diary of Russell Beresford*. Some reviewers spotted the fake diary, some took it seriously, but not Myra, who sent me a cable. "Bravo! But who is spoofing now, dear fraud?" It underlined an uneasiness within me, and I never again used a pseudonym.

II

In Paris I had a friend, Norman Fuller, the representative of a British oil company. I went to visit him early in October. After a few days I called up Armand de La Rochefoucauld whom I had not seen since I had said goodbye to him at Houston, Texas, in 1924. We lunched at Fouquet's and he brought along François de Deservillers, so we were united again. Two days later Armand insisted that I should stay with him in the family mansion in the Rue de Varennes. I found myself in one of the most beautiful and famous houses in Paris. It had two wings enclosing a courtyard whose high gates shut off the street. There was a wicket-gate, opened by a concierge answering the bell. Privacy was complete. The south side of the mansion faced a long garden with tall trees. An absolute country silence prevailed in this terraced domain. A long gilt-mirrored ballroom was the setting for the famous annual La Rochefoucauld-Doudeauville ball, a high mark of the Paris social season. Armand's mother, the Duchess de Doudeauville, occupied a suite on the first floor. In the left wing was the Duke's suite, in the right wing lived Armand's sister Hedwige. She was the widow of Prince Sixte de Bourbon-Parme who won some fame by his efforts, rendered vain, to take Austria out of the war in 1917. Armand occupied a suite on the top floor overlooking the garden. I had a room next to his. His elder brother the Viscount Sosthènes de La Rochefoucauld, and a married sister, the Duchess de Mouchy, lived elsewhere.

I was a little nervous about meeting Armand's mother but I was put at ease immediately. Born Princess Radziwill, she was a member of the great Polish family. Frail, with the pallor of an invalid whose vitality was carefully husbanded, she had nevertheless a zest for life revealed in her brilliant dark eyes. Despite position and wealth she had preserved her sensitivity and simplicity. I had an experience of this. One chilly October day we walked a little on the Quai de l'Arché-vêché. Down on the banks of the grey Seine we watched an old man washing his shirt, a rag of a thing. On that cheerless afternoon he symbolised the hopeless poor of a hard, indifferent city. As we looked the duchess said, "There's something wrong, isn't there, that a poor man should come to that? I feel so guilty, so helpless!"

When I was about to leave after my first visit she held my hand and said, without any embarrassment: "I must tell you that before you came I disliked you intensely! I disliked your name—it was always in everything Armand said. "Cecil thinks that, Cecil said—always Cecil, Cecil! Oh, how I disliked you! I was jealous you see, which was silly for a mother. And now I've told you!" The note in her voice and the smile in her eyes made me her slave. In all places and moods she had this conquering direct simplicity. I see her now, forty years later, walking in the garden with her dog, lying on a chaise-longue while she talked of books and music; at the head of a table deftly drawing her guests into the conversation; or at tea, with the sunset burning through the tall trees beyond the terrace in a setting of gilded boiserie, long mirrors, Boucher tapestries, shaded lamps shining on silver and flowers and her beautiful hands, which had the delicacy of flowers. It was something to have known such a world, soon to vanish in the light of common day.

The duke I found remote, austere. I learned later that his aloofness came not from pride but from shyness. Certainly he was proud. He had married one daughter into a Royal house, he was President of the Jockey Club. One morning he drew me into his study and shyly made a confession. He had just published a book, five hundred pages long, a labour of years. It was a study of his father, who had played an important role in the nation's affairs in the nineteenth century and had been the French Ambassador at the Court of St. James in 1874. The duke presented me with an autographed copy. I expected to find it heavy and amateurish. I discovered that it was full of interest, well-documented and well-written.

The days hurried by. One morning Armand asked me if I would like to see the château he had inherited with his brother from their uncle, the late Prince Léon Radziwill. It was at Ermenonville, some thirty miles from Paris in a domain of forest and lakes. In the eighteenth century it had belonged to a Marquis Girardin who had constructed famous gardens there with an army of Scotch gardeners, the first "English" park in France. The celebrated gardens of the poet Shenstone at Leasowe had provided the model. Of the fifty-six curiosities the marquis had created, only some thirty now existed.

The fame of Ermenonville spread throughout the world when the marquis enticed Jean-Jacques Rousseau to settle there in his last years. Girardin himself had had a remarkable career. He had fought in the Seven Years' War as a captain of the Royal Dragoons, and been on the staff of the ex-king of Poland, Stanislas Leszczynski, father of the wife of Louis XV, living in stately exile at Lunéville. In 1766 the marquis, aged thirty-one, bought the fifteenth-century Château d'Ermenonville, and transformed it. Like so many aristocrats he fell under the spell of Rousseau, whose revolutionary doctrines became the vogue. He invited the philosopher to come to Ermenonville and built a Swiss chalet for him on the side of the lake facing the château, in which Rousseau received queens and revolutionaries. Here he died and Girardin buried him in a sarcophagus built on an island, called l'Île des Peupliers, in the great lake, following his expressed wish. In the French Revolution the marquis was imprisoned. He was liberated but, financially broken, abandoned Ermenonville. In 1794 Napoleon, who had visited the grave, decreed that Rousseau's remains should be transferred to the Panthéon. I saw the tomb still preserved on l'Île des Peupliers.

The château on which Prince Léon's father had lavished money, had a moat. Beautiful woods surrounded the house. In the State bedroom, a feature was the former bed of the ex-King of Poland, brought here on his death at Nancy, the town he had made so beautiful as the capital of his Duchy of Lorraine. This had been the late Prince Radziwill's bedroom. A blue-eyed giant, known as Loche to his friends, he was a member of a family spread across Europe. "It's very provoking," he said, "when I'm in Poland I'm perpetually asked about 'You Frenchmen'. When I'm in France they say 'You Poles!'" He had organised a Polish Brigade and served with distinction with the French army during the First World War, though his family was international. His father, Prince Constantine, had often had Proust as his guest at the château, and he figured in Proust's masterpiece as the Prince de Guermantes.

It was not possible for Armand to go with me to the château as he had another engagement, so I took my friend Fuller with me. The butler showed us over the house. In the bedroom with the royal bed I noticed a pair of ivory brushes on the dressing-table. They were engraved with the Radziwill arms. I picked up one of the brushes, and quickly put it down again, having received from it an indefinable sensation. Remarking on this later to Armand, greatly astonished by my comment, I learned that his uncle Prince Léon, still in healthy middle-age, had been found dead in his bed at the Hotel de Paris, Monte Carlo, when his valet went to his bedroom in the morning. The Prince had returned home from the Casino with a demi-mondaine, Mlle Dalbane, notorious for her adventures, the mistress of a renowned French Deputy. An autopsy on the Prince revealed that he had been killed by an injection of heroin. Mlle Dalbane was missing. She had slipped over the Frontier into Cannes. It was announced that Prince Léon had died from a heart attack. Prince Louis of Monaco, who wished to suppress the scandal and save the feelings of the dead man's family, agreed to this camouflage. In Paris the French Deputy prevailed upon the Préfet de Police not to pursue enquiries. The police had no desire to open Mlle Dalbane's dossier. She died in Paris in old age. Here were all the elements of a James Bond story thirty years before that lurid character had been invented.

On the estate at Ermenonville, among other properties, there was the Moulin du Soleil. It became associated with another singular event. About a year after my visit Armand sold the Moulin du Soleil to two Americans, Mr. and Mrs. Crosby. They were a remarkable couple. Harry Crosby was a nephew of Pierpont Morgan. After graduating from Harvard he worked briefly in the Morgan Bank's Paris branch. A young man of some fortune, he married the former wife of Richard Peabody, of the famous family of philanthropists, who returned from the World War a dipsomaniac and ended his days in an asylum. Leaving the bank in 1927, Crosby and his wife, having literary tastes, founded in Paris the Black Sun Press. Eccentric and generous, they formed a friendship with D. H. Lawrence whose work they admired.

The story of that friendship is characteristic of their impetuosity. Travelling up the Nile Crosby raved over a book he had read, Lawrence's *The Plumed Serpent*. He sent off by overland-camel a fan letter. He had been struck by passages about the Sun God and he asked Lawrence to write him a Sun story for publication in a limited edition by The Black Sun Press. He offered to pay for it in twenty $20 gold pieces. Surprised but delighted by this windfall, Lawrence sent off from his villa near Florence, the required short story, *Sun,* which the Crosbys found awaiting them on their return to Paris in March, 1928. With great difficulty Crosby obtained the twenty gold pieces. One day in their Paris apartment the servant announced a Monsieur Sex. It was a young American, whose actual name was William Sykes—Bill Sykes! Edward Weeks, editor of the *Atlantic Monthly*, had obtained the gold pieces and given them to this young man journeying from America to Paris, to deliver to the Crosbys. The next thing was to get them to Lawrence in Florence. The regulations prohibiting the transfer of gold, the coins had to be smuggled into Italy. Crosby wrapped them up carefully and then went to the Gare de Lyon to find someone on the Rome Express, which left that night, who might be going to Florence and was willing to smuggle the packet in. It was near Christmas. Clad in a mink-lined overcoat, bare-headed, Crosby ran along the carriages looking for "an honest man". He saw one. Finding that he was going to Florence, he asked him if he would deliver the packet. The stranger, leaning out of the wagon-lit just as it was departing, said he would. Crosby told him there was gold in the packet. The stranger thereupon told Crosby his name. "It's Argyll!" he cried. Two days later Lawrence wrote to say he had received the gold pieces. They had been delivered at his villa by the Duke of Argyll. Soon after this Lawrence received another gold packet from his admirer. It was a snuff-box that had belonged to Caroline, the Queen of Naples.

In the spring of 1929 Lawrence went to Paris to find a publisher for *Lady Chatterley's Lover*, now being pirated. He thought that Sylvia Beach who had published Joyce's *Ulysses* might take it. She turned it down, subsequently Lawrence found a publisher who would issue the banned book in English. While in Paris the Lawrences accepted an invitation to stay with the Crosbys for the weekend in the Moulin du Soleil. It was, declared his hosts, haunted. They said that a pillar in the courtyard, against which Lawrence sat sunning himself, had been brought there from the Abbey de Chalis by Cagliostro, who had been in retreat there. They believed that the mill had been built on magic ground, and that Cagliostro and Rousseau as well as themselves, had "felt the spell". They announced that a flock of sheep had walked right through their three-barred gate, and that little fish leaped twenty feet from the millstream to reach a pool above.

Such was the spooky property at Ermenonville to which Lawrence and his wife Frieda came to spend the weekend in March, 1929. The Crosbys liked Lawrence but detested Frieda. She was probably unwanted, as is so often the case with the wives of the famous among celebrity-hunters. There was a dramatic episode. One day, after driving in the woods with his host, Lawrence returned to find Frieda playing the gramophone, which he hated. Exasperated, he took the records and smashed them over his wife's head.*

Did the Moulin cast a spell? It provided a footnote to a tragic event. Shortly after the visit of the Lawrences the Crosbys went to New York. A few days after their arrival Harry Crosby borrowed the apartment of a friend. He was found there with the young wife of a

* *D. H. Lawrence*, Vol. III, by Edward Nehls (University of Wisconsin Press).

Harvard student, both dead, shot. The inquest revealed that the young couple, fully dressed on the bed, had died in what proved to be a suicide pact. Crosby was thirty-two. According to Mrs. Crosby there had been another magic incident at the Moulin. They had had a tombstone carved and inscribed with their names and dates of birth. On the day that Crosby died the tombstone, which had been kept high up on the sun-tower, leapt the balustrade and was smashed to pieces on the pavement below. The widow remarried and lived in a Virginia villa which she restored and in which Salvatore Dali painted the frescoes and Henry Miller wrote a book.

III

After I had stayed a week in the Rue de Varennes, Armand's parents left for their château at Bonnétable near Le Mans. In a few days we joined them. I had been given no hint of the size of this Gothic pile. My large bedroom, with a coffered ceiling and windows overlooking the lake, on which black swans glided, was reached by a wide stone staircase. In the large fireplace a log-fire burned when I went up to dress. On a table by a divan there were masses of flowers and an assortment of books under a big shaded lamp. On one wall hung a fine Beauvais tapestry hunting scene. My dress clothes had been laid out by the valet. I had no time to browse over the books, for the dinner-bell sounded through the château. We gathered in a salon and proceeded to a long dining-room. Its walls bore a fresco of heraldic arms of allied families—Marcillac, Liancourt, Montmorency, Luynes, Estrées, Uzès, Harcourt—they blazed a trail through French history. My table neighbour, elderly, was a bright little woman, the Dowager Duchess de La Rochefoucauld, recently widowed. She was very alert and friendly. One day she said to me: "Let me put you right. I'm an American but the duke didn't marry me for my money, as you might surmise. I hadn't a dollar! He married me for love. He was sixteen years older—a lovely man." Tragedy had touched them. In the hall of the Château de La Rochefoucauld there was a marble statue of a small boy, the only son and heir, who had died. The duchess told me this on a day when we motored with Armand through a forest of October gold to some

296

villages. The purpose of this excursion was to buy the frame of an old
Louis Seize chair for which she had worked a piece of petit-point
needlework. She wanted to upholster the chair in order to make a
present. Three times we set out on this quest. We followed clues into
Le Mans, into villages with antique shops, even to remote farmsteads.
Never had I imagined that so many chair-skeletons existed. In one
storehouse they hung from the ceiling in spidery masses and various
stages of worm-eaten decay, but never the chair whose seat fitted
the needlework. Then one day we were successful and in triumph bore
home the chair. That quest had shown me the French countryside
and ménage as I had never seen them before. Dear little woman, I
gathered she felt lonely and perhaps alien to that over-powering
large clan of the La Rochefoucaulds. "There's nothing so awful, my
dear Mr. Roberts, as being a French widow. It's a profession in
itself. You must dress demurely in faithfulness to the dead, and all your
movements are scrutinised by the living relatives. Well, I've nothing
with which to reproach myself. On his deathbed my darling François
kissed me and thanked me for giving him a happy life."

I was sorry to see her leave. "Come and see me in Paris," she
said, giving me her card, "you're a ray of sunshine. There are so
many bores come out of the panelling in these old châteaux, like
Count B.—who can only talk pheasants and ailments." Poor Count
B., one of the house party, was a bore, but so old-world, beautifully-
mannered and groomed, that he was interesting as a period piece.
He kept mint cachous in a gold snuff-box.

Armand's brother Sosthènes arrived with his lovely young Spanish
wife and tiny daughter. He had recently been on a big game hunt in
Africa. I worked in my room each morning at a table from which I
looked out on the silver lake and down a great avenue cut through the
woods. I was uninterrupted. In French country houses the guests do
not meet until lunch, but one morning a servant brought me a re-
directed telegram. It was from my old grammar school in Nottingham. The headmaster asked if I would distribute the prizes at the
annual prize-giving in November. The request gave me a shock. This
was a "Distinguished Old Boy" role. Was I as old as that? At thirty-
five I still felt quite young, but I accepted the compliment.

In the afternoons if not out driving I walked in the garden with my hostess, discussing books and music. We also made short excursions, one to the near-by little village of La Ferté Bernard. I was surprised to see the names Smith and Johnson over two shop windows. It turned out that I was not the first Englishman to have stayed in the château. In 1348 a British soldier of fortune, perhaps a follower of Edward III and the Black Prince, had made the château his head-quarters. The sojourn of his men could be traced in these English names of their descendants who had settled in the village.

I was sad to leave Bonnétable, deep in its woods like the enchanted castle of the Sleeping Beauty. We had no sooner returned to Paris than Armand proposed that we should spend a few days with his uncle and aunt, the Duke and Duchess de Bisaccia. They lived at the Château d'Esclimont, Gallardon, some fifty miles from Paris. Armand had bought a powerful racing car of which he had recently taken delivery. When we descended to the courtyard in the Rue de Varennes, to leave in the dusk of an October afternoon, I found the new car there, snorting with energy. We got in, bucket seats side by side, our baggage on a grid behind. "Can you drive it?" I asked apprehensively as it leapt under Armand's hands and roared down the Rue. "Certainement!" he replied. As Armand did all things well, I kept quiet. We roared through the Bois de Boulogne, over the Seine, up to St. Cloud, down a ravine, the powerful engine snorting. It seemed to be Count Zobrowski's *Chitty-Chitty-Bang-Bang* over again. Night fell, a soft rain clouded the windscreen, the dark road gleamed before us. The tall trees formed an immense nave through which our quivering headlights cut a swathe. We were going too fast. "Armand!" I called gently, but the reproach went unheard. We roared through the night. Apprehensively, I converted the kilometres on the speedo-meter into miles. Then, suddenly something leapt up before us. It was a very high stone wall with heavy iron gates behind which an avenue of trees continued. The main road took a sharp left-angle turn. The avenue behind the closed gates had misled Armand. Our headlights flooded the gates, the wall, a keeper's lodge. This was death, immediate. I covered my face against glass. Crash! Silence.

So this was Death, the thing speculated upon so much, the mother of all religions, since it inculcated fear in the human mind, which clamours for some assurance of life hereafter, on congenial terms. And now nothing, no pain, no feeling. Strange, not only no pain but I saw, too! What was this white thing fluttering in the deep, dark silence? My soul? Then there was . . . ? But no! It was a shirt, a white dress-shirt. How ludicrous! My portmanteau gaped there among the trees. Then I was not dead. A voice said "Are you hurt?" I answered "No!" "Incroyable!" cried Armand from the ruins of our car. We stepped out of the wreck. In the darkness we could now see a little. One of the great gates stood open, its lower half shattered. There were voices. Lanterns came towards us—searching for bodies? We laughed hysterically. We had smashed the heavy vertical bars of one of the gates and gone in under a crossbar, saved from decapitation by our low racing body. How far was it to the nearest garage?" "Ten minutes," answered the lodgekeeper. "Always I am fortunate, *mon cher!*" cried Armand, for we were unscratched. A gendarme came on the scene. Having inspected the gates, the car, and us, he wiped his brow. "Where are we?" asked Armand. "This is the Château de Rambouillet, monsieur. The château of the President," answered the gendarme. "I am not so fortunate," commented Armand. "My father will be angry. He and the President are not on speaking terms."

A hired car took us to Esclimont. The house party had gone in to dinner, so we joined them without changing, apologising for our late-ness but not stating the cause. There was a company of some dozen guests. The Duchess de Bisaccia, descended from Colbert, the great Finance Minister of Louis XIV, soon put me at ease. She had noticed that I was very pale. One of her two pretty daughters was on my left. The Duke was at the head of the table, he was the younger brother of the Duke de Doudeauville. The table glowed under golden candel-abra. Was it the company, the warmth, the wine, for something hap-pened to me? I felt very gay and light-hearted. I laughed, I talked. Armand looked at me in wonder. Not an hour removed from death, how could I be so jocund? When we joined the ladies in the drawing-room, he told them of the accident. There was general concern. Was I badly shaken, asked my hostess, would I like to go and rest? "Oh, no, not at all. It was marvellous!" I affirmed. Marvellous? Still I talked, encouraged by the smiling company. I recounted incidents in the March to the Rhine, after the armistice, Marshal Foch's entry into

Ghent, the sad fate of Queen Carlotta, widow of the executed Emperor of Mexico, insane, shut up in a convent there, the return from exile of the King of Belgium.

On, on I went. What did I not tell them, borne up by a strange elation? Towards midnight Armand took me up to my room. He seemed proud of me. "You have been a great success. Formidable!" he said. Success, why, how? I was tired beyond physical exhaustion. I lay in bed and dizzily surveyed the room. Rose silk curtains soared to a canopy above me. On a tapestry headcloth hung a painting of a Madonna and Child. Florentine, possibly *quattrocento*. The warm room glowed with soft light. I regarded the embroidered pelmet and curtains, the Louis Seize dressing-table, muslin clad, with mirrors. such a table before which La Pompadour might have sat—*les lèvres comme des roses qui soudain ont fleuri*. I lay back, Armand had gone. Where was I, what had happened, what had I said? I was not sure of myself, here alone. I became fearful, lying on this bed of state, stared at by the Lippi Madonna above me. I resisted a panicky desire to pull the tapestry bell-rope by the bed and rouse the sleeping château. I felt myself going round in a whirlpool with a smashed car, an iron gate and a Madonna who was served with liqueurs and coffee by a liveried footman with powdered hair, wearing white gloves.

The next morning, in daylight, Armand stood by my bed. Was I all right? It was ten o'clock. He had been in twice. I asked him about the previous evening. What had happened to me, had I behaved badly? "Oh, you were a bit delirious, but you were in wonderful form. My aunt loves you!" he replied, and told me what I had said. That afternoon we motored back to look at the gates of the Château de Rambouillet, pretty young Carmen de La Rochefoucauld and her sister, Elizabeth, Armand's cousins, with us. It was incredible that we had emerged alive. The heavy iron bars lay on the ground.

The following two days were spent in the fairyland of Esclimont with its gate-tower clock, courtyard, the high porch carrying the equestrian statue of François I, creator of the château and *parrain* of a La Rochefoucauld, the long lake, parterres, moat and enveloping woods. There was a shoot. The guns had gone out in a brake to the coverts. I stayed behind for I can find no pleasure in massacring birds. My "shooting" was with a camera, among the glories of the château's architecture and its gardens. I browsed in the library and admired the rich *reliures* of eighteenth-century books. My hostess showed me one given to her grandfather when he stayed at the Château de Nohant, a fellow guest with Chopin. The book was one written by his hostess and inscribed ". . . *son ami George Sand*".

One evening before dinner I was the first to go down to the salon. It was empty. A great coal fire burned in the grate. As I stood looking out on the lake a young footman in livery came in. He went towards the grate. From it he pulled out a red-hot poker and came towards me. I had a sudden moment of fear. Was he mad? Was he going to attack me with that terrible poker? Suddenly he stopped in his threatening walk, stooped and thrust it into a can on the floor. There was a great sizzle and a cloud of vapour. Its scent spread through the room. So that was what it was all about! He was fumigating the salon before the advent of the guests. The footman departed with the poker and the can. I reflected that this was a custom descended through the centuries in these aristocratic houses. When next I witnessed this fumigation, forty years later in an old castle in the Ligurian Alps, my host picked up an atomiser, pressed a button and filled the salon with the scent of sandalwood. Thus far have we advanced in a mechanised age.

We visited other châteaux nearby. Deep in the Chevreuse Valley lay stately Dampierre, behind magnificent grilles revealing the façade of the château, its great courtyard and double wings facing the road. It was the seat of the Duke de Luynes. The great hall occupied the centre of the château with high windows at each end looking on to gardens and rising woods. The young duke and his two sisters conducted us through the house. It had many fine paintings, Anne of Austria with her friend the Duchess de Chevreuse (1661), who made for her the magnificent water gardens, Stanislas Leszczynski ex-King of Poland, whose wife made frequent visits. Very notable was the great fresco *L'Age d'Or* by Ingres, who spent several years in the château working on it, leaving a second fresco unfinished. The magnificent library had been lovingly cared for·by the duke's father —"Un homme exquis de la plus fine élégance de manières, le plus accompli de la civilisation si exactement représentée par ce château," wrote a friend. The library held among countless treasures, the letters of Colbert to Louis XIV and Cardinal Mazarin.

My attention was arrested in the great salon by a painting of two small children. Pretty young Mademoiselle Yolande, the duke's sister, told me their history. In the Revolution the children had been confined with their mother in the Tour du Temple, awaiting the guillotine. Each day their mother trained them to mount a chair up on to a wooden table so that their exit should lose nothing of calm dignity before the revolutionary *canaille*. A plain wooden chair and a table, souvenirs of that ordeal, stood incongruously amid the ornate furniture in the great hall.

My visit to Château d'Esclimont came to an end on a bright October morning. We left for Paris by train. As we said goodbye in the lovely courtyard the duchess clung to Armand and I heard her say, with tears in her eyes, "If you see my poor Stanislas, give him my love." Armand explained the scene. "My cousin Stanislas is a naughty boy. He wants to marry an actress they do not approve of. My uncle has forbidden him the house." So despite this historic beauty there was heartache in the château.

As we left the courtyard and drove out under the towered gateway I turned and looked back at this noble edifice. I did not know that thirty years would pass before I was again a guest at Château d'Esclimont, with the same warm-hearted host and hostess.

IV

At the beginning of November I was back home and proceeded to fulfil my engagement at Nottingham in the role of an Old Boy distributing prizes at my old school, of which I had nothing but happy memories. The ceremony took place in the Albert Hall in the presence of a thousand scholars and parents. The platform was not strange to me. I had heard Balfour, Asquith and Lloyd George speak there, and, I, too, had spoken from this platform when a parliamentary candidate. But this new appearance I found the most memorable of all. I did not feel a bit of an Old Boy or entitled to give advice to the young. True I had been about somewhat, written books and accumulated experience on two Continents. As John

Masefield had written: "Like the jovial Huntsman you have 'poltered up and down a bit and had a rattling day'." The distinguished Old Boy on these occasions is usually invited because he has finished well. I was only just half-way on Life's journey, and hoped "the best is yet to be". It wasn't in me on this occasion to play the wise owl. I did not allow my still boyish spirit to be checked, though embarrassed by the fact that the headmaster would refer to me as "Doctor Roberts" on the strength of that unearned degree acquired in America. I did express my envy that they had some fifty or sixty years in front of them, that that might seem a long time in which to do things but they would be mistaken. Life was always too short. The immediate Now was what mattered, not the problematical Future. Alas and alas, I could not know how pregnant was what I told them, for I, a survivor from one doomed generation, was talking to another. Many of them were being reared for the slaughterhouse of the Second World War. Some thirty years later I again addressed the School, in the same role, and found I was talking to the orphans of those youngsters.

V

One day my old chief at the Ministry of Munitions, Sir Burton Chadwick, who had taken me to breakfast with Arnold Bennett one morning in 1917, called me on the telephone. "Bennett was asking about you the other day. He said he hadn't seen you for some time. I think he'd like to see you." Remembering his past kindness to me I wrote to Bennett and asked if I might call as I was now living in London again. Back came a letter in his beautiful script. "I am glad to hear from you and shall be glad to see you. I must say that your name seems to be getting about nowadays quite a good deal, which is very satisfactory."

On a dull December day I went to have tea with him at 75 Cadogan Square, a tall mansion that he referred to with some pride as "a nice thing in houses". It marked his ascent to prosperity and fame. At this time, novels and plays apart, he was earning £3,500 a year for a book column in The *Evening Standard*. He was a good sound critic, most readable, and he became a power in the literary world. Even Beaverbrook, the paper's owner, was a suppliant for his favours.

303

I was shown up into a room on the first floor, his study. Bennett rose from a writing bureau and greeted me. Presently a maid brought in a tea tray and he served me. We talked about various things. Soon I became aware that he was not in an easy mood and stammered very badly. He observed that I had had two novels serialised in the *Westminster Gazette*, which had also serialised his *Mr. Prohack*. "How much did you get for them?" he asked bluntly. I thought it was rather impertinent and evaded the question by saying: "I'm sure only about a quarter of what you got for your serial."* He looked at me sharply and said: "Well, if you don't want to tell me, don't!"

I felt uncomfortable. This was not the former Arnold Bennett I had known, affable, complacent. I noticed he had aged. His colour was grey. I did not learn until twenty-five years later, when Reginald Pound's biography appeared, that he was, at the time of my visit, full of anxieties. He suffered excruciatingly from neuralgia and insomnia. Now sixty, he lived with a beautiful actress in her twenties, by whom he had a daughter. He could not marry her because his French wife, treated by him with considerable generosity, would not give him a divorce. His friends accepted the position. Servants and others did not. A nursemaid left after gossip in the Park, declaring she would not take out "That". The cook was rude to her mistress.

Bennett was at the zenith of his career. Inwardly he was perturbed. He was living grandiosely, presenting to the world a confident image, but he was apprehensive. He tried to increase his output to meet his expenses. He wrote in his *Journal*, for 1926, "At the beginning of this year I resolved to average 1,000 words a day throughout the year but I found it could not be done. I then said I would do 300,000 words in the year. I managed this to the end of March but I doubt if I shall go through the year successfully." In that year, with tremendous industry, he had earned £22,000 gross. It was not enough. He had great hopes of the theatre in which he had had one great success and one mediocre one, but just now his new play, *Flora*, had been rejected by four West End managers. It was never produced.

* It was a good guess. For the serial rights of *Little Mrs. Manington* I received £500. He had just sold the serial rights of *Train de Luxe*, a potboiler, to the *Daily Express* for £2,250. But he could not sell the serial rights of his *Riceyman Steps*.

I did not know that, despite his great reputation, his novels did not enjoy very large sales, rarely exceeding 40,000 copies. "I have never had what I call a sale," he wrote in his *Journal*. "If I have made money by my pen it is the fruit of the fact that I produce as much as H. G. Wells and three times as much as other people." When his novel *Mr. Prohack* appeared, the reviewers accused him of pot-boiling, which was true. Bennett, ageing, became worried. He must have been looking at the younger generation, not with envy, which was foreign to his generous nature, but with misgiving.

During our conversation I felt uncomfortable because of the questions he asked me, which seemed to explain his interest in me. He thanked me for the copy of *Sagusto* I had recently sent him. "Has it sold well?" he asked. "Quite well," I replied. It was obvious he wanted to know how many copies. We began to discuss various authors and books. He said he could not read *The Forsyte Saga*. "I've tried and tried but I find most of Galsworthy's people are stuffed ducks." I was not very surprised by this opinion for authors are often unable to appreciate their contemporaries. Proust could not read Joyce, nor Joyce Proust, and their meeting was disastrous. Conrad could not find anything to justify Jane Austen's reputation. "What is it all about? What *is* it all about?" he exclaimed, baffled. Bennett said he could not enjoy Henry James. "I get bogged down with him, clever as he is. He can never say anything simply, he sniffs about like a dog, and he's a nervous snob." We discussed T. S. Eliot. "Can you read him?" he asked. "No," I said diffidently, knowing that I was breasting a strong wave of acclamation. He looked at me with his cool saurian eyes. "Neither can I—well, perhaps occasionally, but he's a pot of weak tea." He astonished me by saying that he thought Edith Sitwell was a good poet. I suspected some snobbism in this. He had taken an avuncular role with the Sitwells. It was at a time when he was toying with the idea of getting a grant of arms. He had already sketched an heraldic inkpot with pens for supporters, but when the College of Heralds asked £30 for "preliminary research" into his grounds for gentility his common sense asserted itself and he dropped the idea.

After a visit of about an hour I rose to leave. He accompanied me down to the door and thanked me for my visit. I left sadly aware that it had not been a success. The air had been charged. I should have been sadder had I known that he was within four years of his death. He came to a pathetic end. Stricken by a sudden illness, believed to have been caused by drinking water while abroad, living in a noisy and costly apartment, he suddenly found himself, age sixty-four, financially worried and facing death. "Everything has gone wrong, my girl," were his last words as he held his 'wife's' hand and slipped from life. It was a sad confession for a man who had confidently written *How To Live On Twenty-Four Hours A Day*.

Bennett left a large number of friends to mourn him. At his death *Punch* published some verses, written anonymously at the time by Jan Struther (*Mrs. Miniver*) that must have pleased his shade—

Here lies a jester with a sense of duty,
A master craftsman in his art engrossed,
A steadfast friend, a worshipper of beauty,
A kindly critic and a perfect host.

CHAPTER FIFTEEN

Florence, Kitzbuhel, Venice

I

AT THE CLOSE of each morning's work I walked across Hyde Park and Green Park to lunch at my club. One could walk on grass the whole three miles in the very heart of the West End. There was a brief interruption when I had to cross at Hyde Park Corner to Green Park. On a lawn near the beginning of Rotten Row stood the beautiful Diana fountain. The Greek goddess drew her bow above a water basin. Immediately across Hyde Park Corner, before entering Green Park, isled on a plinth, stood the bronze statue of David, surely inspired by Michelangelo's masterpiece, erected as a memorial to the Machine Gun Corps of the First World War. So there stood Diana and David, separated by the London traffic. Her arrow was pointed towards him. I decided to effect their union fictionally and thus I came to write my novel *David and Diana*.

I was very happy in my London rooms, in full creative flood, and fulfilling my ambition. There were others with achievement much ahead of mine. At a lunch party in a friend's studio I met an engaging young man, my junior by seven years, who had already produced two phenomenally successful plays and within twelve months would add to *The Vortex* and *Hay Fever* his delightful operetta, *Bitter Sweet*. Noël Coward had three strings to his bow. He could write, compose music and act; and he was as entertaining off-stage as on.

At the beginning of 1928 I found myself embarked on a new adventure. When I told Arnold Bennett that a company called Film Enterprises Ltd. was negotiating for the rights of *Sagusto*, he said: "Don't get elated, you won't see a penny. I wrote a scenario for them and they paid me with nine hundred shares that are worthless."

My transaction became a pantomime. It got so far that I was sent to Venice and Ragusa, with an American producer and his two assistants, to prepare on location the scenario of my story. Early in March we arrived in Ragusa on the Dalmatian coast. By an odd chance it could not have been very far from that island owned by the Greek lady who was the genesis of my story. But after arrival there nothing happened. We spent a lot of time sitting on the hotel terrace drinking "Cora Vermouth". The first assistant rose early every morning to give himself an enema. The second assistant, a Hollywood Russian, disappeared every morning at ten o'clock. I was told that having lost his wife tragically, he went to mass. The producer spent his time sending cables and trying to persuade the Yugoslav authorities to give him the use of the Ragusa castle for a setting. With all this, and some pleasant motor excursions to places in the neighbourhood, we never got down to writing the scenario. After ten days, exasperated, I went back to Venice. The producer promised to send me the rough-out of the scenario. One day it arrived. I almost collapsed. My heroine's name had been changed, provisionally, to "Miss Cora Vermouth!"

Suddenly the production company was summoned home. There had been extensive publicity. I read one morning in *Bioscope*: "Mr. Roberts is a sensitive and highly emotional type of man, with a wonderfully fluent tongue. He talks business and art without trying to separate the two. The author and the producer have been visiting the Dalmatian coast. Their collaboration has been eminently satisfactory. They return to London on Tuesday with the complete script." All this was sheer fantasy. I did not go back to London with the producer. I went from Venice to Florence thinking it would be pleasant to spend Easter there. The producer and his assistants disappeared after an announcement that the leading lady was "Miss Keir, a beautiful and gifted dancer who, the producer claims, is destined to be one of the world's most famous actresses, and the junior 'lead' is the very promising young film star, Godfrey Winn."

The end of this film enterprise was dismal. It transpired that all the preliminary publicity was designed to raise money in the city for production. It failed. The producer and one of his assistants disappeared over the Atlantic, the other, the Russian, went to Nice.

Here one day he committed suicide. It was revealed that he was a drug addict. He had disappeared each morning not to attend a mass for his dead wife but to give himself a shot in the arm. However, Arnold Bennett was wrong. I got £750, less my literary agent's fee. All the others got nothing but their expenses.

Another little bit of business arranged by my energetic young agent, Mr. Michael Joseph, later a very successful publisher, ran aground. One day he called me to his office at Curtis Brown Ltd. and told me that Lloyd George was writing his memoirs under contract with a publisher. L.G. felt that he should have an experienced author go over his manuscript. Would I undertake this for a fee of £1,000? It would entail considerable work. I agreed, reluctantly. Two weeks later Joseph asked me to see him. "Old L.G.'s gypped us!" he said. "He's got his publishers to undertake the vetting of his manuscript at their cost!"

II

Just before Easter I took a motorbus over the Alps to Florence where I arrived the same evening. I had booked a room at the Hotel Berchielli on the Lungarno. It was the "Bertolini's" of D. H. Lawrence's *Aaron's Rod*. I was awakened at 6 a.m. one day by a frightful shindy of bells below my window. Protesting, I was moved to a room on the front, with a balcony. The view over the Arno to the cypress-clad hills rising above the Pitti Palace was glorious. I learned that the campanile from which had burst the clamour of bells belonged to the little medieval church of SS. Apostoli. According to a legend, a Pazzi had brought back from the First Crusade some flints taken from the Holy Sepulchre. These were deposited in SS. Apostoli. Early each Good Friday morning worshippers brought their paschal candles to be lit by the sacred flints. A priest from the cathedral then took the flints for a famous ceremony outside in the Piazza del Duomo. Here stood a *carro* pulled by two pairs of Tuscan oxen. This vehicle, crammed with fireworks, was connected by a wire with the High Altar. When the solemn mass was celebrated and the *Gloria in Excelsis Dio* was reached, down the wire ran a rocket in the form of a dove carrying fire from the sacred flints. If the dove fired the *carro* the tremendous explosion was regarded as an omen for a good harvest.

When I mentioned to a member of the English colony that I hoped to see Norman Douglas I gathered that he was not approved of. I remarked that I had known Douglas some sixteen years earlier when he was assistant editor of the *English Review* and that he had been very pleasant to me. The next day I met a Major Windram who had an apartment looking down the Arno. He was very hospitable and seemed to know everybody in the English colony. It was he who arranged the meeting with Norman Douglas. "Don't mention D. H. Lawrence to him. They've had a terrific row and are not on speaking terms," he said. We dined in a small restaurant across the Arno that Douglas favoured. I found him very changed. His hair had silvered, his face was very florid. He had coarsened but was still a tall, handsome man, with a fine profile. His manners were commanding and he had an aristocratic air. A fluent linguist, he spoke Russian, Italian, French and German, the last being almost his mother tongue for he had been born in Austria, in 1868. His mother was the daughter of Baron von Poelnitz. It was singular that the two leading English writers then living in Florence should be related to German aristocrats, for D. H. Lawrence had married a daughter of Baron von Richthofen. The Douglas family had owned cotton mills in the Vorarlberg where they had settled. After an unhappy year at Uppingham School, Douglas, aged fifteen, went to Karlsruhe Gymnasium. Later he passed the entrance examination for the Diplomatic Service and went as an attaché to the British Embassy in St. Petersburg, being promoted to Third Secretary. It was there that he learned Russian. When, along with his brother, he inherited the family cotton mills he was well-off for those days, with an income upwards of £2,000 a year. A *bon vivant*, he bought a villa outside Naples, married, had two sons, and was divorced, all this at thirty-two. Unfortunately, his brother made a bad sale of the cotton mills. The capital ran through Douglas's fingers. He had to sell his villa and at thirty-nine found he must live by his pen. He was a hedonist but conservative in his views. Unhappily his paedophilia brought him into trouble with the British and Italian authorities, Joseph Conrad and others broke off their friendship. After working at the *English*

Review he went to Capri. There in 1917 he wrote *South Wind*, which brought him world-fame. A Douglas cult grew, especially with the Americans, whom he exploited mercilessly.

I am not a *South Wind* enthusiast. It is an amazing compendium of oddments of learning, historical, mythological, archaeological, theological and biological, blended with a mischievous wit, but it is not a novel. It fails to create any convincing characters and lacks a theme. The book put Capri on the map, as no other work had done until twelve years later Axel Munthe came along with his phenomenally successful *Story of San Michele*, another mixture. Douglas's two other novels demonstrated that he had not the novelist's gift. The true quality of his scholarly mind, with its command of strong, beautiful English, is best revealed in *Old Calabria* and *Fountains in the Sand*, both produced before *South Wind*.

Douglas was prolific in output at the time that I met him in Florence but he had ceased to be conscientious. He played the "limited edition" racket with a Florentine bookseller, Pino Orioli, his printer and publisher. He had a mailing list of about a thousand subscribers, mostly American, and sold them signed copies at two guineas a time. As he paid Orioli for printing and binding and mailed the copies direct, thus cutting out the publisher and booksellers, he netted a considerable sum. When this "limited edition" field was exhausted, he sold the copyright to a publisher for an ordinary edition. His output got more and more forced. He complained bitterly to an American publisher that rich Americans were wasting their money on fake Italian antiques. The publisher bluntly told him that he had overplayed his market. The signed edition collectors woke up to the fact that he had made suckers of them.

Around the time that I met Douglas he was busy compiling an anthology of dirty limericks, with pseudo-scholarly footnotes. He and Orioli printed the anthology in a "strictly limited" edition. The result was disastrous. A French publisher issued a pirated edition, as also an American publisher, who was sent to gaol for printing the book. There were repercussions with the British and Italian authorities. The Home Secretary prodded the Italians into prosecuting Orioli for publishing indecent books. On the list was *Some Limericks*.

Douglas left Italy for Portugal in 1940, to avoid internment, and eventually reached England. He refused to go to America despite repeated invitations. He detested the U.S.A. which he declared was "a perambulating lunatic asylum". He stayed in England until 1946 when he went to Capri, where he became a patriarchal figure. Along with Benedetto Croce, the philosopher, he was made an honorary citizen. Here until his death he held court. He hated getting old, often speaking of his "slow putrefaction", though he retained his alert mind until the end. He was now over eighty and fortunate in his last years in being installed in the beautiful villa of a kindly Englishman. It was always believed that "Uncle Norman", as he was affectionately called, was in "reduced circumstances" but he had been cunning. When he died in 1952, aged eighty-three, his friends were astonished to learn that he had enjoyed an annuity bought for him by an American admirer, and, all told, he had an income of £1,000 a year. It must be considered an achievement for one who had always advocated a misspent youth. An old friend and Florentine neighbour of his, Reginald Turner, described him as "a mixture of Roman Emperor and Roman cab driver".

When I met him in Florence that Easter of 1928 he was still physically and mentally vigorous, and the obscure assistant editor of 1913 had become an international figure. He was someone to be called on in Florence or in Capri. He had enormous charm if he could be kept away from the animosities he nourished. He remembered me as "a lad out of Nottingham". "I hope you won't turn out as big an affliction as another I know from there," he said. We knew whom he meant. I ignored the reference. Altogether it was a delightful evening. He was a rare conversationalist, or should one say monologist, since he had so much to give. He grew mellower towards midnight and parted from us in a haze of alcoholic benevolence.

III

Someone offered to take me to call on D. H. Lawrence. He was living with his wife Frieda on the upper floor of the Villa Mirenda at Scandicci, outside Florence. I declined the offer for various reasons. He could have no possible interest in me, and I was nervous of the condition in which he might be found. It was reported that he and his wife had violent scenes, they threw pots and pans at each other. I had a prejudice against him for running off with Professor Weekley's wife who deserted her three small children. It had been a great scandal in Nottingham and sympathy was with the betrayed husband. He had shown kindness to Lawrence, his pupil, and was not undiscerning. "I have a genius in my evening class," he told a colleague. In 1912, Lawrence, who had been teaching at a boys' school in Croydon, returned to Nottingham to seek Weekley's aid in procuring a lecturership. It ended in the elopement with Frieda. They were not afraid to face poverty together. When at last there was a divorce Lawrence never paid the £145 owed to the lawyer. He wrote nothing but abuse about the College where he had received tuition.

Aware of all this I did not feel sympathetic towards the man himself. Moreover, I was not carried away, as so many, by his novels. I never could understand what all the fuss was about over *Sons and Lovers*. I did not think the book was well-written. Perhaps I was too familiar with its locale. It seemed to me that Nottingham and its environs were poorly evoked. The obsession with his mother, a frigid type, and the hatred of his father had Freudian overtones. About the time of the appearance of *Sons and Lovers* there was a cult of "the working classes". The upper middle-classes and the aristocracy began to "discover" them. The beautiful Countess of Warwick became a Socialist and made a pet of a Labour leader. Once, when I mentioned *Sons and Lovers* to the sophisticated, monocled Eddie Marsh, he lisped, "Exquisite! What exquisite work!" He had never lived with the working classes or been near them. I had lived on the edge of the Nottinghamshire coal-mining district. I could not get excited about them as revealed in Lawrence's novel, having known them in real life. It was old, drab stuff to me. Again, Lawrence was obsessed with sex, and tirelessly preached the dogma of the phallus. He could not stem his missionary zeal. He collided early with the authorities over *The Rainbow*, in 1915. A London magistrate denounced it as "a work of the utmost depravity". This was in the days before "pornography" had been abolished. It had not yet become a commonplace of an "enlightened age".

Just before I arrived in Florence, Lawrence had sent to Orioli, for printing, the manuscript of *Lady Chatterley's Lover* and was awaiting the proofs. He had written it sitting under a shady tree at the Villa Mirenda. He knew what he was writing. "It's so shocking, the most improper novel in the world," he wrote to a friend. "You will understand what I am trying to do: the full natural rapprochement of a man and a woman; and the re-entry into life of a bit of the old phallic consciousness and the old phallic insouciance." Inevitably the work was adversely criticised and created a scandal. The British and American Customs were driven to seize copies, and thus advertised it. Like *Ulysses*, of which Lawrence had a poor opinion, it qualified for the smuggling racket. America began to buy pirated copies at twenty dollars a time.*

In Florence I heard stories of the discord and dirt in the Villa Mirenda. There was a feminine streak in Lawrence that made him delight in playing the *hausfrau*. He cooked, scrubbed floors, did laundry and needlework. He had a passion for making tea. "Much as I liked some of his work I never had any deep feeling for him as a man," said Orioli. "One always had to be on one's guard with Lawrence. His querulous and chronic distrust of everybody made real intimacy impossible. Sometimes his behaviour made me wonder whether he was not suffering from a persecution mania." Early in his career Lawrence had appealed to Arnold Bennett for financial help. Always generous, Bennett sent him money from time to time. This did not prevent Lawrence, writing to Aldous Huxley, from describing Bennett as "a sort of pig in clover". Norman Douglas gave the same posthumous verdict as Orioli. He wrote to a friend: "Do you realise that no one who knew Lawrence well, as we knew him, was sorry when he died?" On the other hand, Huxley became a devoted friend. "He is one of the few people I feel respect and admiration for. Of most other eminent people I have met I feel that at any rate I belong to the same species as they do. But this man has something different and superior in kind." He wrote this opinion in 1927 and held it long after Lawrence's death. Others grew tired of his phallic obsession, the splenetic storms, the mania for "urgent loins" and "mounting blood". Once he quarrelled violently with a Paris taximan, then, after a stormy

* Lawrence attacked Joyce and Proust. The author of *Ulysses* reciprocated. "I read the first two pages of the usual sloppy English of *Lady Chatterley's Lover*," he wrote.

scene, he admired him. "Did you see his face? Beautiful and human. He lives in his blood that man, he is solid in his blood," he exclaimed. There was never any consciousness of spiritual values in Lawrence's work.

It happened that I was not to leave Florence without meeting Lawrence. One morning I was talking to Orioli in his little bookshop when a tallish thin man and a sturdy woman entered. One glance at the bearded face told me who he was. Orioli introduced me. Lawrence could not know that I had any connection with Nottingham and I made no mention of it. His wife, Frieda, was a fresh-faced, robust-looking woman with a pleasant air. Lawrence had a somewhat bulbous nose, dented in under the brow, a rough tawny beard and moustache. His voice was high pitched. One feature dominated his face: he had arresting bright blue eyes, very clear, with a vital light in them. They possessed you as he spoke. There was something else, contradictory, an aura of death. I knew that he was consumptive and suffered much, bravely. I wondered why he persisted in living in the treacherous Florentine climate, the more so when he told me that he detested Italy, which would have been a surprise had I not heard that he often made contradictory statements. It was obvious that he had called on business with Orioli so I excused myself and we parted very affably. As I walked along the Lungarno I began to regret that I had not visited him at the Villa Mirenda. I had no idea that he was within two years of his death, despite the subtle emanation from his face.

The Lawrence cult has grown since his death, aged forty-four in 1930, and has piled up a formidable library. American editors, professors, endowed researchers, dig over the ground. Legend and fact are entwined. Lawrence when a boy won a scholarship to Nottingham High School. One of his masters had gained a V.C. in World War I. On his death a London newspaper printed a story that young Lawrence had been detected playing with a model gallows and corpse under the lid of his desk. When the master remonstrated with him Lawrence drew a pistol and shot at him, luckily missing him. It seemed to me an incredible story. On enquiry the headmaster told me there was no record of any such event. I asked the newspaper for its authority for the statement. There was no reply.

When Penguin Publications challenged the ban on *Lady Chatterley's Lover* by publishing copies and offering them for sale the authorities took up the challenge. A sensational trial followed. The defence produced among its witnesses a Bishop, a Dean and two other clergymen. Some witnesses went so far as to assert that the book was one that Christians should read because Lawrence was portraying sexual ecstasy as something sacred, a basis for holy life! The Crown badly bungled its case, called no witnesses, and Penguin won the day. Later the Warden of All Souls College published an article pointing out that the gamekeeper and Lady Chatterley had committed sodomy. All this publicity created a tremendous demand for the thirty-year-old book, and there was a sale of half-a-million copies. It might have been entitled *Phallus in Blunderland*, considering what had happened at the trial. The royalty earnings were astronomical. The author, when living, had received £1,615 in the first year of publication and considered it his most profitable work.

There was a story, to which Lawrence gave credence since he thought it explained something Latin about the sexual ferment in his blood. His thoughts turned to a possible mystery concerning his descent. After the battle of Waterloo some English soldiers walking on the battlefield came upon an abandoned infant. They were not sure whether it was French, Prussian or Belgian. They took the child to their camp and the Regiment adopted him, dressing him in a uniform and giving him the name of John Lawrence. The child was brought up as a military tailor. In due time, leaving the army, he found employment at Eastwood, Notts, with the Brinsley Colliery Company, making pit trousers for the miners. From this John Lawrence, assumed to have been born about 1812, the novelist believed he might be descended, being the grandson of the Waterloo baby. This legend confirmed D. H. Lawrence's belief that he had Latin blood. His father, the hated coalminer, was a superb dancer, a gift that helped him to capture Lydia Beardsall, for whom Lawrence had a mother-fixation. Some students of the novelist's work suggest that he received his strain of genius not from his puritanical mother but from his feckless, lightfooted father. The facts, concerning the French descent, are a·little different. Professor Harry T. Moore, a patient investigator of the Lawrence story, tells us that the John

Lawrence who was D. H.'s grandfather was brought up in Nottingham. His mother had married George Dooley, after her Lawrence husband had been killed at Waterloo. Dooley was a tailor and taught John Lawrence, his stepson, his trade. The whole story raises another speculation. Was the Waterloo soldier's widow a camp-follower, and did the Regiment make her a foster-mother, who gave her name to the child? Whatever the truth, D. H. Lawrence liked the idea of possessing Latin blood.

Towards the end of his life he warmed towards his alienated father, whom he had portrayed so bitterly in *Sons and Lovers*. His sister, Ada, reviewing the home life of the Lawrences, wrote: "I wonder if there would have been so much misery in our childhood if mother had been a little more tolerant."

IV

I was home in time to see the buses running all over London announcing the serialisation of *David and Diana* in the *Daily Mirror*, Their fronts had advertising panels, thus for twenty-four hours all over London my name was seen. With natural vanity I went by bus to Mansion House, where seven bus routes converged, and back to Piccadilly, sitting just above the panels. I felt as if I had conquered London.

My Florida friend, Howard Phillips, during my visit to Orlando had extracted a promise that I would spend next Christmas there. We evolved a new route. I would go by boat to Havana, cross to Key West, and take a Florida East Coast Railway train over the Keys to Titusville, where he would pick me up. I would thus combine business with pleasure. After Christmas with the Phillips family I would go north to New York and make a short lecture tour to cover my expenses. I was aware that the novelty of these tours had worn thin. They took some three months out of one's writing life and left one exhausted. You were turned into a "wonder-boy" by advance publicity, blown up to more than life size. I observed that some fellow performers had become blatant professionals. They became more and more desperate in holding the platform. Some developed into charlatans and comported themselves with shameless arrogance or eccentricity. There was the singular figure of the aristocratic Count Keyserling, the German philosopher. He had lost his Baltic estate during the Russian Revolution of 1918. Later he became the president-founder of The School of Wisdom at Darmstadt. His fame came from his book *The Travel Diary of a Philosopher* which swept America in 1925. It was platitudinous and obscure. With its theme of spiritual regeneration it created such a vogue that Keyserling became the prophet of an "uplift" cult, something to which the American public is particularly prone. His disciples formed an élite. They would build a new civilisation out of the ruins of the old, based on a synthesis of the wisdom of the East and West. There was a touch of Prussian arrogance in Keyserling's attitude towards his disciples and audiences. Before he arrived to lecture, his hostess received a printed list of things to be observed when entertaining him:

> The following will help you to understand Count Keyserling's preferences. He is a charming and fascinating guest as long as his wishes are considered. The Count dislikes sightseeing. He dreads overheated rooms. He never attends lectures, concerts, or the like. He never sees anyone later than six hours before a lecture. He does not drink before a lecture. However, half an hour before he has to go on the platform he would like to have served a strong cup of coffee and a sandwich of roast beef or chicken (white meat). He is exhausted after a lecture and does not wish to meet anyone unless he can have a sit-down supper at which he will be served French wines or champagne. The Count refuses to attend dinners with men only. He cannot eat raw fruit, salad, vegetables; only potatoes boiled or mashed. He lives chiefly on fresh fish and oysters, dozens of them on the half-shell, and beef, lamb and white meat of fowl. He enjoys the society of attractive young women.

What was more astonishing than these conditions was that he had no difficulty in finding people ready to conform to them. At Darmstadt he organised an annual conference where he had the deposed Grand Duke of Hesse, with his small court, as his disciples and a backing of moneyed Americans. Hitler persecuted him, withdrawing his passport, impounding his papers and forbidding him to publish, travel or lecture. The privations of World War II, entailing malnutrition, brought on paralysis. He died at Innsbruck in 1946, aged sixty-six. Instead of achieving any synthesis of the wisdom of the East and the West there had followed a sharper division as a result of the Second War.

It must have reassured his hostesses to learn that the Count did not drink. Alas, many of these distinguished lecturers did, excessively. When I lectured at the exclusive Everglades Club in Palm Beach, my hostess, who met my train and conducted me to an hotel, said: "All your hotel expenses will be paid, but they will not include any drinks." I learned that one lecturer drank so excessively that not only did he run up in twenty-four hours a bill of thirty-two dollars, he was so incapable when collected for his lecture that he had to be helped in and out of the car, and leaned very heavily on the reading desk; happily he was surprisingly articulate. I had seen a Lord Chancellor perform at a Bar dinner in a similar state. The brain somehow surmounted the bottle.

My lecture tours had given me a valuable experience of the American scene, as well as helped the sales of my books, but I began to see the danger of following dual roles. The Salpeter interview had revealed that they would be invidiously compared. One afternoon at my club I picked up a copy of *T.P.'s Weekly*, the literary journal of T. P. O'Connor, the famous Irish M.P. It had an article headed *Famous Novelists as Lecturers*. It was complimentary enough but it confirmed my fears:

> Mr. Galsworthy is a speaker after America's own heart. His bearing has that aristocratic distinction which is always so alluring to the democratic States. Mr. Walpole has attacked America from another angle. A robust geniality is the keynote of his lectures. After hearing him speak one quickly realises how the *Jeremy* books come to be written. In spite of his forty years he is still a dashing schoolboy.
>
> Mr. Roberts is the only author of whom it can be said that the speaker is triumphant over the writer. As a novelist, though not undistinguished, he is among a hundred. As a speaker he is a master. Not until we have heard him do we realise to the full his fine choice of phrases, his capacity for apt simile, his power of enforcing us with a swift sentence to visualise a complete scene. He uses no notes, does not even prepare his remarks

beforehand, yet not only does he never falter for a word but his lectures are shaped as beautifully as a well-moulded vase.

Very nice indeed, but you have been warned, I said to myself. It confirmed my decision. I might make a few speeches from time to time but no more professional tours after the one booked for next winter. Thus I resolved, not knowing what Fate had in store for me.

In the middle of August I was back in Venice, en route for Budapest, to join some English friends. It was fortunate that one of these spoke fluent Magyar. Another friend, a Hungarian resident there, Baron Wolfner, destined after the Second World War to languish in a Communist gaol, showed me much hospitality. The capital had emerged from the war with its buildings unscathed. In the early evening one watched from the terrace of the Ritz Hotel the sunset fade, silhouetting the long line of the Royal Palace crowning Buda's hill above the Danube. The night clubs resounded with their famous gypsy orchestras. It was a city of music and gaiety, whose inhabitants had in their veins the commingled blood of Magyar, Slav, Russian, Roumanian, Turk, Tartar, Mongolian and Tibetan races. It seemed to be just outside Europe. The wild horse-men of the Puszta might have been cousins of the Cossacks. At the hour of the Corso, under the plane trees bordering the Danube, I saw more beautiful women than I had ever seen elsewhere in the world. We bathed at Margareten Insel, amid garden cafés, and dined at restaurants perched on the Blocksberg, looking down at night upon the myriad-lighted city of Pest in the plain. On Sunday morning it seemed to be the fashion to visit a series of Turkish baths and hot swimming pools, half underground, famous for their chalybeate and sulphur hot springs. The dim, opalescent pools under rotundas of coloured glass retained the oriental character of the Turkish period.

I left this fascinating city for Vienna, where I lingered briefly. I found Salzburg thronged but not yet obsessed with the cult of Mozart and imported conductors. After this baroque gem I left for a small Austrian town, in the Tyrol, named Kitzbühel, as yet almost unknown except to a few enthusiastic skiers. I had been told of an old schloss that had been converted into a *pension* by a Countess

Château de Bonnétable

The Duke de Doudeauville on his ninetieth birthday with Lise,
his grand-daughter.

Mr. and Mrs. Gene Tunney on their honeymoon.

Lamberg. One September evening I was driven in an old barouche down the quaint Hohestrasse, under an ancient gate and up an incline into the cobbled courtyard of the fifteenth-century Schloss Kaps, stone-built, massive, perched on the foothill of a mountain. I was received in a dark hall whose walls bristled with antlers, and was conducted up a wide staircase into the presence of the countess. She was a middle-aged woman with two children, gallantly battling with the privations resulting from a lost war and a shattered fortune. The painted portraits of dead counts who had once served the Habsburgs looked grimly down in the salons and dining-room. They had been ministers and ambassadors. One of them, governing in Hungary, had been assassinated by a nationalist. The heraldic carving over the main door showed, by the impaling of a Can Grande mastiff and ladder, that the Lambergs had Italian Scaliger blood in them. It was obvious that the countess was making a brave effort to keep the family flag waving. There was a youth, Karl, like a colt. His young sister, shepherded by a governess, took her lessons under a tree on the lawn and was as shy as a gazelle.

The guests were few, for the season was ending. There was an English family, a mother, son and two daughters. The mother was always dressed in black. Her son was about sixteen, her daughters older. I did not learn until much later how sorely Fate had stricken them. The mother was the Countess of Chichester. In the previous year she had lost within a week both her husband and elder son. John, her second son, who had succeeded as the 8th Earl of Chichester, was still at Eton. His sisters were Lady Elizabeth and Lady Prudence. It was singular that I should meet a descendant of the Henry Pelham to whom, in 1743, an ancestor of mine, John Roberts, acted as secretary. Pelham was then Chancellor of the Exchequer before becoming Prime Minister, and was the originator of Consols. John Roberts, of whom I had an engraving showing him with Pelham, was a successful collector of sinecures, a bit of a toady, judging from a letter of his I possess. He seems to have been an unctuous mediocrity, but when he died a memorial plaque was set up in Westminster Abbey; to accommodate it they cut away the top of Chaucer's tomb! So here, after two centuries, a Pelham and a Roberts were together.

I became friendly with this quiet family, still under the shadow of their loss. There was a small lake at Kitzbühel, dark brown, in which we bathed. It contained mud that had curative properties for those suffering from rheumatism. We swam, sunbathed, gossiped and went to the evening Platzmusik performed by a town band in Tyrolean costume.

After ten days Lady Chichester and family left, to my regret. I never saw young John again. Fate had not finished with the Chichesters. Six years later he was appointed an honorary attaché at the British Embassy in Warsaw. Two years later he was *en poste* at Washington, and the next year he became honorary secretary to the British High Commissioner in Canada. On the outbreak of World War II he joined the Scots Guards and was killed in action in 1944, aged thirty-one. He left behind him a posthumous son, the 9th Earl.

Shortly before the Chichesters left Kitzbühel a tall, dark, handsome youth came to lunch. At Eton he had distinguished himself (Victor Ludorum). He was now studying for the Foreign Office Competitive Entrance examination. A former British Consul in Vienna, Forbes Dennis, had settled in Kitzbühel with his wife Phyllis Bottome, the novelist. He practised as a crammer and this confident Adonis lived with them in their chalet. Mrs. Dennis was an ardent disciple of Dr. Adler, the psychiatrist I had heard lecture at the Lamonts in New York. The Dennises sent their wild pupil to Vienna to see Dr. Adler but he was away, and his assistant failed to accomplish anything for the troubled youth. A born amorist, irresistible to women, he ran like a prairie fire through the girls of Kitzbühel. He had announced that "technique in bed is important", something he had discovered at twenty! When he lunched at Schloss Kaps he was confidently handsome and full of charm. We became friendly and used to resort to the Café Reisch where his presence fluttered the Austrian girls. Although he wrote in the after years to the Dennises of "that golden time when the sun always shone", I discerned that he was worried about his future, even though he seemed to be endowed with everything, youth, looks, brains and a background of wealth. His grandfather was a millionaire banker who from a humble origin had risen to be a railway magnate in the United States. At twenty-eight he had been the founder of the first investment trust, a new thing in the stock market.

His father had been killed in the war and he was to lose his youngest brother in the Second World War. He had a gifted elder brother to whom he was deeply attached but he clashed with his mother, a strong-minded beauty, somewhat erratic. He was certainly a dazzling young man and I wondered what his future would be; I could not imagine him as an ambassador. I never met him again after those Kitzbühel days. Then, twenty-five years later, he blazed into world-wide fame with his thriller, *Casino Royale*. He was Ian Fleming, the creator of James Bond, that tough lecher and killer, familiar with gambling dens, spies, whose adventures had sadistic and masochistic undertones. It was success, on a dubious plane. Fleming was too intelligent not to have misgivings about the nature of his raffish hero.

At the height of his triumph Life cheated him. The creator of that hero of superabundant vitality was stricken with heart disease. A few months before his death an old friend asked him what it was like to be so famous. He answered "It was all right for a bit... but now, my God! Ashes, old boy, just ashes!" He died in 1964 aged fifty-six. Within four years of our Kitzbühel meeting, by the unpredictable weaving of Fate's tapestry, I was to be associated with two remarkable women, his mother and his grandmother. But this is a story for another day.

V

Among the guests at Schloss Kaps there was one with the air of a *grande dame*. I was not surprised to learn that she was a Russian, the widow of an ambassador during the Czarist regime. She was referred to as "Her Excellency". She had a companion, a little woman who was a Belgian countess. Demure, she acted as a sort of lady-in-waiting. On fine afternoons about three o'clock there was a ceremony that never ceased to amuse me. Into the castle courtyard came an old landau with an elderly coachman. It was a relic of the Lambergs' former splendour. It drew up at the castle door and waited. Presently down came the little countess, loaded with rugs, and behind her came Her Excellency, very regal with parasol and wearing a large feathered hat. There was a considerable to-do as the two ladies seated themselves. Then, in impressive state, they moved off for their afternoon drive.

By this time I might be considered an established author, with six novels to my credit. One day in the hall Her Excellency, returning my bow, addressed me. She asked "Are you writing anything now, Mr. Roberts ?" I confessed that I was at work on a new novel. The Schloss, turned into a *pension* by a war-ruined aristocratic family, had provided me with a theme that became *Pamela's Spring Song*. "It would be delightful if you would read some of it to me," said Her Excellency. Flattered, I agreed. Few young authors can resist such a proposal, and this invitation came from an impressive *grande dame* who told me, with compliments, that she was familiar with my books. So, each evening after dinner, in front of a log fire in her sitting-room, with a lamp and a samovar on the table, with the mouse-like little countess doing embroidery all the time, I read to them. It was rather like a scene from Chekov, I felt—the country house, the Russian Excellency, the log fire, the samovar, the little countess and the young author. One evening Her Excellency surprised me by saying "Mr. Roberts, I feel quite proud that I am the cause of your being a novelist!" Startled, I exclaimed, "But, madame, how ?" She explained. After the Russian Revolution in which they had lost their estates, impoverished, a widow, she sought to earn some money to keep her son at Eton. In prosperous days, while taking a cure at Bad Homburg she had come to know Mr. Heinemann, the publisher. Fluent in six languages, she applied to him for some translation work, and scouting for foreign books. Later, impressed by her judgment, he sent her manuscripts, particularly those with foreign settings. "That was how I came to read your *Scissors*. I liked it and strongly recommended its publication," she said.

In one matter I have never learned sense. Again and again, obsessed with a book I am writing, I drive myself on to its completion and then collapse. My doctor repeatedly warned me. I was fortunate in my medical adviser. In a way our careers progressed together. One evening in the mid-thirties, after giving a lecture on top of a strenuous four-months' work, I collapsed in the anteroom. My chairman called his young doctor and they took me home. Thus I came to know Walter Fergusson Hannay. He had started in practice by investing in a monocle and a second-hand Rolls-Royce. His surgery was a small backroom in a fashionable West End street. In due time he advanced

324

to Harley Street, and a knighthood, for he became the doctor of a
Prime Minister and his family, the Attlees. Behind the early façade,
which had seemed pretentious, was a man with a gift for diagnosis,
combined with a warm, simple nature. In a sense he was in the literary
set. He was related to Canon Hannay, who had much success as a
novelist under the pseudonym of "George A. Birmingham", and he
married another novelist, Doris Leslie. This was the man to whom I
went every year for a medical check-up. He knew just how to handle
me, a creature too imaginative for serenity. A dozen times I thought
I had a fell disease, consumption or cancer. It was he, poor fellow,
who died of the latter.

In the course of the years he became a valued friend. One day, in
my sixtieth year, after the annual check-up he said: "My lad, you'll
live to be ninety!" Alarmed, I retorted, "Good God! You frighten
me! Long before then I'll have lost my vogue and have eaten up my
savings. When that day comes I'll ask you to quietly put me out!"
He laughed and said: "Oh no, not again, my boy." "Again?—do you
mean to say you have put someone out?" I asked. "Well—it's quite
a story," he replied. "One day at the beginning of my practice I was
called in to attend a lady staying at the Ritz. I was quite elated to
have such a well-to-do patient. I gave her satisfaction and before
she left she said: 'Dr. Hannay, I hope you will always be my doctor
in England. One day I shall ask a favour of you. I'm living on capital
and when I come to the end of it I shall ask you to put me to sleep.'
Being young and eager to please a good patient, I said lightly that I
should always be at her service. I didn't take her seriously, of course.
She was a Russian and you know how melodramatic they can be.
Some years later she returned to the Ritz and sent for me. I asked her
what was the matter. 'Nothing,' she said, 'but the time has come.
I am at the end of my money and I want you to give me a pill that
will finish me.' I told her that I could not do any such thing. She
became very insistent. 'You are an English gentleman and English
gentlemen always keep their word. You gave me your word when
I first called you in and I expect you to keep your promise!' She
became quite a nuisance, so one day I took along with me a colleague,
an alienist, to hear what he thought of her mental state. When we
left the Ritz he said: 'My dear fellow, her obsession apart, she's as

sane as I am.' Well, that wasn't very sane. The poor wretch committed suicide within a year—woman trouble! My patient at the Ritz became such a nuisance that I stopped going to her. Then one day she did it. I picked up a newspaper which had a great splash about a Russian ex-ambassador's widow at the Ritz who had taken an overdose of sleeping pills. So after that experience with Her Excellency . . ." I interrupted him, "Her Excellency—was she a small stout woman, blonde?" I asked. "Yes," said Hannay. "Was her name Madame C—?" Hannay looked startled. "How on earth do you know her name?" "Because," I replied, "that's the name of the lady who recommended Heinemann to publish my first novel!" I then told him the story of my encounter with Her Excellency at Schloss Kaps. Forty years later, again visiting the Schloss as the guest of Count Karl, now a father, I learned that Her Excellency had given Russian lessons to young Ian Fleming.

The novel I wrote and read to Her Excellency, *Pamela's Spring Song*, with Schloss Kaps for its setting, was the story of an English girl who went there for a holiday and had a love affair with the young Austrian Count who, to retrieve his fortune, had turned his castle into a *pension*. Soon after my story had been published I turned it into a play. One evening with a party I went to see *Autumn Crocus*, by Dodie Smith, which was having a deserved success. I could hardly believe my ears. It was the Schloss Kaps story. I went home and tore up my play. It was not plagiarism; this had happened to other authors.

The Schloss gave me another novel. Three years later I wrote *Spears Against Us*. It told how in 1914 war brought ruin to the family at the Schloss. It proved to be one of my big successes, passing through eighteen reprints in the next twenty-five years. I consider it my best novel. In a roundabout way it resulted in the Prince of Wales going to Kitzbühel in 1935 to learn to ski. Young Count Lamberg was a ski champion and gave lessons to the Prince.

VI

From Kitzbühel I returned to Venice to join friends there. In the last years of the Twenties it was an international playground. There was a raffish set to be avoided, led by a vulgar little woman out of the

Middle West. "Elsa", as they called her, was a pushful organiser of routs, treasure-hunts, charity balls, water galas, etc. A malicious gossip-writer, she acted as entrepreneuse between impoverished titled aristocrats, decayed Royalties who acted as decoy ducks, and the moneyed American *arrivistes* who took palaces for the season and gave extravagant parties. An English drunkard, with a good background-name, one night ended by throwing his host's dinner service into the Grand Canal. It was not even an original outrage; in the seventeenth century a vulgar nouveau riche, owner of the Palazzo Labia, gave a banquet and to demonstrate his wealth threw the gold dinner plate into the Grand Canal; but he had been careful to place nets under the water so that he could retrieve his plate after the guests had gone.

I found my own pleasant circle, for whom Venice was a treasure house and not a treasure hunt, so that all my days were filled with much reward. Foremost was my friend "Timmy" Jekyll. I had met him in the war years in London. He had a first-class intellect and a considerable knowledge of art, music, literature and botany. He had won the Newcastle Prize at Eton and shown promise at Balliol. From an accident in boyhood he was troubled by a limp. His real handicap was a complete indifference to time. After Oxford he joined the staff of the British Museum. It seemed likely that one day he might preside over that great institution. He certainly had the Establishment behind him. His father, Sir Herbert, a noted Civil Servant, had been secretary to two Viceroys of Ireland. His mother, Lady Jekyll, the daughter of a wealthy man who had a great art collection, was very public spirited and became a Dame of the British Empire. One of Timmy's sisters married Reginald McKenna, Chancellor of the Exchequer in the last Liberal Government. His other sister married, first, the son of Lord Aberconway, killed in the First World War, secondly, Colonel Bernard Freyberg, the Dardanelles V.C. and later General Lord Freyberg. A cousin married Asquith's son, Raymond. He was one of that brilliant group of young men, the very flower of our youth, that included the Grenfell brothers, Rupert Brooke and Charles Lister, all dead in the World War. In this year of 1928, Raymond's son succeeded his grandfather, the former Prime Minister, as the second Earl of Oxford and Asquith.

Timmy's aunt, Gertrude Jekyll, was the famous garden designer and horticulturist of Munstead Wood.*

With all this behind him Timmy seemed marked for success. Alas, his British Museum career came to a sudden end. I asked him about this. "Oh my dear fellow, it got too tiresome! I arrived one day and found the gates locked." Since then, with a small remittance, he had wandered about Europe enjoying himself. He lived to be over eighty, when he was knocked down outside the Munstead property which he had inherited from his aunt. People were apt to talk patronisingly of "Poor Timmy". It was nonsense. He missed a "brilliant" career, with all the drawbacks such a thing often entails. He enjoyed life. He was a very kind person, devoid of envy; and surely the world needs kindness more than brilliance or success. He gave great pleasure to many and I always see him beaming over a glass of wine and crumbling a roll in some vine-roofed *trattoria*, while he enchanted us with his knowledge and ranging discourse. He greatly enjoyed this wonderful world and had a gift for communicating his delight in it.

Others among my acquaintance were the two Counts Cesare and Gino Visconti, who owned a small palace. There was a delightful old English baronet, turned Catholic, who entertained in a house that was a cave of dangling Holy Infants and hanging pink cherubs. There were the two Cunard brothers, Victor and Edward. Victor distinguished himself as *The Times* correspondent in Rome. He was anti-Mussolini in the Dictator's early days so that pressure was brought on the British Foreign Office to have Victor removed. His elder brother Edward, lethargic, genial, succeeded to the Cunard baronetcy, being the nephew of Sir Bache and "Emerald" Cunard, and cousin of their ill-fated daughter, Nancy.

Victor Cunard had embarked on a brave enterprise. He had discovered a half-ruined palace, the Vendramin-i-Carmine. He restored and furnished it, partly to live in and partly to let seasonally. One day, standing at a dining-room window, I looked across the canal at a house opposite which had on its façade a sculptured Moor's head.

* The Tate Gallery owns a notable painting by Sir William Nicholson, R.A., entitled "Miss Jekyll's Boots", the boots in which she walked about her renowned garden at Munstead Wood. Timmy wrote a Memoir of her.

"That's the Casa del Moro. They claim Othello lived there," said Eddie. My mind then recalled a book of essays, *L'Altana,* by Henri de Régnier, about an old palace he had lived in in Venice whose windows looked on a Moor's head. I read how some forty years earlier de Régnier had lived in this palace through one winter. He described the room in which he worked, looking out at the Moor and how its walls had a Chinese decoration still faintly visible under the dirt. It is singular how a tradition of Chinese art persists in Venice until one recalls that Marco Polo, with his incredible tales of the court of Kublai Khan, created a Chinese craze when he got back to Venice. Obviously I stood in the room where de Régnier had worked. Its walls were now whitewashed. I mentioned this to Victor. He removed the whitewash and under it discovered the Chinese decoration that de Régnier had remarked on.

One day in September Victor had a distinguished guest, a rather shy young man of about twenty-four. He was Prince Umberto, heir to the throne of Italy, destined to reign for a brief time after the abdication of his father in 1946, and then to be sent into exile by the marginal votes of a plebiscite.

I owed my awareness of another writer who had lived in Venice, the bogus Baron Corvo, to young Oliver Messel who came across the Piazza one morning and thrust a copy of *Stories Toto Told Me* into my hand. "Keep it. You must read it. It's quite marvellous!" he exclaimed. I had never heard of Corvo, the malevolent genius who had preyed on his countrymen in Venice until he died there, destitute, unrecognised, in 1913, aged fifty-three. Thirty years were to elapse before the Corvo cult got under way, and fifty-four years before the triumphant dramatisation of *Hadrian the Seventh* brought him posthumous fame. Messel, the donor of the Corvo book, although only twenty-four had already started his distinguished career as a theatrical designer. Cochran, the great impresario of the Twenties and later, had spotted his talent and commissioned him for his 1926 *Revue* and *This Year of Grace* (1928).

I had been only a few days in Venice when I heard my name called in the Piazza. Turning, I was embraced by François de Deservillers in a state of great excitement. He was on his honeymoon. "What luck! What luck!" he cried. "Come and meet my wife!" It had been a swift courtship and marriage for there had been no hint of this when we had met in Paris the previous year. I had four happy days showing them the city. Only one thing displeased him, the gondola. "It's all wrong! The gondolier stands behind and sees everything!" I informed him that gondoliers were born blind.

In the still warm days of October I moved to a small *pension* on the Zattere, the sunny south side of Venice facing the wide Giudecca Canal, with its pageant of liners and merchant ships that passed before my window. The Pensione Seguso was kept by three sisters, thin, medium, fat, all dressed in black. The last was an excellent cook. It was there that I encountered a tall, angular spinster of about sixty who was destined to have a singular effect upon my life. She was a well-known type in Italy. She had deserted America for Europe. Her attachment to Italy had begun when she went as a nurse to the Italian Front during the First World War. Decorated, she became a fanatical lover of the country now her home. By now *Italianitá*, she was a much-loved character. On Independence Day her American loyalty asserted itself and was demonstrated by the children marking her progress. They waved American flags, and held bags of sweets tied up with American colours. We knew that Signorina Grace Cleveland Porter had been that way. The Cleveland denoted relationship with an American President. She had a tiny income and lived in a small back bedroom in the *pension*. She was almost irritatingly cheerful and flamboyant. I was slowly captured by her oozing goodwill. It seemed that in her native Baltimore, where she had lived until her mother died, she had given lectures on Negro Folk Songs, accompanied by her guitar. She had sung her "Mammy Songs" to the wounded Italian soldiers.

Every afternoon around four o'clock Signorina Porter provided a pantomime. She had an Italian friend, a widower of sixty-five. Handsome, tall, white-haired, gentle, he was an artist of some renown. In his early years Riccardo Nobili had been an adviser to Pierpont Morgan when he was making his art collection. Out of that experience he had published a book called *The Gentle Art of Faking*. He lived in a delightful little house with a garden and watergate on the Fondamenta Bonlini in San Trovaso. Every afternoon Signor Nobili arrived at the side canal by the Pensione Seguso in his small dinghy. A houseboy thereupon appeared with a plank which he placed on a step and on the boat's gunwale. Then Signorina Porter appeared. She was a tall, large woman. She advanced holding a parasol, a guitar slung on her back and a large straw hat on her head. She had a mortal fear of the narrow plank. It was like getting an elephant aboard a skiff. Every window of the pension now had a spectator. We rose from our siesta to watch this embarkment. At last, with much coaxing by the houseboy and one of the Seguso sisters, she made it. Signor Nobili was a large man also. Together they completely filled the dinghy and when they moved off under the arched bridge and on to the broad Giudecca Canal the dinghy sank within three inches of the top of the gunwale. We all feared they would be swamped by a passing ship but it never happened. As Signor Nobili gently rowed the boat away we heard the strumming of the guitar and the strains of a "Mammy Song" coming over the water.

One day I was invited to lunch in Signor Nobili's garden. It was a lovely retreat with vine pergola, orange, lemon and peach trees, and faintly musical with water spouting through a faun's mouth into a marble basin. It was a perfect setting for a romance. After lunch Grace Cleveland Porter played her guitar under the peach tree for my host and myself. *La dolce vita.*

CHAPTER SIXTEEN

Havana to Poland

I

AT THE BEGINNING of December, 1928, I sailed for Havana, en route to Florida, to spend Christmas there. The ship was going via the Panama Canal to Valparaiso. It was turned into an aviary by dark-eyed, shrill-voiced Chilean and Peruvian children who never seemed to go to bed. I am fond of children but a hundred of them trilling in small space made the voyage an ordeal. We called at Bermuda, then one bright day of December I landed at Havana.

There had been a sinister incident on board. The second night out I felt uncomfortable in my cabin. I decided to seek a change but hesitated because there was nothing definite to complain of. It was simply that I could not sleep. I got the purser to move me to another cabin. One evening in the bar he looked at me curiously and said: "Will you tell me why you wanted to change your cabin?" I told him that I could not feel comfortable in it, there was something sinister. "That's extraordinary!" he said, "you'd heard nothing?" "Nothing, what could I hear?" He hesitated and then said: "On the last voyage out we had a Cuban millionaire in your cabin. He was a pretty loose lot. He had drinking parties there until after midnight but that was none of my business. One morning his steward came to me, very excited. He said he had been to call the Cuban and found his cabin empty. The steward thought he must have gone up on deck until he saw his clothes lying about. He had made enquiries but could not find him anywhere. We searched the ship without result. His money and papers were in his pocket. Nothing had been touched. He had changed into his pyjamas but his bed had not been slept in. At one o'clock in the morning two women and a man had been there drinking with him. They said that he was quite sober when they said goodnight. What happened we never found out—whether he went up on deck for air, or felt sick and leaned out of his porthole too far, a difficult thing even for a small man, or committed suicide by going overboard, no one knows. His wife met the boat at Havana. There was an enquiry, the police found no clue except a fully loaded revolver in a portmanteau. You are the first to occupy his cabin. You're psychic, I suppose ?" I denied the idea. I asked him to have another drink. Inwardly I was excited. I was searching for a theme for a new novel. At midnight I had the outline of *Havana Bound* in my head.

I stayed three days in Havana storing impressions. My hotel was luxurious but it harboured too many canaries. There was a patio with dozens of them singing madly in the sunshine; I had had enough of human ones. The city was delightful with its palms, plazas and fine boulevards. I can still hear the tinkle of little bells rung by Chinese youths hawking candies, and see the vivid blue sea beyond the fortress guarding the harbour mouth. Then, on a brilliant morning, I crossed by ferry-boat from Havana to Key West, the lone terminus of the Florida East Coast Railroad, a superb engineering feat that bridged islands for two hundred miles up the Florida coast. This line survived several hurricanes but was vanquished finally by the new automobile traffic when a highway linked Key West with the mainland.

On landing, after being "frisked" for liquor, for I was entering Prohibition U.S.A., I mounted my sleeping car to journey north. A crimson sunset over the desolate Keys reminded me of the lonely Venetian lagoons. Florida had not yet become a crowded playground or the launching site of space rockets. There was only a sparse habitation south of Miami. In the fading crimson light my train began the long journey across palm-fringed islands occupied by flamingos and pelicans. The next morning, before dawn, I descended at the hamlet of Titusville, the nearest station for the Phillips home at Orlando.

It was a strange descent upon America. I felt like a Spanish conquistador, a Ponce de León. The mainland was separated from the Atlantic shore by the St. John River that ran one hundred and eighty miles down the coast from Jacksonville, making a wide canal between the mainland and the sea bank. I walked through the silent hamlet

333

down to the river shore. Already a rift of crimson had stained the eastern horizon; above me the stars were bright. I could hear only the far rumour of the sea. I trespassed across the lawn of a small house by the river. I stood there alone. It was an awe-inspiring moment, on that flat peninsula between the Atlantic Ocean and the Mexican Gulf, like the beginning of the world. The dawn came up over the water, the shadows retreated. Then I saw a lonely light gliding over the river; the beat of paddles told me it was a ferry-boat. Soon the incandescent rim of the sun cut the horizon, the day rushed upwards, the sky changed from indigo to rose. A heron cried and fled, a grey ghost over the opalescent stream. On the far bank the palms were black against the flaming sky and then caught fire along their plumey tops. It was still dark in the garden where I stood. I smiled to think how the householder would stare if, raising his blind and demanding who I was, he received the answer: "An Englishman just arrived from London." Two pelicans flapped by. The next minute the growing daylight banished all mystery. Soon I heard the sound of a car and saw the long white beams from its headlamps. It was Howard Phillips from Orlando.

My Christmas was spent in a paradise of sunshine and orange blossoms. There were dances galore and country club dinners. We bathed again on Daytona Beach. We played tennis through the cool nights. There were other, more odd diversions; we danced with "planters" in a wooden shanty to the wail of violins played by "Crackers", natives who could recall the days when the Seminole Indians had attacked the settlers, and the creeks in the Everglades were full of alligators. I was taken to a gospel meeting of the Holy Jumpers. "Jump for the glory of the Lord, brother!" cried a local haberdasher. They jumped and shouted. I learned that I could have seen another sect, a variant of the Whirling Dervishes, the Holy Rollers, rolling on the floor of their chapel in a cloud of dust, calling "Jesus saves!" I heard of a marvellous surgeon. "Sure, he's a man of God. Every time he cuts, he prays." My host was a collector of stories about crackpot natives. "This Florida soil can produce anything!" he declared. He did not live to see it produce, exactly forty years later, at Cape Kennedy, the rocket that took the first men to the moon.

334

One day I visited the new settlement that Howard had prophesied. It had been fulfilled. The forest clearing I had seen two years before was now covered with long avenues of orange trees. We motored out of Orlando over a macadam road where, previously, we had driven over scrubland. Houses had sprung up. On the edge of the settlement rose a large packing shed, an Arabian-white exterior disguising its nature. It contained a canteen and a dancing floor. From a gallery I looked down on rows of girls superintending machinery that sorted oranges, washed, polished and boxed them. Outside, where once the Indians had wandered, was a railroad and a station, named "Dr. Phillips" after my host, who had planted ten thousand orange trees in the wilderness.

In the New Year, 1929, I started north for my lecture tour. When I stepped down from the train the next day at Bradfield, Pennsylvania, the whole town was white under a heavy mantle of snow. There was not a leaf to be seen on the iron-black trees. The air bit me, the temperature was ten below. It seemed another continent. In March I came down from Montreal to give my last lecture at Brooklyn. I hated the cold and the blizzards and felt exhausted and frostbitten. However that was not the impression I gave to Margaret Leland, who interviewed me for the *Brooklyn Eagle*.

Quite significantly Spring's first day brought me tall, reed-like Cecil Roberts. In his perfectly harmonised mauve-brown suit and double reefed fawn-coloured waistcoat, indicative of the perfect taste that accords so well with the set of his high-domed, oblong head and extraordinarily expressive long white hands, Cecil was nothing short of elegant. His, however, is a virile elegance suggesting the lithe strength of a Shelley, or a Byron ready to swim the Hellespont. I have only the proof of his athletic propensities as evidenced by his insistence on springing down the stairs from my seventh-floor apartment, and on nothing stronger than tea . . . Incidentally one remark thrust forth from his enormous cynicism concerned the lavish indifference and waste of Nature—"Nature drops thousands of acorns indifferently and one is stamped into the ground, to take root and grow into a kingly oak, by the foot of a swine, mind you, not by the foot of an artist."

I now envy that "reed-like" appearance. "The slender grace of a day that is dead will never come back to me"—to misquote Tennyson.

II

That winter I had formed a friendship with a young fellow country-
man, Campbell Hackforth-Jones. On coming down from Oxford he
had been sent by his father, a London stockbroker, to get experience
in a Wall Street office. He was there at a singular time when America
was in a mounting delirium of speculation. I delayed my departure to
enjoy his company and the pleasures of New York, a city I always
found attractive and exhilarating. But there was hysteria in the air.
America was dollar-drunk and gin-drunk. Prohibition had boomer-
anged and turned America into a nation of alcoholics. It had become
a fashionable thing to defeat the law, and a test of hospitality to
provide liquor for guests. Vast fortunes were made in this illicit
traffic. Strange concoctions were sold, some of them resulting in
death. At one university I saw a wrecked Fraternity House blown up
by the students' private still. Clubs had their own hidden bars into
which one was led like a conspirator. I was taken to a dance at a
country club. It seemed very respectable with the dowagers sitting
round the dance floor. "Come along!" said a girl I had just danced
with. I was propelled down a corridor into a former bar, closed under
Prohibition. There were couples dead drunk on the floor. Flasks
came out of hip pockets, a girl with her shoulder strap down was
being mauled by a boy in an alcoholic stupor, the hair over his eyes
preventing him from finding her mouth. They were all from respectable homes.

The stock market hysteria reached its apex that year. Everyone
gave you tips for a rise, a quick turnover; the telephone operator,
the bank clerk, the hall porter, everyone was playing the market.
Stocks soared dizzily. I found it hard not to be engulfed. I had
invested my American earnings on sound advice in good stocks.
Should I sell for a profit? Everyone said "Hang on—it's a rising
market."

I had been made a temporary member of the University Club.
On my last day in New York I went down to the club barber for a
haircut. As he removed the sheet from my neck and I tipped him, he
said softly, "Buy Standard Gas. I've doubled. One of the members

put me on it. It's good for another double." As I walked upstairs I reflected that if the hysteria had touched barber-level something must soon happen. I looked at my watch. It was eleven o'clock. I took the express subway train and emerged amid the grey chasms of Wall Street. On the 18th floor of one of these temples to Mammon was my stockbroker, a lady, strange to say, recommended by my literary agent. I told her I wanted to sell my stocks. She looked surprised. "You've done very well, they'll go higher yet. Why sell?" she asked. I told her that I felt it was time to get out. I was sailing at midnight, could she sell them now? "Yes," she said, with a look that implied I was a lunatic. I signed forms. She would telephone me the result by four o'clock. I bid her goodbye, thanking her for excellent service. I did not tell Campbell what I had done when we had our last dinner together before sailing. We did not know when we should meet again. Our reunion was much sooner than we anticipated. He was home within eight months, and became a barrister instead of a stockbroker. There was a resounding crash the following October that shook America. Banks closed their doors, hundreds of victims committed suicide. There were long unemployment queues. The stocks I had sold fell to a half. I had trebled my original investment.

I spent the homeward Atlantic crossing in planning my new novel, *Havana Bound*. It was my method before writing to sketch out the complete story. I planned my novels like a tapestry, but I kept the weaving loose enough to permit the intrusion of a character that might come to life of its own volition. On arrival home I found *Pamela's Spring Song* running serially in the *Daily Mirror*. I had arranged to join Timmy Jekyll in Venice that spring. Before I left, Campbell's Oxford friend, Emlyn Williams, called on me. He was a short, black-haired young man, the son of a Welsh labourer, just down from Oxford. He had been in the O.U.D.S. and had had a play produced there. He was now in London, acting, and writing another play. He stayed for over an hour and I was struck by his beautiful voice. I think we were a little shy of each other, as often happens in meeting the friend of a friend, I regret that I did not see him again until twenty-two years later when I called on him in his theatre dressing-room. In the intervening years he had written and acted in several successful plays, his name prominent on the electric

337

signs above theatres in the West End and on Broadway. Perhaps the most noteworthy one was *The Corn is Green*, founded on his youthful struggle towards an Oxford scholarship and fame. He has told his story delightfully in an autobiography *George*. His deep interest in the psychology of murderers produced another outstanding success, *Night Must Fall*. In both, his acting put him in the front rank.

III

On arrival in Venice I was fortunate in finding a lodging on the first floor of an attractive little house on the Zattere, near the Pensione Seguso to whom it belonged. Its windows looked across a small garden on to the wide shipping canal between the Zattere and the low line of the Giudecca. The passing merchant ships and liners were so alluring that I had to turn my writing-table from the window. I took my meals in the Pensione Seguso presided over by the three sisters and their beloved cat, Moses. One figure was missing, Signorina Grace Cleveland Porter, she of the "Mammy Songs" and the guitar. My enquiry evoked information of a highly romantic character. She was no longer a signorina. She had made a final embarkation from the Seguso and was now the Signora Grace Nobili! She had married her artist friend. The manner of this was singular. That winter Riccardo Nobili had been ill and warned that he might die. He sent for Grace and told her that he would like to bequeath her his villa but there were two difficulties; he was afraid it might create some scandal, also, not being a relation, she would have to pay a heavy inheritance tax. He made a delicate proposition. If they married before his death then it would be natural for her to inherit the villa, and under the Italian succession laws there was practically no tax for a widow. So they were married, bride and bridegroom being sixty-three and sixty-five respectively. But Riccardo did not die as expected. He lived to be eighty and his bride to be ninety-one. They had fifteen years of the utmost felicity in their little house behind the Zattere, which they named *Domus Americorum* because of the many friends that came to it. In their garden I wrote two novels. They were a lovely part of my Venice.

IV

One morning in the Piazza I heard my name called by someone sitting at Florian's. I turned and was astonished to see the unmistakable figure of George Bernard Shaw. I was greeted affably, to my surprise, for I thought I was in disgrace since that episode of his lecture at Nottingham. He asked me to have a drink and introduced me to three persons at the table, Charlotte his wife and a young American couple. "Now, here's something you can do for me," said G.B.S. "I'm told you are an authority on Venice. I wish you'd show the place to my young friends here." I denied the compliment he paid me. Years later, attending a P.E.N. Conference there, Louis Golding said: "Why on earth don't you write a book about Venice—you're a walking encyclopaedia!" I nursed the idea but put it off through the years and a huge collection of notes was filed away. Then in 1960 James Morris wrote his *Venice* and I realised it could never be done better.

In a desire to please a great man I agreed to play the cicerone. I made a rendezvous with Shaw's American couple for the next morning. We do not have the excellent American habit of clearly introducing people. I am bad at hearing names. That evening I tried to locate Shaw by telephone and ask the names of his friends. They had been staying on Brioni Island together. I was unable to find him.

Promptly at ten o'clock the next morning the Americans arrived at Florian's. We spent nearly three hours together when I left them for a luncheon engagement. Yes, they would love to have another tour the next morning. Somewhat embarrassed, I asked them their names. Mr. and Mrs. Tunney. They came from New York. They were a handsome and pleasant pair. The following morning only Mr. Tunney arrived, apologising for his wife's absence. She had a slight temperature. My companion was eager for information and intelligent. He aroused my curiosity. Physically he was magnificent, tall, handsome in face and figure. A lawyer, a stockbroker, a banker? Finally I asked him what he was. "I'm a pugilist," he answered, grinning. I laughed. "Well, you look as if you could be—but what exactly are

339

you?" "I really am what I say. I'm Gene Tunney, the world heavy-weight boxing champion."

I grew to like him, and in Venice we founded a friendship that has lasted all our lives. Little by little in our walks I learned his story. He was the son of an Irish stevedore who had taught him to box from the age of ten. His father took him to a tavern in New York's Greenwich Village and said: "Have a drink in honour of a coming heavyweight champion." "My first hero," said Tunney, "was Jack Dempsey. I was just starting in the ring when I found myself crossing with him on a New Jersey ferry. The 'Manassa Mauler' was famous the world over. He looked like what he was, a great champion. He sat and talked with me for twenty minutes. It was like a meeting between a king and a pageboy."

It took Gene five years in the Twenties to qualify for the champion class. He bought a heavy board and hit it, barefisted, two hundred times a day. He did press-ups on his fingertips. He ran backwards for a mile. He went woodchopping in Canada. The First World War broke out. He joined the Marine Corps and went to Europe. He was just twenty when he became light-heavyweight champion of the American Expeditionary Force. A giant, a perfectionist, he now lived with one ambition, to fight Dempsey. The road to this was a hard one. He fought sixty-eight fights and lost only once, to the terrible Harry Greb who twice broke his nose, for the second time in a fourth match, which he won. Next he defeated the great Georges Carpentier. At last, aged twenty-nine, he was matched with Dempsey, the world heavyweight champion. The contest took place on September 23rd, 1926, in Philadelphia, in a downpour of rain. Tunney flew there and was nearly sick in the plane and when he gained the ground his legs trembled. There was a gate of 120,757 people who had paid $1,885,733. He was a 3–1 underdog. In his memoirs, *A Man Must Fight*, he described the contest:

> The first blow, too high, won the fight for me, but Dempsey sagged. He said later that if I had followed up this advantage I should have won the fight in the first round. I did follow up but Jack had not been in the ring for ten years for nothing. In the

* *A Man Must Fight*, by Gene Tunney (Jonathan Cape Ltd).

sixth round I received a terrific blow on my Adam's apple. The cartilage was pushed into my throat, lacerating the mucous membrane. I coughed blood and was hoarse for several days. When I was the winner at the end of ten rounds Jack was helped by his seconds to the centre of the ring, to shake hands with his conqueror. It was a splendid gesture and his muttered "All right, Gene. Good luck!" was most touching. I was the world heavyweight champion, the Golden Boy of the Golden Age. The fight attracted the largest crowd that had ever attended a sports event up to that time. The spectators came from all over the globe.

The return match was fought at Chicago a year later, when a crowd of 105,000 paid $2,500,000 to see it. In his penthouse at the Sherman Hotel the night before the contest, Gene, a voracious reader, read Somerset Maugham's *Of Human Bondage*, keeping the last three chapters for the final day. The fight proved to be one of the bitterest ever known. Dempsey smashed Gene to the canvas in the seventh round. It resulted in the now-famous "long count". After delivering a smashing right to the cheek Gene won the contest on points. Dempsey was in tears. Gene Tunney had destroyed a legend.

The next day, always magnanimous, aware that one day a younger man might tumble him, Gene called on Dempsey at his hotel. He found him heart-broken over the failure to regain his title. When Gene left, Dempsey said: "Your troubles are just beginning whether you know it or not. Every time you turn round you'll find a process-server." "He was right," said Gene. "At one time I had four lawsuits against me, amounting to $2,150,000! The first three were brought by two blackmailers and a bootlegger, all of whom fled from the jurisdiction of the States after instituting proceedings. The fourth suit went to trial. After a hearing of ten days the jury gave a verdict in my favour in twenty minutes."

Gene received for his second fight with Dempsey a purse of $990,445. At his request Tex Rickard, the promotor, wrote a cheque for $1,000,000 and Gene gave back to him the difference of $9,555. The cheque for $1,000,000, framed, was hung in Gene's study.

As we walked about Venice I tried to satisfy my companion's insatiable thirst for knowledge. He was particularly interested in

Shakespeare, so I showed him Shylock's Rialto and the reputed house of Desdemona, Othello, and Goldoni. We spent many happy hours together and I looked at this handsome fellow with some awe as perhaps the only man on earth who could earn a million dollars, honestly, in forty minutes. I asked him how he came to know Shaw. It was quite a story. Soon after he was the champion he was approached by a Hollywood film company. It wanted him to appear in a film of Shaw's only novel, *Cashel Byron's Profession*, a rather poor story about a prizefighter. Gene asked to see the book. "I read it and told the company I wouldn't do it as I thought the hero was a vulgarian. They informed Shaw of this. He replied, 'I'd like to meet that young man. He must have good taste.' " On coming to London with his bride, in the course of a honeymoon tour of Europe, Gene called on Shaw. "He gave a lunch for me to which he invited H. G. Wells and Max Beerbohm—who invited me to visit him at Rapallo— unfortunately that wasn't possible. G.B.S. and Charlotte have been with us at Brioni Island. What a wonderful pair! I feel very lucky to know them." I asked him about his future—more fights? "No, I've retired from the ring definitely. I shall probably go into business."

So here I was, a guide in Venice to a delightful young man, still the heavyweight boxing champion of the world. In the succeeding years Gene fulfilled his intention and became a most successful business man, a director of sixteen companies. He had made two million dollars in the ring, retiring undefeated. Better, he made a very happy marriage and became the father of three sons and a daughter. It is a success story if ever there was one. There has never been a champion like him, nor is there likely to be another. Gene was never popular with the boxing crowd. They expected a bruiser instead of an aloof Apollo. They called him a "bookworm", a "phoney intellectual", because he did not run around with the riff-raff of the ring and scatter his money on "dolls" and horses, like a typical bruiser. He owns a signed copy of *Of Human Bondage* given to him by Maugham. "The story of your reading my novel the night before your fight was the best publicity I ever received," he said.

Fifteen years after our Venice meeting we met again in the dining-car of the Florida Express. He had a place at Hoby Sound where I visited him and his family. Then, in 1963, passing through New

York en route to Florida again, he gave a lunch for me. He had an office on the 37th floor of the new Pan-American building which has a stupendous vista up Park Avenue, over the golden pagoda tower of the New York Central Railroad. We were now elderly gentlemen, in good health, Gene sixty-six, I, seventy-one. It was a merry lunch in the Sky Club on the 56th floor. The sunshine pouring in on that November day gilded our recall of springtime in Venice thirty-four years earlier.

V

I spent the summer in Venice, happy in my Zattere lodging, mingling pleasure with work. I rose at sunrise each morning and worked through until noon, but there was one annoyance that moved me to make a protest. On the ground floor, window open to the garden, someone kept repeating "da-da-da-da-da" with the regularity of a leaky tap. What on earth was the tenant below me doing? One morning I descended and knocked on his door. It opened to reveal an astonishing figure, a tall, red-bearded youngish man. His pale face was crowned by a golliwog mane of hair. He wore a bright yellow open-necked shirt, red linen trousers and sandals. His general appearance was that of a vegetarian missionary, anti-everything. He was keen-eyed. I told him that his drumming interfered with my writing. "Oh, I'm sorry," he said affably, "I'm testing meters." "Meters?" I repeated, puzzled. He looked more like an artist than a mechanic. "Yes—I'm going over my verses—da-da-da-da-da-da!" he said, drumming his knuckles on the door in illustration. So it was metres not meters. "I'm sorry if I annoyed you. My name's Ezra Pound." I told him mine. We shook hands. His name was familiar to me as a "cult" poet, an American from Idaho. I had once tried to read his poems but found them almost incomprehensible, even in the Twenties, and I was sceptical of his scholarship. He wrote "hermadryads" for hamadryads, "paons" for paeans, "Prosephone" for "Persephone", unless of course these were deliberate transpositions. I found his verse a "puzzlement". Like one of Edward Lear's characters he seemed determined to stand on his head. In retrospect he himself had some doubt about his *Cantos*. "At seventy I realised that

343

instead of being a lunatic I was a moron . . . I've been stupid and ignorant all the way through," he said in a burst of candour. But he republished some of these verses as late as 1967 so his self-disparagement seems doubtful. A pioneer has a right to be inconsistent and variable. His career when we met had already been bizarre. He had been dismissed from a teaching post for an offence more romantic than penal, that of giving a bed for the night to a homeless chorus girl. He had married in 1914 someone who bore the not inappropriate name for a poet's wife of Dorothy Shakespeare. One thing he always showed, a valorous obstinacy in serving his Muse. He descended on London with no means, had known poverty, had existed in cheap lodgings, but always had made a flamboyant figure. The unknown T. S. Eliot owed much to his propaganda, as also did James Joyce.

Pound first visited Venice in 1908 and had a struggle to live. His daughter has narrated how he half-starved and lunched on baked potatoes bought at a stall. Too poor to pay a few centesimi for a *traghetto*, the popular ferry across the Canal, he tramped over the Accademia bridge, making the long detour to the Piazza. It was in this same year that the malignant Baron Corvo arrived in Venice. He remained there until his death five years later, leaving behind him the odour of scandal, and his unpublished masterpiece *The Desire and the Pursuit of the Whole*, an autobiographical odyssey of venom in which he pilloried his Venetian benefactors. Had Corvo and Pound met what would have resulted—a peaceful recognition of each other's genius, or a vicious dogfight initiated by Corvo with his infallible urge for converting every friend into an enemy? If the latter, it was unlikely to have been the fault of Pound, ever generous in recognising a fellow writer's merit.

Pound's circumstances were easier when we met in 1929. He had been living in Italy for many years and would live there most of his life, abusive of "the mercantilist bog that engulfs America". This hostility was to lead him into folly and disaster. In the Second World War he broadcast from Rome Fascist propaganda. When in 1942 he sought to return home with repatriated American diplomats, the U.S. government refused him a passage. By now his name was a byword in America. "So far as the rest of the English-speaking world of letters is concerned he has written finis to his long career," announced *Poetry*, the Chicago magazine, in April, 1942. It was to prove a false prophecy. In 1945 he returned to the U.S. as a prisoner arrested on a charge of treason. He was flown to Washington to stand trial, a much execrated figure. But the U.S. Government had picked up a hot potato. Embarrassed, it had him examined by four psychiatrists. In England or France his end might have been fatally swift. Luckily he was a citizen of a country notorious for eccentric law processes. A rabid public debate ensued. The four examiners produced a verdict couched in flatulent English. "He is abnormally grandiose, is expressive and exuberant in manner, exhibiting pressure of speech, discursiveness and distrait ability." Whether intended to imply that he was a lunatic, a buffoon, or both, the verdict did not support a trial for treason. He was committed to confinement as of "unsound mind" in a Washington hospital where, in comfort, he read, wrote and received visitors.

The enormous publicity established him as a public figure, and boosted the minute sales of his books. Later his friends engineered a rehabilitation. In 1949 they got him the Library of Congress Bollinger award of $1,000, thus implying a semi-official pardon. It set off another public furore, but since there is now little difference between notoriety and fame, Pound emerged from captivity a world figure. He returned immediately to Italy. The U.S. Government had deftly dropped their hot potato, exhibiting a proper magnanimity. More than ever he became the figurehead of modern poetry.

After my meeting with him, I did not see Pound again until thirty-eight years later, in 1967, again in Venice. He was now eighty-two. The whirligig of Time had brought him a tranquil sunset. His attentive daughter was now the Princess de Rachewilz and he was ending his days in her Schloss near Merano, still a strong candidate for a seat on Parnassus.

In my pleasant lodging I worked steadily on *Havana Bound*. Each noon I walked over the Accademia bridge—with one of the great views of Venice towards the mouth of the Grand Canal—to a noon-day seat at Florian's. The warm days slipped by. London seemed so very far away. A friend wrote to say I was not out of mind. "You haunt me twice a day. Your *Pamela's Spring Song* is posterised on all the Underground escalators and lifts. I go up and down with you at South Kensington and Piccadilly Circus. Pamela looks very attractive in her Tyrolean dirndl." This advertising on the Underground was an innovation by my publisher.

Towards the end of August I embarked on a new adventure. Two years earlier, at a Paris dinner party, I found myself talking to a young man a few years my senior. Somehow I mentioned Chopin and how I much desired to see his birthplace. He was astonished that I had never been to Poland. "You must come. Visit us and then see Chopin's home!" he said. He was a Pole, Count Alfred Potocki, a kinsman of the La Rochefoucaulds, his mother being a Radziwill. I did not take his invitation quite seriously but before we parted he gave me his card. His home was the Château de Lançut in the Southern Galician corner of Poland, east of Cracow. I thanked him and said that if ever I went to Poland I would remember his invitation. When I mentioned this to my Polish friend Jan Sobanski, he said: "You should go. It's one of the great houses of Europe. Count Potocki's the head of his line and lives there in feudal state with his mother. It's something that can't survive much longer." I began to read Polish history. It was a country, Chopin apart, for which I had always had great admiration, founded on its heroic resistance to its enemies through the centuries. The Potockis were woven into its chequered history.

In Venice now, with time in hand, I decided to go to Poland. Sobanski said he would be delighted to show me Warsaw where he lived with his wife and child. Everything seemed propitious. I wrote to Count Potocki. He answered, cordially inviting me for a week's visit.

Four days before my departure, walking from the ferry to the Lido beach, I met an acquaintance, an hotel manager. He was in a state of excitement. Serge Diaghilev had just died. His two young companions, Lifar and Kochno, were seized with hysteria. Diaghilev had died leaving a large unpaid hotel bill. The company was dispersed, there was no one to bury the maestro, or pay for the funeral. I suggested that the City of Venice should bury him in style, the Doge of the Ballet. Fortunately his old friend Misia Sert arrived and took charge. His death was a great shock to everyone. Very few knew that

346

Diaghilev was in Venice. I joined the small English colony that attended the service in the Greek Orthodox Church of San Giorgio dei Greci. It was impressively conducted, with Greek rites, crosses and ikons, elaborate vestments and much wafting of incense. It was a setting with Bakst overtones that would have pleased Diaghilev, as also the solemn gondola procession, with the coffin under a canopy, a priest with a great crucifix in the leading gondola, and acolytes chanting, on its way to the island cemetery.

The next day I was in Vienna. It was still hot. I lunched in the Hofgarten where the roses were wilting and dined at a pavilion restaurant in the Prater. I went on to a delightful operetta in the courtyard of the Schönbrunn Palace with its memories of Napoleon's ill-fated son, the Duke of Reichstadt, and of the grief-burdened old Emperor Franz-Josef who had lingered into the twilight of the Austrian empire.

VI

My companion in the train from Vienna to Cracow was a loquacious Frenchman. He had surely one of the most singular businesses in the world. He dealt in catgut for violin strings. He bought much of his material, intestines, in Poland. He was, I suspect, a Jew. He had a sister living in Cracow. "The Poles, sir, are all mad," he said. "They fiddle and dance all night. But they are not the people they were before the liberation of Poland after the war. They have been suppressed, invaded and cut up for five hundred years. They are used to living in a ferment of insurrection. It is their element, they enjoy it. Nothing can crush them. The war over in November, 1918, they start a campaign against the Bolsheviks and invade Russia, who, in turn, march on Warsaw, and so on. Pilsudski pushes them out but the Russian bear is only over the border, waiting. Many believe he will come back and chew them up again. The Turks, the Tartars, the Swedes, the Hungarians, the Germans, the Russians, the Prussians, the Austrians—they've had them all stamping the life out of them, but you can't keep a Pole down. They thrive on aggression. A marvellous race, sir. How odd, their greatest man's a pianist, Paderewski, their best-known another pianist, Chopin! There's

Marshal Pilsudski of course, but the pianists have it. I love them but I couldn't live with them." During this outburst a man in a corner seat, possibly a Pole, must have understood. He looked grimly at the dealer in catgut.

On arrival in Cracow I found myself installed in an enormous room in the Grand Hotel, the former Czartoryski Palace. The head waiter insisted on practising his horrible English on me. He had worked for five years in Reading, Pennsylvania. "Most beautiful place, sir. Ah!" He sighed heavily. I knew Reading, a grim mining town full of Poles. In vain I responded in French, which he spoke fluently. He wanted to keep up his "English".

After dinner I went for a walk. I was not alone. I had the ghost of a friend, five years dead, with me. I recalled how one evening in London Joseph Conrad had talked of his boyhood in Cracow. A sad boyhood. He was about eleven and his father lay dying. Every morning the motherless little boy, who had shared his father's exile in Russia, had walked to school, and every evening, in the dim, panelled drawing-room, he had done his "prep" work by the light of a pair of candles. Before retiring he had been permitted to visit the sickroom. His father could hardly turn his face to him when he gave a goodnight kiss to the frail hand on the counterpane. Conrad recalled his father's funeral, ceremonial, as befitted a patriot who had been exiled by the Russians. A small boy, they honoured his name by giving him the Freedom of Cracow and exempting him from all taxes.*

As I walked in the old town I could see that orphaned boy following the hearse. During Conrad's return visit, in July, 1914, the university librarian had got out his father's letters, written during exile. They had been proudly preserved, letters in which his small son had been mentioned. Conrad had intended returning the next day to copy them, but the next day the Germans declared war on Russia. Conrad and his family caught the last train out of Cracow for Vienna. All around, as they left, the Poles were being mobilised for the Austrian army, since they lived in Austrian Poland. Eventually Conrad reached his home in England via Vienna, Genoa and Gibraltar.

* As a Pole he had no nationality, the Austrians would not concede it, so he remained in Cracow *heimatlos*.

VII

The following morning, after I had breakfasted and gone into the vestibule a thin, dark-haired youth accosted me. He bowed and said slowly: "It would be much honour for me to show you beautiful Cracow, distinguished guest." He said this shyly, carefully. He was poorly dressed but clean and neat. His name was Konrad. Another Conrad in Cracow! He was a student at the university and he delighted me by saying, "If you please, sir, my English is frail but eager." It described his person. For twenty-four hours he was my companion, intelligent, well-mannered, and tactful. "The English are the great gentlemen of Europe. I see at once your Elizabethan air," he said. Being turned into a Tudor relic amused me. His French was fluent, his mother being French, but he insisted on struggling with English. "An accomplishment most desired", he explained. Consequently I found myself turned into a tutor.

We set off for the City Square and the Wawel with the great castle and cathedral on its hill. It was a beautiful sunny morning. I asked if he had heard of another Conrad, the novelist, who lived in England. His face lit up. "Josef Teodor Konrad Korzeniowski! He is our pride! You give honour to mention him—you have read?" he asked. "Not only have I read him, but he was my friend," I answered. The boy stopped in his walk. "So please we go first where as small boy he lived with father." After a few minutes he stopped in front of a house. "It is there he lived when schoolboy," said Konrad. After a silent pause we went on to the great Square, the Rynek. It presented an animated scene with a high towered church at one corner. Part of the Rynek was bordered with old mansions, once aristocratic residences. There was a market with stalls of vegetable and poultry dealers and a crowd of shoppers under the arcades of the vast Cloth Hall that occupied the centre of the Square, a building curiously Italianate so that I was not surprised to learn that the architect had been an Italian from Padua.

The most outstanding object in this vividly busy Square was the fourteenth-century St. Mary's Church, its twin towers dominating the scene. It was built of coloured bricks and the church shone in the

349

morning air. There was a disparity in the two high towers. One stopped abruptly while the other continued upward to a gilded crowning spire. Konrad had a story to explain this. The builders of the towers were two brothers. One of them, outraged that the tower of the other was rising faster than his own, stabbed him. Legend said that the tower of the murdered brother built itself to completion, with a beautiful high octagonal superstructure; the murderer's remained smaller.

A bell struck. "Listen!" cried Konrad, pointing to the tall tower. I listened. A trumpeter played a tune that stopped abruptly in the middle of a phrase. "I tell you the legend," said Konrad. He narrated how in the thirteenth century, when Cracow was a city of wooden houses, fire was a great menace. So a watch was established in the tower of the church. Each hour a bell tolled and from the south, east, west and north windows of the tower the watchman played on his trumpet a hymn in honour of Our Lady—the Heynal. Every trumpeter took a vow to play it at each hour of the day and night, to mark his watch. From the tower he looked down not only on the walled town but he could also see across the Vistula, and the great plain whence came the terrible Tartar invaders who laid the land desolate and sought to burn Cracow. The trumpeter in the tower, therefore, sounded the alarm against two enemies, fire and the invaders. One day in 1241 rumours came from Kiev that the Tartars were on the march again, laying waste the great Ukrainian plain. Kiev fell, Lvov fell. The mounted Tartars drew near the city. The people took refuge in the castle on the Wawel Hill. The town opened its gates to admit the fleeing peasants who joined the citizens in the castle. But one citizen did not seek refuge, the young trumpeter who remained at his post. On taking office he had made the historic oath —"I swear on my honour as a servant of the King and the Polish people that, if there be need, I will faithfully unto death sound upon the trumpet the Heynal in honour of Our Lady each hour in the tower of the church which bears Her name." The Tartars swept down on Cracow. They broke through the gates and the walls, firing the houses, until the whole town was ablaze in the night. In the tower the trumpeter, faithful to his vow, sounded the Heynal on the hour. Below in the Square the astonished Tartars heard him, the only survivor in the burning town. Then in the dawn light one of the Tartars raised a bow and shot an arrow. It pierced the breast of the trumpeter nearing the end of the Heynal. The tune stopped on one glorious note as he died. "Since that day in 1241, at every hour, the trumpeter plays the Heynal and it ceases on the death-note in memory of the trumpeter faithful unto death," concluded Konrad.*

We crossed the Square and entered the church. The interior was very impressive. The central nave was high and long, with stars in a blue ceiling. The light coming in through the stained glass windows, tall and slender, was soft and rich. It fell upon an assembly of towns-folk and peasants in their varied costumes, kneeling in prayer. Bathed in the soft light, they merged in a kaleidoscopic pattern of piety that was singularly moving.

When we left I told my guide that I would like to see the Ghetto as I understood there was a large Jewish population, 30,000 out of some 300,000. He looked surprised. It was not beautiful, it was dirty, overcrowded and smelt. It had once been a strictly separate town on the outskirts of the city. Obviously he was not anxious to show me the Ghetto. The odd semi-oriental tradesmen in their little shops and booths in the Rynek had aroused my curiosity. A friend had told me that "the Polish Jews are the Jewiest of Jews. Poland has never been able to assimilate them. They have swarmed in from the Russian pogroms. We Poles are tolerant but we are conscious of them as an extraneous population that multiplies incessantly."

We took a droshky and drove to the Ghetto. It was a completely foreign quarter, almost medieval in character, swarming with lean, sallow-faced Jews. The men were bearded, some with ringlets. They wore long black coats, their baggy trousers tucked into high boots. Many of them wore little felt hats or peaked caps. The houses were decrepit, in narrow streets. There were six synagogues, all ancient. One of them, built of red brick in the fifteenth century, restored in 1570 in Renaissance style, was beautiful, with stone obelisks at the

* Harold Macmillan in his Memoirs, *Blast of War* (Macmillan & Co.), des-cribes a visit he made with General Alexander, in April, 1944, to the Monte Cassino front. They lunched with General Anders, commanding the Polish Corps. On reaching his headquarters ". . . a trumpeter played a curious and appealing call which ended suddenly, broken off in the middle of a musical phrase". General Anders told his visitors the history of the broken call.

angles. There was a large Jewish cemetery. Some of the children who swarmed everywhere, were strikingly handsome. The quiet was noticeable, there was none of the usual boisterous life of the slums. Everyone seemed to be engaged on secret business. But what business, how did they all get a living? "Some of them are quite rich, sir. Drapers and pedlars who work the country markets," said Konrad.

I left the Ghetto depressed, and somehow hostile without any justification, unless from fear induced by their unbreakable homogeneity, their parade of an indestructible clannishness. I should have been still more depressed had I know what was in store for these poor people. Within twelve years millions of them were doomed to be crammed in barred freight cars and transported to the exterminating gas chambers, gallows and furnaces of Auschwitz, only thirty miles away.

When we came back into the wider streets, with more air and light, it was past noon. I asked my guide to take me to a good, characteristic restaurant. We would lunch and then visit the Wawel. The boy seemed bewildered by my request. "The good, or the most good of high expense?" he asked. "The most good," I replied. He thought a moment. "Yes, please, there is one of high renown, where I have never been." When we entered it looked like an expensive club. The carpets were thick, a flunkey in knee breeches took our hats. It was certainly expensive but good. Strange to zloty notes, I asked Konrad to pay the bill. He seemed stunned. "I am ashamed, it is so great," he whispered. We were bowed out. "That was really excellent. Thank you," I said to restore his spirit. We took a droshky to the Wawel. En route I learned a little about him. He was eighteen. He had two younger sisters. His father, an officer, had been killed at Przemysl. He hoped to become a lawyer like his uncle in Warsaw. His mother taught French in the Lyceum. To earn some money he looked for visitors to guide, hence his presence in the Grand Hotel.

On the way to the Wawel, the great cathedral-and-castle crowned hill dominating the city, we drove past the old university, a fifteenth century Gothic building. The library, the richest and largest in Poland, contained half a million books. But it was not the library he wished to show me, it was a statue in the centre of the fine arcaded court of Nicolas Copernicus, the astronomer. "He was student here in fifteen century!" said Konrad proudly. We continued our journey by one of the grassy boulevards constructed on the site of the ancient walls of the city, as in Vienna, decorated with trees and statues. We ascended the hill and looked over the city, a maze of shining towers, and ancient houses.

We arrived at the castle which had been the residence of kings when Poland was at the height of her power in the fifteenth century. It was still, with the cathedral near by, the ancient heart of Poland, despite Warsaw which had superseded it as the seat of government. We entered the great quadrilateral building, given a Renaissance aspect under later Italian architects. Its former splendour had suffered from fires and pillage. When Poland was dismembered in 1846 the Austrians had converted this royal château into a barracks. They had demolished part of it, taking everything of value to Vienna. The frescoes in the courtyard, glowing with pride in Poland's history, were covered over with plaster. A more enlightened policy, with a less heavy bureaucratic hand, began in the twentieth century. The castle had been restored to some of its former splendour. It still had fine rooms and magnificent tapestries.

We proceeded to the cathedral, the very shrine of the nation, Gothic in the style of the fourteenth century, with eighteen Renaissance and baroque chapels all richly ornamented with monuments to the Polish kings. The 14th-century Potocki chapel particularly interested me. It contained three works in marble by Thorwaldsen, a statue of Christ and busts of Count Arthur Potocki and his mother. There was another chapel with a Potocki bust, Count Wladimir Potocki, who fell at Moscow in 1812, also by Thorwaldsen. Konrad was puzzled by my interest in these busts. "They are a great family. They've a castle at Lançut and a palace here. My mother was teacher in French to them." I told him I was visiting Lançut, hence my interest.

Another chapel had a canopied monument to Casimir the Great. In the ambulatory behind the altar there was a monument to King Jan Sobieski III, the conqueror of the Turks besieging Vienna in 1683. As I examined the reliefs depicting the battle I startled Konrad by saying the King's granddaughter, Clementina Sobieski, had married the exiled claimant to the English throne, James, the Old

Pretender, whom the Pope had recognised as James III. His Sobieski wife gave him two sons, the younger being the Cardinal Henry, Duke of York, the last Stuart survivor, and the elder Prince Charles, famous as Bonnie Prince Charlie. The latter therefore was half Polish. Konrad was quite astonished. I did not inform him that the Old Pretender and his son Prince Charles were so tyrannical that their wives left them and both took refuge in the same convent in Rome.

Under a canopy in the centre of the cathedral was a sarcophagus borne up by silver angels, containing the remains of St. Stanislas, the patron saint and bishop of Poland, slain in 1070 before the altar by King Boleslas. We descended to the Romanesque crypt and the royal vault and found there the tombs of Kosciuszko, leader of the great insurrection begun in Cracow, Prince Poniatowski, Field Marshal of France, who fought with Napoleon, and Adam Mickiewicz, Poland's national poet. There was a fresh wreath on his tomb.

After we had come out of the cathedral we lingered in the grounds of the Wawel, walking by the ramparts. Below lay the winding Vistula in the plain that ran eastwards towards Russia. To the south lay the foothills of the Carpathian mountains, the borderland of Czechoslovakia. When we had descended into the town I told Konrad that I would like to see the Potocki palace. It was off the Rynek, a stately seventeenth-century mansion with a classical façade. Before parting I invited him to dine with me at my hotel. When he arrived that evening he carried a bouquet of flowers from his mother. After dinner I suggested that he should take me to a dancing place. He named a few, of differing quality. There was one frequented by students. Though in vacation time it was full, with four fiddlers for the dancing. I said that it was just what I would like. Later I found myself in a packed den, full of smoke, music and talk. The girls were young and pretty. Konrad brought over two American youths, who were hitch-hiking. One of them could not believe that I had been in Greensboro', North Carolina, his hometown. It was one o'clock when Konrad escorted me to my hotel. They were still madly dancing when we left.

On the morrow I had a full day. We walked through endless galleries. I saw the Czartoryski Museum, then went to the University to see the great hall with portraits of patron kings. When I bade farewell to my guide and paid him he seemed overcome. "It is too much kindness," he said. "All students need money," I replied. I have often wondered what his fate was in the disastrous years ahead, when Poland was massacred. Many years later I visited Monte Cassino, when writing *Eight for Eternity*, my novel about the classic battle on the mountain side. A Polish Corps had fought and died there. After Molotov and Ribbentrop had signed the Russo-German Pact for the elimination of Poland, the Polish prisoners taken in 1939 were interned in Russian camps. Released after Russia was attacked by Germany and anxious to join the Allies, these Polish prisoners made a formidable march through the Near East to the Mediterranean shore, and reached Palestine. And so, entering Europe again, they came to fight and die on the slopes of Monte Cassino. Across a valley on that mountain gleamed the white tombstones of the Polish Soldiers Cemetery. As I looked at it, remote and lonely, with a mountain stillness after the rage of battle, I found myself wondering whether, by the hand of Fate, my young guide, Konrad, lay there, if he had not fallen in Poland.

VIII

Before proceeding to Lançut I made a short excursion from Cracow. I had kept for some time a letter of introduction from Daisy, Princess of Pless, living at La Napoule near Cannes, to her eldest son Hansel, Prince of Pless, a young man of twenty-eight who I heard was at Pless Castle some seventy miles from Cracow. The marriage of Daisy Cornwallis West to Prince Heinrich of Pless XVI in 1891, one of the wealthiest men in Europe, created a great sensation when it took place at St. Margaret's, Westminster. The Prince of Wales, later King Edward VII, and his wife, Princess Alexandra, attended the wedding. The Prince of Pless owned two castles in Silesia, vast Fürstenstein, with its five hundred rooms, and Pless with some two hundred, as well as estates and mines on the border of Silesia and Poland. The young Princess, of great beauty, highly gifted, enamoured the Kaiser Wilhelm II, and a close friendship grew up between them. He was a frequent guest at the two castles.

The fabulous Pless fortunes were somewhat contracted after the

First World War. Worse befell the family after the Second World War when all their properties and estates were confiscated by Communist East Germany and Communist Poland. But in 1929, at the time of my visit, the family still owned the two castles and considerable estates. With the change of frontiers Pless was now in Poland.

Daisy, Princess of Pless, had three sons. "The handsomest boys in Germany," said the Duke of Alba. The eldest, Prince Hansel, was born in Berlin in 1900. He had for sponsors at his christening the King of Belgium, the Prince of Wales, soon to become King Edward VII, and the Kaiser Wilhelm II, hence his additional names Albert Edward William. Prince Hansel had two younger brothers, Alexander and Frederick Cecil Bolko. Alexander, born in London in 1905, was christened in the Royal Chapel of St. James. The sponsors were Queen Alexandra, who held him, giving her name, the Crown Prince of Germany and the Prince of Wales, later King George V. Bolko was born in 1910. The Crown Prince of Germany was his godfather. The two younger sons carried the titles of Counts of Hochberg. They appeared to have everything, a beautiful mother, a father with one of the great names in Germany, wealth and good looks. All the fairy godmothers seemed to have been at their christenings, but a wicked one was also present. A cruel fate awaited them. The two elder sons were to be dispossessed of everything and driven into penniless exile, the youngest to be murdered. All this was hidden in the womb of Time when I hired a car and chauffeur to drive me from Cracow to the Castle of Pless to lunch with Prince Hansel. It happened that Bolko, nineteen, and Alexander, twenty-four, were with their father at Fürstenstein.

The castle of Pless had played an important part in recent history. From the opening of the First World War until the collapse of the Russians, Pless was the G.H.Q. of the German Army of the East. It was used by the Kaiser, the Crown Prince, Hindenburg, Mackensen, and other war lords, and visiting sovereigns, but the Princess of Pless, a wayward, strong character, insisted on visiting the castle. English, a friend of the Kaiser, she was naturally accused of subversive action, spying, and malign influence. Loyal to England and loyal to Germany, her position was difficult and nigh impossible.

With all this history behind it I looked with interest on the great white château, French in style, rising above its lake and woods. The place was magnificent, though Fürstenstein held precedence for its size and treasures. The shifting of the frontier in the post-war settlement brought the castle of Pless into Polish territory as it had once been, and it was given its former name of Pszczyna. En route to Pless from Cracow I passed through the small town of Oswiecim, a name that then meant nothing to me. It seemed pleasant and sleepy but the Second World War was to give it a name of horror throughout the world. The Nazis established there the extermination camp of Auschwitz, the German name of the town. Here four million people were murdered by the Nazis, who brought them in terrible freight-cars from all over Germany and Poland. The first governor of the camp confessed at the Nuremberg Trials to two and a half million victims. Today it is once more named Oswiecim and the Polish Government preserves there a Martyrology Museum.

Young Count Bolko was a Nazi victim in another place. He was sent to what was euphemistically called a 'Re-education Camp'. He was first interned at Gleiwitz and then sent to the notorious Moabit Gaol in Berlin. After much wire-pulling and the payment of $15,000, his release was procured. As he was being driven home he told his father that on leaving he had been given an injection which he would not survive. He died three weeks later.

When after lunch on that sunny September day I returned from Pless to Cracow, leaving the beautiful castle serene above its woods all the murders, horrors and spoliations that were to be visited upon this corner of the world within ten years were quite unimaginable. Forty years were to pass before I should see Prince Hansel of Pless again, when we dined at my London club. Despite the loss of his castles, lands, mines, his total fortune, he was uncomplaining. He was now travelling for an English company as "Mr. Pless", and living with his wife in a small mews flat.

CHAPTER SEVENTEEN

Lançut

I

THE TRAIN FROM Cracow to Lançut ambled along. Every station provided something novel. Unlike the dealer in catgut I found the Poles delightful and vivacious, and not mad. They had revealed much friendliness and the train now provided a ceaseless pageant of beautiful country, so that the journey was all too short. My destination, Lançut, a village that gave its name to my host's castle, was about one hundred miles from Cracow. It was on the line that ran east to Lvov and the Russian frontier, having crossed the whole of southern Poland. We were now in the south-west corner in what had been Austrian Galicia, with Lançut some fifty miles from fortified Przemysl. During the First World War everyone was aware of this Austrian town. There had been a tremendous struggle for the fortress which had fallen to the invading Russians with 900 guns and 120,000 Austrian prisoners. This disaster seemed to threaten the existence of Austria. It was recaptured when Hindenburg and Ludendorff, their troops released after the great victory of Tannenburg in the north, turned to southern Poland and caused the Grand Duke Nicholas to withdraw his Galician army. I recalled how we had all followed the titanic struggle around Przemysl. The pronunciation of its name had sorely tried us; and now here I was only some fifty miles distant from the fortress-town that had loomed so large in the war news.

My train drew into the little station at Lançut. I was pleasantly surprised to find my host, Count Alfred Potocki, waiting on the platform, accompanied by two ladies. He introduced me but, as everywhere throughout my visit to Poland, their names eluded me for a time. Lançut was a village of some six thousand inhabitants, situated in this corner of Galicia where a Latin civilisation infiltrated the Slav. Since the fourteenth century it had suffered repeated invasions. To provide protection from raiding Mongols, Tartars and Turks a Prince Lubomirski had built the castle, and surrounded it with walls and a moat. This had passed by marriage to the Potockis who had remodelled it and made it one of the most luxurious dwellings in Europe, a veritable museum of treasures, as I was to discover.

Passing through the village we arrived at the castle gates emblazoned with the Potocki arms, and entered a great park with avenues of lime and beech trees. In this forest there were successive clearings on whose lawns statues had been placed. It was Versailles in Poland. As we approached the castle I was at first disappointed. It appeared smaller than I had expected. This proved to be an illusion, for Lançut was quadrilateral with a large interior court. The façade facing us was baroque with two projecting bulbous towers, octagonal, copper-covered. The house had three storeys under a long tiled roof. As we drew nearer, the great length of the front became impressive. The colour of Lançut was rose-brick with six pilasters decorating the façade between the towers. There were white stone facings to the windows, those in the top storey being about half the height of the architraved lower ones. There was an entrance in the middle into which we drove. Doors opened on to a hall with four pairs of marble columns.

I was soon overwhelmed by the vastness and splendour of the castle, with its three hundred and eight rooms. There were eight dining-rooms so that one could dine in a new one each night of the week and have one in hand. That evening after dinner an orchestra of some thirty musicians played in the white ballroom, each in a blue livery with crested collars. Later I was to see this orchestra transformed into a brass band for ceremonial occasions. There was a small theatre, a long sculpture and art gallery, a series of salons, and endless corridors that recalled, when I walked down them, a hymn of my boyhood—"a day's march nearer home". The mirrored ballroom rose through two storeys and was lit by Venetian chandeliers. The salons had various furnishing and decorative motifs, French, Turkish,

359

Chinese. I was not surprised to learn there was a Turkish bath in the castle. The library was superb, with boiserie and gilt-rimmed shelves, and tiers of leather-bound books of Polish, French and English origin, stamped with the Potocki arms.

There seemed to be innumerable footmen. They stood along the corridors and flanked the portals of the salons. One of them escorted me to my bedroom. A valet appeared. Soon all my things were disposed of. They seemed poverty-stricken in this ornate frame. The bed was worthy of a French king. My bathroom, even, was a bower of flowers. The majordomo who had greeted me, and one of the butlers—I never discovered how many there were and who was who —spoke a little English, French and German but the servants knew only Polish and we resorted to pantomime. The valet assigned to me had travelled with Count Potocki in England and America. "Peeka-deelee-Hooligan!" he exclaimed with a grin. I looked blank. He made a sweeping movement with his right arm and I knew then he meant Hurlingham, with its polo. He had been there twice with the count for the Champion Cup contest. Later, in a cabinet, I saw sixty-two silver trophies marking the count's tour round the world with his polo team. In the stables there were twelve polo ponies. Fourteen grooms were controlled by a Master of Horse who, in attire and gait, looked as if he had walked straight out of Leicestershire. My surmise was correct. He was English and had been twelve years with the Quorn Hunt. I was introduced to him in the Empire Riding School.

When the valet had departed I examined my bedroom more closely. This was one of sixty bedrooms each with a bathroom. Mine was magnificently furnished. There was a large Louis Seize ormolu writing-desk and a canopied bed with eighteenth-century tapestry hanging. A fine clock made of oriental alabaster had come out of a French workshop. "Rabigeau 1748." I wondered if the doomed Louis XVI had ever looked at its white enamel face in happier days. My query was not so far-fetched. All Europe had been laid under tribute for the furnishing of Lançut. Priceless pieces lined the galleries and salons. The castle could have equipped a notable French museum. Somehow these treasures had survived successive German and Russian invaders who had made the castle their headquarters

Château de Lançut.

Count Stanislas Kostka Potocki. By David.

during the First World War. Much of this furniture and china owed its presence at Lançut to the French Revolution. In August, 1793, there was a sale of the contents of Versailles, the property of Louis XVI and Marie Antoinette. Prospective buyers were informed that: "The furniture of the former Civil List may be exported free of duty." Foreign buyers moved in. The largest were the Russians, Americans, Poles and English. Among the Poles was the Princess Lubomirska, Jan Potocki's mother-in-law, of fabulous wealth. She owned part of the Palais-Royal and the l'Île de la Cité, seven Polish châteaux and 400,000 acres. She bought hundreds of objects. They composed a train of twenty-three horse-drawn wagons that crossed Europe to Poland in six weeks. One of her purchases, standing in a salon through which I passed, was a mounted blue Sèvres vase. Its "pair" was bought by the Prince Regent and is now at Windsor Castle. When Louis XVIII and the Duc de Berry were guests at Lançut they must have had many reminders of their lost palaces. The French émigrés had been warmly welcomed. Other guests had been Queen Caroline of Naples, Madame de Staël, and Kosciuszko before he led the insurrection of 1794 against Russia. John Sobieski III, King of Poland, was at Lançut in 1696. There was a magnificent painting of him in the Grand Salon. I noticed in the library two portrait engravings, one signed "Wellington", dated 1847, the other "Robert Peel", of the same date. Had they visited Lançut? No, but my host's grandfather, Alfred Potocki, had been in London as Secretary to the Austrian Ambassador, Count Dietrichstein, his brother-in-law, and had known them. Later he rose to be Prime Minister of Austria and for eight years was the Governor of Galicia.

I was struck by the Englishness of my host. He had been educated at Magdalen College, Oxford. "When I first visited England I fell at once under its spell," he said. "France I admired, Austria I respect, Germany I don't like. England I've always loved, I'm proud of the Stuart blood in me. Kaiser Wilhelm was my godfather. If only it had been King Edward VII! By an odd chance it might have been the Emperor Franz-Josef. He came here and always tactfully signed our Visitors Book in Polish. He gave my father the Order of the Golden Fleece. On his death I had to return it to the Emperor. When

I arrived at Schönbrunn I was shown into the Emperor's study. Clad in the uniform of an Austrian General, wearing a dress sword, he returned my salute. He looked terribly frail and old—he was eighty-five with much tragedy in his life. He was very kind and gentle, and asked after my mother, praised my late father, and enquired about our estates which I now had to manage. I was with him about ten minutes. Then he shook my hand and said goodbye. I was moved to tears. He died next year."

II

When the hour for dinner arrived a servant came to my room to escort me to one of the salons. After what seemed an interminable journey through a series of rooms I arrived where other guests were assembled. Footmen stood on each side of the doors of an eighteenth-century salon whose ceiling was painted with cupids bearing festoons of flowers. There were Boucher, Fragonard and Hubert Robert paintings. I was surprised to see a fire blazing in a fireplace lined with highly polished brass. The Count presented me to his mother, born Princess Radziwill. Known to all the Potockis as Aunt Betka, she had a formidable presence, the *grande dame* in excelsis. Of "commanding port", out of doors she crowned herself with enormous flowered and feathered hats. Her voice would have cowed a regiment. Four centuries of Radziwill grandees sustained her prestige.

We dined that evening in the vast White Hall. I counted twenty-two guests at the long table decorated with silver epergnes holding orchids and roses. The conversation was mostly in French. I heard little Polish. I wondered who my fellow guests were, for all their names on introduction had passed me by. The ladies were dressed in the height of Paris fashions. Course followed course, the food was superb. A white and gold Sèvres dinner service was used. The dinner was deftly served by liveried footmen wearing white cotton gloves. There were moments when I felt like a super in a Hollywood film. I had not thought there was anything like this existing now in Europe, outside of a royal palace or a Lord Mayor's Banquet. I half-expected a scarlet-coated toastmaster to stand forth and bellow his preamble "My Lords, Ladies and Gentlemen. Pray silence for . . ."

Dinner over, Countess Potocka led the way into the ballroom, past the Winterhalter portraits in the long gallery. Here the orchestra was assembled. I learned that it was the Count's habit, following the Esterhazy tradition whose orchestra had had Haydn for its conductor, to comb the staff, including the stable boys, to discover whether anyone had musical ability, whereupon he received training. As we entered the ballroom the orchestra rose and bowed. After a brief consultation between the Countess and the conductor, it played a Viennese waltz and the guests began to dance.

The following evening we all went into the delightful little baroque theatre. A short French farce was acted by some guests who had come in for dinner. It was well presented. There were moments when my head almost reeled with all that it tried to absorb. I began to delve into the family history, retreating to bed with half a dozen books from the library. The Potockis had lived in south Poland since the thirteenth century. They had distinguished themselves with King Sigismund in wars against the Tartars. In 1660, Stanislas, a Hetman of the Crown, aged eighty-one, defeated the Muscovites. He won the battle of Ochmatow at eighty-six. His two sons fought with King Sobieski against the Turks. In 1770, another Stanislas, heir to immense estates in the Ukraine, tried to found a Polish Republic, but, disillusioned, retired into private life. Ignace Potocki supported Kosciuszko in the 1794 insurrection. He surrendered to the Russians on the fall of Warsaw and was sent to St. Petersburg. After his return from exile he went to Vienna to present a petition to Napoleon for the incorporation of Galicia into the new Duchy of Warsaw. There was Stanislas Kostka Potocki who followed the politics of his elder brother Ignace. He was a remarkable figure. A politician, an author, an orator, he headed the Polish delegation that received Napoleon in Warsaw. After the creation of the Duchy of Warsaw in 1807 he was President of the Council of State. In the Polish Kingdom created by the Congress of Vienna he served as Minister of Education. He wrote much on politics, literature and architecture. He was instrumental in the restoration of Pliny's villa on Lake Como. Because of his classical culture he was termed "The Polish Winckelmann". His book entitled *Journey to Backwash Towns* was very critical of social conditions and caused a storm and his dismissal from office. A reader of one of his books *On Eloquence and Style* must have been the youthful Chopin, for there is a copy of it in the Czartoryski Museum in Cracow bearing his signature on the fly leaf. A magnificent life-sized portrait of Count Stanislas was painted by David and portrays all his panache. It was begun in Rome and finished in Paris in 1781. It shows the Count leaving for the hunt *en habit bas*. The style is a mixture of Van Dyck and the currently fashionable Batoni, who dominated Rome as a portrait painter. It reveals David at the height of his genius and made a sensation when first exhibited at the Paris Salon in 1781. He placed his signature on the gilt collar of the great hound in front of the horse on which the Count majestically rides.*

Perhaps the most remarkable member of the family was Jan Potocki, my host's great-great-grandfather and a brother-in-law of Stanislas. His marriage to Princess Lubomirska's daughter brought Lançut and immense estates into the family. A scholar, everything interested him. When he was twenty-seven, he made with François Blanchard the first balloon ascent in Poland. In 1783 the Montgolfier brothers had ascended in a balloon filled with hot air, later replaced by hydrogen. Then Blanchard experimented with a free balloon in which he created a world sensation by crossing the English Channel. He was invited by Count Potocki to Poland, and from the garden of the Palais Mniszech he made an ascent accompanied by the Count who took with him his faithful Mameluke servant, and his pet dog. Spectators on horseback followed the course of the balloon, which came down an hour later. The intrepid balloonists were escorted back to Warsaw where they were excitedly acclaimed. King Stanislas Auguste struck a special medal with the motto—"The brave are not afraid of the fate of Icarus".

Immensely wealthy, a great traveller, the count went all over the world, China, Egypt, Russia, Spain, Morocco, England, the

* The David portrait was exhibited in London in 1932, and in Paris in 1937. It returned to Rome in 1959, where I saw it again in *Il Settecento a Roma* Exhibition. It made another visit to London, in the International Exhibition held at the Royal Academy in 1968, where, observed Sacheverell Sitwell, in *Apollo*, which reproduced it in colour, "it stole the Show". It is now in the Warsaw National Gallery, one of the Potocki treasures confiscated by the Polish Government.

Caucasus, his curiosity insatiable. A linguist, in eight languages, an archaeologist, he was an intelligent recorder of all he saw. He was a gifted writer in French as well as in Polish. To his scientific writings he added fiction, and his name is preserved by a book of grim stories curiously entitled *Manuscrit trouvé à Saragosse*. It was privately printed in St. Petersburg during an ambassadorial mission. Later it was published in Paris, and went through several editions, the last being in 1958. The Count played a part in the turbulent history of Poland. He was deeply depressed by the fall of Napoleon, and the intransigence of the Czar, which shattered all his hopes for the independence of his country. His health broke. Plagued with neuralgia and a fever contracted at Rhodes thirty years earlier, he fell into a state of melancholy. One day in December, 1815, he decided to commit suicide. Although an agnostic, severely criticised for this by his kinsmen, he called in the chaplain of his domain and requested his blessing. He then picked up his pistol but found he had no bullet for it. He seized a baroque silver sugar bowl, broke from its rim a silver ball, rammed it in the barrel and blew out his brains. He was fifty-four, universally admired. His end caused more sadness than scandal.*

The position of leading Poles like Jan Potocki was always one of great difficulty, of dashed hopes. In the endeavour to preserve their nation they had to manœuvre adroitly and play off their various oppressors. They took office, abiding the day of liberation. The Princess of Pless in her *Diary* for 1905 opens a window on the troubled scene. One of Jan Potocki's descendants, Joseph, a prominent official of Warsaw, under Russian suzerainty, laboured to serve Poland but in one of their recurrent revolts his countrymen turned on him. "During my stay at Cannes," wrote the Princess, "I had a long talk with Helen Potocka. Her husband's life has been threatened. They also threaten to burn his mills. All the schools in Warsaw are closed. She and her young sons, Roman and Joseph, have been sent here for safety by Count Joseph. He blames the Czar and the Grand Duke who would not listen to his warnings and scoffed at the spirit of rebellion that broods over Poland." Between the Russian bear and

* I am indebted for details to Edouard Krakowski's biographical study *Le Comte Jean Potocki*. Edition Gallimard. Paris, 1963.

the Austrian eagle it was difficult for a Pole to find a *modus operandi* without enraging his own people. Jan Potocki had two sons. After the early death of his wife they were brought up by his remarkable mother-in-law, Princess Lubomirska. Immensely wealthy and powerful, she was nevertheless liberal-minded and courageous. She lived in her Paris residence, the Palais-Royal, throughout the Revolution and, as we have seen, bought furniture, pictures and sculpture at the Versailles sale. She had visited Jean-Jacques Rousseau at Ermenonville. She proved to be a remarkable guardian of her two grandsons, Alfred and Arthur, while their father journeyed about the world. The old Princess left them Lançut and the château of Krzesowice. Born into the Napoleonic era they were caught up in politics and warfare. They both served in the Grande Armée and young Alfred was wounded and taken prisoner at the battle of Borodin. There was a striking painting of him in the portrait gallery at Lançut. His son, my host's grandfather, also Alfred, married in 1851 Princess Maria Sanguszko, and here comes a curious link with Joseph Conrad. The small Conrad received her father's blessing. This momentous encounter provided Conrad with one of his stories, *Prince Roman*. He has told us of the occasion in his memoirs.

In 1866 the motherless nine-year-old Conrad had gone to stay with his Uncle Thaddeus. A guest in his uncle's house was Prince Roman Sanguszko, who through the marriage of his daughter was Count Alfred's great-grandfather. The Prince was a famous figure. He had taken part in the insurrection of 1830 and had been sentenced to the Siberian mines. Old, stone-deaf, all communication had to be made by pencil and paper. "How old is this little boy?" asked the Prince when his uncle presented him. Conrad's uncle put down his age. Later Conrad wrote: "I was deeply impressed. What was this ceremony? Was this person too great to be spoken to? Again he looked at the pad and again gave a nod. 'He resembles his grandfather. Give me your hand,' he said. Acutely conscious of inky fingers I put it out timidly. He pressed it firmly and then gave me a final pat on the head. My uncle addressed me weightily. 'You have shaken hands with Prince Roman Sanguszko. It's something for you to remember when you grow up.'" Conrad did remember, and forty-four years

366

later wrote the story *Prince Roman*. It was a tribute to a Polish aristo-crat who had suffered greatly for his country. Standing before the Prince's portrait, my host told me the story of his great-grandfather, who had shaken the boyish hand of Conrad.

Here let me make a diversion. In 1969, forty years after my visit to Lançut, I was the guest of Count Alfred's widow at her Château de L'Echelle, La Roche-sur-Foron. In my bedroom there was an enormous seventeenth-century iron chest, with a secret lock. It required two men to open it and contained many documents, part of the things rescued from Lançut at the end of the Second World War to prevent their falling into the hands of the Russians. After many adventures, bombs, and bayonet thrusts in Vienna, the cases containing these reached the neutral principality of Liechtenstein, ruled by Count Alfred's cousin. Thus these salvaged documents eventually came to the Château de L'Echelle.

The iron chest was opened for me. In it was a mass of documents, charters, honours conferred by the Emperor Franz-Josef, by munici-palities and societies on Count Alfred's father, decoratively set forth on parchments with great seals attached. Most exciting of all were various bundles of letters. There were letters written to Countess "Betka" Potocka by the Archduke Franz-Ferdinand and his wife, assassinated at Sarajevo on June 28th, 1914, a deed that sparked off the First World War. There were letters from the Crown Princess Stephanie, recalling the tragedy at Mayerling, and from Queen Mary in her own hand, from Buckingham Palace and Balmoral.* But most exciting of all was a bundle of letters in spidery handwriting written by Prince Roman Sanguszko to his daughter Marie, Countess Potocka. These letters brought the old patriot who had shaken the small hand of young Conrad very close to me.

Prince Sanguszko's son-in-law, Count Alfred, rose high in the

---

* One of these refers to the Sèvres vase that I had admired at Lançut, of which the "pair" is at Windsor. Queen Mary wrote to Countess "Betka" Potocka a description of her vase. The letter is beautifully written in the Queen's neat hand, without a correction, and records that the vase was bought at the Versailles sale for the Prince Regent, for his residence Carlton House. The blue china vase is mounted on four goat's or faun's feet, with satyr heads on the rim and interlacing festoons of the grape vine, the work of Gaulthière.

service of Poland, then a part of the Austrian Empire. He became a Privy Councillor, Prime Minister of Austria, an Imperial Chamberlain, a Knight of the Golden Fleece, and the Governor of Galicia. He named his son "Roman", after his wife's famous father. There was a splendid portrait of Roman at Lançut, distinguished, with a touch of arrogance which his son, my host, assured me belied his true nature. He had to take refuge in Vienna while Lançut, to which he had given much care, was occupied by the Russians in the First World War.

The army, politics and diplomacy had been followed down the centuries by scions of the Potocki family. They had also made powerful marriages. Count Andrew married the sister of the deposed King of Poland, Stanislas Leszczynski, who had ended his days in exile at Nancy which he made one of the most beautiful cities in France. By virtue of this marriage Count Andrew's children were first-cousins of Louis XV and his wife, Marie Leszczynski.

Fate struck at the family from time to time. In 1908 Count Alfred Potocki, Governor of Galicia, was assassinated by a Ukrainian nationalist student.* The Communist takeover of Poland in 1946 ended the long story of diplomatic service given by the family. The last one serving in the diplomatic corps was my host's brother, George, *en poste* in Paris during my stay at Lançut and subsequently Ambassador to Turkey, and then to the United States until 1940. His cousin Joseph was Ambassador to Spain for twenty years. He also died in exile, in Lausanne.

III

With the castle full of guests it was not possible for my host to give me much personal attention and answer all my questions but he introduced me to his secretary, Pan Starkl, who took a great interest in the family history and the castle's treasures. In my bedroom I found a miniature with a nameplate "Duchesse de Dino". It looked early nineteenth-century. When I asked whether she was the friend of

---

* The assassin was sentenced to life imprisonment. After three years he escaped to the U.S.A. and became a leader of the Ukrainian colony there. Professor C. A. Macartney, the historian, met him in London in 1931.

Talleyrand, who had acted as hostess for the statesman when he was French ambassador in London, and was his devoted attendant until his death, he answered with surprise: "Yes—you know about her? It was painted when she went with Talleyrand to the Congress of Vienna. The Count is related to her. She was his maternal great-great grandmother. Her daughter married the Marquis de Castellane, his daughter married a Prince Antoine Radziwill, and in turn their daughter married Roman Potocki and is the Count's mother. You have it?" asked Starkl. I said I thought I had it. "Simpler, Count Alfred's mother is three daughters removed from Duchesse Dino," said Starkl. "In Poland everybody is related to everybody—we are a peregrinating Almanac-de-Gotha!"

I asked how the Count came to have Stuart blood. "He has Stuart and Prussian blood, though it's a weak strain. Alfred's great-great-grandfather, Antoni Radziwill married Princess Louise of Prussia. She was a niece of Frederick the Great, and the great-granddaughter of George I. There's a mixture for you. I'm making you dizzy!"

A white-haired old man went by. He had three bunches of keys hanging from a belt on his waist. Starkl spoke to him. "That's our clock superintendent. He's been winding clocks here for forty years. The Count's father was a stickler for punctuality. There's a clock in most of the three hundred and eight rooms. The poor old fellow's got to wind them all up within a week. If some of them don't run eight days he's in a mess! But that's nothing. There were once four hundred lamps, all to be filled and the wicks trimmed. And there were sixteen water carts and two hundred fire buckets. Before he died Count Alfred's father laid sixteen miles of water-pipes to bring fresh water to the castle and the stables."

Those stables! I visited them formally on a Sunday morning after Mass, which to my surprise was not held in the castle. We were all taken by coach to Lançut village church. This was a Sunday morning ceremony. Instead of occupying a manorial pew we were in a gallery where we sat in a glassed-in room, as it seemed. The floor of the church was occupied by village folk and peasants. Seen from above, they made a floral pattern with their richly coloured clothes. The men had embroidered shirts, with well-polished top boots, the women many-pleated cotton skirts. On our emerging at the close of the service a crowd had collected to see the castle party depart. There was much curtsying and bowing to the countess. All this coloured movement gave a Russian ballet setting to the departure. Awaiting us, in blue uniforms, with yellow-braided breeches and top boots, was the castle orchestra, this time a brass band. It struck up a lively tune and away we went in procession down the village high street. A Shetland pony drew the drum on a little cart. I felt as if we were going to a circus instead of leaving church, but evidently this was an occasion the Lançut villagers expected and enjoyed. The band played us right up to the castle gates. We were then taken round the end of the house to the stables. We had been brought there for another Sunday morning occasion. As we entered the stables two servants stood there holding salvers from which we took small bunches of carrots for the horses. It was evident that horses were gods at Lançut, despite three Rolls Royces, a Mercedes-Benz, a Packard and other cars. Some thirty horses with plaited manes, ribbon rosettes on their bridles, glossy as silk with grooming, stood in two long lines of stalls, each horse's name engraved on a plaque. Down the middle of the stables ran a drugget. It was more like a hippo-drawing-room than a stables, and one wondered whether a whiff of manure had ever polluted it. The stone polished floor reflected these equine aristocrats. A dozen polo ponies occupied a separate section. Connoisseurs stroked the proud necks and slapped the flanks of these highly groomed exhibits and distributed the rewarding bunches of carrots. The horse-master and his stable lads were at hand, themselves highly groomed, to answer queries and supply pedigrees. My host's favourite was "Khafifan", an Arab stallion, snow-white. There were Polish, Irish, French and English pedigree horses. The thoroughbreds eyed us disdainfully, arching their proud necks and stamping their polished hooves. I speculated on the size of the fortune represented by these sumptuous animals, palatially housed and valeted like royalty. After the stables we toured the orangerie, worthy of Versailles, built by the eighteenth-century French architect who had designed the "gloriette" on a hill, a reminder of Schönbrunn, the great glass-domed conservatory, and the nineteenth-century hothouse where grew palm trees, some thirty varieties of orchids, and other exotic plants. From this nursery came the crimson royal poinsettias and azaleas in the rooms and corridors of the castle. The flowers in my bedroom were changed each day. There was a gardenia supplied for our evening jackets and always a perfect rose on the breakfast tray. I had marvelled at the flawless blooms of the chrysanthemums and asters bordering the drives, and discovered that they were out of the nursery, potted, and at dawn bedded down in the parterres. (They have the same ruse in St. James's Park!)

One morning I was taken to an adjunct of the stables, devoted to a collection of carriages and harnesses covering some two hundred years. There were barouches, berlins, landaus, coupés, all in good condition. There was a great gala coach, lined with yellow velvet, and a gold and blue one in which the Potockis were driven to court in the early days of the Emperor Franz-Josef. There were coach-suites consisting of a salon, bedroom, toilette. Notable among these shining equipages was a black wagon, with peeling leather and a massive undercarriage. Once a month the Potocki ladies had their lingerie sent to a laundress in Paris. The wagon travelled from Lançut to Paris and back, with coachmen and guards, a journey of two thousand miles. The whims of the aristocracy in the eighteenth century! Another exhibit was a rack of whips, French, Polish, English, Arab and Cossack, of every shape and variety, some with jewelled handles. There were also great studded coach-trunks. One thought of the poor horses thrashed to death on the muddy roads of the Continent.

That afternoon at four o'clock, as I sat writing at the Louis Seize desk, a servant brought me a note. The Count asked whether I would like to drive out with him in his six-in-hand. I joined him and found six noble horses attended by three grooms. We mounted behind our host who, reins in hand, was seated on the box with a top-hatted groom in house-livery beside him. Standing behind us were two "tigers", in crimson coats with tan facings, white buckskin breeches, braided silk hats and glossy top boots. The harness and bridles glinted, the brass hubs shone. It was a truly noble equipage. We set off at a good pace, to a merry jingle of harness and a rhythmic patter of hooves. A groom blew a long silver horn. Down the drive we went, over the bridged moat and out into the long wooded avenues with endless vistas. On my bench there was a very pretty, vivacious girl.

We introduced ourselves. She was Cecilia Lubomirska. So we were Cecil and Cecilia. "Do I call you Princess ?" I asked. "No, you call me Ilya, for short!" she replied with lovely laughing eyes. Ilya and I linked arms to feel more safe, sitting high up, trot-trot, the long horn sounding. This was not a Tale of the Vienna Woods but a Tale of the Lançut Woods.

All my life I have experienced incredible coincidences that would seem too far-fetched for my use as a novelist. Again, I jump my reader forward forty years. In 1969, while staying at the Château de L'Echelle, my hostess, Countess Isa Potocka, introduced me to one of her guests. He was a tall, blond young man, H.R.H. Prince Giovanni de Bourbon des Deux-Siciles. He bore the burden of his historic name very nonchalantly. There could be little doubt that he was a Bourbon, the long nose of his pleasant face proclaimed the fact, as also the grace of his manners. Dressed in the period costume of King Ferdinand of Naples (1751–1825), who with Queen Caroline once had much to do with Nelson and his Emma, Prince Giovanni could have walked down the grand staircase at Caserta and have passed for the king himself, the distinguishing Bourbon nose carried down through six generations from Charles III, King of the Two Sicilies. Then one day my young companion startled me. His father, Prince Gabriel, had married Princess Cecilia Lubomirska! Across the bridge of years he evoked not only the vanished Kingdom of Naples but the charm of that girl on the coach from a lost summer at Lançut.

IV

In the ensuing days I pondered constantly over the immense revenue required to sustain this regal establishment. The Lançut estate covered forty thousand acres. Apart from sixty servants in the house there was an army of grooms, gardeners, gamekeepers, forest guards and estate workers. I learned there were several other estates, including a Ukrainian one. There were Potocki palaces, at Lvov where the family had entertained Marshal Foch, at Cracow, Warsaw, and a large hunting box, Julien, much favoured by the Count's mother. What surprised me most was that the estates did not support themselves. My host had large interests in a glass factory, a distillery, timber yards, a bank, sugar refineries, and coal and iron mines in Silesia. These financed the estates. The Count's father and uncle had married Radziwill sisters. Uncle Joseph at Antoniny, on his Podolia property, had kept something of a zoo. There were camels, fierce Arab horses, a lion, and an elephant that was attended by a mahout. Uncle Nicholas was the wealthiest of the family. On his death my host had inherited a mansion in the Avenue Friedland, Paris, which he sold for £150,000, a palace in Warsaw, a villa on the Riviera, and a large farm near to Colombes. This new fortune he invested in a liqueur distillery, a potato-vodka plant, and a beet-sugar refinery. The Polish zloty fell disastrously in the exchange around that time but the Count's investments proved profitable. He was able to increase all the wages on the Lançut estate by 100 per cent.

I never saw an unhappy face all the time I was there. When we drove out the peasants and workers waved gaily, the children frolicked around the Count. It was evident that the family lived on cordial terms with all their dependants. It might be feudal and some-what primitive but there was a Utopian air about the estate, or so it seemed as far as I could see, superficially of course. The Potockis of Lançut were rarely absentee landlords. Count Roman had rigor-ously drilled his son in estate management. Some of the land had been divided into smallholdings, and the Count sustained a flourish-ing agrarian Foundation. It was one of the things King Ferdinand of Rumania had been interested in when he stayed, with Queen Marie, at Lançut in the summer of 1923. She was the belle of the ball given for her after a theatrical performance. She was up next morning at six and visited ten of the cottages on the estate, and charmed everybody.

A most surprising thing to me was the small evidence of the damage the house and gardens had sustained in repeated occupations by Austrian, Russian and German troops during the First World War. The contending armies had swept to and fro over this part of the Polish-Russian frontier. First occupied as an Austrian head-quarters, then by the Russians and the Germans, battles had raged round the house. The Russians had occupied Lançut for three weeks. After their retreat the moat was filled with dead Cossacks and their horses, the grounds littered with abandoned guns and transport. But although many of the farms were destroyed, the barns fired, the horses confiscated, the gardens ruined, the house itself was intact except for the long mirrors smashed in the ballroom.

By the irony of Fate, Count Alfred's cousin, Roman, was fighting with the Russian army, and was billeted in the Potocki palaces, first at Lvov, and then at Lançut. That the house had been spared aroused suspicion when the Count returned to his home, now occupied by the Austrians. "How much did your father pay the Russians to spare this place?" demanded the commanding General. The Archduke Josef Ferdinand, who was billeted with his staff in the castle, refused to receive him on his return.* The Count had only been home three days when an alarm sent the Archduke and his staff fleeing again. The Austrian army retreated from the River San, and the Russian steamroller returned. The terrified Jews in the towns of the Province fled. The road between Lançut station and the estate, made by Count Roman, was impassable. With the Russians now only a few miles off, Count Alfred hastily hid as many of the family treasures as he could. He then began to pack a few belongings, to find that the Austrians had taken most of his clothes and shoes. The Russians were five miles off when he caught the last train westwards out of Rzeszow, crammed with distraught refugees. During the long stops they had to sleep in the fields. In the middle of November news reached the Count in Vienna, where he had joined his parents, that

* Polish relations with Austria were always better than those with Germany and Russia. Prince Clary writes: "Count Alfred was an Austrian officer of the Reserve, a chamberlain to the Emperor, a hereditary member of the Vienna Herrenhaus (House of Lords). His brother George fought in the Austrian army as did all the other loyal Poles. It is obvious that the Poles never forgot the injustice of the tripartition of their country. But whereas they were again and again brutally crushed by the Russians, and horribly treated by the Prussians, they had exactly the same liberties as all the other peoples of the Empire, i.e., liberty of language and education. The administration of Galicia lay in the hands of the Poles; there were High Schools and universities. That is why there was no real discontent in Galicia, except among chauvinists, and why so many Poles served the Emperor loyally as Prime Ministers, Ministers of Foreign Affairs, Ambassadors and Governors. The Archduke Josef-Ferdinand was a very unpleasant man, disliked by most other Archdukes. He was a good soldier but rough and rude, who should never have behaved that way."

Young Prince Clary won high distinction as a cavalry officer in the Austrian army and fought throughout the battle of Cracow.

his cousin Roman Potocki, with the Russian army in the castle, had reported, via the Spanish Embassy, that everything was intact. Then news came that the Russians were in retreat before Mackensen's German army, that Cracow was free, and Przemysl was recaptured by the Austrians. In May, 1916, the Count was back again at Lançut, to find the stables dirty but full of horses, the flower gardens intact, the carriages undamaged, the factories working. Lançut station was burnt out, the forests were in a terrible condition from the indiscriminate cutting of timber by the enemy.

With the end of the war came a currency collapse. There was hunger, and eight hundred typhus cases in the Lançut district. The Count sold some properties, made grants of land, and began to build schools. Effecting drastic economies, he steered his estates through the post-war crisis. It was almost impossible to believe that the lavish Lançut I now witnessed had been restored from ruin. And for what? Within sixteen years of my visit, the castle and its contents, the family palaces, estates, factories and businesses were to fall into the hands of a Polish Communist Government. Poland had been sold down the drain to Stalin at Yalta. The Nazis, with fearful massacres that reached a peak in the Warsaw rising, and with the annihilation of the Jews, only seventy thousand civilians surviving out of a million, had reduced much of Poland to a rubble heap before the Russians moved in and Communism was installed. Count Potocki, in exile, lived to write his country's epilogue: "For us the coming of peace was a mockery. While millions hailed with relief the end of the Nazi tyranny we Poles could not forget that our country was occupied with a million Red Army troops and that we had no rights whatever in the land of our birth. It was enough that we were still alive, scattered all over the world, surviving the greatest and most tragic defeat in Polish history."

Nothing of all this could be foreseen in those days of my visit to Lançut in 1929. Count Alfred and his mother died in Switzerland after the Second World War. Countess Potocka was eighty-nine when she died. In her eighty-sixth year she had taken tea with the Winston Churchills at their hotel on Lake Geneva and had astonished them with the keenness of her mind and spirit, though exiled and dispossessed. Such was the last great hostess of Lançut. All the Potocki estates, the palaces with their treasures, were confiscated. Lançut is now a National Museum.

V

Splendid as Lançut was, it had its rivals near by. These great houses had often been fortresses. We paid visits to some of Count Alfred's relations living in them. At Przeworsk, twelve miles distant, was Prince Lubomirski's castle, standing in a great park. This noble house had a splendid gallery rich with works by Titian, Breughel, Teniers, Vernet, and many family portraits. At Krasiczyn, six miles from Przemysl, was Prince Sapieha's Renaissance castle (1598–1633), considered to be one of the finest in Poland. It stood in a vast park, a great quadrilateral pile with an interior arcaded court, dominated by a high clock tower. There were bastions on each corner of the building, respectively named The Divine, The Pope's, The Royal, The Nobles'. In its long history the place had withstood successive raids. In 1726 the Russians ruined the park, a fire swept the castle in 1852. It suffered in the Great War but here it was, massive, serene. The interior had beautiful stucco-work on walls and ceilings, sculptured doorways, and a circular chapel that held in a niche an exquisite marble tomb of a Princess Sapieha who had died in 1855. And of course, there was a great gallery with family portraits. The castle needed an army of servants, with a family of seven sons and two daughters. The story of those brothers was a saga. One was drowned, one was killed in a Ukrainian rising, one lost his right hand in the First World War, one, shot in the head, had a steel plate inserted, and the eldest, our host, Prince Léon, married to a Potocka, crashed in a plane and landed on his head unhurt. In 1940 the Germans evicted him from his castle and imprisoned him. He was killed by a bomb. His grandfather, Prince Adam, had been known as "The Red Prince" because of his radical views and his efforts to raise the living standard of the peasants. He was the President of a bank that failed. He went out on to a balcony and told the agitated depositors that he, personally, would refund them every penny. One of the richest men in Poland, he impoverished himself by selling his properties to do so.

One question always arose in my mind when I entered these

The six-in-hand, Count Alfred driving.

Chopin, aged 19. Sketch by Princess Eliza Radziwill.

Chopin's birthplace at Zelazowa Wola.

castles inhabited by the historic families of Poland: how long could this feudalism survive with its many servants and estate workers? In the seventeenth century the Potockis possessed 3,000,000 acres and 130,000 serfs; the Radziwills sixteen castles and 583 villages. There were still a dozen princely houses that had survived in a country that had been cruelly dismembered and persecuted by Germans, Swedes and Russians. Their members had again and again led Polish resistance. I had, of course, little opportunity of observing the peasants by whose undying courage the most oppressed nation in Europe had been kept alive. They lived in simple thatched or shingle roofed cabins. The small clusters of hovels that were scarcely villages, with a wide dirt track through the middle, were often fifty miles from a railway line. The automobile had not yet come into general use and stations had to be reached on horseback or by carriage. The long, low, horse-drawn trucks were the transport of everyday life. There were horses everywhere. The vast rolling plains of golden corn gave place to immense forests, dramatically dark. It was still a storybook land, with a goosegirl, a switch under her arm, knitting as she sat guarding her flock.

Three things struck me in the Polish countryside, the universal cheerfulness, the vivid colours, the piety, as expressed by the well-kept churches and wayside shrines. There seemed no question of the people's devotion to their Catholic faith. Perhaps through the centuries it had been intensified by the threat of the Moslem Turks. My Polish friends deplored the dying out of native costumes. Even so, the love of colour was everywhere visible, the little cabins ringed with pots of flowers, the vivid head kerchiefs, the children's blouses, often brightly embroidered. To add to this gaiety of scene there was much fiddle playing. Were Polish infants born with fiddles, I wondered. It is singular that Poland's fame has been mostly spread abroad by two pianists, Chopin and Paderewski, both easily pronounced names—would the latter have prevailed in music, as well as in politics, if his name had been, say, that of one of our chauffeurs, Przezdziecki? I was told that in Warsaw there were a hundred inns where you could dance till dawn to the music of fiddles. The jazz band, gramophone and radio had not yet penetrated and vulgarised with American blare the night life.

377

Often, at Lançut and in other houses I was struck by the paternal air, perhaps part of the old feudalism that prevailed. All the servants seemed cheerful. Their natural courtesy never failed, nor their smiling gaiety. It gave me a shock when first I heard the footmen chiming in on the conversation at table, like members of the family. Once, returning to my bedroom, I found a little group of chambermaids in conference over something. They gave a shriek when I appeared and went off with squeals of laughter. My plaid silk pyjamas had excited them. The valet stroked my vicuna jacket, happily murmuring as if it had been a pussycat. He exhibited a pair of my shoes because inside was the name of a Piccadilly shoemaker. He had seen 'Peekadillee'. The shoes seemed to give proof to the others that he had been there. It irked me that I could not talk with them, for the language barrier was insuperable.

VI

One night about 2 a.m., as I lay in bed reading, I heard faintly a piano being played. I got up and looked out. I saw the window of a room dimly lit from whence came the music. Someone was playing a Bach Fugue. The player was a skilled executant. I stood entranced. Debussy's *L'Embarquement pour Cythère* followed the Bach. Then Chopin, the *Bolero*. Who was the pianist? For half an hour I sat by the window and listened. I was tempted to put on a dressing-gown and investigate but was deterred by an experience of the previous night. I had been awakened towards dawn by what was unmistakably someone snoring outside my bedroom door. After a few minutes curiosity impelled me to get up and open it. On the mat lay a servant in deep sleep. The next day I remarked on this to one of the family. "What marvellous service!" I exclaimed. "*Ah, cher ami,* it's not what you imagine—it's to stop the guests from wandering!" he replied, mischievously. He told me it was a survival from feudal times when an armed retainer guarded his master from nocturnal assault.

I did not go off in search of the pianist, for how could I explain my wanderings to the servants down the corridor, without a word of Polish? When at last I shut my window the pianist was still playing.

378

In the morning I made enquiries. None of the other guests had heard the music. Surely I could not have imagined it all? I settled the question by going to the music room and trying the piano, near a window. The tone was the same. There was music on the rack but none of it was Bach or Debussy. No one seemed to know who was the nocturnal musician. My novelist's imagination began to fashion a story; a castle in Poland, a mysterious pianist heard only at night, the ghost of a music master having a love affair with his young pupil and murdered for his presumption by a jealous count. I used the incident when I came to write my Polish novel, *One Small Candle*, a dozen years later, and made Lançut my "Château Golo".

The music was repeated two nights later. This time I ventured down to the music room. Under a standard lamp sat my pianist, clad in a dressing gown, playing. He was elderly, distinguished in appearance. After listening by the door, not letting my presence be known, I returned to my room. The following morning, walking in the garden I recognised the nocturnal pianist, a fellow guest. I ventured to congratulate him on his playing. He looked somewhat startled. "You heard me? Then I disturbed you!" he exclaimed, put out. I assured him he had given me very great pleasure. He said he was very shy about playing in public. He was not good enough, but he liked to practise, very privately. In his youth he had wanted to be a pianist and had studied under the great Leschetitzky. "You know Beethoven taught Czerny, and Czerny taught Liszt and Leschetitzky, and Leschetitzky taught Gabrilowitsch, Mark Hambourg, Paderewski, and Schnabel. He threw me out. I wasn't good enough!" said the old gentleman, smiling sadly. "I was forced into the army—how few of us are allowed to do what we want to do!"

I told the Count I knew Moiseiwitsch, who had settled in London in 1908. He, too, had been a pupil of Leschetitzky.

"He was a great teacher, and a great tyrant—and he was born here in Lançut a hundred years ago!" said my companion.

Little by little I got him to talk as we strolled in the garden. He was very knowledgeable about Chopin. "I have a very faint link with him," he said. "Chopin's father was a teacher of French. He taught my great-grandmother, and she had gone to his house and heard young Chopin play. A very weak link, of course!" The old

379

Count laughed quietly. I remarked on his good English. Had he lived in England?

"Alas, no!—only a few months at a time. Most Polish families have English or French governesses—we learn their languages almost before we learn Polish. You English are a wonderful people. England is a wonderful country—sensible, sound and never invaded!"

"We had the Romans and the Normans," I observed.

"They were civilised. We've been invaded and dismembered by barbarians—Russians, Prussians, Swedes. Now we are free but they'll come again. Poland is a cockpit."

He picked a flower, smelt it and put it in his lapel, looked over the garden and said quietly: "The world could be such a beautiful place, my dear young man. Think, I once had to shoot a Russian. He was too young and beautiful to die. Horrible! Horrible!"

We had several talks. He asked me if I had seen the Potocki palace in Cracow. I said, "Only from the outside." "Well, if you go again, look at the piano in the music room. It has quite a history. The Countess Adam Potocka was a friend of Chopin. One day she commissioned him to buy a piano for her palace in Cracow. He went to Pleyel's in Paris, selected one and had it sent to her. I've played on it—sacrilege! All the ghosts came out and paraded in the *Marche Funèbre*, so I stopped."

When he left Lançut he gave me his address in Warsaw and invited me to call. I never saw him again. A Polish friend, who was related to him, visiting me in 1935, told me that he had died. So, happily, he had not lived to see his prophecy fulfilled. He was an example of a very fine type, the Polish gentleman of good birth, now "liquidated" or languishing in exile.

The Potocki palace shown to me in Cracow, to which Chopin sent the piano, saw many notable events; the last, in 1935, was momentous. On May 18th the body of Marshal Pilsudski, the greatest figure in Poland's resurrection after the First World War, was followed to the Cathedral by the Government, the Army, the Diplomatic Corps, and the leaders in Polish life. Had they but known, it was Poland's last great demonstration as a free nation. After the ceremony Count Adam Potocki, my host's uncle, received the mourners at his palace.

Among the guests were Goering and Laval, with whom Count Alfred talked. Goering signed the Visitors Book before he left. He seemed much moved by the funeral, but it did not prevent his planes laying Warsaw in ruins four years later, preliminary to Hitler's plan to wipe out the Polish nation. Laval stayed on for dinner after Goering's departure and warned his host that Stalin had come to stay. "He is wise, cold, detached and ruthless. He is completely master of Russia, and everywhere he has an iron grip on the country." It proved a true prophecy concerning the man who, at Yalta and Potsdam, planned the doom of Poland over the heads of Roosevelt, Churchill and Attlee.

VII

One afternoon while out with a riding party I had a slight accident. The Count rode his magnificent Arab stallion, "Khafifan", snow-white, with a great flowing tail, somewhat like the horse in the David portrait of Stanislas Potocki.* My mount, a six-year-old, seemed quiet enough but the bridle and saddle were strange to me. Worse, I had been fitted out with riding boots and breeches that proved too tight, and one leg went numb as a result. All was well for an hour as we rode through the glorious woods but on the homeward stretch we broke into a sharp canter. My mount was rather a bouncer and at moments I thought it was going to do a Lippizaner *courbette* for it backed on its hind legs and reared, tucking in its forelegs. I was thrown, on turf fortunately. There was much concern. A groom wanted to give me his horse but I insisted on remounting my own. It was a bit of painful bravado but I reached home all right. The next morning my left arm was stiff and blue.

The time came for me to leave for Warsaw to meet Jan Sobanski. On the last evening I said farewell to my fellow guests. I made out

---

* I asked the Count if his horse was of the famous Lippizaner stud. "Oh, no," he replied, "much more of an Arab thoroughbred. The Lippizaner is an Iberian horse, descended from the Arab stallions the conquering Caliphs brought into Spain." Niebuhr has a note—"The horses called by the Arabs Khafifani have a genealogy that has been kept for 2,000 years. They are said to derive their origin from King Solomon's steeds."

my tipping list, no easy matter since it had to be done in zlotys. And how many and how much did one tip? Two other guests were departing. I had about a dozen invitations to stay in houses that covered Poland, Hungary, Austria and Spain. As my host shook my hand he said, "You must come again, and soon." As the car turned out of the drive and the long façade of Lançut vanished I was sad. I should have been sadder had I known the fate of that noble house, of the Potockis, of the guests assembled there. So many of them were doomed to loss of their estates, to exile and penury. I was never to see Lançut or warm-hearted Alfred Potocki again.

Certain forebodings travelled with me. They were not those of war. They were of a social nature rather than a militant. I could not help feeling that one day not far distant, such a concentration of hereditary wealth would be challenged. This semi-feudal state, with its great contrast to the common lot of man, provided a rich soil for the seeds of Socialism. Over the border, in Russia, the dark cloud of Communism grew daily more menacing. I did not foresee the Nazi threat from the West that would destroy the old social order and render the Polish nation a prey to the virus of Communism.

VIII

Twenty-seven years later I heard of Alfred Potocki again. This time there was a fairytale touch in the story of his life. I had a Polish friend in New York, the widow of a Wall Street financier. One day she arrived in London and invited me to lunch and told me that she had married her cousin, Alfred Potocki! She owned a beautiful home, the Château de L'Echelle at La Roche-sur-Foron in the Haute Savoie. I promised to visit them. She asked me if I would collaborate with Alfred who was compiling his memoirs. Unhappily I had too many commitments to be able to go to the château for any length of time, and by the perversity of events I delayed going there. One day in April, 1958, I learned of his death. With the editorial help of his cousin, Prince Clary, who had also lost his château and estates at Teplitz in Czechoslovakia, formerly in Austro-Hungary, and of Mr. Haytor Preston, in collaboration, Count Alfred finished his book, *Master of Lançut*, but died a short time before its publication by W. H. Allen. I paid a last tribute to his memory in a *Times* obituary notice, which spoke for a host of his friends:

"The death of Count Alfred Potocki will call to mind a manner of life that has disappeared with the rape of Poland. He was the last Ordynant of Lançut. No one who had experienced the hospitality of that magnificent house, with all its treasures, can ever forget it. The sorrows of his native land and the crushing reverses of fortune could not efface his gallant bearing and natural gaiety."

CHAPTER EIGHTEEN

Warsaw, Moscow, London

I

JAN SOBANSKI WAS waiting for me when my train drew into Warsaw. He had engaged a room at the Hotel de l'Europe facing a pleasant Square. When we dined that evening Jan told me that in about ten days he would be leaving for Moscow on a business mission. He would be there four or five days. Would I like to go with him? This was a startling proposal but being one who never refused an adventure I agreed to go. "Then I must have your passport at once—it's by no means certain that you'll get a visa," said Jan. I did not enquire about the nature of his business and he volunteered no information. Later I learned that it had something to do with a Swedish steel company that he represented. It was his third trip. I found that his wife was apprehensive. "I'm always nervous until he returns," she said. Jan was a good linguist and spoke Russian.

As I lay in bed that night, somewhat excited by the idea of the Russian venture, I began to speculate on the things my room had seen. From below came the music of an orchestra. I got up and went to my window and looked into the street. The gay music seemed to express the unquenchable spirit of this nation overrun in the last thousand years by invaders who made a ploughland of the Polish soil. This hotel had known grim events. Two years after it was opened in 1861 there was an outbreak following the dropping of a bomb on the Russian Governor's carriage. A general massacre followed. Poles flocking for safety to the nearby church were shot down by Russian soldiers. The bodies were carried into this hotel and placed in rows in the foyer until their relations identified them. This was the occasion when the soldiers invaded the Czartoryski Palace from which the bomb had been thrown. They threw the contents of all the private apartments into the Square below and made a bonfire of them. One of the apartments was occupied by Chopin's sister, Mme Isabelle Barcinska. Chopin's piano and all the letters written by him to his family, from his leaving Poland in 1830 to his death in 1849, perished in the fire.

The tune from below changed. They were now playing *The Merry Widow* waltz. Chopin, not Lehár, had drawn me to this city. It would have been more appropriate had they played a *Polonaise*. I closed my window and went back to bed.

I could not have had a better cicerone than Jan. He left his office to take me about Warsaw. I was so full of Potocki history that the family's eighteenth-century palace in which had lived Stanislas Potocki had a very special interest for me. It had a beautiful courtyard enclosed by iron grilles, and pillars surmounted with stone bases. The walls of the salon were decorated with Pompeiian-style stucco-work. The palace once had for an occupant Marshal Murat, commander of the French cavalry. He nourished an ambition to become King of Poland in the reconstructed Kingdom it was hoped Napoleon would create, but his desire to be royal was fulfilled elsewhere, as the brief and tragic King of Naples. He cut an astonishing figure in Warsaw. As vain as he was brave, he dazzled the Poles with his flamboyant uniforms decorated with Orders, aiglets and diamonds, so that he seemed more like a circus ringmaster than a Marshal of France. He gave in this palace a great ball in honour of Napoleon.

There was an older Potocki Palace that had housed Andrew Potocki who had married the sister of Stanislas Leszczynski, the King of Poland. Above its entrance the palace had a balcony supported by four baroque giants. I also visited the old Hotel d'Angleterre. Here on December 10th, 1812, Napoleon had briefly stayed, coming from his disastrous defeat at Moscow. He did not tarry for he wished to reach Paris in advance of the news that might shake his throne. At a quickly convened meeting of Polish ministers he used a phrase, commenting on the vagaries of fortune, that was to become famous—*"Du sublime au ridicule il n'y a qu'un pas"*—it is only a step from the sublime to the ridiculous.

In the Lazienski Park, on a lawn before a lake I saw the public monument to Chopin. It was in bronze, the work of a famous modern sculptor. It showed Chopin, cloaked, seated under an enormous wind-blown tree. It was heavy and grim. Anything more contradictory to the light rhythm of Chopin's music could not be imagined. At the side of this grotesque monument there was a stone platform on which stood a grand piano. From this open-air platform a Chopin recital would be given on the morrow; a charming idea. The following day brought the great event of my visit to Warsaw. I stood in St. Croix, one of the great churches in the centre of Warsaw. On one of the pillars in the central nave there was a modest plaque marking the place where the heart of Chopin was interred. It had been brought to Warsaw by his sister who had attended his deathbed in Paris in 1849, his body having been buried at his request in the Père Lachaise cemetery. I looked on this memorial plaque with much emotion and the whole picture of Chopin's closing days came to mind. When on November 18th, 1848, he had played for a Polish charity at the London Guildhall, he was already doomed, though only thirty-eight. He arrived back in Paris a week later, exhausted. The following summer he moved to Chaillot for better air. There was a typhoid epidemic in Paris. His condition becoming daily more serious, his sister came from Warsaw. Friends went to see him, Princess Czartoryski, Princess Sapieha, Countess Potocka, Baroness Rothschild and Jenny Lind. The 'Swedish Nightingale' sang for him.

In September Chopin moved to a set of rooms in the fashionable Place Vendôme. It was a bold move for his funds were almost at an end. He could no longer give the piano lessons with which he supported himself. He had always had aristocratic pupils who paid well. He dressed and lived elegantly, moving in exclusive circles, keeping a carriage. Just before he died he asked Countess Delfina Potocka to sing for him. The piano was moved near to his bedroom door and the Countess, suppressing her tears, sang for him some songs of Stradella and Marcello. As she ended, his friends, thinking he was dying, fell on their knees to pray, but he rallied and died two days later.

When Mozart died his body lay all night outside St. Stephen's church in Vienna, on a street altar, the fee for a church service not being forthcoming. His body was driven the next morning through a snowstorm, with few mourners, to a pauper's grave. There could not have been a greater contrast than that of the funeral of Chopin, only three years older than Mozart. Both had been *wunderkinder* who had performed before reigning sovereigns. The coffin of Chopin was carried to the Church of the Madeleine where it was awaited by a concourse of four thousand people representing all that was notable in the life of Paris. The coffin passed down the nave to the music of his *Marche Funèbre*. Mozart's *Requiem* was performed by members of the Paris Conservatoire de Musique, with singing by Pauline Viadot, Jeanne Castellane, Dupont and Lablache. Two of Chopin's *Preludes*, the 4th and 6th, were played on the organ. Thus, in grandeur, Paris paid its last tribute to a genius who was a son of Poland and of France. The pen of a great French writer, Théophile Gautier, chronicled the event in the Press. Famous voices had sung for a large congregation at Chopin's funeral. Snow had fallen in silent loneliness at Mozart's.

I was fortunate in the time of my visit to St. Croix. Fifteen years later, following the destruction of Warsaw during the sixty-five days' abortive rising against the Germans in 1944, which the Russians watched from across the Vistula, not moving a foot to prevent the massacre, the church was reduced to rubble. When, after the war, St. Croix was rebuilt with great fidelity, the heart of Chopin was returned and once more reposes in a column in the nave.

II

On my fifth day in Warsaw Jan motored me to Zelazowa Wola, the birthplace of Chopin, some forty miles west. A long desire was now fulfilled. No pilgrim approaching Mecca was ever more moved than I when at last I saw before me, amid the trees in the flat landscape, Chopin's low cabin-like birthplace. Zelazowa Wola! When, a boy of twelve, my music mistress had spoken of it, the name had excited me. It sounded like one of Rider Haggard's Zulu kings. Now, twenty-five years later, here I was, via Cracow and Warsaw, standing on the threshold of Chopin's birthplace. It was a one-storey house with a central door, very simple, not far removed from a peasant's cabin, now converted into a museum in which the Chopin

THE BRIGHT TWENTIES

Society displayed manuscripts, first editions, etc., a visible mute history of a child of genius. Outside, amid a clump of trees, there was a monument to a composer of world fame; inside, the figure of a tiny boy was vividly evoked. It may be only a legend that on the night of his birth a group of musicians, standing in deep snow, serenaded the newborn infant, as was a custom in Poland, but it fits the scene.

The birthplace was on the estate of Count Skarbek, by whom Nicholas Chopin, born in France, was employed as agent. He appears to have acted as French tutor to the family, with his other duties. While thus employed he met a Skarbek relation and married her. In this way his son became linked with the Polish aristocracy. Frederick was their second child. Eight months after his birth Nicholas Chopin was appointed French master at Warsaw High School. He moved his family into the city. Restricted in means, he took pupils as boarders. As soon as his small son received piano lessons from his mother he revealed astonishing aptitude for music. When still a child Poland became a Kingdom or Duchy, with the Czar Alexander as titular King of Poland. The long story of Polish repression had entered another phase. It was in this turbulent atmosphere that young Chopin grew up. At the age of ten he had already created a sensation. A famous opera singer of the day, Angelica Catalani, presented him with an inscribed gold watch. He was chosen to play before the Czar at the Governor's Palace and received a present of a ring. So a boy of fifteen was able to wear a diamond ring given him by the Czar of all the Russias. Only Mozart could match this, having performed as an infant prodigy before the Emperor of Austria and Marie Antoinette, and been decorated by the Pope.

On the occasion that Chopin appeared before the Czar he played his first composition, a *Rondo in C minor*. It was published as *Opus 1*. At sixteen he was the pride of the Conservatoire of Music, fêted and invited to play at all the great houses. He performed for Prince Czartoryski, Prince Sapieha, Count Potocki and Prince Radziwill. While visiting Berlin he had played in the palace of Prince Radziwill. It was here that my Lançut hostess, Count Alfred's mother, *née* Radziwill, had been born. In the Nazi regime the palace became Hitler's Chancellory. The dictator's office had once been her

388

birthroom. Prince Antoni Radziwill was Governor of the Grand Duchy of Poznan. He had married the Princess Louise of Prussia. A musician, he composed the first musical score of *Faust*. Chopin was a frequent guest at his country house. Two delightful sketches of him were drawn by the Prince's daughter, Eliza, one made when he was sixteen, another when eighteen.

After giving recitals at Vienna and Dresden Chopin wrote to his family of a visit to the magnificent home of Prince Clary at Teplitz:

> Dec. 26. 1829. Dresden. I was invited to the Castle by the Prince and Princess Clary. This is important—a sovereign family possessing enormous estates and the town of Teplitz itself . . . We have been everywhere. We were also at Dux, in the palace of the Wallensteins.* In the evening instead of going to the theatre I dressed, put on the white gloves of my last appearance in Vienna and at half-past eight I went to the Prince's. That evening I played four times and the Princess desired me to stay longer at Teplitz and dine with them on the following day but not wishing to leave my friends I declined with many thanks.

By the end of 1830 Chopin, now twenty, was becoming restless. He was determined to try his luck in the greater world of Paris. Many of the Polish aristocrats had houses there. Possibly there were other reasons for his departure. Young Poles could be conscripted for service by the Russians. Forty-four years later there was another young Pole who hurried out of Poland for a similar reason and became a sea cadet in Marseilles, Joseph Conrad. There may have been, also, an emotional reason. Shortly before Chopin left Warsaw in 1830 he had dedicated his *Concerto in F minor* to a fellow student, Constanza Gladkowska. Her rich parents opposed the attachment to Chopin, hoping to marry her to an aristocrat. Rebuffed, Chopin cancelled the dedication of his *Concerto*. When he published it later he dedicated it to Countess Delfina Potocka. This marked the beginning of a lifelong friendship with the Countess. There is a

* The castle at Dux was where Casanova wrote his famous *Memoirs* and ended his days there as Prince Wallenstein's librarian.

"When Chopin played in Teplitz, the young Prince Clary he mentions in a letter to his mother, was my grandfather Edmund (1813–1894)"— Prince Alphonse Clary.

singular story connected with this. In 1941 a Madame Czernicka said that she had discovered some letters written to Chopin by Countess Potocka. They were of a sensational nature and suggested a lurid sexual affaire. When the Chopin Society, to whom Madame Czernicka offered the letters, asked to see the originals she failed to produce a single letter. The society had no hesitation in calling them spurious. The obsessed woman appeared to have had some kind of sexual trauma regarding Chopin, whom she could never have met since she was born long after his death. It is true that the beautiful Delfina Potocka was said to have had many lovers but there was not an iota of proof in the letters that had passed between her and Chopin that their relationship had ever been anything but innocent.

Returning from Zelazowa Wola we called at Walewice to see the eighteenth-century château that had been the home of Countess Marie Walewska. Unfortunately the owner was absent but a servant took us over it. No hesitation was shown regarding the famous liaison between the Emperor and the lovely young Countess. There was a carefully preserved Napoleon room, with period furniture. She had been married at eighteen to a rich old Count who had grandchildren of the same age as his pretty wife Marie. There is something of a parallel with the Byron-Guiccioli liaison, where the old husband again seemed acquiescent in what was going on with his girl-wife. When Marie Walewska died she was buried in the family grave at Walewice—"all passion spent". But she was a nicer character than Napoleon's faithless Marie Louise, who deserted him after Elba. She never went to see him, neglected her son, the Duke of Reichstadt, and took a paramour, the one-eyed General Neipperg, whom she married after Napoleon's death, whereas Marie Walewska crossed Europe and visited him in exile. As for their son, he proved a credit to both of them. The Bonapartes recognised young Walewski who, when he was sixteen, escaped from Poland to London and Paris, to avoid being conscripted in the Russian army, like Chopin and Conrad. The French refused Russia's demand for his extradition. King Louis Philippe sent the twenty-year-old youth, born within ten weeks and fifteen miles of Chopin, secretly to Poland, to aid the revolutionary leaders, who in turn entrusted him with a mission to London. He became a naturalised Frenchman when a Warsaw rising failed. On the succession of Louis Napoleon, Walewski was sent as Envoy Extraordinary to Florence and Naples and, later, as Ambassador to London, where he announced the coup d'état to Palmerston. In France he became successively Minister of Foreign Affairs, Minister of State, Senator and President of the Chamber. There must have been a close bond between those two young Poles in Paris, Walewski and Chopin. In 1837 one was earning his living as a journalist, one as a pianist. The two young men knew each other. "Mr. Walewski's cousins inform me that he will soon arrive here," wrote Chopin's father to his son in Paris in 1833. "If so, ask him to bring a copy of your *E minor Concerto.*" It is singular that although Alexandre Walewski was born at Walewice he was conceived at Schönbrunn Palace, Vienna, where, in 1809, the twenty-year-old Marie slept with Napoleon and gave him news that she was expecting their child. In this same palace lived and died his legitimate son, the Duke of Reichstadt. The half-brothers never met.

III

A whole week passed and I had not yet received a visa for the Russian excursion despite much wire-pulling. The matter was complicated by the fact that the British Government was in disfavour with the Russians and diplomatic relations were still ruptured. Jan continued his efforts but our departure had to be postponed. "It would be easier if you were a Japanese!" he said.*

Meanwhile, I continued my sightseeing in this most pleasant city. I walked by the Vistula and admired the panorama from the Royal Château, now become obsolete, a place of sad memories for the Poles, recalling tyranny and insurrection. It was with special interest that I looked at the Palais Tepper. It had once belonged to the banker of King Stanislas II and saw many magnificent receptions and balls given by that prosperous financier. It was here that Talleyrand

* In February, 1924, the new British Labour Government recognised the U.S.S.R. as the *de jure* rulers of Russia, being the first major Power to do so, and appointed a Chargé d'Affaires to Moscow, not an Ambassador. Until 1929 King George V opposed receiving an ambassador from a Power that he regarded as guilty of the murder of his cousin, Czar Nicholas II and family.

resided, from December, 1806, until May, 1807. He faced the dual problems of dealing with the political structure of Poland and tactfully assisting the Emperor in his liaison with Countess Walewska for which, in a way, he was responsible; for it was at a great ball given by Count Potocki in honour of Napoleon in January, 1807, that the Emperor first met the Countess and became madly enamoured, though he wrote to his Josephine, sitting at home in Paris, complaining that he was lonely, that he loved her above all women, that he could not permit her to take the risk of joining him! "I believe that his Walewska affaire was the only genuine one he ever knew after the divorce of Josephine," said Jan, "and I'm of the opinion that if Marie-Louise had not presented him with a son and heir he would have divorced her and made young Walewski his heir—and perhaps have married his mother! From his record the boy would have made a very good Emperor if Napoleon had not lost everything at Waterloo."

I explored the beautiful Rynek (Grand' Place) whose sixteenth- and seventeenth-century houses were to disappear for ever in the Nazi bombings. Proud of their work, they made a film of the destruction in Warsaw at the beginning of the war and officially exhibited it at their Embassies throughout Europe, freezing the marrows of foreign governments with this evidence of what would happen to them if they opposed triumphant Nazidom.

The days passed all too rapidly. The weather was golden. The city had a French gloss about it. Off the Rynek I made a personal enquiry. Zadia, my alluring friend of the Russian Ballet in London, after returning home to Warsaw in 1920 where she was living with her aunt, had invited me to visit them. She was teaching her aunt English, "so that she can talk to you". Much as I would have liked to go, my editorship had held me, something Zadia could not understand since she always did just what she wanted to do. Now here I was in Warsaw, nine years later. I had learned that she was dancing with a Spanish company in South America. Perhaps she had now returned home and, if not, her aunt could give me news of her. I had her Warsaw address but not having faith in the amount of English she could have learned from Zadia, I asked Jan to accompany me. We found the house, an old four-storey one in a street off the Rynek, but were baffled in our attempt to find Madame Klukowska. The house had been divided into four apartments whose windows were gay with potted plants. We tried each floor. The top one ended our quest. An old couple living there told us that Madame Klukowska had died five years ago in the apartment below. They had known her niece the ballerina but had no idea of her present whereabouts.

IV

My visa came at last with the accompanying documents. There was one singular stipulation, I had to supply nine photographs, in triplex, in three positions, front face, profile and back—for shooting? The Warsaw-Moscow express left at 8 a.m. It was about one hundred and fifty miles to the frontier beyond Brest-Litovsk with its grim memory of March 3rd, 1918, when Lenin and Trotsky had had the humiliating Peace Treaty forced upon their exhausted country. The Germans had got rid of their costly Eastern Front and could concentrate on the Western.

The long train crawled across the monotonous plain. We were an hour late when we drew into the frontier station. We had to detrain to pass the Customs and immigration officials. The bright red Soviet flag with the hammer and sickle device fluttered over our heads. On the Russian platform armed guards with their wooden, peasant faces looked forbidding. We had to detrain on the Warsaw platform where we were kept waiting for half an hour before being herded by the guards into a long shed. The Customs officers examined each piece of baggage suspiciously. They were puzzled by Jan's supply of toilet rolls, a necessary asset. No one smiled or said a welcoming word. "We shan't see a smile again until we get back to Warsaw," said Jan. He warned me not to talk with anyone on the train. It was an unnecessary warning, no one attempted to. We were a cargo of mutes. After two hours we pulled out of the station. (Warsaw-Moscow express!) We were now on Russian soil. The train crawled on through the dreary landscape. We had passed the endless Pripet Marshes in which millions of Russian soldiers had died in the First World War and where Hindenburg had made his name. Swamps alternated with flat agricultural plains from which rose solitary wooden church domes. The approach of autumn touched the dense

o   393

forests with gold. We passed through small stations whose platforms were filled with drab peasants sitting by bales of luggage. It looked as if all Russia was on the move.

Our ancient wagon-lit was comfortable, with heavy mahogany fittings. The dinner in the restaurant was fair but there was a general grubbiness, the porcelain cracked and chipped. The sun had gone down in what looked like a prairie fire. The black night descended. Our Express became something of an express at last. I am a bad train sleeper. Twice I raised the blind to look out. One could almost feel the darkness, like a piece of black velvet. On, on, on, then the dawn over the undulating landscape and, at last, Moscow.

We were registered in an hotel a few minutes off the Red Square. It had a faded splendour. To dinginess it added dirt. William Plomer, staying there on his way back from the Far East, a few months earlier, opening a napkin at dinner, unhoused a large cockroach. I feared bugs in the bed but slept unscathed. After 9 p.m. we were locked in, or locked out, according to which side of the entrance you stood. "We shall be followed from the moment we go out until we come in," said Jan. "Be careful what you say to me. Our conversation may be tapped." We had large iron bedsteads in our communicating rooms. The service was surprisingly good but glum. The water was scalding hot. I had a red-headed chambermaid who smiled and talked a little English. She astonished me by saying her name was O'Brien. She had had a Russian mother and an Irish father, an engineer from Belfast who had been employed by a Volga steamship company. She was born in Russia.

"It's rather singular," observed Jan, "that though our rooms adjoin I have a Polish-speaking maid and you have an English-speaking one. It may be thoughtful service—or something else. Be careful!"

As soon as we had unpacked we went out. I was impatient to see the Red Square. It was a short distance so we walked. Presently we arrived at the Square. It was a long, vast open space, a rectangle nearly three-quarters of a mile long. It bore no resemblance to the Piazza at Venice except in one respect, the end of each was shut in by a church of semi-barbaric splendour. The cathedral of St. Basil was a mass of coloured domes, gold, green, red, chaotic in grouping but

394

achieving a bright magnificence. It had been built by Ivan the Terrible to commemorate his victories; it dominated the Square. Now desecrated and deprived of its function, its nine altars stripped of their sacred vessels and ikons, the cathedral had been transformed into a national museum. Nothing of its inner desecration could be surmised from the exterior grandeur of the cross-surmounted domes that soared, balloon-like, into the clear September sky. As with the Taj Mahal, it fulfilled all expectations aroused by its renown.

The Red Square was dominated on one of its long sides by the reddish high brick wall of the Kremlin. In this vast space what spectacles had been enacted down the centuries; the battles with the Tartars, the massacres, knoutings, executions and sadistic orgies of Czars and Boyars. Here, on a Palm Sunday, had ridden on a mule the proud Patriarch before the devout gaze of a hundred thousand kneeling peasants. Here, by the Kremlin walls guarding the Citadel within, had stood the frustrated Napoleon, watching the flames of the burning city that preluded the disastrous retreat across the snow-covered plains in October, 1812. A legend about this, said Jan, was in error. The city had not been deliberately burned by the Russians. Some of the inhabitants had carelessly started a fire on the night following the entry of the French. The people fled before the flames that destroyed three-quarters of the wooden-built houses. Napoleon's army lingered from September 14th to October 19th, incessantly attacked by Cossacks and armed peasants.

As I looked at the long Kremlin wall, with its fishtail parapet, I noticed something familiar about its architecture, which seemed foreign to this Russian scene. I recalled other battlemented walls of this nature; those of Verona, built of the same reddish bricks in the same style. I was not surprised to learn that the Kremlin owed much to the two Italian architects of the fifteenth century, Antonio Solari, and Ridolfo Aristotele Fiorvante of Bologna. The latter had fled here from Venice. He met disaster in trying to straighten the campanile of St. Angelo. The morning after the scaffolding had been removed the campanile collapsed. Fiorvante knew the penalty one paid to the Signory for failure. He fled from Venice to Moscow, thus avoiding the fate of Sansovino, who had been thrown into prison when his façade of St. Mark's Library had collapsed.

V

Each day I grew more and more depressed by the utter drabness of Moscow and its people. One did not see a well-dressed person. The grimness of their existence was written over them, as over the whole city. Everywhere one saw only the dour faces of a people that had exchanged the tyranny of the Czars for that of the Commissars. The middle-classes, under the stigma of the parrot-word "bourgeois" had been exterminated as well as the retrogressive and irresponsible aristocracy, tyrants at home and playboys abroad. Stalin had embarked on his merciless Five Year Plan. Six million smallholders, Kulaks, the backbone of Russia, whose sturdy independence offended Stalin, were to be expelled from their farms, to wander destitute, or to be sent to their deaths in the labour camps of the Siberian wastes. One result of this repression was a near famine. Outside the foodshops I saw long queues of miserable women, all ill-clad, their heads swathed in the universal babooshka. I went into a huge new store. The merchandise it offered was pathetically poor, the prices fantastic. Any little shop in an English village was an emporium in comparison. One evening we visited a popular café that had a balalaika orchestra. It was vividly dressed and played with great gusto. It was the only spontaneous note of gaiety I had encountered since our arrival but somehow a miasma of gloom hung over the thronged tables. The people had faces that registered nothing yet they belonged to a nation that had given us Tchaikovsky and the incomparable Russian ballet. They were kind and polite in little ways.

I asked Jan if he thought the Five Year Plan would be achieved. "It may be, and if it isn't there will be another Five Year Plan, no matter what it costs in political slavery," he replied. "In all my business transactions I'm impressed by their zeal. They've surrendered their liberty, intoxicated by slogans. Poor devils! How rewarded would you feel if you had to share a room with nine others, in a cracked tenement building with one cold water tap, and an informer on each floor? Papa Stalin has promised them paradise, and is giving them hell to reach it. They've seen no white bread or butter since the war but they've been promised honey tomorrow. The immediate drive is for steel, steel for industry, steel for armaments, steel for ships, steel for power. They're making handcuffs for civilisation."

As prophesied by Jan, every time that we went out we were followed. Our two attendants were ludicrously obvious. If we took a droshky, they took a droshky. If we walked quickly, they walked quickly. Once, Jan pulled me suddenly into a side street. "Pretend to be looking in this shop window, and wait." In a couple of minutes our attendants turned the corner, and walked on pretending they had not seen us. The next morning when we left our hotel they were there. Jan raised his hat, mockingly. They returned the salute, solemnly. "We've become so attached I believe we could borrow a few roubles off them, poor devils!" commented Jan.

One day a Russian friend called on us. He was related to Jan by marriage, a Communist, a professor at the University. He had been two years at Oxford before the war. "He wears his communism like a glove. He has to live," said Jan. The professor offered to take me over the Kremlin citadel, such parts of it as were shown, while Jan was out on business. He proved to be a man of considerable culture, Moscow-born. We avoided politics. I learned that the fantastic Uspensky Cathedral, with Indian cupolas in the Lombardo-Byzantine style, was also the work of the Italian, Fiorvante. The Church of the Archangel, flamboyant, had been built by a Milanese architect in the sixteenth century. It contained the tombs of the Czars, except a notable one, that of Boris Godounov, a Czar familiar to me because of the opera of that name and Chaliapin's acting and singing in that role. This Czar's body was taken in 1606 to a monastery at Zagorsk. A belfry, holding the chief bell in Moscow, had been built in 1532 by another Italian, Petrocchi. An English architect had made a contribution to the city. The tower above the Gate of the Redeemer, one of the Kremlin's three gates, with a famous peal of bells, was his work, dating back to 1625.

When we were half way down the Red Square the professor pointed to the Kremlin wall. "Next year we are building a mausoleum which will house the body of Lenin, who will be visible to all. Just over there!" he said, and added, with a wan smile "But this time it will be the work of a Russian architect." We went to the State Library.

It contained twenty million volumes and claimed to be the third largest library in the world.

Learning of my interest in the Bolshoi Theatre, the home of the famous ballet, the professor took me there. The season had not yet opened. He introduced me to an official he knew and we were shown the dark auditorium from the vast stage. It was something to stand on a stage where ballet history had been made. My guide told me that his youngest daughter was enrolled in the School of Ballet. Did I know Madame Isadora Duncan? Evidently he had not heard of her tragic death. He was greatly moved by my account of her end. "I did much work for her when she was here to found a ballet school for children. She not only taught them but she fed them. She was like a beam of light penetrating the dark storm. She had a magic. She was a spirit moving over dark waters," he said. There was such emphasis in his tribute that I was startled. I looked at him and ventured a question—"Were you in love with her?" He stopped in his walk and replied gravely, "All we young men were in love with her. She seemed as immortal as the Winged Victory of Samothrace. It is hard to believe that Death could touch her."

VI

The day of departure arrived. I was sorry to leave with so much unseen in this bizarre capital of Russia, with its mixture of the baroque, oriental and modern, with its ill-fed, ill-clothed, sad-faced people, dumbly heroic in the fortitude with which, out of centuries of repression, they marched on into a doctrinaire future that would shake the world. They were now in the era of Stalin, at whose hands millions would meet their deaths.

My visit had been a great experience. One day I hoped to come again when this vast nation had moved into happier times. Much that I had seen I used when I came to write *Pilgrim Cottage*, three years hence. Before departure I tipped my chambermaid. There was a revealing incident. She accepted the tip somewhat fearfully. Suddenly she sat on a chair, took off a shoe and placed the note inside it. "We are not allowed to take money," she said in a low voice. "When we go home we are searched in case we take knives, forks and spoons, or food." As she said this she tried to smile through the sadness of her eyes.

On the train to Warsaw I asked Jan if he was satisfied with the business he had done. "I think so but I never can tell with these suspicious moujiks. The more I do business with them and study them the less I understand them. It's impossible to know just what a Russian is. Not 20 per cent of them in the whole Empire are pure Russian. The rest is an amalgam of a score of races all hating Moscow and controlled by it. They have exchanged the knout for the tank. Their slave labour-camps and prisons are more, and fuller, than they were under the Czars. I heard this from a friend of mine two days ago, a Russian journalist. No one knows the real figure of those in them. You can't count sand." He estimated that half a million were deported to the labour camps every year. "It's a guess. No one knows how many don't reach that end. Nearly all trials are faked and secret, and the executions are summary and hidden. I'm afraid they'll destroy the world. They've got rid of God and substituted an automaton. They are encouraged by our home-grown Bolshies, mostly sloppy young intellectuals. We have them, you have them. America has them. By the time they grow older and learn sense the damage is done. I suppose it's the price we pay for freedom and free speech. I confess I'm scared."

VII

I stayed a week in Warsaw after my return there. Ceaselessly entertained, I found it impossible to present many of the letters of introduction I had been given at Lançut. I vowed I would come to Poland again, my heart warmed by all the kindness I had received. Jan and his wife saw me off. I was never to see them again. Ten years later he was killed fighting the German invaders. Two years after the close of the Second World War I learned of the fate of his wife and small son. A bomb destroyed their apartment house in which not a single person survived.

On the homeward journey via Berlin and Paris I halted in Berlin. *Das Leben Ist Eine Kunst* said a motto across the lounge of the Adlon Hotel. If only the Germans had lived up to it! The country was still

399

war-shaken, wailing over the Treaty of Versailles, with Hindenburg as the father-figure, and five million unemployed. I heard little of an agitator named Adolf Hitler, and saw no swastika-banded youth marching and chanting, though others told me of them and of an upsurge of aggressive nationalism. Next year Hitler would get a hundred of his party members into the Reichstag. Within a decade this demoniacal, uneducated house-painter would ruin Europe.

When I reached Paris the golden leaves were fluttering down. Along the Champs Elysées the pavement cafés were thronged. I encountered at a party a young Spaniard, Salvatore Dali, black-haired, famine-thin, with stiletto moustache, who informed me that he had joined the Surrealists. I startled him by asking him what these might be. That very morning I had lingered over a painting of his in an art dealer's window. It was of a lion's skin hung over the leafless bough of a peach tree in the middle of a yellow desert. It cost fifteen pounds. If only I had bought it!

On arrival home I learned that Nancy Cunard with African brace-lets on her skeleton arms had invaded London with her lover, a negro pianist, and had raised the banner of racial equality in Bloomsbury, having thrown a party in a swimming bath. She clashed with her mother, Lady Cunard, and published a fulminatory pamphlet denouncing her.

It was good to be home again with my books and pictures and a log fire crackling in the grate. At the parties of a retired British Minister to Nepal I met a rumpled, vivacious and witty young man of twenty-three, John Betjeman. He was penniless and without a job. He shared a flat, rent free, with a promising young politician, Hugh Gaitskell. Then one day he got a job on an architectural journal. His verses began to be quoted. We founded in this year a lifelong friendship that was to run concurrently with his brilliant success.

Soon I began to refuse social engagements as I wished to concentrate on *Havana Bound*, which I had begun in New York and written intermittently in Venice and Lançut. I was now approaching the last two chapters. I worked for three hours each morning and then walked along the Serpentine and through Green Park to lunch at my club. I loved London, with Nelson high on his column, the ducks by the beautiful suspension bridge across the lake in St. James's Park, with the snowy pinnacles of Whitehall down the shining water to the east, and embowered Buckingham Palace to the west. I loved the long Grand Canal-like vista of Pall Mall with its Venetian-style clubs, ending in the Palladian façade of the National Gallery; when the road gleamed after rain one almost saw gondolas instead of taxis on it. I loved the bright buses with open tops designed for lovers who could pull the weather canvas over their knees and secretly hold hands. And where else in the world, in the company of old ladies, could you be served with afternoon tea and a biscuit during the interval at a theatre matinee?

The Twenties that had opened so light-heartedly and full of promise were drawing to a doubtful close. We were badly governed and not aware of it. Lloyd George, who had led us to victory, had been deposed. In the last year of his life, lion-maned, he would enter the House of Lords, which he had once held up to riotous ridicule. At present he vainly tried to summon his depleted ranks and produced a plan to save England that no one would listen to. Ramsay MacDonald and Stanley Baldwin went in and out of Downing Street like the figures on a Swiss chalet-clock. They proved incapable of devising work for two million unemployed decaying on the dole, as demoralising as it was inadequate. Winston Churchill, again out of office, was bricklaying at Chartwell and becoming more and more alarmed. "The eventful years through which we are passing are not less serious for us than the years of the Great War. They belong to the same period. The grand and victorious summits which the British Empire won in that war are being lost," he told an audience. No one believed him. No one thought there could be another war. The League of Nations would look after us. To underline the folly of war a German, Erich Maria Remarque, had written a bitter novel, *All Quiet on the Western Front*, which had a phenomenal success. To keep us grateful and chastened R. C. Sherriff had leapt to fame with his brilliant play *Journey's End*, a heart-searing epitaph for the heroic dead. Our easy confidence had been shaken by the crash in Wall Street, which had left a trail of bank failures, unemployment and suicides across the United States. This calamity had brought from New York my friend Campbell Hackforth-Jones and thus I was taken to his home, bursting with lively brothers and sisters. It was presided over by a bearded patriarch, a very symbol of the City, and by a Juno-like, warm-hearted matriarch whose hospitality embraced two scribes, youthful Emlyn Williams and myself.

It was astonishing how much money there was about, all paper. The golden sovereign had gone for ever. The war had produced a heavy crop of knighted profiteers. When I shopped at Harrods Store before Christmas I felt I was in a Rugby scrum. The money had got into different hands and the accents had changed. Vanishing maidservants refused to wear white bows on their heads, waitresses had invaded the not-so-exclusive West End clubs, and page-boys in buttons, once well rewarded by sixpence, had almost disappeared. There was a note of social equality everywhere. Jack was better than his master, who couldn't strike. Everyone swore he was ruined by high taxation, and ordered a new car. The Establishment, with its Edwardian snobbery, had been shaken. The slave-wages of office clerks and workmen were no more. Miners no longer lay on their backs in danger and darkness for thirty shillings a week. Shop assistants no longer worked penal hours. People of the lower classes ceased to be stigmatised by badly-cut clothes. The frock coat had become a sartorial joke, preceding in obsolescence the Court débutante's three ostrich feathers. England was on its way to becoming a land fit for typists to wear silk in. There was a note of hilarity in our steady march to national bankruptcy. The fewer the waves Britannia had to rule, the brighter seemed the voyage. On the horizon gathered the clouds of the Great Depression.

CHAPTER NINETEEN

The End of the Decade

AT THE CLOSE of 1929 I finished my novel and was out of bonds, except for the hard labour of revision. On the last evening of December I went to a New Year's Eve party given by friends who had a penthouse apartment in Westminster. There were some forty guests. The noise was deafening; as the cocktails went down the voices went up and people grew more affectionate as they grew more inarticulate. To escape the noise of the long room I went out on to the terrace. There was a fine view over London to the Surrey hills. In the foreground rose the black silhouette of the Houses of Parliament. The white face of Big Ben, its hands moving towards midnight, shone in the great tower. Westwards, there was a silver flash of the Thames, lit by a moon emerging from scudding clouds. The air was mild. There was a stillness over the scene but lights in various windows told one that not all London was abed.

For a few minutes I fell into a reverie. I thought of all that a dying decade had brought me; the first sweets of success after long labour; the struggle for independence, and the loss of the one dearest to me in all the world just as I had gained it; my editorship, with the whirr of the presses after midnight; my first novel in a bookseller's window; the United States from Niagara Falls to Florida; the stupendous first entrance into the Piazza at Venice; my nervous breakdown and the end of political ambition; Winston Churchill shouted down at West Leicester; laconic President Coolidge at his desk in the White House; Havana, Key West, and the orange groves at Orlando; Cracow with the trumpet of the Heynal from the steeple; Lançut, with its salons, horses, woods; Chopin's birthplace, Warsaw's gaiety, Moscow's grimness.

In our literary world new stars had arisen. Proust had appeared with his great novel in translation. We were all reading Aldous Huxley who had given us *Antic Hay, Those Barren Leaves, Point Counter Point,* all delightfully ironical. *The Constant Nymph* made a sensational entry and the post-war Bright Young Things all wanted to be taken for nymphs, with Lady Diana Cooper as patroness, though she was now a nun *par excellence,* who had returned from performing *The Miracle* in the United States. There had appeared another Lawrence, more concerned with the sands than the glands, a young hero in sheik robes who had given us, with well-organised publicity, the acme of prominent reticence, *The Seven Pillars of Wisdom,* unanimously acclaimed a work of genius. Harold Nicolson, a diplomat of The Establishment, had enrolled in the Lytton Strachey Debunking School. In *Some People* he had made fun brilliantly of stuff-shirted statesmen, and endorsed the comforting belief that "our betters" were often pompous humbugs. There was the proletarian D. H. Lawrence again in the limelight, with the banned *Lady Chatterley's Lover.* A lively cross-Channel smuggling traffic grew up in copies of this and of *Ulysses* by James Joyce, after *Fanny Hill,* the first to plough the phallic field. Another book had appeared of which little notice was taken, *Mein Kampf* by Adolf Hitler. With his scrub moustache, dank hair, he seemed a ludicrous figure of no real import. We had survived what seemed a very real menace, the General Strike.

My reverie was broken. Out on to the terrace, through an opened door, came the wailing of the gramophone. They were dancing to it, a strange rhythm was being brayed into the night expressing the current cult of negro music, American in origin. The radio had created a craze for music, classical and jazz. Conductor-fetish had begun, with Toscanini, defier of the Fascists, as its god. There were bright spirits around. Noël Coward had stormed London with *The Vortex, Hay Fever* and *Fallen Angels.* There was the invention of the new colour film. Walt Disney's Mickey Mouse, a star-comic, entranced us with his joyous baiting of the cat-bully; children squealed with delight, and I with them at this reversal. We experienced more serious achievements. Alexander Fleming had discovered Penicillin, a miraculous antibiotic that would save millions of lives.

What a wonderful ten years these had been, but they held also a sense of loss and retrogression. The flower of our youth lay in the war cemeteries, impoverishing our future. I wondered what would be the story of the next ten years, bringing me to middle age. Mercifully none of us knew that within a decade Big Ben's light would be out and in a darkened scene searchlights would be stabbing the murderous skies.

Both terrace doors opened, the guests came streaming out. The gramophone was now playing Coward's latest success, *Bitter Sweet*. My reverie was broken by vivacious voices. Big Ben drew nearer to midnight. Maids appeared with trays of champagne. A sudden anticipatory silence possessed us. Then, as the hands of the great clock converged, there came the first sonorous stroke, the voice of Britain over the world. We counted the measured beat; the last wave of sound died in the night. We raised our glasses in cheerful greeting to the New Year. The Bright Twenties had passed into Eternity.

The End of the Third Volume of this Autobiography.

INDEX

INDEX

Bryseis, S.Y., incident of, 289–90
Burlington House (Royal Academy), 192
Burns, John, 43, 148
Buxton, Noel, 131
Bynner, Witter, 56
Byron, Sir John, 80
Byron, Lord (the poet), 106, 216, 263
  Byron Centenary Lecture (author's), 235
  connections with Nottingham, 80, 235
Byron, Reverend Lord, 80

Cagliostro, Alessandro, 295
Cahn, Sir Julien, 125, 127
Caine, Sir Hall, 153
Cambridge Union, 184–5
Cambridge War Memorial, 54
Campbell, Sir Malcolm, 284
Campbell, Mrs. Patrick, 46
Cannan, Gilbert, 68, 69
Carlotta, Queen of Mexico, 300
Carmania, S.S., 197
Carnarvon, Lord, 192
Carnaval, Schumann's, 78
Carnegie, Andrew, 342
Carnival (Compton Mackenzie), 82
Caroline, Queen of Naples, 361, 372
Carpenter, Edward, 131
Carpentier, Georges, 340
Carter, Howard, 192
Caruso, Mrs. Dorothy, 205
Casati, Marchesa, 263
Casimir the Great (of Poland), 353
Cassino, Monte, Polish Corps at, 351, 355
Castellane, Jeanne, 387
Catalani, Angelica, 388
Cayuga, Lake, New York state, 285, 286
Cecchetti, ballet maestro, 146
Cecil, Lord David, 274
Cecil, Lord Robert, 65, 131
  Corfu incident and, 159, 160, 161
  letter to author, 132–3

Chadwick, Sir Burton, 31, 154, 303
Chaliapin, Feodor, 397
Chamberlain, Sir Austen, 279
Chamberlain, Neville, 163, 180
Chancellor, Beresford, and family, 189–91, 192, 193
Chaplin, Charlie, 150, 188
Charles I, King, 193
Charles, King of Two Sicilies, 372
Charnwood, Lord, 33
Chesterfield House, demolition of, 147
Chesterton, G. K., 66, 260
Chicago, 211–13:
  Evanston (Higbees' home at), 279, 285
  Executives Club, 212, 279
  Mediæval Club, 279
  Rotary Club, 212
  Tunney–Dempsey fight at, 341
Chichester, Dowager Countess of, and family, 321–2
Chichester (John), 8th Earl of, 321, 322
Chopin, Frederick, 301, 346, 377, 378, 379–80, 385–91
  Chopin Society, 387–8, 390
  early life and career, 386–91
  death and funeral of, 386
Chopin, Nicholas, 388
Christian Apostolic Church (forerunner of Christian Scientists), 211
Churchill, Lord Randolph, 166, 204
  Lord Randolph Churchill (Winston Churchill), 174
Churchill, Sir Winston, 13, 65, 123, 150, 161, 187, 232, 401
  Americans' interest in career of, 203–4, 225–6
  Brendan Bracken and, 168, 172, 175, 176, 177–8, 179, 180–1
  Chancellor of the Exchequer, 204, 219; and War Debts issue, 219–20, 222
  early political life, 162–3, 164–8, 174, 175

Churchill, Sir Winston—*cont.*
edits *British Gazette* during
General Strike, 261
guest of Count Potocki, 375
meeting with Mussolini, 261
meetings with author: at West
Leicester, 173–4, 176; after
interview with Coolidge, 229–30
relationship with Beaverbrook,
245–6
U.S. lecture tour, 38, 43, 60
West Leicester by-election cam-
paign, 162, 168–9, 171–2, 173–6,
403
Winston S. Churchill (Randolph
Churchill), 60
Civil Liabilities Commission, 13,
189
Clary, Prince Alphonse, 12, 374, 382,
389
Clifton-Bruce family, 77
Cobb, Irvin, 207
Cochran, Sir Charles (*Revue* 1926),
329
Colbert, Jean Baptiste, 299, 302
Collier, Constance, 45
Collins, Professor Churton, 89
Collins, Michael, 167
Colonna, Princess, 138
Colony Restaurant, New York, 79
Columbia University Club, 25
Columbine (Compton Mackenzie),
82
Colvin, Sir Sydney, 179
Compton, Edward, 81
Compton, Mrs. Edward, 81–2, 83,
84, 86, 255
Compton, Ellen, 82, 83
Compton, Fay, 82
Compton, Viola, 82, 83, 84
Conan Doyle, Sir Arthur, 33, 38, 40,
255
Conan Doyle, Denis, 210
Conrad, Joseph, 13, 66, 83, 92, 148,
151, 255, 305, 310, 366–7, 389
boyhood and early life in Cracow,
348–9
friendship with author, 349

Conservative Party, attitude to
Churchill, 204
Constant Nymph, The, 262, 404
Conway, training ship, 17
Cook, A. J. (miners' leader), 149
Coolidge, Calvin, 210, 217, 230,
279
background and career, 217–8
interviews author, 220–4, 403
War Debts issue and, 218, 222
World Court proposals of, 223
Cooper, Lady Diana (Lady Duff
Cooper), 146, 263, 404
Copernicus, Nicolas, 353
Corfu incident, *see under* Greece *and*
Mussolini, Benito
Cornell University, 270, 285–6
Cornwallis-West, Daisy, Princess
of Pless, *see under* Pless
Cortot, Alfred, 138
Corvo, Baron, 329, 344
Courage (J. M. Barrie's rectoral
address at St. Andrew's Univer-
sity), 70
Covent Garden Opera House, 78,
79
Coward, Sir Noël, 45, 404, 405
feud with the Sitwells, 147
Cowdray, Lord, 117
Craig, Gordon, author's meeting
with, 134, 136
Croce, Benedetto, 312
Crosby, Mr. and Mrs. Harry, 294–6
Cunard family, 263
Sir Bache, 264, 328
Sir Edward, 263, 264, 328
Emerald (Lady), 150, 328, 400
Nancy, 104, 263–4, 328, 400
Victor, 263, 328–9
Czartoryski, Prince, 388
Czartoryski, Princess (friend of
Chopin), 386
Czernicka, Madame, 390
Czerny, Karl, 379

Dahon, Renée (Madame Maeterlinck), 39

Marsh, Eddie (Sir Edward), 44–5,
88, 168, 228–9, 231
Masefield, John, 13, 35, 53, 56, 151,
302–3
Massine, Leonide, 13, 78, 79–80,
146, 188
Master Mariners, Company of, 154
Matthews, Lester, 83
Maugham, Somerset, 242, 341, 342
Maxwell, Elsa, 327
Mdivani family, 204–5, 209–10:
Alexis, 204, 209, 210
David, 204, 209
General, 204
Nina, 204, 210
Rousadana, 204, 210
Serge, 204, 209, 210
Messel, Oliver, 150, 329
Mills, Emma, 29, 30, 31, 32
Misia (Sert), 210, 347
Mitford, Nancy, 150
Moiseiwitsch, Benno, 33
Mond, Sir Alfred (later Lord
Melchett), 154
Montgomery, Alabama, lumber
camp, conditions in, 50, 52
Montreal, 201–2, 203, 210, 277
Montreal Star newspaper, 201
Moore, George, 264
More, Sir Thomas, 228
Morgan, Evan (4th Lord Tredegar),
95, 97, 104
Morgan, J. Pierpont, 18, 294, 330
Morosini, Countess, 263
Morrell, J. B., 66
Morrell, Lady Ottoline, 100
Mozart, Wolfgang, 386–7, 388
Muir, Professor Ramsey, 121
Muller, Pastor (Jack Laing's Swiss
tutor), 105, 106, 112–14, 140
family of, 112
Munstead Wood, 328
Munthe, Axel, 311
Murat, Marshal, 385
Murray, Mae, 209
Mussolini, Benito, 137, 138, 161:
Corfu crisis and, 157–60
March on Rome, 137, 158

Mussolini—*cont.*
meeting with Churchill, 261
death of, 143

Napoleon, 293, 363, 364, 365, 385,
390
retreat from Moscow, 385
Negri, Pola, 209
Neguchi, Yone, 34
Neipperg, General, 390
Nelson, Lord, 80
New Orleans, Tulane University
213–4
New York, 203–7
Newman, Cardinal, 179
Newstead Abbey, 235
Nicholas, Grand Duke, 358
Nicholas, Prince, of Rumania, 210
Nicholas II, Czar, 391
Nicholson, Sir William, 328
Nicoll, Sir William Robertson, 68
Nichols, Robert, 33
Nicolson, Sir Harold, 404
Nijinsky, Vaslav, 78
breakdown of, 188–9
Bronislava (sister), 189
Romolo (wife), 189
Nobili, Riccardo, 330–1, 338
North Carolina—
Greensboro', 354
Raleigh, author's visit to State
Legislature at, 285
Northcliffe, Lord, 129
Northumberland, Duke of, 149
Nottingham—
Byron's association with, 235
Graham Greene's description of,
258–9
D. H. Lawrence's early life in,
313, 315
Bernard Shaw's visit to, 255–7
Lytton Strachey's letters from,
265–6
University College, 265, 266
Nottingham Journal, the—
author's editorship, *see under*
Roberts, Cecil